Another in the Fire

D1557844

Another in the Fire

Aaron Reed

Copyright © 2021 Aaron Reed

All rights reserved. No part of
this book may be reproduced or
used in any manner without
written permission of the
copyright owner except for the
use of quotations in a book
review. For more information,
write:
permissions@thereedwriters.com

This book is memoir. It reflects
the author's present recollections
of experiences over time. Some
names and characteristics have
been changed, some events have
been compressed, and some
dialogue has been recreated.

ISBN:9798491016620

www.thereedwriters.com

Dedication

For Anne,
with deepest respect.

For Reksmei,
with pure adoration.

Table of Contents

Acknowledgments

Perhaps my greatest blessing is having been born into an amazing family. My mom, Viki, my dad, Steve and my sister, Heather never failed to remember me in prayer, and continued to regard me with their patient love throughout the years I was MIA and largely unlovable.

I treasure my twenty-five-year friendship with Dr. Ellen Bassuk, who has stood by me throughout the entire journey.

Hugs to Courtenay Lange for being my primary reader and for offering her brutal and necessary criticisms, and thanks to Lange Portraits for the photo editing.

Thanks to Vinny and Joann Kame for their kindness, and for Jo's precise line edits.

Sincere gratitude to my editor, Sarah Chaves, who was super fun and relatively painless to work with.

Love to Curtis Brown, Jim Buckley, Dr. Brian O'Neill, Albert Jovel, Barry Bradford, and to Edgar Roberto Medina Garcia.

Love also to Erik, Cheryle and Kristin Benson, the most amazing family.

Thanks to Carlos Alberto Velásquez Eussa and Francis Farinas de Velásquez for their overwhelming kindness.

My deepest appreciation to Luis, Olga and Alba Liz for opening their hearts and home.

Thanks to Jaime Lopez for his exceptional legal services.

Thanks to Jessica Wolff for her technical expertise.

Warm regards to Linda Cadariu and Kathy Wilson for planting the seeds.

Prologue

Phnom Penh
August 2015

Weighing out my last gram, I placed it on the cutting board and crushed it to powder. After spilling the dust carefully into a small plastic pharmaceutical baggie, I rolled the baggie up like a joint and taped it up as tight as I could make it. Pulling my pants down to my ankles and covering the tootsie-rolled baggie with K-Y, I laid on my back with legs in the air and painfully inserted the package into my rectum. Shouldering my pack and pulling the rolly, I gave one last glance around my Cambodian house before shutting the door, closing it all away with a new padlock.

Bogotá
August 2015

It was 4:30 in the afternoon when the plane landed at El Dorado International in Colombia. Most passengers had deboarded when I was shaken awake by a stewardess. "Sir, we've landed. Please gather your things and-"
I sat bolt upright, wiped my chin and did as I was told. My head felt three feet thick and my vision out of focus. I was the last one to walk off the plane. Hitting the first bathroom I glanced at my

disgraced reflection. The area around my numb lips and chin where my girlfriend Lyda had smashed me in the face with a brick only a few days prior had turned a yellowish-purple and the square gauze covering the hole in my cheek hung askew, held there by a rumpled piece of surgical tape. I took a face bath in the sink, shaved, swabbed the hole with H2o2, then replaced the dirty gauze with a fresh one. Pieced back together, I made my way to customs, cleared, then hit the airport bank where I changed dollars for pesos. Walking onto the street, the air felt cool on my skin; Crisp air, carrying me back briefly to my Michigan childhood in Autumn. Shaking off the pleasant reverie I sucked down two cigarettes, climbed into a yellow and handed the hotel address to the cabbie.

Prior to the trip, I'd done zero research on Bogotá or Colombia or anything related to its language, culture or customs. I hadn't purchased any sort of guidebook to the city, nor had I checked out the Hotel Lourdes where I'd be staying. I spoke no Spanish and had no desire to learn. Complete and utter apathy. The ride from the airport to the hotel I noticed was entirely urban, snaking through city sculpture and neighbourhoods that reminded me of San Francisco's Mission district. Paying the driver, I climbed out and took quick inventory of the street.

All the low buildings were different shapes and sizes but attached, each sharing a wall on the left and the right. Hotel Lourdes was a small four storey upright situated in the middle of the block on Calle 63. Directly to the right of the hotel was a squat building with a large pink neon sign that advertised *Sex Shop*. To the left was a Dollar Store. The rest of the street was lined with cheap phone shops, small dingy cafes and restaurants offering empanadas, arepas, dark bars blasting salsa, and knick-knack emporiums selling umbrellas, plastic Jesus dash ornaments, rubber chickens and everything in between. An impressive homeless population roamed up and down the street, begging, laying in alcoves. Bukowski would have felt right at home here, and so would I. Silently thanking Sand, my Nigerian *jefe*, for not having

2

booked me into some Four Seasons bullshit, I walked into the Lourdes and checked in.

Dropping my bags, the first thing I did was relieve myself from the baggie. Washing it off in the sink, I then took a light bulb out of one of the lamps, cracked it against the sink, took a broken spoon-shaped shard, filled it with a good pile of ice and lit up. Sucking the scentless smoke through the straw, I immediately felt the rush spread through my body instantly restoring my head to perfect clarity. Holding the smoke in my lungs for as long as I could was like enjoying a tall drink of water after crawling parched through the desert for days under a punishing sun. Instantly satiated. Except with ice, there was never any true satiation. Every hit demanded another, then another, over and under and around and through endless tunnels of more! A solid hour of non-stop inhalation left me feeling sorted, so I ventured out to get a better lay of the land. I didn't go far, about a block toward each compass point before heading back to the room.

I couldn't have cared less about being in Bogotá, or anything about being in the Latin world again. I'd already been through Nogales, Tijuana, Juarez, Mazatlan, Puerto Vallarta, Antigua, São Paulo, Quito, Tena, Papallacta… I figured one more Latin American city was just like all the rest. Spent the rest of my first evening ensconced up in the room attaching my laptop to the free Wi-fi streaming The Cure, The Brian Jonestown Massacre, Habib Koite and other favourites.

I walked down to reception and notified them I did not require any room cleaning. Then I went and bought a new Samsung Galaxy copy phone/tablet along with a local SIM card, called Sand and gave him the update. Hanging the Do Not Disturb sign on the knob, I got down to business and over the next 24 hours I did nothing but crouch naked on the floor loading glass after glass smoking myself silly into a nail-biting wall crawling masturbatory delirium. When the stash finally expired and I was finished scraping and then licking the resin off the remaining glass shards I collapsed back into the bed sheets and pretended I was dead until I finally, finally was able to disappear into the coveted nothingness of dark velvet sleep.

On the morning of the 20th I woke to Sand's call. "Brother, my friends are ready to meet you. There is an Olympica store down the street from your hotel. My friends will be in front of the store in one hour. When they arrive, they will send you a text. Prepare yourself to go with them. They will give you the package and deliver you back to the hotel."

I climbed out of bed, walked down to reception, nodded like a zombie to the girl behind the counter and filled two paper cups full of black coffee. Back in the room I guzzled the scalding fuel, revived with a cold shower and pulled on some clothes. Exactly one hour and five minutes later the call I'd been waiting eight days for finally came.

Approaching the Olympica, I felt somewhat composed. My feet met the pavement in cadence with the mid-morning hustle of the street. I was surprised to find myself so alert after five days of sleep alternating with such a treacherous quarrel with sobriety. Two very tall Nigerian men stood in front of the store, stood out like sore thumbs. "You guys speak English?" I asked.

"Yes."

"You guys thirsty? I'm going to get some Coke. Want anything?"

They declined.

Minutes later, when I emerged from the grocery store, they motioned me into a waiting cab. The tallest guy, clearly the senior jefe, sat shotgun while his sidekick sat next to me in the back. Meeting with the jefe and receiving the package was always a bit awkward. A cordial rapport, and maintaining a certain decorum was always necessary and expected, but at the same time, neither party wanted to divulge unnecessary information, each wanting to ensure anonymity. After exchanging fake names and the bare minimum required, we rolled through the dirty city in silence.

The distance from my hotel to the pick-up was uncomfortably far. After nearly an hour snaking through traffic, the senior jefe instructed his lackey to wait with me on the street in front of a sporting goods store. We both lit up and stood smoking through the tension. About five minutes later, another yellow cab pulled up and the senior jefe climbed out, handing me a small backpack that, from the initial heft, weighed in around three or four kilos. The exchange involved nothing more than that. I shook their hands, thanked them and climbed into the cab. Overcome with a last-minute surge of paranoia, I rolled down the window and motioned the boss over for one last pow wow. "Bro," I whispered. "You know the dogs at the airport… they can sniff this shit out from miles away."

"No worries, my friend." He whispered into my face with stale breath. "This is professionally packed. No way the dogs will smell anything." And with that, I nodded to the cabbie who guided the car back into the flow of the day. At the hotel, I sauntered through the lobby with my kilos, nodded to the cutie behind the desk and buried the backpack in the room under my heap of dirty clothes.

I shot off an email to Sand: *Package received*. Within the hour Sand emailed my return ticket and wired cash to cover my return expenses. At this point in my muling career, I'd developed a superstitious six-tiered ritual surrounding the pre-flying day. It was necessary strategy to board the plane looking as presentable as possible. After picking up the cash at Western Union, I embarked on my pre-flight activities.

First purchase: A white dress shirt. After wandering the neighbourhood, I stumbled upon an upscale dress shop and selected a pure cotton snow white long-sleeve button-down.

Second purchase: Shoeshine. The plaza surrounding the *Nuestra Señora de Lourdes* was bustling with impressive pedestrian traffic. Several shoe-shiners were lined up in front of the cathedral.

The man gave an excellent shine, and even set me up with new laces.

Third purchase: A new backpack, designed to match my black boots and khaki pants, making me out to look like just another anonymous Joe. I found a brown and black L.L. Bean type rip-off that rounded me out nicely.

Fourth purchase: A haircut, complete with ear, nose, neck and eyebrow trim.

Fifth purchase: A three-pack of new boxer shorts. I'm not crystal clear why I'd adopted this into the regime. In retrospect, perhaps it was some attempt to ensure that if (and when) I got popped, I'd have enough underwear to walk into prison with.

And finally, the sixth preparatory purchase, getting a massage. The idea behind this inclusion was simple; I wanted to remind myself that everything was cool. I was relaxed, and all would go according to plan. Living in S. Asia for eight years, I had experienced (literally) hundreds of massages in Vietnam, Laos, Thailand, Malaysia, Singapore as well as in Cambodia. I'd developed a healthy addiction to them and believed entirely on the therapeutic experience for both body and mind. After searching the neighbourhood for an hour, I finally stumbled on *Ikonos Estética y Belliza*, Ikonos Aesthetics and Beauty. It was a hair salon full of good-looking stylists all sitting around thumbing through beauty magazines. Not a customer in the shop. The single sign in the window offering "Massage" lured me in. After miming my need for a rub down, I was ushered into a tiny back cubicle filled with a massage table, a sink and a small armoire filled with massage lotions, towels and the like. After disrobing and wrapping up in a towel, the masseuse came in, dimmed the lights, and proceeded to give me one of the worst massages I have ever received. It was so bad and awkward that I cut the hour into 30 minutes, mumbling excuses (politely in English) why I had to leave. They understood not a single word. After leaving a sizable tip, I made the dash.

Out on the street, I shouldered my new backpack full of my new purchases and began walking. Instead of heading back to the hotel, I diverted towards the cluster of mountains, the *Cerros Orientales*, that form a natural hedge along the Eastern edge of Bogotá. The urban sprawl eventually gave way to a congested and low-lying *favela* type neighbourhood that butted up against the towering wall of the mountains. I wandered the barrios for an hour, lingering in the dusty, ill-maintained parks littered with trash and overgrown with weeds. *This could very well be your last stroll in freedom for a while.* A part of me already knew that my four-year, drug fuelled sortie into complete irresponsibility and unaccountability was about to come to a screeching halt. Another part of me welcomed it. Looking back now, I should have seen the terrible premonition for what it was: an omen.

Night fully swallowed the city by the time I reached the hotel. I situated the package on the bed and unwrapped it. The coke had been "professionally" packaged into the hardcovers of three enormously sized children's books. There were also four rolls of fax paper, each containing large flat baggies of coke wrapped in plastic and hidden in the rolls. I laid out my new outfit for the next morning's flight, packed the hardcovers and the paper rolls into Lyda's purple rolly, lining them with my clothes, and tidied up the room.

Turning on the laptop and booting up Skype, I was hit once again full in the face with yet another brick. Li, my ex-wife, had sent along a photo taken earlier that day of my daughter on her way to her first day at Kindergarten. My daughter, dressed impeccably in a cute blue top and wrapped in a neon pink and yellow pullover, a flower headband in her hair, a backpack strapped confidently around her shoulders and wearing an excited smile, pierced the camera with a heart-melting gleam in her eye. I called her. She spoke excitedly about her adventures from her first day at school. I continuously had to keep muting my microphone and blanking the screen so she wouldn't hear or see my sobbing. "I'm coming next month to see you, baby girl. We'll be together for your birthday."

"Ohhh Papa! I will be so happy to see you. I miss you so much. Papa?"

"Yes, honey?"

"Will you take me to ride the ponies in Half Moon Bay?"

"I sure will. And I'm going to bring you lots of surprises from Cambodia."

"*Aahhyyii,*" she squealed. "I love you so much, Papa!"

Exhausted from the day and from withdrawal, from solitude, from failure and from life's prosaicism I killed the light, set the alarm for 3:30 am and eventually dozed off feeling profoundly sad and very, very alone.

Waiting in line for my flight check-in, I pantomimed a frantic and professional conversation on my phone so I'd appear in the surveillance cameras as just another uptight working stiff trying to close a deal on his way to a flight. After presenting passport and itinerary to the agent, she frowned over my insane flight schedule and remarked with a hint of suspicion, "Mr. Reed, why such an extensive flight itinerary?"

"I waited until the last minute and that schedule was all I could get." I answered lamely.

She shook her head, processed my stack of boarding passes, then situated Lyda's rolly onto the conveyor. The last thing she did was scribble *TSA* onto my initial boarding pass with a thick red marker, along with her initials. Swallowing my paranoia, I accepted my documents with a smile and headed for the gate.

The pre-boarding call was announced. "*People travelling with small children along with first class passengers.*" General boarding followed. I waited until final boarding call when the lounge area was completely deserted. Shouldering my carry-on and arranging my boarding pass, I was the very last passenger to check in. I approached the ticketing agent, an attractive woman in her thirties with all the normal trimmings of an airline stewardess. I placed my boarding pass and passport on the counter and offered her a robotic smile. She flipped open my passport, glanced at my ID page. "Yes, Mr. Reed. Please come with me," she stated matter-of-factly. "The police want to ask you some questions." In one fluid motion she gathered my passport and boarding pass and maneuvered around the counter.

"OK," I answered, with no reaction or apprehension. "Will the flight wait for me?" I asked.

"Of course. *If* the police dismiss you, you'll be allowed to board."

In that moment I should have been riveted with fear. I recall feeling very nervous, but not in the situation's reality. I felt nervous because I was walking alongside the pretty woman with nothing to say. I felt tongue-tied, panicked like being at a party and not having the suave and debonair to charm. We walked about fifty yards to the end of the concourse, then descended an escalator to the ground floor. She led me to an unassuming and unmarked grey steel door and knocked.

The door opened to a windowless room the size of a two-car garage. About twenty cops, a mix of men and women stood around. A large stainless-steel table was set in the corner. A small collection of tools like surgical instruments were neatly arranged. The centerpiece of the room was made up of the largest and most beautiful K-9 specimen I had ever seen.

Lyda's purple rolly was on the table. An officer greeted me and asked me if I spoke Spanish. Hearing my answer, a cop with cutely cropped auburn hair and large cinnamon eyes stepped up and introduced herself as Erica Velásquez. "I will be your legal interpreter." Ms. Valasquez gestured to the regal German Shepherd. "Bronco smelled something in your bag. Will you please open your bag for me?"

"No problem." I fished out the key from my backpack and opened the rolly. All the cops gathered around. Two of them pulled on latex surgical gloves and began unloading and placing my things on the table. The three hardcover books and the rolls of fax paper were just as I'd packed them—stacked and arranged next to my clothes. Bronco stood stoically staring directly at me, his majestic tongue lolling long and wet from his mouth.

Without a word, Ms. Valasquez picked up the hardcovers with her latex hands and passed them around for everyone to examine. Everyone in the room appeared bored. They'd seen this a thousand times before. Books gathered back on the stainless steel, she selected a scalpel and asked my permission to cut one of the books open. I nodded my consent. When the blade punctured the fabric, a small explosion of white powder burst out onto the cover. For everyone in the room, it was as expected. No reactions. Business as usual. She looked at me and asked, "And what do you think this is, Mr. Reed?"

"Looks like cocaine to me," I offered, politely naming the elephant in the room. I shot a side glance at Bronco. He nodded.

Ms. Valasquez then reached for a chemistry test. "Mr. Reed, this is a simple test called a narco-test that will determine the contents of what you're carrying. I will swab the powder and if it turns blue, that will indicate a positive test for cocaine." She swabbed the Q-tip with the chemical solution and immediately after it touched the powder, the white cotton tip turned colour of the most beautiful azure sky. The officers exchanged winks, smiles, high fives, and with *atta-boy* slaps on the shoulders, one by one began heading for the exit. My final seconds had ticked off the clock. Game over. What followed then was a loosely translated rendition of the Miranda Rights, a quick frisk down, and then the bracelets finally clamping firmly around my wrists.

Before being led from the room, I turned to Bronco, and with a surge of primordial respect I offered the gorgeous beast a nod, perhaps even a slight bow, congratulating him for a job well done.

Chapter One

San Francisco, Colachel, India, S. Asia
2004 - 2008

My fiancé's family owned a small condo in N. Lake Tahoe. Li and I had driven from San Francisco to enjoy a picturesque holiday with my parents who'd driven up from Phoenix. The weather was fairy tale perfect, everything covered under a blanket of immaculate white. Icicles dripping from skeleton trees. Early Christmas evening, skiers were enjoying a six-foot base on the mountains, clear skies, the temperature floating in the mid-forties. After a delicious dinner, we curled up on couches in cozy quilts to hibernate comatose with stuffed bellies.

On the other side of the world, the undersea Sumatra-Andaman mega-thrust earthquake had sent a Tsunami hurling into the Southern tip of Kanyakumari, India. Waves recorded at four and a half meters swallowed up two inland kilometers of the densely populated coastline. We watched silent and stunned as the news feeds flashed reports of the chaotic devastation.

I liked Li even before meeting her. Curtis, my oldest friend who I'd known since college was Li's colleague. Employed with UCSF as social workers in San Francisco's Tenderloin, they worked with triple diagnosed clients transitioning from the streets to assisted living, carrying with them the impossible baggage of mental illness, retardation, and various addictions. Li had invited Curtis to her birthday party in the Sunset district, and he'd invited me along as a third wheel. I didn't want to go.

"C'mon." Curtis coaxed. "You need to get out of your shell. Yeah, Li's cool. Super good at her job... yeah, she's cute. C'mon, let's go for the free beer!" Reluctantly, I agreed to tag along.

The party was a typical San Francisco back yard BBQ with lots of beer, attended by kind social worker types hanging out and having fun. A good crowd. Li, dressed in a silky and sexy Chinese pantsuit circulated easily, attending to her guests. I could see she was amiable, well-liked. I was immediately attracted to her Asian-American ethnicity. Long, black hair. Tiny body. Cute, round face. Guzzling beer with Curtis, I watched her make her rounds through the crowd. At one point she greeted some new arrival with a dramatic but playful karate kick, and I was instantly hooked. A week later I called her, and she agreed to see me.

We held a lot in common: A mutual compassion for the disenfranchised—people who'd been dealt the wrong hand at birth. Li had some international travel under her belt. After graduating from Cal State Long Beach with a degree in Fine Arts, she'd taken off on a diagonal trajectory to live and work in a small, rural African village during a two-year stint in the Peace Corps. We shared a compatible interest in music. She introduced me to the rhythms of Fela Kuti, and I tried to entice her with my tastes at the time. She warmed to Radiohead, but couldn't seem to understand my passion for the Butthole Surfers. After nine months of wearing her down, I finally received my first kiss.

Li was attending First Baptist Church of San Francisco. The church attracted me with its progressive outreach and global community service focus. I enjoyed Pastor Phil Busbee's humble homilies, and the way every word was spoken softly and sincerely from his heart. I learned that FBC had a working relationship with a Pastor named Sunil working out of New Delhi, who was mentoring a young pastor by the name of Mahadevan way down in India's Southern State of Tamil Nadu. In January of 2005, Li and I met with Pastor Phil and expressed our concern for the catastrophic events in S. India. He agreed to send us to conduct a damage and needs assessment in the small village of Colachel where Pastor Mahadevan and Usha, his wife, had started a church plant.

After a twenty-two hour itinerary we landed in Mumbai, then hopped an eighteen hour train down to *Thiruvananthapuram* in the Indian state of Kerala. From there we hopped a bus that carried us down to Tamil Nadu. Mahadevan and Usha greeted us at the bus station and delivered us to his parents' house where we spent the next five weeks pampered by our host's gracious hospitality and acclimating to their Hindu traditions. Mahadevan's church was made up of about ten people who met each day in a tiny one room cubicle that doubled as a community outreach center. What they lacked in membership, they made up for with awe-inspiring spirit. The dusty, one-road-town of Colachel was truly the ends of the earth.

The coastal village is situated twenty kilometers from the southernmost tip of the country—a mere 220 miles from Sri Lanka. The ancient village had emerged around the fishing industry. The small port had been constructed without a sea wall, allowing the freak wave to rush inland at a height of fifteen feet, leveling the entire coastline and estuary to the ground. Concrete bridges spanning forty meters set dilapidated in the surf, toppled from their foundations like discarded children's blocks. Entire communities had been erased and sucked out to the depths of the Arabian Sea. Touring the devastation had a peculiar effect on our voices. Walking the beach and the affected areas, we spoke in whispers, as if our normal volume might disturb the somber ambiance of the crowds of people picking through the rubble.

"Why are there so many children?" I asked Mahadevan.

"They are the orphans. They have nowhere to go. They stay here every day looking for their families."

Returning to San Francisco, Li and I met with Pastor Phil and his wife Claudia at their house and shared our impressions over dinner. Throughout the next year, FBC responded by creating a budget and a fundraising campaign, raising money for the construction of an orphanage for the children wandering in the surf.

In the Spring of 2006, Li and I were married at First Chinese Baptist Church in San Francisco's Chinatown. It was a grand celebration, complete with a traditional Chinese feast and dragon dance. We spent the next two months preparing for our return to India, where we would lead *Team Colachel*—a group of eighteen volunteers from FBC to support the opening of the orphanage. I was dreading the trip. Of all the countries I had been to, India had proved to be the most challenging. The poverty had a different feel to it than I had experienced in other countries and left me in a state of profound sorrow. And then there was the heat—bearing down all hours of the day like an anvil on my head. The dust. The lack of culinary variety—subtle variations of rice dal breakfast, lunch and dinner. The sensory overload of the otherworldly Hindu lifestyle and traditions left me reeling in a state of intense culture shock—*cultural electrocution*! Despite my personal challenges, the opening of the orphanage was a success, and the trip created many lasting friendships and inroads between two very different cultures.

With India in our rearview, Li and I said goodbye to *Team Colachel* and embarked on our honeymoon. The itinerary was extensive, but chill. First stop: The Kingdom of Cambodia. We spent a week entranced in Siem Reap, touring the ancient temples of Angkor Wat before moving on to zany Phnom Penh where the desperate reckless city and the dark genocidal tourism of The Killing Fields swallowed me whole. From there we dipped down to the resort town of Sihanoukville on the Gulf of Thailand where we discovered marijuana and shroom pizza, enjoying a string of lazy do-nothing daze. Then on to enormous Bangkok—hopped a bus down to the Thai islands where we wrapped up our summer tour of S. Asia in a beach bungalow guzzling cold Singha and salivating over spicy Pad Thai and steamy octopus soup.

On the heels of the best summer of my life, Li and I returned freshly married to San Francisco and did our best to integrate back

14

into our ordinary lives. Renting an ocean front apartment in the idyllic coastal town of Half Moon Bay, we settled into routine. Each day Li commuted forty-five minutes up to the city to continue her social work while I resumed teaching my students on the coast. Our jobs provided us a consistent regularity. I was able to entertain the luxury of deciding whether to drive my car or ride my Harley down the Pacific Coast Highway to work. On weekends, we stood on our balcony sipping wine, catching glimpses of leaping dolphins, or the occasional whale breeching the surface of the undulating ocean. Our first year of marriage was a good season, but I could feel those dreaded words of *ordinary*, *routine* and *regularity* begin to gnaw under my skin. I couldn't seem to shed the mystique of S. Asia from my mind.

I began researching teaching jobs overseas, and in February, I attended a Search Associates three-day recruiting fair up in the city. I was offered high paying teaching positions from reputable schools in Egypt and Vietnam but turned them down. My heart was set on Cambodia. My first interview with the reps from Northbridge International School, Cambodia went very well. On the final day of the fair, the NISC headmaster called and scheduled a second interview. I killed it and was offered the job. Within a month, Li and I said goodbye to friends and loved ones, packed up our lives, and in the early summer of '07 landed in Phnom Penh.

Our arrival came on the heels of the country's long and painful reconstruction. In the 70's, the Pol Pot Regime, in their attempt to convert the entire population into a nameless and faceless agrarian society had killed off a third of the entire population. Following the genocide, the country plunged into civil war, leaving the country's social, physical, political and economic infrastructure in complete shambles. It wasn't until '97 that the Khmer Rouge finally came to accept the government's amnesty and turned in their guns. But the unrest and violence continued when in that same year, a political clash outside the National Assembly left 125 wounded and 19 dead. The first parliamentary elections took place in '98, and as a result, Cambodia entered ASEAN with full membership in April of '99.

Li and I landed. Retrieved our bags. Cleared Customs and hailed a cab. The traffic was utter chaos; red lights and stop signs ignored by all. No laws. Cops hid in bushes around the intersections and leapt out occasionally to collect bribes from violators. A quick two or three-dollar payment and you were on your way. At 6:00, all law enforcement vacated their posts and returned home, leaving the entire city to its own devices. At dusk, the city experienced a shift change. The police vanished, replaced with an ocean of young girls who filled the cluttered streets and girlie bars with their skimpy dresses and coquettish taunts at the legions of (S)Ex-Pat tourists in pursuit of young flesh.

Li and I settled into a spacious and airy second-story two-bedroom flat in the *Daun Penh* district of the city. An excellent location, within walking distance to Hun Sen Park, to the Mekong River and all the touristy international restaurants that lined its muddy banks. Our enormous balcony was a patio really, overlooking Wat Botum, one of the largest Buddhist temples in the city. The invisible saffron-robed monks filled the still afternoons with their singing bowls and hypnotic mantras. Exotic birds nesting in the blooming bougainvillea filled our yard with strange songs. *Unruly. Exotic.* I fell instantly in love with the mysterious extremes of the lawless and developing urban thrall.

With my new teaching position and the advent of the school year, I dove headfirst into new and demanding professional challenges. Northbridge International was a high-end school, providing a progressive education to the students whose families could afford the $20,000 yearly tuition. My students were the sons of millionaire foreign investors and the daughters of Khmer Royalty. My class load was rigorous. In addition to teaching 9th grade Language Arts, 10th grade English and World Lit, 11th and 12 grade AP studies, I offered the electives of Speech and Debate and Music and Culture. My income provided Li and I a lifestyle of luxury. I bought us both motorbikes to tool around the city, and hired a part time housekeeper to maintain our domestic needs. Naomi, a young girl from the provinces, kept our home perfect and filled our bellies with her excellent Khmer culinary skills. The school atmosphere offered me both a renewed professional focus and an English-speaking social circle. The transition into my new life came with comfort and ease. Li's acclimation was another story.

Li's transition proved both abrupt and unsettling. Back in San Francisco, she'd devoted herself and her skills to her job to the point of defining herself by her profession. She'd spent years building her reputation around the city as a damn good social worker. Surrounded by her family, along with a dependable social circle, she'd created a somewhat insular existence that provided consistency and professional satisfaction. For Li, our move to Phnom Penh proved to be an upheaval. Each day I rode away happily to work, leaving her alone in an unfamiliar home with no friends and no job. And each day I returned to face her sullen circumstance, defined by her depressive slump and morose temperament. "Relax!" I encouraged. "There's no need for you to work. Enjoy your time. Do whatever you want!"

We began exploring S. Asia with frequent weekend excursions to Bangkok and Saigon. I booked the tickets hoping the sojourns would inspire her in some way, dislodging her from her lonely funk. Our quick escapes into Thai and Vietnamese mystique were enjoyable and provided necessary respite from the insanity of Phnom Penh. Cheap accommodations. Feasting on delicious street food. Attending cultural shows. Soaking in the scents and stimulations of new and peculiar landscapes. But the frequent honeymoons always came to an end; resulting in my return to work and Li sinking further into a state of serious depression that I had no idea how to rescue her from. A glimmer of hope came from New Bird.

We stumbled on the restaurant while exploring our new neighborhood. New Bird was a sorry hole-in-the-wall on Street 240 just a five-minute stroll from our house. The proprietors, Lika and Virya, were a young Khmer couple who both spoke passable English. Lika was sassy and cunning, clearly the brains and the brawn behind the business. Virya impressed me as a typical uneducated Khmer dolt, content on doing nothing. Making a simple payment, his parents had purchased for him a low rank into the Cambodian Army, affording him a monthly salary that he would enjoy for the rest of his life. Virya had drawn lucky in his marriage and into his co-owning and managing New Bird; riding the coat tails of his ambitious, entrepreneurial wife. Li and I enjoyed their company and began spending a lot of time at their little restaurant. Lika expressed interest in learning how to cook Western meals, and Li often prepared dishes in their kitchen for Lika and Virya to sample. I encouraged Li's friendship with Lika, as it provided her a much needed and healthy social outlet.

One sunny afternoon while sipping beers on New Bird's patio, I spotted an ex-pat strolling down the street sporting a Jerry Garcia T-shirt. I waved him over to join us. Short-cropped hair, nerdy glasses, Mike was a transplant from some small farm suburb of St. Louis and had been in the country a few months. He'd landed a job at one of the small English Academy's and was spending the day tooling around town getting to know the city. Our mutual affection for The Grateful Dead and P-Funk sealed us as fast friends. We exchanged numbers, and soon began hanging out regularly on weekends.

I quickly learned that Mike's clean cut, down home Mid-Western appearance was a thin veneer. One evening, after ordering our fifth or sixth round, he explained with an utmost sincerity, "Aaron, as much as I love The Grateful Dead, I love drugs as well. Ecstasy, pot, shrooms, coke, you name it!"

"Yeah, some of my best memories of college was going on my first Summer tour in '91. I toured with The Dead for the next two summers as well. Changed my life!" I answered.

Mike took a swill and shook his head. "Damn! I wish I'd seen Jerry."

"You never saw Jerry?" I gasped.

18

"Naw man, I jumped on a bit too late after he died in '95."

A few years and half a generation younger, Mike had missed the boat. "So, I take it you're a Phish fan?"

"Yeah, they're cool. But I'm really more into Widespread Panic." I hadn't heard of them. "Fuckin awesome band… in the same vein and style as The Dead and Phish. Fucking Widespread Panic. I followed 'em around and seen 'em dozens of times. Nothing better than a Panic show on acid." After declaring himself a devoted Panic Fanatic, he added, "And I've dosed over five hundred times!"

"What's your best acid memory? The most vivid trip experience you've ever had?"

"One time I was at a Panic show with my best friend at the time. I turned to ask him if he wanted a beer and his head launched three feet off his shoulders and bounced around on a spring like a Jack-In-The-Box." Mike exploded laughing. "BOING! Fucking most terrifying and beautiful thing I ever saw."

Mike was kind, smart and up for anything. When our work weeks ended on Friday the party began, often lasting the entire weekend. Both of us were new arrivals and hadn't yet connected into the underbelly drug scene of the city. Our stimulants through those first two years were limited to throwing darts and shooting pool at The Walkabout, bar-hopping around town and getting sloshed on cheap drought beer.

My first year at NISC proved enjoyable and productive in every way. I was challenged professionally daily by both my administration and my students, and rose to the occasion. The experience slowly but surely taught me to become a more seasoned educator. My professional environment, my financial and social stability, and now my friendship with Mike served to further my sense of security and success. I enjoyed my job. Had more than enough cash. And now had a friend who I sincerely enjoyed hanging with. Li, on the other hand, had none of these things, and her lonely existence continued to fuel her daily bouts of depression. The more I assured, the further she regressed. The more I encouraged, the deeper she slipped into depths of personal conflict and cultural drowning. My resolve to rescue her from her heartsick lack of joy was sincere, albeit, short lived. I tried, and in retrospect, probably didn't try hard enough.

Our existence was enviable. Wealth providing a comfortable lifestyle. Exotic travel at our whim and disposal. As our first year abroad ended, NISC foot the bill for our return to the States to spend the summer with family and friends. After my first year at the school, I'd managed to save $32,000. I sunk the entire load down on a modest single-family home in Casa Grande, Arizona; One of the best housing markets in America. Aiming to rent the house, it was my first attempt in life at a serious investment. Aside from my ambitious stake into real estate, Li and I enjoyed the extended vacation. I held high hopes that the lengthy holiday would rejuvenate her resolve. It did, but only temporarily.

Returning to our life in Phnom Penh for my second school year, Li fell instantly back into her miserable trajectory as if determined to make the worst of the situation. To complicate matters, by September, the U.S. financial markets had collapsed, and the housing bubble imploded. Spanning back to the 1860's—in over one-hundred and fifty years of America's modern housing market—I had invested at precisely the worst moment. Two months after purchasing my investment property in Arizona, the house went underwater. I had lost my entire life savings. Despite the financial crush, I continued to relish the extremes of living as an ex-pat in The Penh while Li continued her decline.

3:30 every Friday I'd make a bee-line out of school back to the house intent on ripping it up with Mike, leaving Li sitting at home alone mulling her sad existence. "Why don't you go hang out with Lika at New Bird? Maybe have her teach you some new Khmer recipes?"

"Maybe..."

"I noticed you still haven't even unpacked your paints. You're extremely talented, Li. Why don't you start painting again?"

"Not inspired..."

"There's a lot of local ex-pat club-type groups and social organizations. Have you checked those out?"

"It'll be morning soon in San Francisco. I guess I'll just try and Skype my sister."

"I've got a long weekend coming up. Let's take another trip! Want to go back to Bangkok or Saigon for the weekend? Maybe Singapore?"

Crickets. My typical *male driven* problem-solving advice was exactly what she didn't want to hear.

I continued with my futile efforts to resuscitate Li to life by extending our itineraries to Kuala Lumpur, Hanoi and Laos. Our frequent sojourns were enjoyable enough, though always ending plunked back into our routine in The Penh with Li's collapse, returning to roost on her stagnant nest.

The treadmill existence of married life fell on my neck with unbearable weight, comparable to what every bride and groom experiences while taking photos at their wedding. Throughout the first fifty pictures, the smiles are believable. After the hundredth shot, the smiles begin to droop. Everything after that resembles the stretched, taut and forced grins of an elderly cobbler sequestered in his tiny shop stooped over a pair of worn leather shoes deciding whether to apply stitching to the tears or abandon the project altogether.

Uncertainty is the most treacherous slope to negotiate. I loved Li and love her still. But at the time, I found myself pulled into an impossible and existential ouróboros; a fatal and serpentine shape that would eventually teach me that I wasn't made to successfully endure the spiritual demands of the institution of marriage. In his thought-provoking book, *Sacred Marriage*, Gary Thomas poses the challenge that the milieu of marriage was not designed to make you happy, but rather, *holy*. Each day I continued living in The Penh, my concept of holy dissipated into resembling an abstract pull-up bar that I had once had a firm hold on, my grip slowly slipping. When Friday evening rolled around, I would kiss Li goodbye and set out to meet up with Mike and prowl the city.

21

I was both frightened and enamored by the city's reckless pulse. The lack of police presence cloaked the city in a peculiar sense of tense freedom. The thriving sex industry left me puzzled. The sight of young girls selling their bodies in order to send money home to their provincial families stretched my comprehension into impossible directions. I loathed the idea of poverty-driven solicitation. But in a country where prostitution had been all but ignored to the point of becoming legalized, I found myself conflicted to the point of re-negotiating my moral compass. It didn't take long for me to take the fall.

Li enrolled in Khmer classes and gave valiant effort in learning the local colloquial expressions. Having become somewhat fluent in *Ewe* during her two years in Ghana, she had a knack for languages. Her time spent with Lika over at New Bird gave her a regular venue for practice and in a matter of months she was able to converse quite well. Her linguistic acclimation opened professional doors, and she eventually landed a part time position working at one of the local NGO's devoted to working with young girls who had fallen victim to the city's viscous prostitution and human trafficking epidemic. This quickly led her to a full-time social work position in a shelter providing emergency housing and counseling to rescued girls. She was once again plugged into a job and a cause that she believed in. Her new professional challenges elevated her from the doldrums, providing her with new focus and an encouraging social circle. At day's end, we'd both converge back at the house and exchange the colorful vignettes from our days. Li and I enjoyed cooking together. Preparing chicken parmesan, I spoke about my students and complained about school politics. Cutting veggies, Li spoke with passion about the girls at the shelter and the sordid tragedies they had come from. The portrayals she gave of her clients were far more interesting than anything I had to share.

Fresh from the American Southwest, Li and I had an insatiable passion for delicious Mexican cuisine and had pretty much perfected the art of the Tex-Mex taco. Once a week we'd declare *Taco Night* and spend an enjoyable evening sipping beers, preparing the ingredients for our regular taco feast. Over dinner one night, Li shared her latest news from work. "We sent a rescue van out to Wat Phnom last night. That's a hot spot where a lot of young sex workers congregate," she explained further. "When the van pulled up some of the girls scattered. Some of the girls don't want to be rescued. We managed to take a few girls back to the shelter and process them in."

I knew about the prostitution around Wat Phnom. I knew it well. Names of the few girls I'd met there flashed through my memory. I hadn't yet crossed the line, but I did remember clearly a recent drunken escapade. One Friday night, after parting ways with Mike I'd motored over to the famed Wat Phnom to check out the scene. Lots of young, ragged looking working girls standing in the shadows waving and calling out to passing motorists. I pulled up to a small cluster of ladies and was immediately surrounded. "Hi, where you from? I go with you handsome man? You like young girl? You want party? You want boom boom?"

Trying to converse, I quickly learned that this was the extent of their English. One girl suddenly jumped up on the back of my motorcycle, wrapped her arms around my waist and whispered into my ear. "C'mon. I go with you. They not speak English but I can speak. C'mon, you take me and we have good party."

I took Srey Mom to the International Guesthouse, bought a six pack in the lobby and paid for a cheap room. Once in the room, we cracked beers and stumbled through some awkward silence. I asked her if she was hungry and ordered a pizza. Waiting for the delivery, Srey Mom disappeared into the shower and minutes later emerged wearing nothing but a white towel wrapped around her wet, dark skin. She took a seat on the bed and flicked on the television. The pizza arrived and we both ate ravenously. Then more awkward silence. Finally, I turned and assured her, "Srey Mom, you are very pretty and seem very cool, but I don't want boom boom tonight."

"Up to you." She gave a simple shrug and cracked another beer.

"But can you give me a massage?"

Tightening the towel around her skinny body, she motioned for me to lay down and proceeded to give me one of the best deep tissue massages I had ever had. After the massage we killed off the rest of the beer, exchanged phone numbers. I delivered her back to her spot in the shadows of Wat Phnom. Just as she was climbing off the bike a car pulled up. She chatted with the John for a few seconds and then off she went. Over the next four years I would see Srey Mom dozens of times. She was a sex worker and a single mother with an infant child. She spoke English and was fun to hang out and party with. I often arranged clandestine meetings with her in guesthouses around the city. We became friends. Ours was a symbiotic relationship, allowing me to keep one foot dangerously dancing into the enticing world of Phnom Penh's underbelly, with my other foot planted firmly on the slippery slope of moral integrity. I paid Srey Mom well for her massage services and for the party. I never once slept with her.

One evening while dicing tomatoes and shredding cheddar for our weekly taco feast, Li discussed the pangs of her new job and the intricacies of Phnom Penh's prostitution scene. "The women are the prey and the men are the predators," she explained. "There's so much focus on getting girls off the street and not enough focus on arresting the John's who finance the industry. If we could somehow shift attention and resources on eliminating the John's…" Portraying a fascinated naivete, I slumped in a sort of guilty silence. I was much more aware of the industry than she knew.

"It's an interesting approach," I concurred. "So many pigs out there using their monetary superiority to exploit the disenfranchised." As I said this, the blade of my knife nicked the tip of my finger oozing blood into the tomatoes.

Our second year living in The Penh proved far better than the first. I continued to acclimate well to the school, to my classes, and had developed a healthy rapport with my students. Li's devotion to learning the language carried her into the Khmer culture and her employment with the NGO helped re-establish her identity. We kept regular company with Lika and Virya at the New Bird restaurant. The many nights we spent sipping beers there, it became obvious by the lack of customers that the restaurant was doomed to fail.

In a last ditch effort, Lika decided to expand the menu. She wanted to add a new string of Tex-Mex dishes that Li had taught her in order to lure in more tourists. Li and Lika met regularly in the New Bird kitchen; Lika eagerly absorbing Li's cooking tutorials. The menu additions did boost the business a bit, but not nearly enough. The current lease on the restaurant was due to expire. And that's when Lika approached Li and me with her savvy business proposal.

Lika wanted to relocate the restaurant to a more active and touristy part of town. Her vision included leasing a hole-in-the-wall and completely renovating the place from the ground up. Hardwood floors, brick walls, dim lighting, original oil paintings, full bar, fully air-conditioned and a completely overhauled Tex-Mex menu catering to the city's ex-pat clientele. Lika's entrepreneurial skills were lethal. She pitched well, and her enterprising mind was creative and convincing. Lika asked me to invest $9,000 for a 49% stake in the new business. Lika would hire staff and manage the place. Li and I would be silent partners and not have to do a thing. When she threw in the perks of unlimited free beer and free food for the duration, I handed her the cash.

Li and I drafted a business contract and suddenly found ourselves in partnership with Lika and Virya. Lika scouted and found a prime location down in the touristy section and just steps from all the Riverside traffic. She signed a two-year lease and within days, construction began on the new joint. To Lika's delight, I christened the place *Casa Lika*.

The restaurant opened to much fanfare. From day one, the place enjoyed a comfortable ambiance throughout the week and was packed out every weekend. We hosted children's birthdays and booked private parties. Many of the students and staff from my school became regular customers. Casa Lika quickly became a darling of the local press and was dubbed "The Best Mexican Restaurant in Phnom Penh." *Travel and Leisure Magazine* gave us an excellent review, expanding our profile to the global tourist industry. The restaurant became mine and Li's second home. When we weren't working our day jobs, we were helping in the kitchen and chatting up customers. I loved the fact that any time of day I could stop in for a free meal, and spent many weekends perched at the bar with Mike, drinking for free. The income we took in was small, but significant. Small enough to cover our monthly rent, and significant given the fact that Lika (with no help from her lazy husband) ran the entire show with whipcrack efficiency. Aside from Li and I directing the marketing end and happily participating in the restaurant's events, we did very little. The investment seemed to be paying off.

Perhaps the biggest dividend came from the fact that Li's depression remained constant, but far less intense. Her employment with the NGO gave her focus, and her nights at Casa Lika seemed to provide her with a healthy social outlet. We continued vagabonding around S. Asia, taking pleasure in the spontaneous and rewarding sensory stimulations, enjoying what we could of our normal and somewhat stagnant marital continuum. Our marriage seemed to be enjoying a subtle revival of sorts. And then I met Kunthea.

Dusk fell over the city. Another Friday night. After kissing Li goodbye, I raced off to meet up with Mike at our favorite joint. The Walkabout was an open-air bar set on the outskirts of Sorya Mall, just a stone's throw from the epicenter of Phnom Penh's central red-light district. The Walkabout was set slightly apart from all the sleaze bars that lined street 51. Ex-pat sex tourists loved the cheap beer and the laid-back casual atmosphere. Free-lancing sex workers filled the place, as it afforded them both freedom from the constraints of working in one of the pimp-driven girlie-bars, and the autonomy to pick and choose their Johns. The bar doubled as a hotel, renting cheap rooms to the constant flow of horny customers that contracted hourly with the bored hookers.

I loved the moment pulling up to the bar. Walking in and seeing Mike's nerdy, smiling face. Ordering beers. Exchanging serious and meaningless stories of the week. Throwing darts, shooting pool and flirting with the working girls who caroused the place. Knowing that for the next two nights I was free to float whimsically about the city, my weekends with Mike assured me I still possessed myself.

Early Autumn in 2008, after another boisterous night with Mike we stumbled into Mei Lien's, an unassuming bar somewhat removed from the strip. The place was completely empty. U2's *Electrical Storm* played on low volume. Two working girls were shooting drunken pool in the back. An older woman, the obvious Matron of the place, sat fat behind the bar fanning herself. A girl stood close to her collating receipts. Thin. Tall. Straight black hair reaching the small of her back. Dark skin. Dark eyes. Dark ambiance. My jaw hit the floor. Collapsing into a booth, I pointed her out to Mike. He gave her a once over and shrugged. "Yep. She's a looker. They all are, Aaron. Khmer women are the most beautiful women in the world. Why do you think I moved here?"

"Mike, I'm serious. That one is drop dead gorgeous perfection!" It was nearing closing time. This was our last stop in a pub crawl that had spanned the last eight hours and I knew I was talking in gross hyperbole. "I mean… *look at her*! I'm already nervous. I hope she doesn't come over to take our order."

The woman stood and approached. Mike ordered while I simply stared. She returned with the beers. "I'm sorry but we close ten minute. You want order more now? Because no more in ten minute." While I continued staring, Mike doubled up on last call. The girl dismissed us with a sad smile, placed our order with the Matron, and then began closing down the shop.

As we were draining our last of the night, the fat Matron came over and sat down next to Mike. "Where you guys from? I not see you in here before." It was a kind greeting from the proprietor, aimed at roping in new customers. "My name Mei Lien. This my place. I know it small, but we make good drinks here and the girls good company."

Mike pounced on the opportunity. "Actually, my friend here is interested in that girl over there." Drowning in a facial blood rush, I could have killed him. I was wasted, and in no respectable form for conversation. Mei Lien gave a quick whistle, and before I knew what was happening the gorgeous girl slid into the booth next to me. Mei Lien introduced her. "This is Kunthea." In my drunken stupor, I politely took her hand and then dove silent and headfirst into my last two beers while Mike sat grinning at me from across the table, enjoying his moment.

Lying in bed the following morning, fighting through severe hangover haze, images of the previous night came slow until Kunthea finally emerged. Her thin face encapsulating manicured brows arcing over mysteriously vacant eyes. High cheekbones. Full lips. Rounded chin and sharp jaw line. Stunning simplicity. Her commanding beauty gently dissolved in a slim aperture of tired, graceful sadness.

Throughout the day I stumbled through my routine with Li, unable to shake Kunthea's face from memory. After dinner that evening, I made up some excuse to leave the house and headed back to the bar. It was closed. I returned the next night and when I walked in, my heart collapsed. Kunthea, along with every working girl in the bar, was crowded into a booth in full ecstatic orgy surrounding some fat guy singing along to *Piano Man*. The table was littered with overflowing ashtrays, empty Coke bottles and a half empty fifth of Jack. The guy was having himself a grand party, throwing bills around the girls laughing, drinking and curling into his arms like kittens. Kunthea sat one girl removed from his grip, but close enough to burn into my brain. I greeted Mei Lien, mumbled some excuse for my quick departure, then locked eyes with Kunthea before making my exit. Her sly wave and shy smile sent me invisible out the door.

I returned the next night. Early on a Tuesday. Mei Lien greeted me from behind her bar as if I was her longtime friend. The place was completely empty. "Where is everyone?" I asked. "Where's Kunthea?"

Mei Lien poured me a draught and shot me a coy smile. "She's in the back with the other girls. They get ready for the work. You like Kunthea?"

"Yes. I want to pay her bar fine."

Mei Lien gave an absent nod and disappeared through a door. Minutes later she appeared with Kunthea in tow. I threw down two bucks for the drink and another ten for the rights to take Kunthea out of the bar for the entire evening.

Kunthea offered me a bashful smile and implored me with her dark eyes. With her hand curled into mine like a small leaf, I led her into the beginning of a nightmare that would eventually devour the next two years of my life, ultimately ending in the destruction of my marriage.

On the street I saddled the cycle and sturdied the bike. I accelerated gently down the street as if balancing a porcelain teacup. "Where we go?" She asked into my ear.

"I want to take you to your house."

"No." She protested. "You not come my house. My family not know I work in the bar."

I pulled to the curb. Killed the engine. "Kunthea, I paid your bar fine, so you don't have to work tonight. You don't have to spend time with any customers, or even with me. I can take you to your house and you can just spend time with your family or whatever it is you want to do. It's a free night for you."

She studied me curiously. "Why you do like that?" To her, my actions and intentions were somewhat bizarre. The bar girls were paid to drink, entertain and negotiate sexual favours for customers. They weren't paid to enjoy nights off at home with their families.

The dynamics were too complicated to explain. "Because I like you. And I want you to have the night with your family." After uncomfortable silence, I added, "If you don't want me to know where you live, I can take you close to your house and then you can walk or take a moto home."

She finally agreed and directed me through the narrow streets to the Vietnamese Friendship Monument. She climbed off the bike. "My house very close. I can walk from here." I knew the neighborhood well. Kunthea lived on the North side of Hun Sen Park. Li and I lived on the South side. From where we stood, I could look across the park and see the end of my street. Kunthea and I lived in the same neighbourhood.

"Have a good night, Kunthea. I will see you again soon."

She gave me a quick hug. "Thank you, you do good for me." She walked a few paces, then turned. "What your name again?"

Her simple question sliced me in half, reminding me that I was nothing more than a John, or a David, or a Joe. "Aaron. My name is Aaron." With a furl of her hair and a casual wave she turned. I stood and watched her weave through the night traffic and disappear down a dark alley.

Over the next several nights I showed up at Mie Lien's, paid Kunthea's bar fine and dropped her off near her house. It was a win-win for everyone. Mie Lien was making money (of which a small portion was paid to Kunthea.) Kunthea was spared the dark existence of having to slave away in the bar eight hours each night kowtowing to piggish customers; able to enjoy time at home with her family. And I was able to go to sleep at night without sordid phantasies flashing through my mind of sweet Kunthea selling her soul in the city's complicated sex-industry. Falling asleep next to Li, I'd convinced myself that my intentions were good, even to the extent of being *spiritually* directed while my moral awareness was slowly eroding into zones of forbidden play. It was a sick dynamic; my sacramental vows to holy matrimony suddenly absorbing the pure and permanent stains of my primal and reckless blood lust.

The weekend came. "Hey Mike. Can't meet tonight. I'll catch up with you next weekend." I didn't want him, or anyone to know about my recent obsession. For now, Kunthea was my secret, and

I wasn't yet ready to share her. After telling Li I was leaving to meet Mike I made my way to Mie Lien's, paid for her bar fine and the two of us made our exit. Only this time I wasn't taking her home. "Kunthea, would you like to go to dinner with me?" She readily agreed and directed me to a small food stall near her house. We talked easily over a cheap but delicious Khmer dinner about my life in Cambodia, her family and her young son. I was entranced by her spontaneous laughter. At one point I asked her age. She was thirty, nine years my junior. After dinner, I dropped her near her house and enjoyed a prolonged good-bye. She didn't rush off, per usual. After chatting a bit, she hugged me, and left me reeling with a gentle peck on the cheek.

Saturday night was a repeat of Friday, only better. After dinner we went for drinks. After drinks we went for a stroll along the Mekong riverside. The night was getting on, but I wasn't ready to take her home. There was nowhere to go. My place was out of the question, and she wasn't yet ready to show me where she lived. We ended up checking into the Asia Hotel, a mid-range urban high-rise with quaint and well-maintained rooms. Still on my best behavior, we spent the next many hours ordering appetizers from room service, flicking through channels, and sipping wine on the eighth story balcony overlooking the enticing lights of the insane city. Around 2:30, Kunthea reminded me that this was always the time she went home after work and that her mother and son would be expecting her. We checked out, and I delivered her back to her dark and deserted neighborhood. Before leaving, we held each other through a long embrace, ending with a kiss. It wasn't long before my weekend infidelities with Kunthea developed into a full-blown affair.

My relationship with Kunthea co-existed with my marital demise. Every second spent with her was another lie spoken to Li. I maintained my clandestine movements under the constant hum and terrifying institutional churn of a mindless backhoe slowly clawing away my moral awareness. It was a tense process. Tense in the sense that my dangerous and continued liaisons led me to deceive myself, defile my vows, and destroy my marraige through subtle cunning and terribly invisible violence. The destruction became mechanical; my selfish will marching forward like a relentless and mindless army content on annihilating anything that interfered with my path. I found myself living in constant pantomime with Li, terrified of being discovered. All the while wandering deeper and deeper into the dark, hideous corridors of the fun house, lying inert under Kunthea's serpentine prowess, laying my head in the lap of Delilah waiting for the guillotine to fall.

The emotional novelty I derived from Kunthea pulled me further and further away from Li, leaving her alienated and bemused. The sexual gratification I derived left Li curling into the sheets alone, wondering where her husband had gone. Entering December, just three months into my affair, the ebb and flow of my marital rhythms had dissolved into utter chaos. In an attempt to rescue both Li and me from our daily discord, I booked us a three-week Christmas holiday in Laos. After kissing Kunthea goodbye, Li and I made our way to the airport and hours later, touched down in the Capital city of Vientiane.

Laos. One of the undiscovered jewels of S.E. Asia. Strolling through the lazy streets of Vientiane was like stepping back fifty years in time. Rural, underdeveloped, poor, and with only thirty people per square kilometer, Laos is a mysterious and fascinating playground for global voyagers bent on exploring off the beaten path. Li and I rented a 600 cc Honda Transalp and set out to discover the country. I had it in the back of my mind that the experience would also help us rediscover and save our marriage.

It was the trip of a lifetime. Over a thousand kilometers spanning ten days. Negotiating the switchbacks through the misty rugged highlands of the Annamese Mountains was the single most exhilarating biking experience of my life. After three days we finally reached the former Laotian Capital city of Luang Prabang. Dating its origins back to the 7th century, the romantic UNESCO World Heritage City provided Li and me a fitting place to reopen closed doors and reacquaint. We found a little B&B tucked down a quaint and quiet alley.

Afternoon on Christmas Eve, we browsed the Luang Prabang market for a Christmas tree. Li discovered a two-inch tall potted evergreen and put it in her pocket. Back in the room we set the small tree on top of the television, drew the blinds and made awkward love for the first time in months. I withdrew and quickly disappeared into the bathroom. When I came back into the room Li was on her back with her legs drawn tightly to her chest. "What are you doing?" I asked through an amused chuckle.

"Making sure our baby doesn't leak out." Our daughter's conception was our last-ditch effort at saving our nearly murdered marriage.

Returning to Phnom Penh refreshed and with new orientation, it was only a matter of days before I found myself immersed fully back into Kunthea's delightful witchery. My reaction to Li's pain reflected little more than disdain, flavoured by a frightening peppering of apathy. Snapping her wings, the pinions of my deceit became a mere exercise of lying. Lying to her. Lying to myself. Content in the process of destroying her and eroding whatever was left of my pathetic *id*, I found myself ready for the descent. Despite Li's extensive accommodations, eternal patience and relentless attempts to make sense of my ever-increasing absences, I continued my path headfirst down the rabbit hole, searching for my evaporated joy. All the while, Gary Thomas' admonitions slamming like a reckless ocean through my deteriorating conscience. *God's primary intent for your marriage isn't to make you happy... but holy.* The words made sense. I understood them with perfect clarity yet gave zero exertion in the application.

I recall fragments of a day, standing face to face with Li in our flat, wandering through the endless rooms of our collapsing marriage. Her small body. My defiant ego. Her fierce and terrified eyes. My selfish center demanding everything and giving nothing. What was left of her willing spirit clinging childlike to whatever was left of my sane comprehension, and the sudden downward swipe of my careless vision. "I don't want to be married anymore. I don't love you anymore." My tongue; a scythe cutting her off like an atrophied limb.

Apprehensive baby steps wading the shallows eventually lead to exploratory depths highlighted by hues of bemused wonder and pure terror; Waking one day to piece together the vague journey that led you to this present and deplorable existence. An honest mind, will at some point pause and try and piece together the broken fragments of the past—all the obliterated memories—all the buried treasures—in an attempt to justify the looming present one finds himself drowning in.

Chapter Two

Phnom Penh, Bangkok
2009 - 2012

A few weeks after returning from our fantastic adventure in Laos, I paced through the house gnawing my fingernails like an expectant father. Li emerged from the bathroom with a calm smile and handed me the test. "It's positive." I hugged her happily. And I was sincerely happy. Not ecstatic. But happy enough. Li seemed happy as well. Not thrilled. But happy enough. With all the ups and downs over the past year, along with my constant lack of emotional and invisible presence in the house, she'd become impossible to read. Li's depression continued, as did my affair with Kunthea.

A Friday evening in January, I'd just finished arranging dinner onto the table, timing it perfectly for Li's arrival. I stood on the balcony listening to the chanting monks across the street, admiring the way the shadows grew long on the ground from the tips of the Wat Botum stupas. Predictably, Li pulled up on her moto at precisely 6:00. Unlocked the gate with a clatter. Pulled her moto into the courtyard. Locked the gate. Her movements resembled a worker ant. I greeted her coming up the stairs, took her backpack from her arm. "Dinner's ready!"

She disappeared into the bedroom with a heavy sigh. "Do I have time to shower first?"

When she finally joined me at the table, she slumped into her chair. "Do you want to pray?" I asked.

"Why don't you?" She demurred. After reciting a laconic *blah* we started in on the already cold meal. Filling the silence, she recited the trivialities of her day, her week, her life. She spoke about the impossibility of rescuing young prostitutes, her frets of pregnancy and about missing her family back in the States. At 6:46 I was clearing the plates. "What are you doing tonight?" She asked.

"Ah, nothing special. Meeting up at The Walkabout with Mike, as usual. Throw some darts. From there maybe… who knows? Probably get some late-night grub somewhere… I'm not really bent on hanging with him too long. I have a short story I'm working on so I'll probably call it early and check into the Asia Hotel and work. I'll be home in the morning."

An hour later and in a fury of sweat I withdrew from Kunthea and lay panting. She climbed on top giggling, gyrating playfully against my impotence. "More! More!" I pulled her down and buried my head into the crook her neck, erasing myself into the flow of her raven black hair. Through the thick strands I stole a glance at the clock on the nightstand. 8:24. "What we do now?" She sang.

I covered myself with the sheets, reached for a Marlborough and asked for a beer. Kunthea pranced to the fridge like a child, grabbed two beers, cracked them both open and leaned her breasts against my chest while lighting my cigarette. "I want you take me out. I want go dancing." I watched her move naked and mysterious around the room through coils of smoke. "I want you take me to hair salon so I can have my hair curled pretty. I want go swimming! You take me to the beach one day?"

My liaison with Kunthea was in its fourth month when one Friday night, in our usual room at the Asia Hotel she suddenly smothered me with kisses. "I want you meet my son and my mother. Can you come my house tomorrow afternoon?"

A long and narrow alley angled deep into an urban village far from the main street. Her street was authentic Khmer. Villagers stared as I passed. *Barang's* seldom (if ever) wandered here. Sidestepping stray dogs and scurrying chickens, we came to a small door. Kunthea unlocked it and I followed her in. Her poverty was more severe than I'd anticipated. Lit by a single low-watt bulb, the entire domicile consisted of one windowless room that tripled as a bedroom, kitchen and family room. The walls and low ceiling were peeling grey in serious need of paint. Neatly arranged and tidy, but depressing. Kunthea immediately set to task folding a large pile of clothes heaped on the bed. A short, frumpy lady with silver hair like a Brillo pad sat on the bed in her pajamas (it was 3:00 in the afternoon) watching Khmer soap operas on a small black and white. Kunthea introduced me. I bowed in supplication. Her mom responded with a fake smile, giving me a suspicious once-over.

Just as I was wishing the ground to open and swallow me whole, a small boy raced through the door and squealed into Kunthea's open arms. She twirled him around, threw him playfully onto the bed and then shot me a tired smile. "This my son. His name is Youngbin." Noticing me for the first time, the boy examined me with wide eyes. Like an adorable, miniature soldier, he stood quick and presented himself rigid in his blue and white school uniform. I didn't know whether to salute or shake his tiny hand. Instead, I knelt and gathered him into a hug.

I held him at arms-length. "Youngbin, do you speak English?" He gave a firm nod. "How old are you?" The boy held up five fingers. He then moved into the kitchen area. Seconds later, he presented me with a plate balancing an apple, a banana and a collection of rambutan—a small fruit the size of large grapes protected with an outer layer of furry spines. I'd never eaten rambutan before. I picked one up and examined it. Youngbin took it gently from my hands and gave me a lesson on how to crack it open. The two of us sat silent on the floor enjoying the delicious snacks. What Kunthea's priggish mother lacked in hospitality was made up by her adorable son. Over the next hour, I made multiple attempts to communicate with the mom through Kunthea's translation, but she had none of it. Her responses came in icy glares, grunts, and at best, an occasional forged smile. Seriously bad vibes from that one.

Over the next many months, I visited the house regularly, often spending entire weekend afternoons with Thea and her family. Much like his mother, Youngbin was a gentle, funny and inquisitive child. The ice between me and Thea's mom eventually began cracking under the warmth of my relentless positivity. But it wasn't until I began speaking the language of dollars that she began offering her sincere and smiling acceptance.

Always inquisitive but never intrusive, I continued to pick up random glimpses into Thea's life whenever I could. For small dollars, I'd gained her physical affections. It was her biography I was sincerely interested in. So far, I'd pieced together that her father had died when she was in her teens, leaving her mother to care for Kunthea, a brother and two other sisters. Left destitute and embittered by her husband's death, Thea's mom had withdrawn the children from their early education and entered them into the provincial workforce as farm laborers. After coming of age, Thea had fallen into Mie Lien's hands through a friend who had recommended her the job. Leaving her family back in Kandal Province, Thea headed for the big city. During one of our earliest dates, she had explained to me while sipping beer and flicking through channels in our room at the Asia Hotel, "I never go with customers. Never!"

But here you are with me. My thought was of course both rhetorical and unspoken.

Thea's sad, fluttering lashes possessed immense persuasion. Whenever an unexpected cost came up in her family, all eyes and expectations fell on me. At first, the expenses were nominal: An extra 5 kg's of rice from the market, or an unpaid electric bill. From there, things suddenly escalated to my being presented with hand-scrawled doctor bills to treat the mom for her sudden and frequent illnesses. One Saturday afternoon I stopped in for a visit and found Thea in tears. Youngbin's school fees? *Uumm... OK.* I agreed with gritted teeth. *How can we deny Youngbin's educational pursuits?* My monthly subsistence trickled out, along with my adamant insistence that Thea quit working at the bar. My pleas fell on deaf ears. To bring the matter up was an automatic trigger for hysterics. "What can I do?" It was her eternal question. "I must take care my son! I must take care my mom!"

My weeks were spent in the flat with Li, struggling daily through a marriage we both no longer loved. Each day we came home with nothing to look forward to but to embrace our evening routines. We ate. Cleared dishes. Negotiated silence. Pretended to attend to each other from the uncomfortable corners of our silent house.

Li continued in her pregnant depression. Confronting her sorrow, I encouraged her to devote her time and attention into the restaurant. She spent most nights there, away from our constant emotional drain. Casa Lika was doing well, attracting a constant flow of customers and providing Li with an alternative to staying at home to endure the not so subtle nuances of my brooding. At the end of each month, Li and Lika would meet, tally receipts and we'd be given our cut. We continued to pay our rent from the profits, but our dividends had dipped noticeably in the recent months. We pointed this out to Lika. "Do not worry." She assured. "Common this time of year. The low season. Things will pick up." Her constant brush-off came with her casual, entrepreneurial smile. And we believed her.

Li had begun to show, her small tummy swelling with hopes of our marital rescue and happier days. Discussions ensued surrounding the particulars of the birth. Faced with the choices of hiring a midwife for a homebirth, having the birth locally or dealing with the implication of having the baby abroad, we decided on the latter. Neither of us were brave enough for the homebirth scene. The local hospitals we went and toured were rudimentary. We elected to have the baby delivered in Bangkok. The school was providing me with excellent insurance and would cover full pre and post-natal care at Samitivej Sukhumvit Hospital, one of the best medical facilities in Thailand.

Li entered her sixth month. We began preparing for her living arrangements in Bangkok where she would spend the last trimester in a rented apartment located near the hospital. I would remain living and teaching in Phnom Penh, commuting to Thailand on weekends. It was a good arrangement. The flight from Phnom Penh to Bangkok was a quick forty-five minute jaunt, allowing me to be with Li during the months leading up to the birth. At first glance, it seemed that the pregnancy was healing aspects of our marriage. Li and I were preparing for the birth of our child and together entering the mindset of *family*. It felt good. Closer examination showed my efforts constantly shaded by the burdens of my other adopted family, and the tensions that came from my continued lies and deceit. Balancing my two existences was like walking a tightrope woven with frayed strips of gossamer. It wasn't a matter of guessing *if* the line would snap, but more a question of *when*?

Sunday morning, September 13th. I groped through the dark for the phone. Li's voice sounded a lifetime away. "You may want to go to the airport. She's coming."

Li and I had already worked out protocols. I was well prepared for the call. I leapt out of bed, grabbed my packed bag sitting by the door and within minutes was racing through the streets towards the airport.

Flights between Phnom Penh and Bangkok departed daily on the hour. I caught the first flight of the day and landed at *Suvarnabhumi* Airport in record time. The immigration robot took a particularly long time examining my passport. "Please Ms., you can see this is my ninth or tenth time to Thailand. Please hurry. My wife is in the hospital delivering our baby!" This encouragement only slowed the robot further. She shot me a faceless expression, and then finally and without a word, stamped my passport. I ran the length of the terminal and fell huffing and puffing into a cab. I handed the driver my pre-printed instructions and directions to the hospital written in Thai. The driver kicked into gear, weaving through the dense morning Bangkok traffic.

Arriving at the hospital, I took the stairs double-time to the fourth floor and presented myself gasping at reception. After three hours of airports, pure urban hum adrenalin rush, chaotic traffic, regimented immigration, whiplash and flash I finally stepped into the delivery ward. The hospital wing was pleasantly lit. Tranquil. Silent. Nurses in starched-white floated ethereal up and down the corridors. A young girl led me calm and smiling down a short hall and showed me to a room. I glanced inside. In the center of the room, Li reclined with wild hair and face still glistening. Her labor had been quick. She'd delivered just two hours after arriving at the hospital. Three young nurses hovered over her like ghosts. I stepped delicately into the peculiar dreamland and kissed Li on her forehead. As Li had given her best effort at delivery and succeeded, I'd also given best effort to be there, and failed. We passed the uncomfortable moment of my missing the birth, then focused on our daughter wiggling and cooing in Li's arms.

Li and I spent two weeks living in the rented Bangkok condo before returning with our daughter to Phnom Penh. I gave best efforts attending to her every need, while learning the ropes of being a new papa. As any father knows, the first year is quite uneventful, save for a lot of diaper changing, sleepless nights, and learning as you go.

Closing my third year at NISC, Li and I made our third trip State-side to spend the two-month summer holiday, but this time carrying the baby. Both sets of grandparents, extended family and friends were waiting to see the nine-month-old new arrival to the family. Li was back in her family element and couldn't have been happier. It was refreshing to see her smiling again. Typical of the ever-increasing chasm that continued to grow between us, I found myself on the opposite end of the spectrum.

After three years of living abroad, half a world away from anything and everything *American*, setting my feet on U.S. soil was like stepping onto the moon. I hated the States. I loathed George W's residual quagmire; all the while cautiously curious and enamored with the image of Obama emerging as the risen Christ.

41

I despised the fact that going out for breakfast at a moderate restaurant in Los Altos ran a bill of twenty-five bucks. At one point I found myself wandering the aisles of Walmart. Everything about the experience felt filthy. American consumer culture. On my third night back, after the jet-lag had worn off, after laying my daughter into her crib, I collapsed angry into bed like an infant stunned in a foreign cradle ranting small limbs at an ominous and unfamiliar sky.

Two weeks after arriving, the novelty of family and friends had waned, and I felt the suffocation beginning to set in. After three weeks, I was climbing the walls and gnawing my tongue. I loathed the neatly cut lawns and perfectly planned grids of American suburbia. Each morning I greeted the predictability and the safety and the daily treadmill existence with a groan, and when dusk settled, I longed for the risqué lawlessness of Cambodia. I wondered about Thea. I stared at the calendar and ticked off the days until our return. After a month, I had had enough. With Li's blessing, I changed my flight and headed back for The Penh.

Clearing customs, I took a tuk-tuk to the house, dropped my bags and headed straight to Golden Sorya Mall. I walked into the bar excited to see Thea. She wasn't there.

"Is she out with a customer?" I asked Mei Lien.

"I not see her long time. Don't know anything."

At Thea's house, her mom greeted me with her typical suspicion, shook her head and slowly closed the door.

Heading back to Sorya Mall, I spent the next hour walking up and down the streets, peaking into bars and restaurants hoping to spot her. Nothing. I returned to the house nauseous. It was three in the morning and in the thick of jet-lag, I was wide awake. On the spur, I suddenly convinced myself that I needed to smoke a joint to help myself simmer down. It was a ridiculous and spontaneous urge. It had been fifteen years since I'd smoked marijuana. I didn't enjoy the buzz. Even so, I called Mike to tell him I was back and to see if he could meet up and get me high. No answer. I then ventured out into the lawless night to see if I could locate my own score. My footsteps naturally headed for *The Building*.

Erected in 1963, The Building was the city's most notorious slum. Spanning four city blocks, the massive four-story complex of deteriorating concrete crammed 500 extended families and squatters into 468 one room cubicles. Unmonitored by the city's civic authorities, plagued with poverty and poor sanitation, the place was a rat-infested lawless entity unto its own and falling apart at the seams. A classic example of urban neglect and decay. The Building was famed as Phnom Penh's epicenter of prostitution, drugs and crime. A quick ten-minute walk across Hun Sen Park delivered me into the heart of the exciting chaos.

3:30 am and the place was in full swing. Within seconds I was swarmed by ambitious pimps peddling a line of silent and jaded girls. Pre-pubescent, expressionless and clothed in rags. "This one for you. So small. No pussy hair! You like? Special price for you!" Walking past the melee and further into the shadows I spotted a cluster of teenaged thugs smoking a joint. I walked up and asked for a hit.

"You have marijuana? I want to buy." My inquiry was met with curious, blank faces. The language barrier complete, I pantomimed holding a pipe to my mouth. One of the boys stuffed a small piece of folded paper into my hand. "Five dollar!" He demanded. I paid him, then made my quick exit back to the house, anxious to smoke.

With no rolling papers or pipe, I reverted to my college dorm days and fashioned a bong out of a tin can. I unraveled the small envelope and stared blank at the contents. Instead of grass, the envelope contained a tiny mountain of shattered glass. I had no idea what it was or what to do with it. Determined to catch any high at that point, I sprinkled a tiny pinch onto the bong and lit up.

The first ride was orgasmic. Straight into a celestial orbit. Dating back to college I'd transversed the gamut of altered states: Pot, X, acid, coke, along with various forms of psilocybin. I thought I'd done it all. But nothing had prepared me for this lunar launch! I then decided to variate the experiment and crushed out three fat lines onto the coffee table. The sensation of inhaling raw ice up the nose is equivalent of receiving a sudden and violent punch to the center of your face. The tiny crystals cut and slice into your mucous membrane like a zillion tiny razors. Face immediately numbs. Eyes water profusely, completely blurring vision for many minutes. It's like receiving a blast of military-grade pepper spray. After falling back on the couch and gouging fists into my eyes I made my way blind down the hall to the bathroom where I shoved my face under the spigot and inhaled water into my scorched nostrils in an attempt to extinguish the inferno, feeling the rush of the toxins gently enter my heart and pulse throughout my body like a warm river, crystal clear, life giving rapture. Reinstated, I sat back down on the couch and loaded another bowl.

Despite my severe jetlag, the small contents of the envelope kept me flying for the next two days. With my lips affixed to the bong, I inhaled all the strength and energy necessary to relentlessly scour the city searching for Thea. After a few hours running around the city like a dog foaming at the mouth, it was back to the flat for a re-fuel. Search for Thea. Get high. Repeat. Soaring into my third day without sleep, just as the sun began bathing the city into its sickening night, I finally spotted her seated outside some random bar entertaining a customer. I took a seat incognito at a bar across the street, ordered a drink, and spent the next torturous hour pinned to her every move.

She was wrapped head to toe in black. Black heels. Nylons. Sexy sleeveless black dress. Her eyes painted perfect with black mascara and eyeliner. She maintained a well-trained and elegant posture, enticing her John with her black soul. Her long black hair fell in perfect curls around her shoulders and down her back. She leaned with elegance and lit her client's cigarettes with exquisite grace and laughed at his every slurred word. I observed her from the shadows, shaking furiously in methamphetamine-fueled delirium. I thought I loved Thea. I knew I hated her John. In vivid detail, I created a fantastic fantasy of following them both to their shitty hotel room, slicing his throat and leaving him squirming on the floor in his own blood; then turning to smother Thea under the pillow she used to fuck on. I wanted to smoke more of whatever it was I'd scored at The Building. I quickly and easily settled on the latter. The ice served a dual and contradictory purpose of dulling my intense jealousy, and at the same time, gave me fuel to chase Thea around town all hours of the day and night. Balancing what was left of my marriage and my extra-curricular relationships involved an impossible landscape of clandestine movements and deceptive dialogues resulting in a constant and exhausting existence. Fixing my lips onto the pipe proved so much easier. Pure escape. By the time Li and my daughter returned four weeks later, I'd waded waist-deep into a threatening *I only use on weekends* addiction to crystal methamphetamine.

Entering my fourth year at NISC, my contract was due to expire. The well-loved principal had retired and been replaced. The new administration, headed by one Mr. Crawford, came armed with classic small town American pedagogy, waving loud and insensitive flags of ethnocentric idealism. The free-thinking AP curriculum was suddenly overtaken by the didactic and International Baccalaureate (IB.) The collaborative governance that students and staff had enjoyed the past three years was suddenly obliterated by a new top-down oligarchy. Exceptional, tenured teachers who'd been working at the school on decade-long contracts were suddenly fired. Crawford's integration into the tranquil NISC family manifest in a violent and exasperating shakedown with heads rolling.

As the school year neared its end, I handed in my resignation. My free-thinking and student-centered approach wasn't appreciated by the Crawford regime, and I simply didn't want to work any longer under his didactic governance.

Li and mine's tenure at Casa Lika was also coming to an end. For months, we had been mystified at the discrepancy between the steady business and the lack of income we were being handed from Lika. The number of receipts she remitted to us at the end of each month had plummeted with no numerical or visible explanation. It didn't take long for us to connect the dots. For nearly a year, Lika had been trimming the receipts, along with our share of the profits. When we sat down with Lika and Virya, they were astonished and offended at our inquiries, stormed out of the meeting and very quickly axed all ties with Li and me. Within a month they severed the lease and liquidated all assets from which we saw nothing. Lika and Virya, our friends and entrepreneurial partners, had taken us for countless thousands, and then simply disappeared.

My madness over Thea continued slipping further and deeper into the darkest mire. My contributions to her mother and family had become less generous and I was no longer welcomed at her house. I managed to track her down on a few occasions—always in a bar setting. The experience of having to sit there watching her schmooze customers was excruciating. She had become a working girl. I'd become a frantic babysitter, trying to make sure she didn't leave with any clients. Though in the end, I was the one left stuck in the corner sucking my thumb.

Chapter Three

Phnom Penh
Autumn 2012 - Spring 2013

Li was constantly absent, preoccupied and tired; the earmarks of an excellent mother. We began discussing the possibility of moving house to accommodate our new orientation to parenthood. I valiantly responded to her exhaustion by encouraging her to fly back State-side for a short holiday to rejuvenate with her family. In her absence, I agreed to take on the onus of finding a new place in the city. It was a smoke screen to veil my every-increasing addiction and infatuation with Thea. The absence of Li and the baby was exhilarating and horrifying. Beholden to no one, the city was mine. My addiction was mine. I had designed the scheme and embraced it with all the vigor of Annie Dillard's moths content on diving into the flames with a voluntary and sincere suicidal apathy.

After a fruitless day of searching for a new flat, I pulled into GSM in search for some action. A girl emerged alone out of the Sorya Mall crowds and paused on the sidewalk deciding which way to go. She took her time coming down the street, stopping in front of stores and bars to examine potential clients. When she finally reached me, I could easily see she held all the visible points of an entertaining companion ready for the long night. She was young. Twenty at most. Tall in heels. Thin wrists. Long, slender neck. A dark-haired angel adorned in a black lace dress like some nineteenth century rococo working girl coming un-done at the seams. She froze me with steel eyes. Thea's eyes, as I recalled, still held a fragment of life. This girl's glare had disappeared far into an intimidating nothingness. In the center of her cherubic face, her blood red lips cracked a grin. Her vacant stare failed to support her smile.

"Handsome man, you want lady?" She wasted no time.

Neither did I. "Yes. I want a girl who smokes ice."

She climbed behind me on the back of a moto and directed me ten minutes away from the lights of Sorya Mall into one of the city's darkest ghetto. The place made The Building seem like a resort. *Boeung Kak*, formerly known as *The Lakeside,* was a sodden section of the city that had been swallowed up and spit out by the inspiration of potential urban development. Once tucked neatly on the shores of *Boeung Kak* lake, the community had been a thriving tourist destination. Over the past few months, the ninety-hectare lake had been entirely landfilled by the government and no longer existed. Countless businesses went under. Four thousand families had been evicted and displaced. The remaining squatter community covered a half square mile that now resembled a wasteland of urban decay, social annihilation, and addicts roaming aimlessly.

My nameless dead-eyed girl took me by the hand and led me up a flight of stairs into a pitch-dark corridor. I held my hand against the wall to steady my pace. She knocked twice on a door and whispered something in Khmer. The door immediately invited us into a dark hovel lit only by candles where I was greeted by fourteen curious eyes.

The most prominent eyes fixed on me from a small woman set cross-legged like some tranquil Buddha holding a baby to her naked sagging breast. She motioned for me to sit. Her narrow face warmed the room with a wide smile and her dark eyes laughed with brilliance. "I am Sana."

All around Sana, an orderly circus of children, all under the age of ten, tumbled over the floor. Half amused, the children greeted me with feigned curiosity before diverting attention back to their playthings. The final set of eyes observed me briefly from the darkest corner of the room. A few feet away from the rolling children, a small shirtless Khmer man reclined on the family mat, giving best effort to loving the last live vein in his skinny arm.

Sana set her sleeping baby gently onto a dirty pillow, swabbed the last drop of milk dripping from her swollen nipple and rearranged her blouse. The man in the corner slipped the needle from his arm and placed it into a small wooden box up on a shelf out of the children's reach. He then pulled a makeshift shower curtain, separating himself from the rest of the room.

Sana was kind and gentle. Her English was good. She took my order and made pleasant small talk while weighing out the crystals onto a small digital scale. Deal done, my companion and I rose to leave. On my way out the door, Sana located a scrap of paper and wrote her number down in red crayon.

Next day as the sun neared high noon, I was back at Sana's door ready for my re-up. The scene in her humble room was drastically different from the night before. The H junkie was gone and only two children remained. Her eldest daughter looked after the youngest baby while Sana portioned my order onto the scale. Her tiny fingers expertly loaded and lit the bong and the two of us spent a half hour blowing through a hoon. She spoke with a resigned calm about her poverty, accentuating her story with the delicate and fluid motions of an Apsara dance.

Fingers, wrists, body, feet, head. Aside from her gorgeous smile and fluid voice, everything about Sana was tiny. She reminded me of a brightly painted songbird, in constant motion and with a pleasant canticle dripping from her lips. I slouched to match her tiny posture. Her English was limited and broken, but she worked her way through short sentences with careless confidence.

Seeing Sana on a daily basis, we quickly became close. I was bringing in a lot of cash into her otherwise impoverished household while she kept me in product. After scoring, Sana and I would load up and pass hours chatting and playing with her kids. One afternoon I arrived and she was out of product. The two of us climbed on a moto and rode to *Phsar Chas*, another ghetto neighborhood near the Riverside. I followed her into a massive tenement building. Side-stepping a few rats, we hiked up the dark stairwell four floors to the very top of the structure. The door opened a crack and the face of a kind looking grandmother appeared. We entered a tidy room not much bigger than Sana's place. Sana and I sat cross-legged on the floor as the granny eased herself into a hammock and began cooling herself with a paper fan. Sana introduced me to Ehoi.

Ehoi barked out a shrill sound and out of nowhere, a small child magically appeared. Under Ehoi's orders, the child vanished into the adjoining room and then re-appeared seconds later balancing three cups of tea and some crackers on a tray. I sat sipping silent as Sana and Ehoi exchanged Khmer pleasantries. After some minutes, Ehoi dismissed the child from the room. Once the child was gone, and in one fluid motion, Ehoi reached behind her back and withdrew a gigantic cellophane bag full of ice, along with a pipe. She handed the package to Sana who busied herself with preparing the session.

The quality of Ehoi's product was top grade, far superior to Sana's. After sampling, I threw down a hundo and was thrilled to see Ehoi portion out nearly double of what my hundred would have scored me at Sana's house. I immediately exchanged contact info with Ehoi, my new contact and supplier. Ehoi spoke broken English. Sana translated that I was welcomed to stop by anytime. As we were leaving, I caught glimpse of Ehoi handing Sana a large was of bills—commission for Sana bringing in a new and profitable customer.

When my supply ran out, I made my second pilgrimage to Ehoi's for a re-up. Near midnight. On the way I made a swing through Sorya Mall to check out the scene. The cesspool was in its usual nocturnal swing. Music pumping. Neon flash. Young girls browsing Street 51 taunting the legion of Johns congregating at tables around flowing beer bottles. I stopped into Mei Lien's to catch a glimpse of Thea. She wasn't there.

Rolling into *Phsar Chas* alone was unnerving. The neighborhood was famed for its day-time petty theft and night-time all out thuggery. The four flights up to Ehoi's door offered no lights. I groped my way through the cement corridor by the light of my phone. I took a seat on the floor. Ehoi appeared nervous. No child summoned. No tea offered. The door to the adjoining room remained open a crack; enough for me to catch snapshots of another adult in the flat. Arms and legs moved about in strict masculine fashion. Definitely a man. A man in uniform? A black uniform with a small rack of badges affixed to the breast. A cop? Overwhelmed with bad vibes, I got up to leave. Reclining in her hammock, Ehoi made a *tsssst* sound and motioned for me to stay put. I obeyed. Minutes later, the door to the adjoining room opened. Sporting short-cropped hair and a neatly trimmed mustache, the man stood small, starched and handsome in his Khmer military uniform. Black boots polished. Pants and shirt pressed to perfection. He examined me with a glare of abusive authority. He motioned for me to join him. I walked into the room. He closed the door and invited me to sit.

The space was no bigger than a walk-in closet; a spartan bedroom with nothing but a bed and a side table. We sat across from each other on the floor, knees touching. The man eyed me suspiciously for an uncomfortable moment. He then placed his palm on his chest and greeted me with a friendly smile hinting mischief at the corners. His voice sounded like a country gravel road riddled with potholes. "My name Hout." He announced. "Master Hout!"

Mirroring his motions, I slapped my chest hard and looked him in the eye. "My name is Aaron!"

When I did this, Master Hout threw back his head and exploded in peals of laughter. He then reached behind him and placed two objects between us. The first was a black revolver that landed on the wooden floor with a thud. From the drawer in the nightstand, he withdrew a small wooden box and laid it next to his gun. Flipping open the lid, the container resembled a small tackle box with four squares of small partitions, each containing a different drug. Master Hout leaned over his stash and initiated my orientation. *"Nih ne?"* He pointed. "Heroin! Very good. Very strong. *Nih ne?* Ice! *Haey now tinih?* Ecstasy! *Nih ne?* Marijuana!" Master Hout didn't speak, he barked. Each syllable shooting from his taut mouth like a curt and ungracious military command. A venomous viper bite.

Over the next few hours the Master prepared samples of his wares for me to taste. I was familiar with his supercharged ice, but the rail of pungent black tar sent me spiraling downward into a peculiar lull that I'd never experienced before. A half tab of very trippy X managed to pull me from the depths, and I eventually leveled out with a bong full of kind weed.

Writing down calculations into a small steno notepad, he kept meticulous record of everything I ingested. With my tutorial coming to a close, the Master handed me a small paper sac containing a myriad of drugs, along with a very clear mathematical diagram of assets and expenses. Marching me to the door, he handed me a bill of sale with a smile. Ehoi sat up in her hammock, offering her best translation. "Master Hout… he say… you sell everything. He say you come back… give him money." And thus began my career as a strung-out, drug dealing entrepreneur.

Exiting the Master's house, I was completely and utterly trashed. I gave best effort to present understanding and understood absolutely nothing. I wandered down the dark stone stairwell bracing myself like a cripple. Emerging onto the street and overwhelmed with the psychological weight of public scrutiny, I sought out the nearest dark alley and collapsed to the dirt spewing my overdose over stone walls in explosive vomit. Once purged and relieved from my psychological torment, I righted myself, hailed a moto taxi and once again entered the city. It was dawn. I was in no way, shape or form fit for public consumption. I tried to focus and saw only blur. The sun rose, watering my eyes like contagious sores. I loved my immediate blindness, and the way it bored into my conscience with all the fail and futility of an empty threat. I loved the fact that I couldn't see reality. On the back of the moto, I threw my head back and cackled like a fiend. Racing blind through the morning streets offered me a peace bordering an indescribable and undefinable suicidal abandon.

I eventually found a newly constructed flat situated on street 330 directly in the center of town next to the *Toul Sleng* Genocide Museum. The furnished two-bed, two bath, full kitchen, family room came with a high balcony offering an expansive view over the entire neighborhood. Li and the baby were due to arrive in four weeks. I plunked down the payment, signed a year lease, exited the guesthouse and moved into the new spread carrying nothing but my backpack. I spent my afternoon wandering through the rooms, sucking on the pipe, getting to know the place. I dashed an email to Li announcing the positive developments.

One early afternoon, after parting ways with Master Hout, I returned to the new house and tried reviving in a cold shower. Saturated in a soaring high, I danced through the rooms like an insane marionette: Strings pulled by my extended absence from Li. Not directly associated with my being away from her, but more from the sense of freedom that grew from our progressing alienation. It was a strange and complicated emotion. Despite our marriage being on the outs for years, a certain part of me missed her and left me lamenting over memories of our better days. The distance from my estranged and beloved daughter was another story. I missed her terribly and was elated and anxious to hold her again. I constructed a large calendar and hung it on the wall. Whenever Li called on Skype, my daughter and I together would make big X's, crossing off the days until her return.

With my mouth permanently affixed on the pipe, I easily convinced myself that my productivity was directly associated with Li's absence. I had found our new flat and had begun prepping it for Li and the baby's arrival. I had also networked with Sana, Ehoi, and now Master Hout. In a blur of abstract days, I'd managed to climb the consumer ladder from small-time street buyer up to face-to-face top-tier exposure and employment with one of the most prominent dealers in the city.

Sorya Mall, with all its filth and debauchery, became my playground and center of distribution. Utilizing Bopha, Srey Mom and a few other working girls, I put the word out that I was open for around the clock service. Within twenty-four hours my phone was ringing off the hook. Ice was my biggest seller. The hookers were my most frequent customers, snapping up hoons: a small and cheap quantity weighing .37 grams. Heroin was the next big seller: Too expensive for the girls, but popular amongst the American ex-pats living and working in the city. The X and the weed moved too slow. Hout's pot wasn't that great and his price on the X was too expensive. In the ensuing days I quickly became Hout's favored pet; a most productive lackey, unloading my daily supply, making him a shit ton of cash and returning the following day for more.

Master Hout's jurisdiction centered from his little flat in *Phsar Chas* and extended west along the riverside covering the neighborhoods of Central Market, *Boeung Kak* (where Sana lived) and all the way into *Tuol Kork*—covering a four square-kilometer radius. I moved freely, untouched, even respected under the shadow of the Master's enormous reputation. Even the cops turned a blind eye at my arrival. I was *known*.

Shooting off Street 51 there was a neighborhood alcove known in common circles as *Ice Alley*. Spanning about three city blocks, the place was constructed of interconnected shanties providing ghetto housing for the lowest echelon of societal displacement. With its proximity to Sorya Mall, many of the working girls of the city lived in the wooden rattraps and cement blocks with their extended families and called the neighborhood home. I entered the alley with the hope of running into some working girl friends and unloading some hoons. Aside from some grandmothers sweeping their afternoon stoops, the alley was dead. Exiting the alley, my heart dropped into my stomach when I caught sight of Thea.

Many months had passed since I'd last seen her. Her sudden presence bent my already warped mind into impossible directions. The brief sight of her launched a sudden and relentless onslaught of mental implications spanning canyons of sorrow. Dressed in a loose fitted white dress that brushed lightly on her naked thighs, she walked alone, face painted in sexy make-up and head held high with an air of fragile certainty. Poised on long, thin legs, she appeared perfect. Always perfect. I recalled MacGrath's lovely expression. *Ah, that woman in the mask, that chimera of a night, that fancy of an hour!*

I followed her for only a few seconds before she vanished into the Shanghai Bar. I stood mute in the shadows gnawing my tongue in a violent urge to chase her, tackle her, bathe her with my tears, rapture her into the depths of my vice-grip arms and smother her to death with kisses resembling nails.

Shanghai was situated in the center of the strip. Decked out in modern American décor, the large room offered an extensive bar and dance floor. Always full, the place doubled as an unrepentant whorehouse; packed nightly with a hundred or more scantily clad working girls milling about the thirsty and hungry ex-pat patrons looking to score. Famed as one of the busiest girlie bars in the city, the place did well to define The Penh's mechanical industry of sleaze. Movement in and out the front door resembled an army of ants. Ex-pats entered, only to re-appear minutes later with a sad girl draped over their arm en route to dark and cheap motels scattered around the dark corridors of the city.

I entered the bar and scanned the place. Thea was nowhere. I ascended the stairs up to the roof top. The place was humming. Guetta's *Titanium* blasted from the pumping sound system. Milling madly through the noisy crowd, I paused with brief introspection, viewing myself through the hundreds of eyes that suspiciously followed my frantic movements. Stumbling through tables and chairs, it dawned on me how wasted I was. Ducking into the WC, I took a long piss and endured the awful minute of facing myself in the mirror. I smiled, trying to convince myself that I didn't in fact look like absolute shit. Days without sleep painted my eyes with dark circles and my dilated pupils roamed wild trying to focus. I was covered in a sheen of sweat that bled into the collar of my T-shirt. Descending the stairs like a blind cripple, I turned the corner and spotted her through the crowd. She was behind the bar taking orders and serving drinks. I knew I wasn't in any shape to present myself and ducked out. Back at the house, I showered, changed clothes and readied myself for a more appropriate presentation.

I returned to the bar at quarter to two. The busiest time of the night. Scummy Johnny's ordering last call and making last choice of the girl they'd take home for the night. I took a seat at a table on the patio directly in front of the fan. Waited. My stakeout afforded me a view through the window. I could see Thea pouring drinks, making nice with customers and closing the place down for the night. My high anxiety split in two directions. I was nerve-racked over the thought of actually speaking with her again. And the very real possibility of seeing her come out of the bar with a companion sent me into an irrecoverable mental skid. Too much tension. More than I could handle. I decided to give her (and myself) fair warning. A young waitress with dyed blonde hair appeared and began stacking chairs, closing the patio for the night. She smiled sweetly. "Handsome man, you want one more drink? You want lady? We close ten minute."

"Thank you, no. I'm waiting for Kunthea. Can you please tell her that Aaron is here?"

The girl paused. "Who you wait for?"

"Kunthea." I pointed. "The girl behind the bar. I'm her friend."

The girl followed my finger and stared at Thea through the window. "Who?"

"Kunthea. Right there! The girl with long hair talking with that guy."

The waitress wrinkled her nose and shrugged. "That not Kunthea. That girl name *Sara*."

56

It was common practice among working girls to disguise themselves with a *nom de plume*—an invented pseudonym to help disguise their identities and distance themselves from their working girl realities. *Sara*. Hearing the name was like a Hank Aaron homerun swing connecting with my skull.

The bar emptied. It was around 2:30 when the lights finally dimmed and the blinds were drawn. Thea was among the last of five girls to exit. The group chatted for a minute and then dispersed, with Thea walking quickly to the street.

I emerged from the shadows. "Hi Sara."

She whirled. Out of context, she looked me in the eye directly and studied me curiously for a moment. She took a few steps, and her impatient face melted into a grin. "Oh my God! Aaron?"

I stood and approached her cautiously. "Hi Thea." She offered me a hug. We held each other in silence. Li and mine's affections had long since evaporated. Thea's embrace was the first taste of intimacy I'd felt since I had last seen her nearly a year ago. We stood on the street catching up like old friends. She gushed me with questions, and I gave her all the answers she wanted to hear. She said she was exhausted and asked me to take her home. Hailing a tuk-tuk, we rode through the melting night back to her old familiar neighborhood. I walked her down the dark alley to her door. "OK. My mom and Youngbin, everyone sleep now," She whispered. "You come see me tomorrow?" She leaned in and placed a bashful kiss on my lips. And with a running start, I took the dive off the old familiar cliff, free-falling a thousand feet straight back into the churning whirlpool.

I showed up the following day. Her door was open. I peaked in. Youngbin leapt off the bed and nearly knocked me down with a locomotive hug. Thea's mom stood, pressed her palms together in polite supplication, mumbled something in Khmer, then squeezed past me and disappeared down the alley. Our meeting was brief. Thea explained that she had an appointment with Youngbin's school and needed to go. She discouraged my offer to come along. "Please, you meet me at Shanghai tonight. Two o' clock, after my work?"

At quarter to two I slipped my head through Shanghai's front door and caught Thea's eye through the throng of customers. She gave a wave and returned a happy, tired smile. In the tuk-tuk ride, she took hold of my hand and leaned her head heavy on my shoulder. Up the long stairs and into the flat I led her through the rooms with an enthusiastic tour of the place. Her grin was forced, polite at best. I asked her if she was hungry. She opened the fridge and placed three eggs, bread, jam, and an apple onto the counter. She vanished down the hall while I whirred up her breakfast. Arranging it all neatly onto a tray, I carried it into the bedroom. The light was off. She had dissolved into the thick comforter with the longest strands of her dark hair flowing over the white pillow. I set the tray onto the nightstand and ran my hand lightly through her hair. She rolled over with a sigh. Propped herself up against the headboard. Brushed her hair from her hazy 3:00 am eyes and cooed. "I'm so tired." Her breath came like an artist's apprehensive brush stroke onto a terribly conceived canvas. She picked at her meal. I laid down next to her in the half dark tragedy of our warm and terrifying reunion.

"Why you come looking for me again?"

"I never stopped looking for you. I was afraid to come by your house. I know your mom doesn't like me."

Silence.

"Thea. You awake?"

"Yes."

"Why did you stop work at Mei Lien's? I tried to find you there a few times."

She took a nibble of her apple and stared at me; her face shrouded in the tired gloom of the room. "Oh... no customers there." She whispered. "No tips. Shanghai have many customers. Many people drinking. I can make more money. You know, Aaron, I give my mother money. Youngbin have to go to school." She sat up further and took a small bite of her cold eggs. Dipped the bread into the strawberry jam. "Why you come look for me?" She repeated her question.

"I love you, Thea. And I can't stay away from you." We passed a comfortable silence. I shattered it by asking, "Why did you change your name to Sara?"

She stabbed me with a sudden and doubtful glare. She reached up and like a playful kitten, slapped me on my nose. "Silly man. You not love me. Only sleep now. I so tired." She kissed me and then disappeared deep back into the sheets and was instantly asleep. I wrapped my arms tight around her trying to pull her back. I lowered my face into the curve of her collarbone and listened to her breathing dip deep into a swirling and violent dreamscape.

I spent the night and into the morning in the front room smoking incessantly while Thea slept. A few times I heard her cry out and lingered in the hall to see if she was OK. Watching over her, it was clear her slumber was plagued with sleep terrors. Every so often she would explode into sudden bursts of movement and groans. I held her through her convulsions while her mouth dripped saliva onto the pillow speaking in a hushed chorus of incoherent tongues.

Around eleven I left the house and rolled over to Khmer Kitchen, Thea's favorite restaurant, and loaded up on pounded eggplant dip, *samlor korkor*, caramelized fish with green mango and spring rolls—all her preferred dishes. Once again balancing the banquet on a tray, I roused her lightly to a brunch in bed. She ate ravenously, talking casually about Youngbin's school and the burden of looking after her mom. When I asked about her job at Shanghai, she became impatient, dodging my pointed questions, stating simply, "I never go with customers!" After our lunch she showered, dressed, did the dishes and cleaned the kitchen. "I have to go back home now, Aaron. My mom not know where I am. I help Youngbin with his schoolwork. Please, you take me?"

Dropping Thea back at her house, she left me in the alley with a long, warm kiss. "So, I'll come to Shanghai again tonight at 2:30?" I asked. "You can come back to my house or I can take you home. Whatever you want." Twelve hours later I again pulled up to the bar to watch the exodus of the last-call drunks filing out the front door with their young Khmer trophies. I took a seat on the patio and watched Thea clean the bar and close the place down. She hopped on the back of my moto and wrapped her arms around my waist. "Where you want to go, Thea? You want to come to my house?"

"I go home. My mom sick and I can't stay out." Pulling up to her place, I parked and walked her to her door. She interlaced her fingers into mine and leaned against me with the full weight of her melancholy.

My early a.m. Thea pick-up's at Shanghai became the norm. It was my benevolent act to ensuring her purity, along with giving best efforts to worm my way back into her graces. Waking at noon, I'd begin my day at Master Hout's, getting high and loading up on my stash for the day's deliveries. Afternoons and evenings were spent rolling around the city dishing crystals around Sorya Mall, making house calls to scummy ex-pat junkies with the H and partying with customers. Around midnight, I'd return to the house, force feed a meal, shower, smoke up and then roll over to Shanghai. Most often I simply delivered Thea home, but on the few and happy occasions, she came back to my place. We quickly fell back into our heated and hopeless relationship, absorbing each other into our daily routines. Our renewed passions were short lived; disrupted by Li's September return.

By the time Li and the baby showed up, my 24-hour delivery business had blossomed into a lucrative operation. My daily meetings with the Master never failed to launch my busy schedule. Profits were consistent—pulling in about a hundred dollars a day. But given the fact I was inhaling half my earnings left me with just enough to eat, pay bills and dash small cash to Thea whenever she asked. I loved the thrill and the reckless illegality of the occupation. Making my own hours. Living my sleazy nocturnal existence. Dishing hoons left and right through Sorya Mall. High every waking hour. I enjoyed my company with the working girls. I felt at home wandering the dark alleys, huddled over bubbling bongs in $5 rented rooms sharing free smoke and listening to the girls discuss their sad and transient lives. And my sporadic nights with Thea were filled with relational satisfaction and emotional fulfillment I hadn't enjoyed in years.

Li and the baby arrived at the airport on a night flight connecting through Seoul. I met them at the airport juiced to the gills. Despite months of separation, Li greeted me with her usual banal affect. Waiting to retrieve her bags, she examined me under her precise stare. "You look terrible." It was true. I'd been awake for three days and hadn't eaten in four; my only nourishment coming from a constant ingestion of meth and guzzling Coca-Cola by the liter.

Having just endured a twenty-hour flight with our baby, Li appeared haggard as well. I took my sleeping daughter from her arms and nuzzled her while Li hailed a tuk-tuk. She opened her eyes, reached up and touched my face. "Hi Papa." I felt mule-kicked realizing our baby was now a toddler. We arrived at the house just past 1:00 am. Carrying all the luggage up the stairs, I was excited to show Li the new flat. "The landlord lives on the main floor with his wife. Very nice people. You can see, Li, it's a great central location. And the place is brand new. We're the first tenants. I think you're gonna love it!" I had done well securing and furnishing the place for the family's arrival. I walked her through the rooms, giving her the tour. "So? What do you think?"

"Yeah, it's nice." She quipped, with all the enthusiasm of a corpse. I could have walked her into Prime Minister Hun Sen's palace and her reaction would have been the same. After unpacking essentials, Li made a quick sandwich from the stocked fridge and collapsed. I put our daughter to bed in her new room and fell asleep next to her.

Having my daughter again renewed and thrilled me to no end, but Li's sudden presence spooked me completely. We had learned to endure each other, in exchange for sharing our child. Her arrival shattered all pleasant equilibrium. She came in like an overzealous cleaning crew scouring the already spotless flat, spraying my tranquil existence with her constant and polarizing mental disinfectant. Her lack of enthusiasm for anything was nothing new. I fed off her apathy. It only took two days for me to clearly see the impossibility of cohabiting with her and maintaining my blazing habit, illegal business and reckless lifestyle.

Li returned to her former social work position, providing services for girls rescued off the street while I continued supplying the same population with all the ice they required. The irony was too thick for me to fake my way through. Every minute I spent with Li I felt like a bug under a microscope. I developed a constant and hideous hallucination: Li as an unhappy and sadistic child kneeling in the dirt holding a magnifying glass searching out worms to paralyze and fry; and me as the worm sizzling under her focused and precise lens. Li spent her days acclimating back into her work. Her identity. I passed the days playing with our daughter, lulled under her charms, and at the end of the day giving reports to Li about my pretend and continuous job search. Li was a wonderful mother. And I, an adoring but terribly distracted father. A week after their arrival, I announced that a marital separation was in order. The passion to end the marriage, albeit destructive, was clearly on my end while Li seemed to have little passion for anything at all.

I took up residence about five minutes away, renting a second storey flat in a fine three-story mini-mansion on the other side of the Dyke Road. The house was in the extreme south of the city where the burbs butted up against rice fields. The street didn't even appear on the city map. It took a fifteen-minute moto ride to reach Hout's each day, and I was still relatively close to Li and my daughter. The idea of being off the grid and far away from the chaos of Sorya Mall was appealing. The new location induced a crucial alteration in my business scheme. Instead of providing my usual 24-hour delivery service around town, I decided my clients now had to come to me. I liked the anonymity of my new neighborhood. It was deathly quiet, providing me a solace away from the constant madness I found myself becoming lost in. A place I could comfortably repose in my decay. The very fact that I needed this solace was testament to my rapid descent into treacherous water. I knew this. I was aware of it. Offering a vague and lazy nod in the right moral direction was followed by zero vicissitude. I simply didn't care.

Living for so long and weathering Li's depression, it had become impossible to discern the precision and scope of her observations. Her baseline was banal, at best; an even and blasé temperament fluctuating between boredom and disapproval. Had she caught on to details of my illegal and extra-curricular activities?

Despite Li's constant encouragement to find gainful employment, I continued to shelter my clandestine identity. I was making money and that's all I cared about. I couldn't tell her about my drug dealing as the mainstay of my daily income. I weathered her persistence like a cloistered, elderly grandfather enduring the *drip drip drip* of a leaky faucet. In January, she called with "…good news! I have a colleague here at work. Her husband is the science teacher at Hope International School. They are looking for a part-time high school English teacher. I spoke with the Headmaster, and he said he would be interested in interviewing you."

Hope International School was well-established in Phnom Penh. Its student population was made up largely of kids whose families were involved in Christian-based NGO's and missionary work in and around the country. Ensconced in my flat blazing through hits off the glass, I queued up their webpage and weighed the option.

Pros: The school was small. Small classrooms translated into a minimal amount reading and grading papers and assessments. I'd only be teaching part time. The school was just a four-minute moto ride from my new place. *Cons:* The school followed the IGCSE; a British-based curriculum I had no experience with. According to the school's mission, teachers were expected to "… reflect the love of God in their relationships with the students, and try to incorporate a biblical worldview into their teaching…"

Loading another rock in the glass, I mulled this over. The pros were strong. In addition to having Li off my back, I'd be pulling in additional income, all the while still able to maintain my business with Master Hout and my frequent liaisons with Thea. The cons were weak: Nothing I couldn't fake my way through.

I made an appointment and met with the Director. He was a *nice*, elderly gentleman who gave his best to enthuse cutting edge philosophy but, tried as he might, couldn't hide his old school rigidity. He loomed large behind his gigantic wooden desk. Bespectacled with grey hair and beard, the way the sagging skin on his throat wobbled like a chicken's crop when he spoke made me shift uncomfortably in my chair. The interview was predictable—the Director running through the usual litany, and me maintaining one step ahead of his didactic questions. I'd just come off smoking a quarter gram and sat opposite his inquiries, feeling odd and extremely high like a mischievous schoolboy writhing under the meticulous scrutiny of observation. Everything about the school and its governance reeked of archaic establishment trying its best to break through into progressive education. My CV was competitive. My experiences at NISC were impeccable. My references, reliable and tight. As the old guy hemmed and hawed his way through the tension, I decided to take full control.

"Sir? Do you mind if we take this moment to join together and pray over this divine appointment?"

Together, we bowed our heads. Laced with dazzling mercurial exhortations and sincere piety, I hefted that prayer and deposited it directly onto the footstools of Heaven with all the sincerity of a preacher poised at a Lake of the Ozarks pig roast tent revival. And no sooner than the Director and I had both voiced our *Amen's*, I was offered the job to begin the January, Winter semester.

It was a good gig. Three hours per day. Fifteen hours per week. An ideal job allowing me to maintain my daily sacrosanct rituals of addiction, whoring and deceit. The school's governance even threw in the bonus for my daughter to attend the pre-school free of tuition along with medical insurance for the entire family.

The students I greeted on my first day were delightful. The girls were well dressed, refined in their spiritual modesty. The boys sat clean cut and still. The entire class, respectful and eager for instruction. I found myself faced with an eternal legion of porcelain faced shiny freshmen and sophomores ginning at me with painful enthusiasm. Ninety percent of them were children of Christian missionaries. And fresh from my house where I had just said good-bye to Thea and had drained a full glass of Master Hout's finest product, I greeted the class tongue tied. I had no idea what to say.

It took a few days of getting to know the kids before I finally settled in. My four years at NISC, and my AP and IB certification had prepared me well. The students were charming. Hard working. Willing to please. But I didn't like the new IGCSE curriculum. I found it didactic and rigid like the IB, and oh so… *Bri-ish*. The book list was loaded with unfamiliar titles. I decided to embark on an in-depth study of Oscar Wilde's, *The Importance of Being Earnest*.

Each morning I showed up high and sleep depraved, stumbling through the farcical comedy in which the protagonists assume fictitious personalities to escape their onerous social obligations. Life imitating art, I was certainly qualified as a first-hand example of what I was teaching, but having never read the play, I made up the entire curriculum as I went along. In a dismal reversal of effective pedagogy, I gave my best efforts to keep up with the students. I survived my first month at Hope by showing up to class stoned, faking my way through lessons, pacifying my students with intriguing ambiguity.

After departing the Master's place one night with a large bag of candy, I was roaring through the streets on my moto when the front wheel hit a pothole. I woke half-conscious on the asphalt. I remember staring up at the sky and laughing like some alien drug fiend—entranced at the fragile cotton clouds threading over the weak luminescence of the half-moon like breathed-on strips of tinsel. I felt no pain. Everything hilarious. I found my feet, righted the moto and rolled home at an idle with a peculiar numbness shooting up my leg. Back at the house, I lit another glass, then hobbled into the bathroom to check my injuries.

My left ankle was grotesquely twisted. Staring into the mirror, I watched the three-inch gash on my neck empty a rivulet of blood over my right shoulder trickling down my chest. I spent the early morning alternately sucking on the pipe and wrapping myself in home-made butterfly bandages creatively constructed from masking tape and fabric strips scissored from my pillowcase. I hobbled into my classroom just after sun rise. I have the vague memory of a concerned student offering herself as a human crutch, supporting me to my desk. "Mr. Reed! Oh my, what happened? Let me help you!"

Weeks later, I woke dazed in an empty classroom. Wiping the drool off my face and desk, I focused in on the clock. Half past six in the evening. The kids had long gone. The school was deserted and dark. The last thing I could recall was spouting some abstract lecture to a room full of bemused faces. I heard a *swish swish* in the hall. The school's Khmer janitor entered the room, leaning his full weight against his cart of cleaning supplies. I stood and gathered my things. Mr. Khieu was small. He clapped me lightly on the shoulder and filled the room with his gigantic grin. "Goodnight Mr. Reed. You working too hard. Time you go home."

Three months after being hired, I found myself full circle— seated back in the Director's office. The *nice* Headmaster adjusted his glasses and paralyzed me with an uncomfortable silence. Reverting to my initial bogus strategy, I offered to pray over our audience.

The Headmaster nodded patiently and raised his hand, as if placing an oath onto the thick and uncomfortable air. "Before you do, I'd like to share some information." Out of his desk came a stack of yellow post-its. "These are dictations I've taken from students, fellow staff members, phone calls and meeting with parents over the last two months." He began flicking through the notes, reciting...

"Mr. Reed sometimes seems like he's distracted in class. Mr. Reed gives interesting lectures, but sometimes he seems like he doesn't really know the material. Mr. Reed never grades our papers... we turn them in but never get them back... I don't know what my grade is. Mr. Reed never gives any formal feedback. Mr. Reed is often late for morning orientation, and we don't get the daily announcements. Mr. Reed seldom attends staff meetings. Mr. Reed never returns my emails or phone calls."

Setting aside the notes, the Headmaster paused, politely waiting for my response. I had nothing to say. He straightened his tie and buried me in a long sigh. "Aaron... spanning my entire career in educational administration, I have never met a teaching professional who has offered so little to a student body..."

Chapter Four

Phnom Penh, Bangkok
Summer 2013

Freshly fired from Hope, I maintained my downward trajectory with sharp precision and renewed vigor. Li and I continued sharing custody of our daughter. Feeding my addiction, my pursuit of Thea and balancing fatherhood proved impossible. As Thea continued to appear in, and disappear out of my field of vision, all focus fell to securing her purity and devotion. Each night, with devout fervor bordering on sainthood, I rolled up to Shanghai intent on bringing her safe and secure back to my place. On the nights she was there, we'd return to my flat to live out our fairy tale pantomime as farcical spouses, charmed and devoted beloveds. The nights she was invisible catapulted me into a simple and pure suicidal madness. I knew where she was and would spend hours rolling around the city gritting teeth, gnawing my tongue into bloody foam with my brain electrocuted into an all-out blitzkrieg searching furiously for her and her John. And always the next day her text would arrive. "Sorry about last night, Honey. Me and my friends went for drinks… Sorry about last night, Honey. I was sick and went home… Sorry about last night, Honey. My house owner was making trouble for my mom and my son… Sorry about last night, Honey. My pet unicorn escaped and I got lost in the magic jellybean forest trying to find her."

Evaporating quickly between my deteriorating life with my family and my hoped-for life with Thea, I held a vague awareness of both my fall and the fall-out, but couldn't find any integrity or passion to care.

In the first week of May I showed up to take my daughter for the next twenty-four hours. Li asked me to sit. I listened as she laid out her innovative and meticulous proposal. "I think it's important that she grows up knowing her grandparents and her cousins. I want to take her back to the States for the summer. I've researched flights." She slid a Cathay Pacific itinerary onto the table. She'd taken time to highlight details in yellow. "As you can see, we'll depart next month, early June. Spend the summer with my parents and extended family. And then we'll return the first week in September on the 4th in time to celebrate her birthday."

My blurred vision was instantly cured. My black lungs suddenly cleansed with a gush of fresh air. The idea of relief from Li's constant presence brought a smile to my face. Practical exoneration from responsible fatherhood filled my cluttered head with sudden peace. It all looked good to me. I cared nothing about Li's departure. I offered her an absent hug.

At the airport, Li passed me my dozing daughter and I took her into my arms. I nuzzled my nose onto her hair. She smelled clean and pure; everything I wasn't. I rubbed noses with her. She opened her eyes. I stared into her galaxy. "Papa will see you soon."

She gazed into my eyes. "Love you, Papa." She cooed. I inhaled the impossible scent of her innocence and baptized her curious expression in a flood of my apprehensive tears. With Li and our child back in the States for the summer, I was free to devote all my focus to distraction and all energy into absolute lethargy.

A partial reason why an addict uses is to distract from the reality that they're an addict in the first place. Sustaining an addiction proves extremely hard work—often staying awake for five, six, sometimes seven days straight to maintain sales, network with other dealers and users, and party with your customers to keep the ball rolling.

My days throughout the spring and into the summer (and greatly to my landlord's chagrin) had taken on a rather static pattern of chaos in the form of a consistent merry-go-round of reprobates coming and going from the flat at all hours. The day's first order always came in around nine o'clock with Nick showing up for his morning heroine blast. An hour later, Nick's roommate James would arrive with his hypo and disappear into the bathroom for his morning fix. Selling H bummed me out. I only had Nick and James as customers, but I found their engagements intensely depressing. It's difficult to say exactly why, but my experiences with the H clientele were different from the tweakers I dealt with all day long. There was an underlying element of sadness I sensed from the mainlining junkie's that I didn't pick up from the ice-heads. I pitied them, often throwing an extra smidge of powder on the scale in some obverse measure of compensation for their tragic and pathetic predicaments. They were pleasant enough to deal with; passive, polite, but always seemed to shoulder a shroud of doom reflected in their shifting eyes like a smoke trail left from a freshly extinguished candle. The hours straddling midday brought a second wave of customers, mostly working girls pulling up on motos, ringing the bell, noisily running up the stairs to get their hoons, then running back down the stairs and slamming the gate before rushing away back to their clients.

My supply chain was still plugged directly into Master Hout. He was tickled pink that my H sales had increased. His constant appearances, along with all other foot traffic were observed under the suspicious stares and frowns of my landlord and his family. The pleasant vibe between myself and the family quickly evaporated; our daily cordial exchanges dissolved into quick greetings or nods in passing. In order to quell the rising tension, I decided to change up the dynamic of Hout's regular deliveries and reverse the process by traveling to his house in order to pick up my daily rations.

Hout woke each day at noon. The day he and I agreed to work together, he had explained in his ever-expressive way (waving his Makarov 9mm in one hand and his snorting straw in the other) rule number one: Under no circumstance should I ever call him or arrive at his place before noon. Once the working girl traffic trickled off, I'd call him to schedule my mid-day arrival. Fueled up on delicious, lip licking amphetamine inhales, I'd race through the traffic and pull up to his building.

Hout's rule number two: Never draw attention to yourself. Hout's neighborhood was rough, even in the daytime. No place for a white boy carrying drugs and large amounts of cash. Preparing for my daily arrivals and nightly cash drop-offs at his place, I'd disguise myself as a Khmer construction worker. Filthy tattered jeans, a long sleeve plaid shirt that covered my white arms, sneakers and riding gloves. To hide my white *barang* face, I wrapped my head in a turban.

I never had to knock. He was always waiting for me. Once inside, I would pay my respects to his family, kissing his children and respectfully embracing Ehoi. Hout and I would then sequester ourselves into his bedroom, sit cross-legged on the floor and immediately begin devouring as many drugs as we could manage within the next half hour, while simultaneously weighing and packaging small baggies of this and that to be distributed throughout the city to the legion of waiting customers. Long trails of coke snorted greedily up nostrils, package a few baggies… two or three trails of H, prepare a few more baggies… a half dozen inhales of ice, a few more grams weighed and packaged… topped off with a nip of ecstasy and away we'd go. Hout and I would emerge from the dark recesses of his building into the blinding blaze of a Phnom Penh afternoon with our eyes bulging kaleidoscope style, hidden behind dark shades while trying our best to maintain composure; saccharine grins pasted over our faces hiding our urge to gnaw our tongues off under the effect of pure Heaven-high saturated joy. We'd climb on our motos and off we'd zoom, speeding through the city with faint iridescent trails of bliss pouring from our eyes and hot air balloon-sized vacancies where our minds should have been.

I returned to the house just past 1:00. My phone rang and displayed an unrecognizable number. I answered and heard what sounded like a loud motor. After a few seconds, I heard Thea's voice speaking to someone. My heart began pounding out of my chest. "Thea? Thea, can you hear me?"

"Aaron?" The roar of the engine and the sound of wind whipping into the receiver was deafening.

"Yes, Thea. I can hear you. Where are you? Are you coming to the house?"

"Now I go my house in the province. Goodbye." Click.

Collapsing onto the stairs, my entire body started shaking. I must have dialed her number twenty times before finally giving up. I was sick, stomach spasms threatening to explode out of my clamped mouth. I wanted to scream, vomit, cry and destroy everything around me. With no one to turn to or speak with, I locked the door and proceeded to destroy the only thing available: Myself.

I wandered through the house from room to room five or six times. Cold sweat. Packed and drained the glass five or six times. Panic. Tried calling her again five or six times. Heart pounding. No ability to focus thoughts. In a complete mental rage and blackout, I felt the dull thud of my fists smashing against my cheekbones and skull. Hyperventilation. On the floor, rolling, thrashing. Screaming into a pillow. Fists clenching my hair. Ripping. Pulling. Fingers clawing at my face. Fists pummeling my skull again and again and again. It was the first time in my life I had ever displayed physical self-abusive behavior. And it felt fantastic.

Thea's announcement that she was on her way to the province was a dull and rusty scythe disemboweling me of all hope and semblance that I'd been pitifully clinging to. Her sudden disappearance. Her phone shut off. I knew what it all meant. It was the rug pulled out from under me. The cleaver cutting off my tongue. The wooden pegs driven deep into my ears. The verdict recited in monotone from the faceless and laughing All-mighty judge finally sentencing all my remaining emotional capacity into the darkest depths of the animal soup void. *Fuck you God.*

What followed my violent self-injurious assault can only be described as a temporary and suspended sphere of overwhelming serenity. I slowly emerged back into a state of semi-awareness, laying on the floor, staring at the ceiling, childishly and softly humming one of my daughter's favorite nursery rhymes. Despite all the rage, the sleeplessness, and the effects of the four or five different drugs pulsing through my veins, I suddenly felt enveloped and gathered into angel wings of clear and crystalline perception. My usual urge to sit and suck the glass seemed a silly and useless exercise; like offering a band-aid to a man who had just had his legs cut off at the knees.

Slowly I stood, made my exit, locked the door. Floated down the stairs, saddled the moto and rode to the outskirts of the city. Watching the urban sprawl melt into flat farmland, water buffalo wading neck deep in shallow mud ponds, sparse clusters of palm trees bending, I turned onto Route 2, a rustic two-lane highway that angled into Kandal Province, rural Cambodia. There was no hurry, really. I already knew what I'd find, or more accurately, what I *wouldn't* find, once I arrived. An hour later I reached the tiny village of *Kaoh Thum* where I loaded my bike onto the ancient ferry and chugged across the Bassac River, a tributary of the Mekong. I continued another fifteen minutes down the dirt road leading to Thea's village.

I'd been there eight or ten times before. I was known by the villagers as Thea's *barang* boyfriend; the American with a money tree growing in his backyard. The commune consisted of fifteen or twenty bamboo and thatch huts scattered along the dirt road. I rolled up to the grandmother's house, parked, and immediately noticed the absence of the village children who normally swarmed my moto whenever I arrived. I walked up to the bamboo veranda. It was late afternoon. Thea's extended family sat lazing on the low platform. I smiled at her cousins, aunts and uncles I recognized, bowed low in supplication to the grandmother, and then turned with a smile and faced Thea's mother. Despite the radiating heat of the afternoon, I stood there presenting myself small and chilled to the bone.

"*Saum chomreab suo. Sruosaear rsiel la. Khnhom sangkhumtha anak teangoasaknea mean sokhpheap la ning rikreay.*" Nodding to each person, I greeted the family and wished them health and happiness. The social climate from the entire family was one of absolute and pure loathing. My smiles and bows were met with blank stares. I stood shrinking in the afternoon shadows, decimated by the family's icy embrace. After an awkward pause, I inquired after Thea. "*Kunthea anak nowenea?*"

Hearing her daughter's name, Thea's mom averted her eyes from my face to the ground, shuffled herself off the bamboo platform with a grunt, then waddled into the dark hut without so much as a word. Left facing the rest of the family, I again asked for Thea. "*Kunthea anak nowenea?*"

One by one, Thea's cousins, aunts, uncles and all remaining family members shook their heads, scooted themselves off the stoop and wandered away into nearby hovels, some toward the fields and others in the direction of the river, until I was left standing utterly and completely alone.

I rode back to Phnom Penh, my head resisting torturous thoughts of Thea somewhere, with someone, doing… Dizzy with nausea, denying the reality, I entered the city well after dusk. Stopping in at the flat to collect my stash before rolling into town for my nightly sales, I noticed an email from Li. News flash from the States: In no uncertain terms, she was contemplating quite seriously filing for divorce. Curious news I quickly shrugged off, denying this reality as well.

For an addict, the words *alternate reality* do not serve to paint a quaint catch phrase or a slick sound byte. The alternate reality of an addict is the peculiar phenomenon comfortably created and adopted in order to re-define existence and contextualize their fragile, delusional enormity. Avoiding pain.

Golden Sorya Mall was up to its usual swing and tempo, music blasting from the rows of bars, drunks swaying with one foot on the sidewalk and the other in the gutter, neon pulse, sex tourists prowling and flirting with the hundreds of tramped-up working girls enticingly strutting their young bodies. I joined the ranks, occasionally running into acquaintances, shelling out hoons and quarter G's to customers known and trusted. The night was crisp, autumnal. The vibe on 51 was happy, positive, the hookers laughing and playfully taunting passersby. With Thea somewhere entertaining some client, literally *working* through the horrors of her existence, I roamed the streets burdened under the dual weights of unrestrained freedom and profound loneliness, giving best efforts to keep thoughts of my wife and daughter from my relentless consciousness.

A text came in from Rumpelstiltskin Mike asking for a hoon. His one room efficiency was a block away, situated down a narrow corridor in *Ice Alley*. Cheap street deals (often consisting of bunk drugs) and cheap blow jobs (from the skankiest working girls) were contracted here. Rumpelstiltskin Mike was an American ex-pat who suffered from degenerative scoliosis, permanently planted in Phnom Penh. In his rare moments of standing, he measured up to just over five feet. I guessed his age around sixty or sixty-five. His white hair curled Santa-Claus fashion down past his shoulders in a natty, unkempt swirl wildly framing piercing blue eyes, thin lips that emitted a creaky but kind vocalization, and a severe nose. His long bony limbs seemed to bend and kink in impossible directions while leaning on his cane. He appeared like a troll and moved like a grotesque marionette. My imagination sparked his most appropriate place squatting under some bridge in a Brother's Grimm fairy tale, waving his stick, waiting to chase or haunt children into nightmares. He claimed that back in the seventies he had made a million dollars promoting concerts for notable bands like The Police and Fleetwood Mac. He had long retired, taken up permanent repose in Phnom Penh, living off his financial nest egg, feeding a relentless H addiction and his insatiable appetite for young girls. *Really* young. Despite his pushing the limits of pedophilia, Rumpelstiltskin Mike had secured his place in my ever-expanding mosaic of colorful friends.

I knocked, and he answered, "Open!" I hadn't heard from him for a few weeks and was sincerely happy to see him. He was reclined in his typical position with his usual layout of tinfoil, lighter and small lump of black tar H lined up on the nightstand beside his tiny bed. After exchanging our usual warm greeting, I locked the door, pulled up a chair, began assorting my stash and paraphernalia next to his and the two of us got right down to business. After each of us had sampled the other's wares and caught up on random gossip, Mike asked perceptively, "So what's on your mind, Aaron? You seem outta sorts today."

He listened attentively while chasing the dragon, nodding occasionally, while I explained the situation of Li threatening divorce and Thea's disappearance into the provinces. We sat in silence for a few orbiting minutes while our large ingestion of ice and heroin mix settled in. Finally, he gave a long sigh, and murmured almost inaudibly, "Well, you know how it goes. *You can take the girl out of the bar, but you can never take the bar out of the girl.*" And with that, he crossed his bony fingers on his chest, tilted his head back into the pillow, and nodded off. Sage wisdom from good ole Rumpelstiltskin Mike. Grandpappy Mike. Not to disrupt the whispers of lonely truth echoing in my ears, I tiptoed to the door, closing it softly behind me.

Out on the street I spent the next hour trolling up and down 51, in and out of the bars and game rooms, dishing hoons and halves and shooting the shit with customers. Strolling past G-pub someone called my name. I turned to see my morning H customers, Nick and James, along with their other roommate Will, huddled around a table littered with pitchers of beer, half-emptied glasses and overflowing ashtrays. I wasn't in a social mood, but politely joined them. As always, the conversation centered on drugs, hookers and potential scams going on around the city. My ears pricked up when James mentioned a mutual friend of ours,

Ricky, who had just come into a sizable quantity of high-powered MDMA. I made a mental note, suddenly developing a mad thirst, thinking some good Molly is just what the doctor ordered to alleviate my depression over Thea's recent stunt. Weary of thinking and with nothing to say, I bid the fella's farewell. On the way back to the house I stopped off at the pharmacy and picked up a handful of valiums. The pharmacist, in his broken Khmer/English explained the daily dose. "You take 40 mg each day." Back at the house, with the intention of slicing my raging high in half, I gulped down 200 mg's and quickly collapsed into sweet oblivion.

Thea's call came two days later, jerking me from sleep. Her soft and reluctant "Hello" fired my rage and snapped my spine at the same time, rendering me to puddles. "Thea, are you OK? Are you back in Phnom Penh?"

Thea's arsenal of charms reached into the very depths of Hell. An hour later she showed up at the house with her long eyelashes, her soft sighs, her supple body, her exhausted posture, offering no explanation or reason for her recent disappearance. Walking the fine line of pummeling her with inquiry and coddling her injured and furious spirit, I chose my words carefully for fear of pissing her off, breaking her completely and losing her altogether.

"*Where the hell have you been?*" translated into, "Thea baby, right after you called I went to your village to see if you were OK. You weren't there."

"Um, I must have been visiting my Aunt down the road. She's sick."

"*Everyone in the village treated me like shit when I asked where you were. I Google translated everything through my phone into Khmer so they could understand what I was saying. They knew where you were, but they didn't want to tell me. Explain what's going on right now!*" was changed into, "Honey, I asked everyone where you were, but no one would even speak with me. I was so worried about you."

"You know they can't understand you. They didn't know what you were asking or what you were there for." Sigh.

"*I called you fifty Goddamned times. You didn't answer your phone because you were off fucking some sex-tourist for cash you dirty whore!*" morphed into, "Love, I was so worried about you. Why didn't you call to let me know where you were? What have you been doing for the past few days?"

"Oh, you know how reception is in the country-side. And besides, my phone was dead and there's no electricity to recharge the battery. I was visiting my family. Why are you asking me all these questions?"

"*Thea, your money-grubbing sick pimping mother is making you go with customers, isn't she?*" Converted to, "Baby, is your mom putting pressure on you to work more? Is she asking you for more money?"

"You know my mom always wants money. She doesn't work because she says she's too tired all the time taking care of Youngbin. I work so much at the bar, but it's not enough. What can I do?"

"*Liar! Get your shit. Get the fuck out of the house now and out of my life forever!*" was mumbled, "I'm so happy and relieved you're back. Stay as long as you need to. Sleep now, and I'll take care of you. I'll always be here for you."

Hinging on her every syllable, digesting her every breath, clinging to her every phrase, she filled my head to capacity with her lies, and I chose to believe every word.

Placing her teacup onto the dresser, she climbed into the bed unsteady like an exhausted child and curled into the sheets. I climbed in and tried to spoon her, but she wriggled away. Within minutes, she was gone. Listening to her soft snores, I laid there with my arm draped over her hip, watching the rise and fall of her shoulder. I knew where she'd been, how long she'd been there and what she had done. The only thing I didn't know was who she had been with. Slipping from the bed, I silently picked up her purse and left the bedroom, closing the door behind me.

In the living room I rifled through her bag and immediately discovered a thick roll of twenties wedged into her change purse. $180 cash. The equivalent of over a month's wages at the bar. Scrolling through her text messages, I discovered a text from some random number that came in the morning she had vanished. *Sara, I'll pick you up at the bar at 2:00. I'm so excited to see you.* Using her phone, I dialed the number, sat and closed my eyes.

A voice came crawling into my ear after the third ring, elderly, frail, European, elated. "Sara?"

I took a deep breath and calmly engaged. "Hello. My name is Aaron. I'm sorry to bother you. But I'm in a situation that I think you might be able to help me with."

"Yes?" Then hesitation. "Um, why are you calling me from Sara's phone?"

Another deep breath. "The woman you know as Sara is my girlfriend. I understand that you recently traveled with her. Please know there's no problem here. I'm fine. *Sara's* fine. I just want you to understand that she and I have been having some problems in our relationship lately. I didn't know where she went when she took off with you. I was worried sick the entire time she was gone. She's back here with me now. I'm not angry with her. If anything, I'm broken hearted. Can you please tell me what has happened over the past few days?"

To my surprise and chagrin, the man cordially introduced himself. "Very well then. Aaron, my name is Jim…" After an awkward start, he naturally fell into a tender and expressive narrative of what had gone down. "I'll give you all the details because I can appreciate your situation. I can't imagine how hard it must be trying to maintain a serious relationship with a bar girl. I met Sara… your girlfriend, about a week ago one night at the bar she works at. I'm from Belgium. I come to Cambodia once a year to, well, you understand…" He trailed off. I understood perfectly. Jim was the stereotypical wealthy Euro sex-pat who enjoyed his annual frolic in The Kingdom with the girls of GSM. Clenching my fists, biting my tongue, I waited for him to continue. "Anyway,

I bought her a few drinks, enjoyed her company. I found her remarkably different from the other girls one usually meets—she was respectable and kind. After an hour or so in her company I invited her to go down to Sihanoukville with me for a couple days. She agreed."

With my blood pulsing to the boiling point, I also experienced a certain calm from the way Jim was divulging Thea's sins. The simple fact that he was taking the time to share any info at all, along with his gentle way of speaking resulted in a peculiar and soothing effect on my mental chaos. "I hired a taxi and we rode down together. We stayed at the Ochheuteal Beach Guesthouse, a place I often stay when..." I knew the place. My stomach turned hearing the name. Ironically, Thea and I had stayed there on our last trip to S'ville. Listening to Jim's gentle voice give description, I could only wonder if he and Thea had stayed in the same room as she and I had?

He continued speaking like a perfect gentleman. "After arriving and having dinner together, we enjoyed drinks on the ocean and then went for a walk along the beach. She held my hand. It was very romantic for me. I took her back to the room. But once we got back into the room, I could tell that she was nervous. I could tell she just wasn't interested in anything sexual. We slept in the same bed, and there was a little kissing, a little touching, but that's as far as it went. Like I said, I could tell she was quite uncomfortable. And I'm not one to force anything on anyone. To be honest, Aaron, this was a very big disappointment for me."

A huge wave of relief swam over me, but I couldn't help asking him to clarify. "Jim, I really appreciate your info, and I just want to make sure-"

"-It's as I said," He assured, cutting me off. "Nothing happened. There's no reason for you to be upset with Sara. You can rest assured, she behaved herself like a lady and I, a complete gentleman."

"And how much did you pay her for her time, if you don't mind me asking?"

"Her fee was $200 for two days."

After thanking Jim, I hung up, deleted my call off the phone log, slipped the phone back into her purse. Creeping into the bedroom, I sat gently on the bed and watched her sleep for a few minutes. Hating her poverty, loving her spirit, hating the financial pressure her piggish and indigent mother placed on the family, loving her gentle sadness, hating myself for not being able to rescue her completely from the horrors of her demographic, I loved her to a sickness. Technically, I was still married to Li, but divorce proceedings were already in motion. It was in that very moment that I decided to marry Thea, and began planning perhaps the most pathetic engagement in the history of the world's courtships.

Thea woke around eleven the next morning, called her mother, then asked me to take her back to her house. Her mom had returned from Kandal and she needed to get home. When Thea keyed in, the room was full of her family. Placing Thea's bag on the floor, I squatted and gave Youngbin a high five. I stood and hugged her sister, then bowed to her pimp mom who greeted me with a grunt. Thea walked me back to the street and thanked me.

"Why do you thank me, Thea?"

She suddenly fell flat against me, holding me deep and close. As quickly as she had embraced me, she pushed me away, then disappeared back down the narrow alley.

Half an hour later I pulled up to Sana's place. I hadn't seen her since she had handed me off to Ehoi. She appeared like an absolute sunbeam. Dressed in her typical yellow sari, the bright fabric set well and stark against her long black hair always spun up into a comical sprouting twirl atop her head. I spent the next few days hunkered down in her one room cubicle with her and her children climbing over me like an army of giggling monkeys. Thin as a rail, her small head came only up to my chest, but her strength and longevity was that of an ox. She often stared with dark, unblinking eyes, her arms moving gracefully whenever she reached for her children. She regarded everything around her with a genuine care and love, and interpreted life with a peculiar perception of hilarity. I loved spending time with her and her family. Despite the squalor she lived in, she made the absolute best of her hand. She had perfected the art of multi-tasking: balancing two toddlers—one on each knee—while cooking noodles over her single coil burner and taking long pulls on the glass.

She offered her uncensored history. Ten years earlier, in her late teens, Sana had been a street girl like most of the uneducated girls in Phnom Penh. She then elevated herself out of the profession and became a major processor and dealer in Tuol Kork, but eventually had to drop out of the scene when she started having her babies. Angelo, her H-head junkie husband that I had met was now gone. She didn't know where. Sana shared her small room with her mom and three children. Her mom worked as a seamstress in some shop near Orussey Market on the other end of town. I enjoyed her as well, as whenever she was around, she treated me with thoughtful and genuine Khmer kindness, like I was a most treasured and welcomed member of the family.

In turn, I offered Sana my story as well. My history included my coming to Cambodia, my failed marriage to Li, my love for my daughter, and my complicated infatuation with Thea. One afternoon, with the children sprawled out peacefully on the floor mat, I handed Sana the half G that I'd just picked up from The Master. She loaded up a glass and we began a marathon smoke session that lasted well into the evening. "Sana, I've made up my mind. Once my divorce from Li comes through, I plan on marrying Thea."

Sana's ever-present smile melted into a pool of swirling concern. "You know, Aaron. Khmer girls not like normal girls. Especially a bar girl. The bar girl does anything she needs to do to survive. And you need to think about her family. If you marry a bar girl, then you also marry her family." After a lengthy pause she asked, "You love Thea's son?"

"I like him." I answered. "He's cute. Smart. Funny. A good boy."

After folding my answer into her lap, Sana asked, "And do you love Thea's mom?"

"Not at all. I don't like her and she doesn't like me. She's a lazy mother. She doesn't work. All of her three daughters work in the bars and she just sits at home and relies on them to support her. I see her no better than a pimp."

"I know you love Thea. I know you want to marry her. Rescue her. Can you also agree to spend the rest of your life with a cute young boy and a mother you do not like?"

I stared at Sana, waiting for her to curtail her confrontation with a sudden explosion of laughter. Perhaps an offer to condone the wedding? At the very least, agree to attend the ceremony as a happy guest offering blessings, lighting incense and throwing rice.

Sana melted me with her kind smile. Her silence spoke volumes. I writhed under the lens of her strict care and friendship. Her cautions were perfectly clear, and like everything else in my life, I gave no heed to the warnings.

Riding behind me through the Tuol Kork traffic, she guided me through the city to an off the beaten path market near Wat Phnom. "This is the best place in the city for diamonds." She explained. "All the rich Khmer and Chinese buy here."

Sana and I spent the next half hour perusing the lighted glass showcases at the thousands of brilliant rings and dazzling stones. The diamond world was completely unknown to me, and I felt like a fish shopping for a bicycle. Sana engaged the seller in discussion over a handful of her selections while I stood by staring and nodding dumbly. She finally selected one of the rings boasting an impressive stone centered between two smaller diamonds and set within a curvy white gold circular design. Through Sana's translation, the shopkeeper highly recommended the ring and offered some sort of certificate of authenticity along with it. I laid out five hundo's onto the counter. The seller placed the ring into a box lined with a red puffy cushion, handed me the receipt. Thanking Sana for her time, I passed a small piece of crystal along with a twenty-dollar bill so she could catch a ride back to Tuol Kork.

With the ring in my pocket, I rode over to Thea's house. She was alone, curled into a nap on the bed with Youngbin. "I have a great surprise for you, Thea. You need to tell your boss that you won't be working at the bar for a week. I am taking you on a mystery trip. You will need your passport."

"If I need my passport, does that mean you are taking me out of Cambodia? Are you taking me to Thailand? Vietnam?" She asked with dazzled eyes. She called the bar and after haggling with her boss, managed to secure a short five-day sabbatical.

"Yes, Thea. I'm taking you out of Cambodia. But I can't tell you where because it's a surprise!"

In all her thirty-four years, she had never once stepped foot outside of The Kingdom. She threw herself into me and squealed, "Oh Aaron! Are we going on a plane? I've never been on a plane before. I have dreamed and hoped all my life to ride in a plane. Please take me on a plane!"

Not to be outdone by my hasty and thoughtless purchase of the least expensive ring I could find, I arrived on the morning of July 13th at Thea's place in a taxi. I was wired, hadn't slept in three days, and was packing a nice baggie of pulverized product in my pocket to see me all the way to the border. The cabbie situated her things into the boot, we climbed into the backseat and began our six-hour ride to Thailand. Thea was silly with anticipation, texting her friends, calling her family, relaying her excitement like a Cinderella being whisked away to the Royal Ball in her pumpkin coach. En route to Poipet, I instructed the driver to pull over for rest room breaks on the hour so I could duck into the wooden outhouses along the way to inhale lines from my last pick-up from Hout. Snuggling in the back, blazing through the farmlands of Kampong Speu, Pursat and Battambang Provinces, Thea and I enjoyed the reckless and spontaneous road trip vibe listening to music, chatting like silly lovers. By the time we reached the border I was high, crawling out of my skin. Thea had fallen asleep with her head in my lap. I caressed her cheek. "Wake up baby girl. We're here." She sat up and gazed wearily out the window.

After clearing customs, we schlepped our way a quarter mile, dragging our rolly's through a scorching heat to the *Aranyaprathet* bus depot. The 7-11 exchanged my dollars for Bhat. Thea and I piled into a white micro-bus along with ten other tourists bound for Bangkok. Thea slept most of the way while I enjoyed my tongue-gnawing, wild-eyed stare out the window. When we started rolling into the outer sprawls of Bangkok, Thea stirred awake and stared out the window at an explosion of sights and sounds like a child licking the window of a candy store. I was just starting to feel my four-day high beginning to wane.

We checked into a small guesthouse just off Kao San Road, the area of the city famed the world over for its non-stop 24-hour backpacker nightlife. Thea, humming some happy tune joyfully inspected the room and began unpacking her things while I collapsed into the bed, heavy from withdrawal. Curling into the warm sheets, feeling my blood turn into an iron sludge, I vaguely recall the icy temperature of her hands on my skin as she tried her best to rouse me.

9:00 am the following morning, Thea shook me from the deepest sleep. My first instinct was to reach for the glass. Realizing I had no product, I pulled myself awake with a groan. Thea had to practically dress me, pulling my clothes on like a spunky pre-teen dressing a rag doll. She'd been up since 7:00 and had arranged a half day city tour.

Collapsing into a tuk-tuk, our first stop was Wat Pho, which housed the Temple of the Reclining Buddha. I'd already seen the attraction, many reincarnated lifetimes before, on one of the many trips to Bangkok with my wife. I lazed in the tuk-tuk watching Thea stroll around the temple by herself, taking snapshots. She took a moment to purchase a handful of incense sticks from a bald female monk, stood at the foot of the enormous Buddha, lit the incense, held it to her forehead and bowed many times in supplication. Lounging in the tuk-tuk, I stared in awe at Thea's display of religious reverence. Her minutes of fluid devotion with her Buddha impressed me, reminding me how over the past few years, my own spirituality had been reduced to pure corrosive hatred. I had come to loathe everything and believe in nothing.

Thea keyed us back into our tiny enclave and served as my crutch to the bed at the end of the day. No doubt disappointed at my piss-poor performance she hissed, "What's wrong with you? Why are you sick?" Throughout the past many months of my spiral into addiction, I'd managed to hide it all from Thea. Since the day we met, I'd always been enamored with her naivete, and gave every precaution, albeit deceptively, to maintain it. Curling into the thick sheets, I waved her off with a groan. Minutes later, after listening to her quiet symphony in the bathroom, I felt her freshly oiled and perfumed body slithering in her silk negligee press into my aching skin like a bulldozer rolling me into the grave.

When I woke, she was gone. I lay still, loving the dark nothingness of the room. A conversation came leaking through the door from a tourist down the hall arranging a Bangkok city tour with the front desk clerk. *Not recommended*, I thought, *especially if you're a junkie without product vacationing with the intention of engaging a gorgeous Khmer girl who's unaware of your addiction and as innocent as a lamb*. I fumbled for the remote to check the time. The eerie glow of the flatscreen filled the room. 12:22.

I had packed a baggie of six valium for this exact occasion. My effort to search my backpack for the stash demanded every ounce of focus and muscular coordination. My muscles were cement. I was all thumbs pulling the zipper of my pack, searching the pockets. Brain haze. Visual vertigo. Tactile impairment.

Thea keyed in, closed the door behind her; her face moving like an orbital satellite exploring the room's noir. Her doe eyes spotted me in the bed, the contents of my pack strewn about the floor. She sat down next to me, placing her icy hand on my forehead. I swerved from her touch and continued searching my pack for the valium like a zealous pastor thumbing the pages of the Bible for the crucial, anesthetic verse and finding it non-existent. The small jewelry box containing the ring toppled onto the floor. Thea picked it up. Opened it. She held the ring to her eyes, curiously examining it as if gazing through the beauty of stained-glass possibilities.

"Will you marry me, Thea?" I mumbled from the dark recesses of my confessional.

She slid the ring onto her finger, stared at me. A sad smile. She kissed my forehead like one would kiss a child, accepting my proposal with the conviction of the sincerest of unbelievers.

Chapter Five

Phnom Penh
Summer - Autumn 2013

I crossed back over the border with my new intended bride on the 17th of July. The cab rattled into Phnom Penh just as the Wednesday evening rush hour was thickening. After her five-day sojourn, Thea explained she needed to spend time with her mom and Youngbin, which matched perfectly with my need to spend time with the glass. After dropping her off at her room with hugs and kisses, I made a bee-line for Hout's. The relief that came from the first inhale filled my lungs and pulsed through my veins, dripped down my throat like discovering an oasis of ice water in the barren Sahara.

Properly stoned, I left the Master's and made my way over to GSM to see how many sales I could drop. The trip to Thailand had set me back a grand and I wanted to make it back as quick as possible. Parking the bike, I hadn't walked ten paces before a tall, kind-looking and alluring working girl approached me and quickly pulled me into a recess between two buildings. Fishing a wad of crumpled Riel from her tight jeans, she addressed me by name and told me she needed a hoon. With my paranoia alarm hitting a high note, I walked away. She followed, lacing her arm through mine. I stopped and explained, "Listen, I have never met you before. I don't know you and I don't know what you want."

"Oh, you know me," she corrected, playfully pushing my chest. "I'm Srey Neang. You met me last week. I'm friends with Chan Ti and Srey Leak and..." She continued name dropping.

Some names I recognized. Others I didn't. This tall and slender body with flowing hair framing dark wide eyes and thick lips was doing her best to wear me down, and easily succeeding. With Thea snug back in her room with her family, the idea of enjoying Neang's enticing company clouded my reasoning. The depressing ride home to an empty house, and my complete inability to exist alone with my pathetically dependent self was easily replaced with the reality of Neang's cheap companionship and someone to party and pass the empty hours with.

I loved the working girls. I'd developed an insatiable and unhealthy appetite for their company. All of them. Most of them lived with one foot in the gutter, constantly searching for their next meal, and often sleeping in the streets while constantly on the prowl for their next John. I gave Neang a quick tour of the house. She immediately opened the fridge and stared at my small inventory of food. While she showered, I prepared her a massive plate of scrambled eggs and buttered toast. Emerging from the bathroom, she sauntered into the living room all bronze arms and legs with wet black hair dripping and wearing nothing but a white towel. Sitting cross-legged on the floor, she set into devouring the meal while I started weighing out the night's festivities with Yo La Tengo streaming in the background.

With both of us more interested in the ice than anything sexual, we enjoyed a great night together. Neang's English was better than good, her laughter infectious. I loved the way it bounced off the walls of my empty flat, pushing further and further away the reality that, with Thea safely back with her family, and my wife and child back Stateside, I was truly alone. The fact that I had just taken a fiancée meant nothing. By this time in my free fall, the only two things that drew my loyalty were myself and the glass. Neang's presence... anyone's presence for that matter, went far to further distance me from having to ponder over the monster I had become.

The feeling that comes when the morning sun begins its first delicate creep through the blinds, and you're barricaded away from the world with a gorgeous girl's head cradled in your lap, and a small mountain of ice piled up next to the glass, is simply indescribable. Neang and I eased grinning into the day saturated in a perfectly balanced tranquility. I alerted my morning H customers that they were no longer allowed at the house and arranged to begin delivering their orders. Other than me speeding off to re-up with Master Hout, and dumping off my afternoon deliveries, Neang and I stayed completely and safely sealed up and away from all worry, fear, anxiety and anything else related to the real outside world. I was enamored, and quickly fell prey to her unpretentious and child-like mental expressions, entranced by her raw ability to laugh through her horrible existence, and enslaved with her pure and primal sexuality. I'd lost all immunity to the moments when she'd take me by my hand like some toy and lead me to the bedroom, breathing an adage no doubt taught to her by some former client, "Come with me silly, I have something I want to show you."

Over the next three days, Neang never once left the house, and proved to be the ideal guest. Quiet, respectful, a great conversationalist and outstanding cook. I remained with her, smoking, deliriously grinning at all fleeting notions of responsibility and hissing at God to go fuck himself. When I'd arrive back from deliveries, I would discover that she'd completely cleaned the place, or had taken the opportunity to move the furniture around, or had a delicious Khmer meal waiting on the table. It was three days after her arrival when I eventually ended up forcing her, kicking and screaming, back out onto the street.

Sunday morning, July 21st, Neang and I were sequestered away in our blissful primal utopia when I followed up on James and Nick's tip-off regarding Ricky coming into some good Molly. I wanted to score some for me and Neang. Ricky and I were both dealers, and had crossed paths several times, be it on the street, at parties, and wherever else dealers collide. But because his habit and immersion centered on the heroine scene, and mine in ice, we pretty much ran in separate circles. I didn't know him well, but I liked him. He displayed a polite patience while dealing with others, and I recognized and admired his quiet sadness. Tall, reluctantly handsome, Ricky held a striking physical and facial resemblance to Perry Farrell; mirroring Farrell's gentle demeanor and aptitude for loving kindness.

Ricky answered screaming into the receiver. "What? Can you speak up? Hey Aaron! How you doing, Mate? Yeah… yeah, I can meet you for sure. Yeah, whatever you want, I got it. I'm the man! Sure… I'll meet you at my place. Now? Sure, let's meet now…"

Neang slithered in the sheets as I kissed her goodbye. I made my way through the early, lazy Sunday morning traffic towards *Wat Koh*. Ricky's one room efficiency set perched atop a four-story dingy apartment high-rise situated in a back alleyway off Street 63, just around the corner from where Nick, James and Will were flopping. Climbing the stairs, a knock on his door went unanswered. Standing on his balcony, I watched the warm sun climb over the city. I dialled. He answered, shouting into my ear over blaring club music pulsing in the background. "What? You're at my house… now… yeah okay I'll be there… coming now… yeah bringing a friend… see you soon…"

Twenty minutes later, from my birds-eye view, I spotted a tuk-tuk round the corner of the alley and pull up to the building. Ricky climbed out, then turned to help an unknown companion out of the small vehicle, as if assisting an elderly lady from her carriage. They paid the driver, then disappeared into the building, only to re-appear around the corner where I waited at his door.

Ricky, despite his wild, gnarled hair and rancid alcohol breath, greeted me with a hug in his typical gush of kind-hearted optimism. He then turned and introduced me to his friend. "Yeah brother, this is a friend, John, I met a few days ago." John and I exchanged smiles, shook hands and followed Ricky into his room. John un-shouldered his massive backpack onto the floor and collapsed with a wince into Ricky's only chair. Leaving the door open, Ricky moved to set a pot of tea to boil and continued his loquacious, animated soliloquy. "Yeah man… me and John been hanging out all weekend… going around town… doing this and trying that and checking all the places out together. I'm like his tour guide because he just came up from Sihanoukville after traveling all around S. Asia… doin' the backpacker thing ya' know? Yeah, John's quite a guy… been all around the land, ya' know? Laos, Thailand… he just came to The Kingdom a week ago… bus from Saigon… kickin' it down in Snookie and then I ran into him a few days ago…" Motioning to John, Ricky asked, "Say John, when did we meet? Today's Sunday, yeah? Must have been a few days ago, right?"

John reached into his backpack, uncorked a half empty bottle of red wine, took a large swig and set the bottle on the floor. Gave a grunt. Mumbled something. It then occurred to me that Ricky and John were neck deep in an all-weekend bender. Nearing 9:00 am on a Sunday morning, and they were completely plastered: Ricky riding the celestial whims of sincere euphoric black-out, and John, dangerously close to tumbling down the steep stairs of incoherence. Hoping to revive them both, I took out my stash, packed a large glass and passed it around. Ricky accepted it with a gush of grateful enthusiasm. John politely refused, instead taking another grand gulp of the red. Using the wine bottle as a crutch, John pushed himself upright to a kneeling position, then kind of half walked, half crawled out onto Ricky's balcony. Left alone, Ricky poured tea. Then he and I conducted an unhurried deal, measuring out our products, exchanging ice for Molly in a fair and professional manner.

Walking onto the balcony, Ricky and I stared at John doubled forward in a lawn chair trying to wrestle off one of his socks. His face was twisted in agony. When John finally pulled the sock off his foot, the source of his pain became evident. His foot was swollen to the size of a football, the skin stretched tight in a bruised myriad of red, orange, black and purple.

Ricky and I bent down and examined it. "Damn, John!" Ricky gasped. "Somethin seriously and truly wrong with your foot, bro!"

Falling back in the chair, John lunged for his red, took another monster swig, and offered his story through a series of groans. "Ah, happened when I was walking on the beach down in Sihanoukville. I think I stepped on something, or something cut it. Hurts like hell."

"How many days ago was that?" I asked.

"Oh, four, maybe five." He took another gulp of the red.

"Listen John, your foot is really infected. You need medical attention… like *now*. I live across town about twenty minutes, but near my house is *Sokhapheap Thmey*, a very good western clinic run by an excellent clinician. I've been treated there a few times for this and that. An Aussie woman named Gloria runs the place. She's super cool. It's open 24 hours, so no trouble getting you seen. How about you come with me. I'll drop you off there and you can get that foot checked out. Seriously, man. You need some medical attention for that."

Ricky nodded furiously, affirming my advice. John again lifted the bottle to his lips, sucked the red hard, then set it down on the floor with a thud. He stared at his foot, then stared into the empty space of the room contemplating his options. "No man. Thanks anyway, but I think I'm just gonna hang around here and self-medicate."

Ricky and I exchanged glances. I shrugged. "Suit yourself. It was good to meet you. Take care, John." I shook his hand, gave Ricky a hug and made my way down the four flights of stairs to my moto. Being a Sunday, the city traffic was sparse, and I crossed town in about fifteen minutes. Fumbling for my keys to unlock the house gate, my phone rang.

Ricky's voice was strange. He spoke in a hushed whisper, rapid, and I couldn't make out was he was saying. "Hey Ricky, slow down buddy. I can't-"

"-don't know what… came into the room… laid down… I don't think he's breathing…"

Back on the moto, I raced back to Ricky's, took the four flights and knocked softly. Ricky's voice came faint from the other side. "It's me, Ricky." I whispered.

The door opened a crack. Ricky peered out. I entered. He quickly shut the door and bolted it behind me. There on the floor in the center of the room, John lay on his back. Arms at his sides. Eyes closed. Peaceful. The room was eerie in shadow, the only light bleeding through the thin, yellowed fabric hung over the window. Ricky and I stood staring dumbly at John's massive body. I kept watching and waiting for the rise and fall of his chest. It never came.

I eased down cross-legged on the floor next to John's body and lit a smoke. "Ricky?"

Ricky began pacing circles around the corpse, running his fingers through his dark, gnarled hair. "I don't know, man. After you left, he finished the rest of the wine and then he just crawled in here and laid down. We were talking for a while and then suddenly, he stopped talking. I thought he was sleeping, so I tried to wake him up to get onto the mattress…"

The next ten minutes was nothing but scrambled brain activity, trying to gain focus and realizing none. Ricky paced the small room babbling a string of tangential narratives, flinging his hands, smoking furiously. "I met him just a few days ago… some bar I can't remember… fucking bars and strippers… a lot of H and ice and booze… he was traveling S.E. Asia…" Ricky's non-stop ranting and his panicked train of thought was escalating my anxiety. Obliterating my ability to focus. Standing, I unbolted the door, pulled Ricky onto the balcony and sat him down in the lawn chair. We spoke in hushed whispers, mindful of the neighbors living just a few meters away.

Ricky eventually calmed. Listening to him re-trace his and John's movements over the weekend, and the comradery they had shared, I kept thinking how strange it was that two people who had just met could have managed to forge such a close and sincere friendship in such a short time. His compassion for John was overwhelming. When I pried for clarification, Ricky turned to me, his eyes brimming with tears. "He was just such a nice guy, Aaron… oh what the hell am I going to do? He has a family… *a family* back in London…" Ricky was working himself back into hysterics. "He was good bro… one of us, *you know*?"

I did know. I knew from his description that Ricky and John had spent the weekend consuming tons of alcohol and doing a shit-ton of drugs, and it quickly became clear what must have killed him. I suddenly had the vision of a dozen Khmer cops swarming the place. As Ricky was unraveling, I began gathering his loose strands, gaining clarity for him, for the both of us. "Ricky, you holding stuff in the house right now?"

"No, not really. Just a bit of my personal H and maybe a few grams of the MD. Why?"

"Ricky, we need to get you out of here." I glanced at John's enormous body. "I can't think straight here, and neither can you. Gather up all the drugs, whatever you got. Clean the place. *Now.* Is there a guesthouse where you can hide out for a day, just so we can sort through this shit without having to stay here?"

Ricky stared, nodded, his eyes taking on a sudden lucidity. Ricky spent the next half hour wandering around the place like an ADHD child trying to make sense of an intricate puzzle, fumbling, gathering, packing and then unpacking things into his small and tattered backpack while I sat chain-smoking on the floor next to the body. His problem-solving skills at that point were non-existent. He kept peppering me with questions interspersed with incoherent ramblings that I kept trying to filter out so I could think. I answered him in silence, hoping my non-engagement would spur him on to hurry with his packing. The party had suddenly turned sour, and all I wanted to do was get myself and Ricky away from there. Ricky stumbling around, me crawling out of my skin with impatience, and John laying just an arm's reach away from me. Finally, I stood and told Ricky I'd meet him downstairs. "Hurry up, man!" I slipped out the door and descended the stairs to the moto. Ten minutes passed. I called him.

"Ricky, quit fuckin' around! Get down here!" Minutes later he emerged from the dark stairwell, climbed onto the back of my bike and off we went.

Ricky barked directions to the Happy Guesthouse on Street 107 near Orussey Market, about four blocks from his place. "It's a good place... small... this cool family runs it and they stay out of your business. It's out of the way... I've stayed there a few times." We checked him into room 208. Once inside and without a word, we both emptied our respective stashes onto the old wooden desk and began preparing our fixes. While Ricky lined his foil with tiny dollops of H, I crushed some stones and packed the glass. After getting our heads straight, we passed some tenuous silence before recanting the details.

"I don't know man," Ricky stammered. "I knew his foot was fucked up because he was walking kind'a funny... you know? With a limp, but I never knew it was *that* bad. He told me he got hurt, but he didn't really complain about it much. We just hung out all weekend in the bars, drinking and, ya' know... The first time I saw his foot was with you this morning." We sat smoking, remembering the grotesque disfiguration. Ricky sat upright and smacked his forehead. "Damn Aaron! If only he would have gone with you to the clinic, this would have never happened. He wouldn't have..." Falling forward, Ricky's head landed with a thud on the table and he suddenly burst into uncontrollable dyspnea. "Oh my God, I can't believe this is happening... I can't believe he's dead!"

Seeing Ricky with his head on the table, cradled in his arm, sobbing, unleashed in me an avalanche of compassion. I'd only known him on the periphery for a few months but in the moment, I offered him the very best of my friendship. "Ricky," I said, shaking him from his miserable reverie. He raised his head and looked at me through his dark, swollen eyes. "I am your friend. And I'll try my best to help you through this. We'll figure something out."

Hearing this, he leaned forward and wrapped his arms tightly around my neck, his continual sobs abating, and his incoherent mumblings dissolving into whimpers.

We passed the next hour considering the predicament and brainstorming options. In any Western country, the line of action would have been simple. Call the police, report the death, go down to the station, recount the events, sign papers. But in Phnom Penh things aren't that crystal clear.

The Cambodian National Police are rotten to the core. Cambodian cops appear regularly on global watchdog lists. "…one of the country's most corrupt institutions," observed the Heinrich Boll Foundation. General Neth Savoeun, the Supreme Commissioner of the National Police (and an in-law relative of the Prime Minister,) is constantly cited for human rights abuses. And the corruption enjoyed a trickle-down effect, all the way from the top brass down to the peon cops who roamed the streets extorting money from the poor and prowling around for their next hand-out. The police in Phnom Penh were shameless about their corruptive methods, often attempting to wrestle motorists off their motos on the street, citing imaginative offenses and demanding cash payments on the spot. Their methods were brazen and sick, but I understood where it came from. Cops in The Penh average a monthly salary of $150 to $200 and they have to make money somehow. Nevertheless, this allowance didn't make the Cambodian National Police any less ominous. In both Ricky's experiences and my own, we knew the police were to be entirely and strictly avoided.

We both recalled the widely circulated story about an expat recently discovered dead in one of the upstairs rooms at The Walkabout. When the police showed up, they proceeded to demand a payment of a $1,000 from the bar's owner just to remove the body.

"…and I don't have a thousand dollars." Ricky confessed. "Not even close! And I'm illegal. I don't have an up-to-date visa. Hell, I don't even have a fucking passport!"

"Yeah," I agreed. "I have no idea what the police will do if we call them. They'll sure as shit sweat us down and try and extort us for all we have. Especially when they see we're foreigners."

"For all we *don't* have." Ricky corrected.

After a second round of inhales, we reconvened our congress.

"What about notifying his family?" I suggested. "You say he has family in London?"

Ricky thought about this for a moment. "Yeah, that's what he said. I know he has an address book and a bunch of papers in his backpack. Probably a passport, too. But even if we notify his kin, the first thing they'll do is call the police here and then we're right back to having to deal with them."

Options seemed risky and few. In retrospect, I know that Ricky's best move would have been to alert his Spanish Embassy for protective purposes; and then contact the British Embassy to pick up the pieces surrounding John's death. But for two unemployed drug fiends huddled in the Happy Guesthouse who hadn't slept in days, it just simply didn't occur. A plan was reached to simply get rid of the body. Ricky and I agreed he should remain at the guesthouse for the next twenty-four hours to get some rest and clear his head. We agreed to meet up again at midnight, at Wat Phnom, a public and outdoor central social hub in the city where two ex-pats would attract the least attention. From there, we would devise a plan and wash our hands of any repercussions or suspicion.

"Hey man, I need a re-up. Ten units. Can you meet?" Mighty's voice coaxed me back to consciousness.

I focused in on the time. It was eleven o'clock, an hour before my rendezvous with Ricky. "Yeah, I can do that." I dressed quietly, not to disturb Neang passed out on the sofa.

After meeting Mighty in an alley near GSM and filling his order, I buzzed over to Wat Phnom to meet up with Ricky. Wat Phnom translated into English as *Hill Temple*. The temple was a venerated place of worship situated atop one of the only hills in the city. A roundabout circled the hill that served as a tourist attraction by day, and the hot spot for the city's cheapest and sleaziest prostitution by night. I parked the moto and took a seat on one of the benches, lit a smoke and waited for Ricky to show. I kept an eye out for Srey Mom, thinking a massage would feel good right about now. Being Sunday night, there weren't many girls around, and both auto and pedestrian traffic was sparse. 12:15 and still no sign of Ricky.

The following day I phoned him around noon and was relieved when he finally picked up. "Hey Ricky. Everything Okay? Dude, I went to meet you at Wat Phnom last night like we planned but you stood me up. Where were you?"

His voice was unhurried, calm. "Oh, I went out walking for a while and must have lost track of time. I'm still at the guesthouse if you want to swing by."

"Have you been back to your place?"

"No. Just hanging here all day watching TV."

I wanted to reach through the phone and strangle him. Before I could berate him for his negligence, he added, "Come by, why don't you?" As casual as if inviting me to afternoon tea.

Half an hour later, he peered out at me through his chained guesthouse door. His room was in typical Ricky mode: TV tuned to some random cartoon channel; clothes littered over the floor. Yawning, still in boxers and a T-shirt, he flopped back into the bed. "There's some pork rice there if you're hungry," he offered, pointing to a half empty carry-out Styrofoam.

"Ricky, where were you last night? I waited at Wat Phnom at midnight to help you with this shit. You pulled a no-show. I called you a thousand times, but you didn't answer." He pulled himself upright and stared at me incredulously, as if I had suddenly grown three heads. I stared back at him. "Have you forgotten the shit-

99

storm you have back in your place? Are you clear on how serious this is?"

Pulling himself together, we sat down at the wooden table and each lit a cigarette. Fifteen minutes later, we were browsing along the outer shops of Orussey Market with a list of supplies Ricky had written for the task at hand. Latex gloves. Face masks. Rope/twine. Large thick tarpaulin. Re-entering Ricky's place was like creeping back into a black infected womb where birth had been given to a sick and nauseous nightmare. It was in fact, a tomb, with John's body laying just as we'd left it twenty-four hours earlier. With face masks and latex gloves pulled taut, we arranged the large blue tarp on the floor and proceeded to roll John's huge body into the center of the fold. Once positioned, we folded the tarp over him, ensconcing him like a cocoon. The entire process only took a few minutes but seemed to last a week. Rigor mortis had already set in. His stiff body held the consistency of half dried plaster. Pushing his arms and torso into the tarp felt like trying to force a stiff piece of cardboard into a flimsy paper envelope.

Beyond physically exhausting, the experience was overwhelming and emotionally draining. A total mind-fuck. With John wrapped away, Ricky and I hurried out onto the balcony, pulled off our masks, lit cigarettes and collapsed like two spent rag dolls. I'd had all that I could handle for the day and told Ricky so. We made plans to meet again at midnight, following Ricky's scheme to carry the body out of Ricky's place, then disposing of it in some unassuming part of the city.

It was mid-afternoon when I unlatched the gate to the house and rolled my moto into the parking area. My landlord greeted me with a frown. I listened patiently as his bubblegum popping, twenty-something daughter translated that she had suddenly become engaged, and they needed me to move out so she and her new fiancé could move into my flat. Obviously uncomfortable and clearly pissed, they were giving me notice to clear out. It was a well-crafted fiction, and certainly not a surprise. With my constantly revolving door of hookers and tweaking ice-heads, I'd finally worn out my welcome. My landlord and his family were good people and had every right to enjoy their house without having to deal with my shenanigans. They asked that I vacate by the end of the week.

Walking into the flat, the place smelled of freshly cooked Khmer food. Neang had cleaned and a big spread was waiting on the table set for two. She peppered me with questions I had no head space to deal with. "Where have you been? Why you gone so long? You have ice? I want smoke now." Neck-deep into Ricky's mess, I needed Neang out and told her she had to go. Over the next hour she stormed around the place, gathering her things, breaking dishes in the sink while screaming at me in Khmer. I handed her two twenties, hoping to calm her rant and hasten her exit. She took the two bills, ripped them up in my face and threw them over my head like confetti. I was finally able to walk her down the stairs. The timing couldn't have been worse. When we got to the courtyard, she continued her screaming rant right past my landlord who stood by with his daughter, both shaking their heads. Climbing on the back of a moto and stabbing me with her eyes she parted with a warning, "You think I'm a dog and you just put me out? Okay Aaron, you see what happens!" It was clearly a threat—one I had no space to process.

At midnight, Ricky answered his door and ushered me back into his hell. John's giant blue cocoon remained the permanent fixture in the center of the room. Ricky was brewing a pot of tea and offered me a cup. After sipping and sharing a monster glass filled with excellent ice I'd just procured from Hout, we began discussing our next move.

"Can't just carry him down the stairs and out into the alley." Ricky observed. "He's a giant. He's got to be over six and a half feet tall. Must weigh over 230 pounds!"

"So, what do you propose?"

"Well, I know this tuk-tuk driver who's a customer of mine. Maybe we can get him to help us carry him down, load him in the tuk-tuk, and then ride him out into the countryside and burry him in some field somewhere way out of the way?" The plan was a logistical nightmare. The thought of bringing someone else into the circle—a Khmer nonetheless—sent the buzzers and whistles screaming. Yet, in the moment, there seemed little else we could do.

"Call your friend, Ricky. If you trust him enough. But just remember, a Khmer tuk-tuk driver makes his living by networking all over the city. They deal with a wide range of people and gossip runs rampant. You need to really trust that this guy isn't going to talk to anyone about these two foreigners who hired him to dispose of some dead guy in some field. Get what I mean? Call me when you've made arrangements and I'll come lend a hand."

The next three days were typically chaotic, packing up my things and searching for a place to move. My meetings with Hout remained consistent, in sync with my deliveries around town. Mighty had suddenly increased his daily orders.

Ricky's call finally came on Thursday. He answered the door wearing his face mask, latex gloves and rubber boots. When I walked into the room the stench leveled me to the floor. John had been lying dead for four days. The body had gone into *active decay*. Ricky had opened the tarp and John's remains had begun to liquify. Unidentifiable body parts floated in the black liquid. I could see dark crimson stains had coalesced on the floor where fluid had leaked through the folds and creases of the blue tarp. His flesh had melted, filling the room with putrescine; the scent and essence of death that drips into your nostrils, seeps into the fibers of your clothes, burns into the pores of your skin, and burrows into the deepest depths of your relentless memories. In that moment, I knew Ricky's lackadaisical and delayed response to this fucked-up, urgent and bizarre situation had finally sealed his fate. And yet, his comportment remained calm, unrealistic and detached to the severity of his reality.

Straining to breathe, Ricky handed me a mask and a pair of gloves. "Ricky, this is really bad." I gasped. "Do you have any idea how much trouble this has turned into?" I asked, trying to gauge his sense of the real world. He wandered about the room in a daze, gathering a green plastic bucket and a handful of rags and towels. Kneeling next to the tarp, which had ballooned out to resemble a giant blue kiddie pool taking up most of the room, he began mopping up the stains of human soup and wringing out the towels into the bucket, leaving red smears and black whorls on the floor.

"Have you contacted your tuk-tuk friend to see if he can help?" I asked. He mumbled something about not being able to track him down.

"Ricky, I can't stay here, man. I'm sorry bro, but I can't breathe. Way too intense. Way to fucking intense." I explained to him the situation with my landlord; about having to move and told him I'd check in on him in a day or two.

My voluntary engagement with Ricky's macabre phantasy continued to wear me down, bleeding into my own personnel complications. Fired from Hope school, stumbling through my second eviction in six months, and ripping through what remained of my extended Visa credit, I continued to spiral deeper into my addiction, while supporting myself by running all over the city for Master Hout. It had been a month since I'd seen my wife and daughter off to the States and I hadn't once spoken to either of them. I hadn't seen Thea in days. Parallel to Ricky's morbid predicament, I could feel my own death, circling, tightening, slowly closing in around me.

On the morning of my final day in the flat, I'd packed all my things and had arranged for a tuk-tuk driver and his vehicle to help me move out, but still hadn't found a place to relocate. In the eleventh hour while madly scanning the local online postings, I discovered a listing for a place about ten minutes down the road. House 62B on Street 53BT. I raced over to check it out, met the family, and moved in that same afternoon. The place was a large one-bed, one bath with spacious living room, newly remodeled kitchen and second story balcony overlooking a quiet residential street fifteen minutes removed from the city center. It seemed like a good location to maintain my deliveries from, yet far enough removed from the urban chaos to ensure a respite from the madness. Spacious windows allowed for ample sunlight. Anticipating Li's and daughter's return in early September, it was a place I could see my daughter happy in.

Lugging my boxes, crates and bags up the stairs leading to my door, I constructed a mental list of New Home Resolutions. With Thea still living across town with her mom and son, I held an intense enthusiasm and every intention to protect my new home from the mayhem that had plagued me ever since returning to The Penh. I desperately wanted a respite from the stress and madness of entertaining working girls. No more *femme fatale* drama at the house. I also resolved to cut myself out from the H scene completely. I informed Nick and James that I was no longer supplying. They were good enough guys, but I found their hollow intensity a bit too depressing. John's recent OD and Ricky's disturbing ongoing predicament probably had an influence on my thinking as well. I needed distance from intensity; a vacation from all the sadness I suddenly felt myself swimming in. Despite Li's divorce threat, my heart was set on her returning with our baby so I could continue pursuing and building a relationship with my daughter. I had no idea how I was going to break the news to Li about my engagement to Thea. Like everything else, I'd likely fall off that bridge when I came to it.

I spent my first night in my new place alone, unpacking, loading glass after glass, streaming my playlists from Violent Femmes, The Smiths and other euphoric anthems. The Wi-Fi connection was quick. Situating and organizing my new lease on life was fun. And the latest stash I'd picked up from The Master was clean and super-charged.

Sunday morning. August 12, 2013. I blinked into consciousness after a fitful collapse into a stretch of typical spasmodic sleep. Reached for the glass and lazed through multiple inhalations before planting my feet firmly onto the floor. With the invigorating emptiness of the new day, I dressed quickly and enjoyed a half-hour stroll through the quiet Sunday morning streets to the market where I loaded up on a carton of eggs, and enough fruits and vegetables to sustain me through the week.

Rounding the corner to the house and happily swinging my groceries, I was greeted with an ensemble of uniformed cops standing around a patrol car parked directly in front of the house. I was immediately spotted, my initial inclination to turn and run thwarted. Keys in hand, I walked confidently up to the gate and was instantly encircled. It was then I noticed Ricky seated in the back of the cruiser.

One of the cops approached me and inquired in near perfect English. "Are you Aaron Reed?"

"Yes, I am. What can I help you with?"

Another cop reached and opened the car door. Ricky climbed out, hands and feet cuffed in chains. Finding his balance, he faced me, appearing like some pasty paper-mâché Laotian marionette. Weak. Fragile. Grandfatherly. Aged a thousand years since I'd last seen him. Tired of wading ankle deep in the throes of human waste, tears brimming over the dykes of his eye lids and unable to contain his pure sorrow and crystalline terror, he stared into my eyes. His face brightened, barely. His lips parted thin enough for a fragile "hello" to leak out. I reached to catch it but missed; his weak voice slipping through my fingers.

"Do you know this man, Ricardo Blundell Perez?"

"I do." Suppressing my urge to gather him tightly into my arms and fly away, I extended my hand. We exchanged a formal handshake and a screenshot of horrific eye contact that none of the cops saw.

Ricky's voice was soft, weary. "I need you as my witness, Aaron. They came last night and arrested me. They're keeping me at the police station. I need you to tell them what happened, so they believe me."

"We would like you to come to the station." The cop inserted himself quick, cutting off Ricky's and mine's exchange. "We have questions we want you to answer concerning the case of your friend."

"Now?"

"Yes, now. The station is near Ricardo's house. You come with us now. You ride in the car with Ricardo but no talking."

The cops referring to Ricky as *Ricardo* was confusing; a mental blitz orienting me to the gravity of the situation. I asked permission to carry my groceries into the house. The police agreed. I unlocked the gate, hiked the stairs, dropped the groceries on the kitchen counter, then ducked into the bathroom with the pipe, frantically inhaling the rest of what I'd left in the bowl. Minutes later, I rejoined Ricky and the cop crowd on the street, climbed into the back of the squad car and rode across town next to Ricky in absolute silence.

The station was just around the corner from Ricky's place. Ricky was led away to a cell, and I was seated in a bare walled interrogation room with nothing but a dirty institutional conference table and two chairs. Additional chairs were brought in to accommodate a string of four new cops who took seats at the table. These guys were dressed in uniform suits with bars and ornaments on their pockets and shoulders. Investigators. Notepads flipped open. According to the clock on the wall, my interrogation began at 9:04 am. Little did I know that news of Ricky's arrest had already leaked into public knowledge from the press. Gossip was running rampant on the Khmer 440 on-line community forum.

My identity. My history in Cambodia. Details about my family. Past work experience. My relationship with *Ricardo*. My recollection of the events on 21 July surrounding John's death. Recanting the details, I suddenly realized that Ricky had been living in his tiny apartment with John's rotting corpse for the past twenty-one days. "How did you end up discovering the situation at Ricky's apartment?" I asked.

"The smell. The neighbors called us and asked us to come. We went there and discovered the body."

After two hours of constant Q and A, the cops asked if I needed a break. I asked if I could see Ricky. I was led down the short hall and around the corner to a single brick cell no bigger than a walk-in closet. Ricky stood from his seat on the floor and met me at the bars. He thanked me for coming. Thanked me for everything. "What do you need Bro?" I asked.

He appeared bedraggled but managed to speak with a hint of his typical enthusiasm. "Two things." He responded automatically. "First thing is I'm really hungry. Can you go to my favorite restaurant on 172 and pick me up a Tonado sandwich?" I knew the place and promised to go as soon as the police released me. "Second, please call my friend in London. Her name is Savina. She's an old family friend and when you tell her what's happened, she'll know what to do." I asked the cop standing by for a pen and paper. As soon as I jotted the number the cop motioned that my time with Ricky was finished. I hugged Ricky through the bars and told him I'd see him again soon.

I asked the cop if I could go for a smoke and was ushered out to the street. I offered a cigarette to my sentry, the two of us smoked in silence. Back in the station, I was seated again in the same chair, surrounded by the same cops, and for the next two hours, was peppered with the exact same litany of questions. With the clock ticking to just after 1:00 pm, I was again granted a smoke break. Seated back at the table, I was also offered a Styrofoam container of Khmer noodles which I devoured while launching into a third round of the same answers to the same repetitious questions from the same faceless cops. By the time the interrogation wrapped up, the clock was spinning near three in the afternoon. After six hours of quizzing, at 3:27 in the afternoon, with my brain turned to complete oatmeal, I was told I was free to go. I walked out dazed into the blinding sunlight and started walking toward street 172.

Ricky's favorite restaurant was a small dive that served a mixed concoction of Khmer dishes and poorly made Western favorites. A Tonado sandwich was the Khmer mis-spell and mis-creation of a western tornado sandwich consisting of a baguette filled with cheese and various meat products. I ordered it up along with a side of fries, then walked back to the jail. The cops wouldn't let me deliver it to Ricky so I handed it over to them hoping he would actually receive it.

A creature of habit, my steps automatically turned and wandered over to GSM. Sunday afternoon, the place was deserted. I then walked blindly to the Riverside, soon finding myself on the outskirts of Hun Sen park, eventually strolling up to Thea's small room. The door was open. I peeked inside. Thea's mom sat on the floor cutting veggies into a small colander. I greeted her respectfully, slightly bowed with my hands pressed in supplication. "*Niak sok sabai teh, Bong.*" Seeing me, she went rigid, diverting her concentration back to her paring knife. I scanned the room for recent signs of Thea... a purse, an article of clothing, anything. There was nothing. After waiting a few uncomfortable seconds, I inquired about Thea's whereabouts. "*Bong, soum toh. Kunthea noew ey nah?*" She shrugged her shoulders, shook her head, kept cutting away. I repeated my question. She slowly stood, waddled to the door and closed it softly in my face. I dialed her number. Her phone was shut off. Thea missing once again. Unaccounted for on a Sunday afternoon. Dismissing the horrific possibilities from my mind, I repressed the urge to vomit and took a moto back to the house.

It was near dusk by the time I unlocked the gate and trudged up the stairs. Home again, alone again, my cluttered mind battling empty spaces. Scant sleep in the past thirty-six hours, six of which I'd spent surviving a rigorous police shake-down with my friend now arrested and housed in a Khmer cell for harboring a rotting corpse in his house for the past three weeks.

Collapsing into bed, I mechanically packed and lit the pipe. My attention and obsessions fell on random objects scattered about the room. A half empty bottle of water left on the nightstand. My dirty clothes bag half full, the top folded over like some mischievous gnome's cap. My laptop with a blank screen. Overflowing ashtray. My Bible spilling out onto the floor from a crate of books I had yet to unpack. Everything composing my life appeared perfectly random. Viscous. Chaotic. Pristine. All trivial matters, really. After getting super high I shed my clothes and wandered naked into the bathroom. Staring into the mirror, I couldn't recall the last time I had smiled.

Chapter Six

Phnom Penh
Autumn into Winter 2013

To:aarononthecoast@yahoo.com
From: Licambodia@yahoo.com
Date: Mon, 12 Aug 2013 GMT

Jonah Chapter 1(NLT): But the LORD hurled a powerful wind over the sea, causing a violent storm that threatened to break the ship apart. Fearing for their lives, the desperate sailors shouted to their gods for help and threw the cargo overboard to lighten the ship.

But all this time Jonah was sound asleep down in the hold. So the captain went down after him. "How can you sleep at a time like this?" he shouted. "Get up and pray to your god! Maybe he will pay attention to us and spare our lives."

The sailors were terrified when they heard this, for he had already told them he was running away from the LORD. "Oh, why did you do it?" they groaned. And since the storm was getting worse all the time, they asked him, "What should we do to you to stop this storm?" "Throw me into the sea," Jonah said, "and it will become calm again. I know that this terrible storm is all my fault."

Instead, the sailors rowed even harder to get the ship to the land. But the stormy sea was too violent for them, and they couldn't make it. Then they cried out to the LORD, Jonah's God. "O LORD," they pleaded, "don't make us die for this man's sin. And don't hold us responsible for his death. O LORD, you have sent this storm upon him for your own good reasons."

Then the sailors picked Jonah up and threw him into the raging sea, and the storm stopped at once! The sailors were awestruck by the LORD's great power, and they offered him a sacrifice and vowed to serve him.

Last Saturday I heard a message preached by Pastor Herman of ALCF. He preached on this passage and the familiar story of Jonah. He mentioned that storms in our lives have 3 causes. 1- it's nature, it's time and it just happens (there is no cause). 2- other people's sin and disobedience 3- our own sin or disobedience. He said that we all find ourselves at some point in relationship to a storm. We either just came out of one, we are in one, or we are headed into one.

Aaron, you and I have been in a storm for the last 3-4 years. I feel that I have been trying to row the boat to shore, trying to dump the cargo out to make the boat lighter—but nothing has worked to make the storm go down. These last 10 months in Phnom Penh have been very difficult for me especially in my relationship with you. I won't go into details here nor will I defend, argue, or justify my position.

Mei and I have been sailing with you on a boat that has gone through very rocky waters. The boat seems to be falling apart and the storm is getting more violent. I have heard God's message and it is simply this: throw Aaron off the boat. God has prepared a great fish for some time and how can that fish get to you if I keep you on the boat? For this reason and others, Mei and I will not be returning to Cambodia.

It was 7:00 am in San Francisco. I dialled Li on Skype. Her voice came crackling through the speakers. Flat, dead, with a hint of nauseating sweetness. I extended my fingers through the thousands of miles of trans-Pacific cables with the hopes of snapping her neck with pure precision. After a few deep breathes, I offered best effort to release my grip, my voice instead finding a calm and patient chime. "Hi Li. How are you?"

"Fine. And you?" Her response formal. Practiced.

"What's up, Li? I just got your email. Am I reading this correctly? You and Mei aren't coming back?"

Her voice came over the wire like a fishhook hitched into my gums, dragging me back through the murky past months. Her litany was never-ending, reciting everything I'd done wrong, my neglectful and miserable attempts at being a husband, my pathetic efforts at fatherhood, my self-preoccupation, my unemployment, my frequent evictions, my reckless spending, blah, blah, blah. Her content alone was enough to raise my hackles, but it was her monotone, emotionless drone that really raised the mercury. After she'd decimated my character and left me for dead, she trailed off, leaving about a half minute of dead air hanging between us. I took a deep inhale, positioned my mouth over the laptop mic and shattered the silence. "YOU HAVE NO RIGHT TO TAKE MY DAUGHTER WITHOUT MY PERMISSION!" She responded to my explosion by simply killing the call. My efforts to call back went unanswered.

Rage boiling to overflow, I tumbled out of bed grabbing the glass in the process. I sat broken and naked on the floor, packing and sucking glass after glass with furious determination. Determination for what? Resolved to reduce my heart rate and murderous fantasies. Bent on annihilating myself. Convincing myself that my wife deceiving me and illegally abducting my daughter back to the States had everything to do with her selfish motives as a mother and her existence as a lousy and manipulative wife and certainly nothing to do with everything or anything I was involved in. I resolved to escape the day's crystal-clear reality that with my wife's checkmate, I was heading into a skidding tailspin that I would not have the focus, integrity or fortitude to recover from.

Hours after informing me of her desertion and the abduction of my daughter, Li sent another bomb chiming into my inbox. She had filed for legal separation with the Sunnyvale Superior Court a month ago—the same week I'd been in Thailand engaging Thea. She had to wait another six months until she established the residency requirement before amending the legal separation into a formal divorce. Further, she had enrolled our daughter into the Los Altos school district. Starting September, Mei would be in the *Little Clouds* class with Miss Lori.

On the heels of Li's desertion and setting up her and my daughter's new life back in California, I received an email from my mom.

To: aarononthecoast@yahoo.com
From: Vikchik@yahoo.com
Date: Aug 30, 2013 at 4:46 PM

I have not been able to get the image of our last video Skype visit out of my mind. I hadn't seen you for almost a year and was shocked to see how much weight you've lost and how gaunt your face was. We are very concerned about you. Whatever you are involved in in Cambodia has changed you. Please look carefully at what's happened. Your wife is gone, your family is torn apart, you have no job, your body is breaking down and we see you living in fear and anger. Nothing about that is healthy for you and your family.

Reading my mom's message, in my heart of hearts I knew that her every word was true, and I couldn't have cared less.

Li's desertion and abduction of my daughter leveled me completely. By the time of Ricky's arrest, my addiction and daily intake had come to the point of far outweighing any income I was currently generating. My cash flow had dwindled to near nothing. Li's reference to my reckless spending was a direct indictment to my latest credit card activity which, no doubt, she had been tracking online. Over the past three months, I had been drawing heavily on the account, supplementing my ever-dwindling drug sales with multiple cash advances.

Everything I held a passion for was slipping through my fingers like granules through the narrow neck of an hourglass. My wife and daughter, kissed goodbye and not returning, re-established back in America. Any ability I once held for gainful employment, evaporated like the smoke trails from my pipe. My family, crying out my name from half a world away, too far away for my ears to hear. My mother had spelled everything out in her profound email with the simplicity that a child could have understood. But therein lay the problem. In the chaotic mind of an addict, it isn't a matter of the addict not being aware of the problem; it's the addict's apathy that continues to feed and perpetuate the insatiable cannibal dynamo.

The only thing that remained consistent was Thea. Throughout August and into September we saw each other regularly. She continued working at Shanghai. I continued eking out my own living by picking up from Hout and dishing product all over the city. She continued to live in her hovel, supporting her pimp mother and Youngbin from the scant income that the bar (and her extra-curricular activities) paid her. I supplemented her salary with random dashes of ten's, twenties, an occasional fifty—trying my best to keep her sudden and random weekend disappearances to a minimum. On occasion, she would come to stay a night at the house. My greatest relief came when she would call near closing time. I would pick her up as the bar emptied, take her home, tuck her in, and watch over her like a mother bear protecting her young. She would sleep through the night before returning to her slave life with her lazy and cruel mother whom I hated and blamed for Thea's constant sadness and exhaustion.

One wet night while out on deliveries, I decided to drop by Thea's room to see if she'd arrived home from Shanghai. It was quarter past two. The door was slightly ajar. Her light was on. The window, open. I peaked in and saw the shapes of her mom and son asleep under thin sheets. Thea sat in a chair in the corner, removing her make-up and talking on the phone. I paused before pushing the door open and listened for a moment to her sweet voice. The rain had abated, and I didn't have to strain to hear her every word. "Hi Honey, it's me. Can I see you tomorrow? And you can help me?" Giggles. "Yeah, that would… that will make $320. Thank you so much, Baby. Yes, I miss you too much. OK. Goodbye."

Stomach convulsing, I turned and quickly retreated down the dark alley, holding my hand over my mouth. I didn't make it to the street before the vomit came exploding between my fingers. Dizzy and reeling, I found myself sitting on a bench in Hun Sen Park about a half block from her place. I didn't recall walking there. A stone's throw away was the playground where Li and I had spent countless evenings pushing our daughter on swings, chasing her through monkey bars, treating her to vanilla and strawberry ice cream cones which she'd buried her face in and then gazed at us through the blissful eyes of her candy-coated giggling innocence. I imagined the dark and empty playground fully lit, full of parents lounging, conversing, keeping one eye on their frolicking children. Sitting there alone like some decrepit, abandoned grandfather, the memories flashed like an endless film noir. I sat alone, staring across the dark park; Reality falling onto my worthless existence like a thousand-kiloton bomb landing like a feather onto the crown of my wilted head. My wife, now permanently gone. My daughter, now 12,635 kilometers away, too far to hear her laughter or her breathing. And now Thea, my beloved and holy mistress, evaporated into an image of a groaning whore, staring at me through a black veil, white blind eyes rolled up into her forehead, slithering tongue.

Following three days of constant ice ingestion and red wine blackout, I resurrected myself, dressed and showed up to Thea's room at dawn. Throwing wide the door, she gushed smiles over me while trying to push Youngbin out and on the way to school. "Hi Aaron!" He paused to give me a happy hug, and I held him warmly, knowing this was the last time I'd ever see him. I'd met him when he was four. He was now nine, and on his way to another semester of Khmer private school that I had paid for. He was a good boy. I loved his infectious giggle. I watched him as he followed Thea's mom, who passed me with a grunt, out the door and down the alley to the street. With the house cleared, Thea led me by her warm hand to the bed, greeting me with all the false sunshine of the day. "Aaron, I so happy you come see me. Why you come see me so early?"

I nodded, staring absent at the floor.

"Youngbin," she continued. "He so naughty at school! The school call me last week and tell me Youngbin make many problem. I have to go to the school and talk with the people there." She said this while rolling her eyes, then smacked my thigh playfully, continuing, "And my Mom she still very sick. She can't work, you know, and…"

"Thea. Please stop." I released her hand with a quick shake of my head.

She brushed her hair from her eyes and pierced me with uncertain concern. "Aaron, you know me and my family have many problems. You not want to know? You angry me for something?"

I inhaled, exhaled deeply. Nodded. "Yeah Thea. I'm angry about…"

In her typical Khmer avoidance, she quickly stood and began tidying up her small room, pulling the worn comforter over the bed and clanging pots and dishes into the small sink. As she worked pulling the room together, holding her composure, I wearily explained what I'd heard while standing outside her door. She absorbed every word as smug as a murderer stands before the judge with her ever-present assurance tucked securely away in her pocket. When I finished my prosecution, she turned to me with a sympathetic smile and scolded me lightly. "Aaron, why you think like that? I *never* make a phone call like that! I think you hear my sister that night. My sister have boyfriend in Germany. He send her money sometimes, you know? You not hear me that night. You hear my sister."

Thea. Demon of deception. Artist of evasion. The high priestess of twisted lies and tearful alibis. In my deepest heart I'd

116

known for a long time what our dynamic had been. We'd managed to exist in our ongoing charade for years; her poverty and familial pressures manipulating her, *literally*, into grotesque positions, copulating with my willingness to believe and exist in her specious sphere, each lie and every instance of her disappearances and my torturous nights alone laid like a wreath of flowers adorning both our graves. Each of us buried alive beneath our decayed hopes, self-delusions, eulogies and condolences.

After having the body destroyed and the soul dismembered, a prostitute's survival and greatest triumph depends largely on her ability to disassociate from their unwanted reality and trauma. Thea had found the strength to accomplish this process; The *mental removal* of herself. As Thea's ultimate devotee, I had embraced the polar opposite. The more she learned to evaporate her mind, body and soul from her reality, the more I moved to immerse myself in it, anchoring her down in the process. The tension this created had simply become unmanageable. The bridge spanning between us had inadvertently succumbed to an irreversible corrosion. There was nothing left connecting my alternate reality to hers, or hers to mine. The only remaining thread that kept us tied was the fact that we still shared common injuries stemming from the same onslaught. Mentally fucked and spirituality annihilated. Together we'd been left gangrenous, with no other option left except to finalize the physical severance and our spiritual amputation.

Another deep inhale. Bracing myself for the impending eruption, I whispered, "Thea. It wasn't your sister I heard. It was you. I *saw* you, through the window, speaking on the phone. I heard every word you said." Before she could explode, I asked calmly for the ring. "Please give me the ring back, Thea. We can't marry... can't continue like this."

Surprisingly, she slowly took a seat next to me on the bed, placed the ring into my hand and kissed me lightly on the cheek. With my eyes welling with tears, I stood and walked quickly to the door, closing it softly behind me.

I rode across town to Sana's and found her still lounging in bed with all the kids tucked in around her, a *mélange* of tiny arms and legs. Her mom, crouched in the corner preparing breakfast, greeted me with a warm smile and invited me to stay and eat. Thanking her, I took a seat on the bed next to Sana and explained what had happened. Sana slipped from the bed and disappeared into the bathroom. I prepared a good-sized glass while she bathed. When she came out, she quickly dressed, and together we devoured the glass. Minutes later we were riding through the morning *Tuol Kork* traffic towards *Psar Thmei*.

Sana presented the ring along with my receipt back to the seller we had purchased it from. Sana explained the failed engagement, and that I was there to return the ring and collect the refund. The shopkeeper gave me a sympathetic smile and began lining up her monocular and testing kit onto the top of the glass display case. Sana kindly expressed her concern and lent her condolences. "I'm so sorry, Aaron. Are you OK, my friend?"

"Yeah, I guess. It just sucks that it had to end this way. I really thought we were going to make it. I really *believed*, Sana. Just too complicated and so fucking sad." Sana had been with me through many of my trials and horrors concerning Thea. She knew the details. And being a former working girl herself, Sana knew the impossible intricacies and relational complications the profession entailed.

Just as I was beginning to tear up again the shopkeeper removed the monocular from her eye and delicately placed the ring onto a small chamois atop the glass counter. She spoke to Sana in a soft Khmer that I didn't like the sound of. For the next two minutes, Sana maintained the conversation, asking questions and receiving information in a poised and professional exchange. Finally, Sana turned to me. Unable to look me in the eye, she translated the dialogue. Two days prior, a woman had brought this exact ring to the shopkeeper, had sold the diamond back and had replaced the original diamond with a cubic zirconia stone—a fake diamond.

Overcome with a gush of nausea, and fighting off a sudden sense of vertigo, I pulled up a photo of Thea on my phone and showed it to the jeweler. "Is this the woman who sold back the original diamond?" I asked.

The merchant gave a knowing nod.

"And what is this fake diamond worth?" Sana asked the jeweler.

"The ring is pyrite. The diamond is glass. It's worth nothing." She replied.

Leaving the jeweler empty-handed, I dropped Sana back at her place and declined her invitation to come in.

I was back at my house by near noon, frustrated to the explosive point at Thea for her deception and cunning. So sweetly had she placed the look-alike into the palm of my hand, brushing my cheek with the weight of Judas' kiss. Preparing for a long afternoon of abuse and escape, I placed a quarter gram stone into the glass. Admiring its purity and brilliance, I laughed at the realization of how similar Thea's need for the diamond reflected my need for ice. For her own tailored reasons, her drug of choice had become money. And she could never get enough. My drug was obviously the meth, and like Thea, I could never get enough. In addition, I'd garnered the habit of possession. Attempting to possess her even more while I failed to possess myself.

Dusk settled into my flat with the enormously pleasurable dissolving of the sun. I opened the blinds to the night sky, welcoming the reality of another wasted day. Naked on the floor, like a crouching cat dazzled with nip, I recalled a passage from years ago, reached for my Bible and began flicking quick through the immeasurable pages of folly and deception in an attempt to summarize Thea, whom she'd become, what she'd done, justifying my hatred and my further mental descent. The wisdom of King Solomon defined my pain, anointed my comprehension, blessed my ears.

With her great persuasion she entices him; she lures him with her flattering lips. He follows her on impulse, like an ox going to the slaughter,

like a deer bounding into a trap, until an arrow pierces his liver, like a bird darting into a snare—not knowing it will cost him his life.

Now, my sons, listen to me, and attend to the words of my mouth. Do not let your heart turn aside to her ways; do not stray into her paths. For she has brought many down to death; her slain are many in number. Her house is the road to Sheol, descending to the chambers of death.

-Proverbs 7:22

Chapter Seven

Phnom Penh
November - December 2013

Since Thea's desertion, I'd pretty much fallen off the map, retreating deep into Ice-land, binging four, five, six days without sleep; as long as I could go until deprivation would trigger massive hallucinations, paranoia, exhaustion and finally, blessed unconsciousness. Holy void.

Coiling into a grub-like fetal position, I wept through memories of playing in the park with my daughter, and raged against my wife's ploy and successful abduction of my baby back to the States. Of course, *I* had no ownership in any of this. The fact that I'd deceived my wife with unfaithfulness for years; had burned through more than $10,000 in the past ten months and was riding a habit the size of Niagara had nothing to do with anything. My introspective lens had long since snapped shut, replaced with a grossly skewed and darkened sense of reality through which I groped along blindly with zero insight. Each situation presented as a canvas for me to fling my twisted psychological projections onto. No capacity for accountability. I was *not* the failed husband, or the truant father. *My* role was *victim*. And reaching for the glass, I played my character to my own standing ovation.

Since the day of Ricky's arrest, Khmer 440, an online forum spinning all things gossip in the Kingdom had been buzzing like a pulsating neon sign announcing all things coarse, vulgar, exaggerated and gross regarding Ricky's case.

Re: A Spic, a Yank and a Dead Brit in Phnom Penh
Post by Elekid» Fri Nov 28, 2014 10:07 PM
Earlier today the Spanish suspect appeared in court for a hearing. He denies killing the British national but admits that the body was found in his room and that it was him wrapping the body in plastic. Apparently he did this because he was scared people would suspect him as the killer and because he was staying illegally in the country (without passport.)

Re: A Spic, a Yank and a Dead Brit in Phnom Penh
Post by Elekid» Sat Nov 29, 2014 1:48 PM
Loeuk Um, who conducts autopsies for the Phnom Penh police, said that Connell died from a drug overdose. Um Sopheak, a deputy prosecutor, said that as a result of that information and Perez's testimony, he changed the charge to "hiding a body."

Re: A Spic, a Yank and a Dead Brit in Phnom Penh
Post by vladimir» Sat Nov 29, 2014 7:55 PM
Alice in Blunderland. A Spanish guy, an American, and a dead Brit wrapped in clingwrap walk into a forum. And an investigator called Look,... Um. It's a bad joke.

I had been in touch with Savina, Ricky's family friend and advocate in London. We'd volleyed numerous texts and had finally met face to face on a short Skype call. She appeared forty-something, attractive, all business, clearly concerned about Ricky's well-being. She wired some cash via Western Union to provide for Ricky's immediate needs at Prey Sar Prison, along with a shopping list that Ricky had provided her with. I spent an afternoon riding around town, visiting various merchants at Russian Market and *Psar Thmei*, purchasing a blanket, a pillow, various clothes and food items.

Waking groggy after a twenty-eight hour sleep marathon, I saddled up the moto. Concern, obligation, curiosity, perhaps a twinge of guilt moved me to the outskirts of the city and into the surrounding countryside. The prison was located about 20 kilometers outside the city, but the pot-holed dirt roads demanded over an hour to negotiate. Nearing the fortress, I stopped at a roadside shack and spent the remaining dollars Savina had wired on anything I thought Ricky could use. Turning off the main road onto a two-track, winding my way slow through peacefully deserted fields dotted with skinny cows, the prison eventually came into view surrounded by low Beng trees and tall palms standing stationary, wilting in the still, stifling air. I parked the moto and obtained my parking ticket.

Next stop was a small shack built of ill-fitted wood walls and thatched roof; just large enough to house an ancient student's desk behind which sat a non-descript man dressed in a tattered tan police uniform. After flicking through the pages of my passport, he passed it back and asked for twelve thousand Riel, the equivalent of three dollars. Receiving the money, the man gave a grunt and nodded me on to the main entrance of the prison.

Here I was greeted by a brown-skinned frowning boy standing in sneakers, wrapped in tight jeans and draped in a police shirt three sizes too large with a Boston Red Sox baseball cap set askew on his head. Porcelain faced, pre-pubescent, he couldn't have been more than ten. After a lazy pat-down, he demanded sixteen thousand Riel. Pocketing the money, the boy motioned me into a narrow hall that led to a small waiting room.

The room was busy with three more guards examining parcels being brought into the prison by a queue of family members trying to get in to see their loved ones. Groceries, fruits, razors, vegetables, toilet paper were pulled out of bags and boxes and lined up onto a short wooden counter. Items were examined, questions asked, answers given. When my turn finally came, a guard emptied my bag and began picking through the contents. Eye-balling me with intense suspicion, the man asked me where I was from. "*Khnhom mok pi a me ri ch*," I replied. Handing him my passport, the man tossed it aside without even so much as a glance.

"*Anak trauv chamnay bram dollar.*"

Shelling out another five dollars, I gathered the spilled groceries from the counter and moved on to a doorway where the people queued before me were filing through. The door opened to a spacious cage about the size of a two-car garage. Four large picnic tables filled the space. Prisoners in orange jumpsuits were led into and out of the cage to meet their loved ones. They came and went, led like mangy curs shackled hand, waist and foot. The inmates spoke hushed, rapid, heads hung on elastic necks that bent in grotesque proportions, trying to explain themselves with hands laden in irons, spirits decapitated where mind joins the soul. Anxious wives rejoined, explaining the dynamics of unpaid rent and hungry children. Surrounding the human cage, birds flitted from tree to tree singing their morning joy songs around mothers huddled together weeping with their sons in quiet congress.

Ricky eventually appeared, led like a dog by the same boy guard who had frisked me on my way in. Gushing me with smiles, I stood to hug him. We stood for a lengthy spell flooded with good and horrible memories before taking our opposite seats at the table. He appeared in fine health but with emaciated spirit, like some rambunctious grandfather recently told he only has two months to live. He wrapped his arms around the bags of groceries and provisions. "The food in here is shit. Rice water. The water is rancid. Maggots swimming in it." We spoke of John's death, the confusion of the aftermath, the police showing up, his arrest. "They're saying I *killed* him, Aaron. You were *there*. You *know* I didn't do it!"

"I know, Ricky. I know."

The visit lasted exactly fifteen minutes; abruptly silenced by a guard tapping Ricky on the shoulder with a baton. "I'll come again, Ricky. Be strong, Bro." As he was led away, he turned and said something over his shoulder which I didn't catch.

Throughout November into early December, Ricky's case received a lot of press coverage, which I followed intently. In a hearing on November 28th, Police Lieutenant Loeuk Um, who had examined the body of the deceased, told the court that John had

124

died of a drug overdose and was not murdered. The real relief came the following day, on the 29th, when the Phnom Penh Post reported that the judge had dropped the murder charge, reducing the charge to "…hiding a body."

The two final axial tilts of the year both occurred within days of each other in the first week of December. In the height of its high season, Golden Sorya Mall had swelled with its annual tidal wave of tourists, sex-pats and Euro-trash backpackers looking for a good time. Bars were filled to capacity by eleven every night of the week. Oceans of alcohol poured, drugs were sold, smoked and gulped down by the handful, and the poor working girls flooded in from the provinces to meet the insatiable demands of the clientele.

Friday night, while peddling my wares, I ducked into one of the fish arcade game rooms where a dozen or so Khmers sat emptying their pockets and hammering on the game control buttons. After dishing out a couple hoons, I turned to make my exit and came face to face with Lyda.

I'd first met her months ago, on some random lonely night, and had taken her back to the flat for a night of entertainment. I vaguely recalled a bottle of red, some smoke and a lazy night of couch lounging, Khmer television and enjoyable conversation. Her English was not good, but passable. Her company had been enjoyable, chill, her manners polite, and most important of all, no trouble the following day. I had simply paid her, and she'd gone on her way without any complications or drama. Eye to eye, she took the moment to step back and tuck her white T-shirt over her flat belly into her tight-fitting jeans. Flashing me a coquettish grin, she simply said, "Aaron."

"Oh, hello. Uh… Lyda, you remember my name?"

"Yeah," she shrugged. "Why not? Everyone know your name. You remember me too." We stood shifting through a brief, uncomfortable silence. "So, what now?" She asked. "Where you go?"

"Ah, you know, just hanging out."

"You have ice?" She whispered. "I want smoke with you."

Li and my baby in the States and not returning. An empty flat waiting for me. Nothing to do and nowhere to be. A pocket full of ice. An available ice-head with a gorgeous face and killer body. Deciding my next move wasn't difficult.

With Thea, all my original pious intentions had dissolved in a fruitless fit of spiritual sacrifice and moral crucifixion. Our sexual hilarity and innocent liaisons had quickly slipped into my penetrating and failed attempts to rescue her; further feeding my strategies of manipulation and control. Lyda's sudden appearance offered me distraction from Thea's absence; a new and enticing pond by which to recline, stare at the sky and stagnate by. I was immediately charmed by Lyda's perfectly lithe figure and frail appearance; intrigued by the self-inflicted scars running the length of her forearms testifying to her impenetrable Khmer warrior mentality; hypnotized by her banal approach; enticed by her lust for smoking ice and enchanted by the fact that she never smiled. My destroyed soul instantly loved her human ugliness.

She found Pink Floyd and the BJM boring. "Ohhh, this music make me want to sleep!" She preferred the White Stripes and Sonic Youth. "This good music. But maybe you turn down little bit? I like soft sound." Amiable in her disposition. Deferential in her opinions. She spoke very little, gorgeous in her silence. She asked for a change of clothes. I handed her a T-shirt, along with a pair of sweats and a fresh towel. She disappeared into the bathroom. Half hour later, she joined me on the couch, emanating her intoxicating scent of clean skin and wet hair, her tiny body invisible under the oversized clothes. We stayed up all night lounging on the couch, smoking, chatting, burning through glass after glass, exchanging foot rubs. She offered nothing, promised nothing, and seemed to expect the same. She moved slow through candlelight, preparing the glass, peering wide-eyed through the blinds at the moon, pouring tea with the grace of a ghost. And just like that, I acquired my new roommate who came with a one-way usherance into the indelicate depths of authentic, psychological hell.

My phone went off at 3:45 in the morning with Rumpelstiltskin Mike requesting a half G. The thought of going back out into the whirr of the city and leaving the ethereal utopia with Lyda was crushing, but at the rate Lyda and I were devouring my stash, I felt I had to make up some cash if it was available. I uncurled myself from the couch and began weighing out Mike's order onto the scale. Fingering the empty glass, she asked, "I come with you?"

"No. You stay. I won't be long. I'll be back in one hour." Leaving her with a small rock to entertain herself, I kissed her lightly on her forehead, like a father to a child. I left her there, alone, her black hair slithering around her slender neck, her lips slightly parted, her thin wrist navigating the mouse over song selections, her dark eyes staring at the screen like fathomless black holes.

The city was a ghost town at that time of morning, and I reached GSM just after 4:00. I wanted to do the deal quick and get back to Lyda's warmth and charms. Parking the moto, I rushed through the Ice-Alley maze, ascended the dark stairs to Rumpelstiltskin Mike's. Knocked. Behind the door, his high thin voice announced, "Open!"

The scene was as I'd left it two weeks ago: Lights dimmed, casting everything in the tiny room in a perpetual state of geriatric inactivity and heroin induced lethargy. With his mange of unruly wiry white hair, ever-smiling Rumpelstiltskin Mike peered out from under his bedsheet with a bright smile and tired eyes. "Ahhh, Aaron. Come in! Come in!" He spoke in a William S. Burroughs-like drawl, observing me in a shadow of fascinated boredom. I took a seat next to him on the bed and politely declined his offer for a chase of the dragon. With a shrug, he fired the foil and filled the room with the sweet scent of Asian black tar. We exchanged our normal pleasantries. "I've been getting some good stuff, really good stuff over in *Yung Jo*. I need a pick-me-up. You bring something for me?"

I handed him his half G. He motioned to a crumpled wad of cash on the nightstand. I scooped it up and tucked it into my pocket without counting it. He asked about Thea. As he prepared his next foil combining his H with my ice, I gave him a quick narration of the pathetic engagement in Thailand, Thea's clever stunt of selling back the diamond, my discovery of her infidelities and the details of the break-up. Inhaling a deep pull off the foil, he listened intently, exhaled, then nodded off for a few minutes. I sat quiet, respectful, waiting for him to come back. When he blinked his eyes open, he managed to pick up right where we left off. "Yeah, I'm sorry to hear that, Aaron. But you shouldn't be surprised." He chided lightly. "It's near impossible to sustain a real relationship with any girl in this town. The ingredients of poverty, sex and love simply don't mix. Trying to combine the three will always result in heartache. The poison and fatal cocktail. Every time. The Johns desire love. The girls desire money. Somewhere in-between these two things lies a misery that can't be defined." The sage had spoken. I sat mute, absorbing his painful wisdom.

"Listen Mike, speaking of misery, I need to get going. I got a chick waiting back at my place."

"Of course you do. Just remember this." Rumpelstiltskin Mike lifted the foil to his face, lit, and inhaled a dizzying pull through his pursed lips, then exhaled through his nose. Focusing his dilated pupils into mine, he advised, "I've lived in this miserable town for a miserable fifteen years, and never once have I seen any guy realize a positive thing to grow out of a relationship with a Khmer whore. As beautiful as they appear, with their silken hair, full lips and endless eyes, all of them are broken... shattered to the core. And in order to ensure their continued survival, they'll think nothing of lying to you, manipulating you, *destroying* you if it means an extra dollar in their pocket. They'll promise you everlasting Heavenly pussy galore. They'll convince you *every time*, that you are everything to them, while in reality, you are nothing. We fall at their feet. We love them. Adore them. Sucking their toes, sucking shit out of their sweetly perfumed assholes. They *allow* this to happen, they *tolerate* us, as a means to their necessary survival." Sitting up in the bed, he took another long pull, then continued. "Unless you're able to provide unlimited cash flow into their lives and into the lives of their mothers and fathers and their starving children and sisters brothers and cousins, the girls in this town *never* love. They don't know *how* to love. The Khmer term is *Srey Kouc*. That means *broken girl*, and they aren't called that for nothing. Through their forced profession, they've learned and mastered how to *unlearn* love, disassociate from the very concept. They only know how to *tolerate*. And this they do with the sincerity of a ravaged and grateful child."

I sat poised, transfixed, hinging on Mike's every word. His sermon seemed to float down like feathers from the heights of Heaven, and I heard none of it.

A thunderous knock at the door silenced Mike's sermon. It was a rapid and belligerent knock that had *cops* written all over it. "Did you lock it behind you?" He whispered.

"Always." I mouthed back.

We sat frozen, eyeing our drugs lined out on the nightstand: Baggies of ice, H, lighters, a cooking spoon, crumpled foils, an overflowing ashtray filled with half smoked spliffs. Another three terse knocks in rapid succession, followed by a voice bellowing from a mouth I could imagine pushed right into the door jamb. "C'mon Mike, I know you're in there. Giddy-up!" Placing the voice, a big smile spread over Mike's face and his eyes began twinkling. "Well, I'll be damned! Go on, Aaron. Answer it."

I slid the deadbolt. The door flew open under an enormous weight pushing me back into the room. Six and a half feet, 265 pounds of mass slammed the door, fixed the deadbolt, then lumbered past me directly over to Mike. Their reunion put me at ease. Warm smiles, a heartfelt handshake. Nothing short of bizarre. Like watching a gigantic grizzly bear embracing her disoriented, long lost cub. The giant turned, unshouldered a

Laotian-embroidered man-purse and began emptying its contents onto the nearest chair. "I brought something for you, old buddy. Something I *know* you're gonna like!" While he was filtering through a pile of knick-knacks, he half turned to me and extended his huge meaty hand without eye contact. "I'm Ike by the way. *Big* Ike. Me and Little Mike go way back, don't we Mike?"

Mike... *Little* Mike gave a sincere nod from his bed. "Indeed. Indeed." Little Mike then offered formal introductions. "Ike, this is my friend, Aaron. Aaron, this is my friend Ike... known as *Big* Ike for obvious reasons."

Big Ike addressed me, again with no eye contact. "Good to know you! Damn good to know you!" I cringed under his salutation. One of my pet peeves: Someone presuming to know you without knowing you at all.

Big Ike finally found what he was looking for. Shot me a quick surveying glance before presenting Mike with a folded-up piece of paper. I made myself small, observing the gift-giving ceremony. Big Ike stood over Little Mike, showering him with an ecstatic grin. His head was huge, with closely cropped curly hair the color of a large cement brick fixed directly atop his wide shoulders. No neck. Mammoth arm flesh protruded from a tight-fitting T-shirt that displayed a psychedelic four-armed Indian Shiva god seated on a throne distributing blessings. His body maintained an enormous, invasive presence. He appeared, gestured and demanded attention like some WWE wrestler exuding a sense of international entitlement, though with a hint of commercial humility that I found attractive. Like a wide-eyed, long-lashed anarchic schoolboy sprinkled with a dash of charm.

My perceptions of Big Ike proved true. I watched as Mike unfolded the paper and a small plastic baggie fell into his lap. He held it like a child up to the light while Big Ike proudly divulged its contents. "That there is a smidge of the finest China in Asia today! Super fucking potent! Use that with parental supervision! Ha-ha-ha! Scored it about a week ago while crossing over the Burmese/Thai border. Finest shit there is!"

Holding the small baggie close to his eyes, Mike beamed at Big Ike.

I abruptly asked Big Ike, "You moving shit from Burma into Thailand? What's that border like?"

Big Ike turned to me, shining a thousand smiles. "Easy as butter, my friend. Butter on a piece of warm cinnamon toast on a lazy Sunday morning." What followed was an unsolicited gush of CV, travelogue and bragging rights without any caution whatsoever. Big Mike spoke with a fascinating bravado; a pure Hillbilly spirited with his heritage. "Born August 9, '66 in Mindon, Louisiana in the good ol'e fucking U.S. of A! Graduated Alexandria High School in Alabama. Figured out quick I didn't belong there. Needed to see the world. Knew I had a thing for the gorgeous Asian female specimen, so I headed over to S.E. Asia and by-golly been here ever since!"

Without discussion, the three of us directed our attention to the nightstand, and each began fiddling with the paraphernalia, ready to sample each other's wares. Rumpelstiltskin Mike (now christened Little Mike) emptied Big Ike's gift into a spoon and started cooking, while Big Ike and I each began preparing our respected rocks. I simply dumped mine into a small glass, while Big Ike went the more laborious route, expertly preparing a foil. We all finished at the same time. Little Mike, by *gift-right*, lit and took a long pull of his dragon, while I and Big Ike silently agreed to satisfy our curiosity by sampling each other's product. After holding in our inhales, we all exhaled in unison, filling the room with an enormous toxic cloud.

Little Mike's chin instantly hit his chest, and he spent the next five minutes completely red-lined, nodding in and out of consciousness. Big Ike's ice was also quite good—just as strong as mine, with an instantaneous lift along with a chemical syrupy sweetness that my product was lacking. "Good high… sweet taste." I remarked.

Big Ike shook his head in an enthusiastic *yes* to my compliment. While holding in his second hit, he returned his

131

favorable review of my product, his voice ratcheted two octaves higher than normal. "I like yours too! Clean. Glassy. Strong acceleration, but mine tastes sweeter, don't you think?"

"Definitely. Taste goes to you, while the smooth goes to me." I quipped. This sent us into a sudden eruption of chuckles, like a pair of nerdy Siskel and Ebert's giving a two-thumbs-up review of our favorite entertainment.

Little Mike then righted his head, opened his eyes and focused into the room like a newborn realizing life for the very first time. "Goddamn... strong..." He drawled, before taking up another trail and nodding back out again.

Big Ike and I smiled over Mike's indulgence and continued taking pulls. "So, where you getting your shit?" I asked. "It's obviously different than mine. And what are you paying if you don't mind me asking?"

"Get my shit locally..." He rejoined between puffs, "...from some Nigerians I've been working with for over a year now. They give a good price, but they're always late. They keep me waiting around an hour or two like some cheap street whore. And you?"

"My supply is Khmer. Some crazy fucker living down in the slums just off Riverside. He's consistent, never keeps me waiting, but I think I'm paying a bit too high."

Big Ike raised his bushy eyebrows, questioning my price.

"$55 a gram. Straight up. No breaks." I divulged.

"Pretty expensive if you ask me. I'm only paying $40 a G for mine."

After toking through a silent minute, Big Ike continued. "Maybe we can make an arrangement? I'll split your difference. If I sell you G's for $47.50, that's putting $7.50 into my pocket on each G, and leaving you with a savings of $7.50."

"That's reasonable." I answered. I filled another glass, while Big Ike prepared another foil. "And I appreciate your honesty. But what's up with the waiting around bit? I hate waiting around. With my current gig, I roll up, pay up and I'm on my way. Simple as that."

Big Ike shrugged, exhaling an enormous plume. "Well, I guess it comes down to whether you want to work for a psychotic Khmer or a lazy Nigerian?"

Apples to oranges. "Just how tardy is your Nigerian? I asked.

"How crazy is your Khmer?" He rejoined.

We both shared the laugh, shrugged the joke. A savings of $7.50 per G was appealing, especially considering another mouth now to feed in the form of Lyda waiting back at the flat. I'd been in the game long enough and also knew that once I got in with Big Ike, it would only be a matter of time before I'd be able to exercise my savvy and work my way up to meeting his supplier and cut him out entirely. The idea of going from $55 per unit down to $40 was the draw. The deal was sealed with a handshake. Big Ike suddenly stood, swiped his stash into his pocket and shouldered his man-purse. "Here, take my number and give me a call whenever you want to hook up." After exchanging info, he moved to the door. "Hey, you know anyone who wants to fly?"

A direct and simple question. But one that shifted seismic weight to my miserable existence. In ten crisp syllables, it was as if I'd been granted a window through which to escape all the horror of the past year. My numerous evictions. My firing from Hope school and inability to hold respectful employment. The mental and emotional bite marks left from my gnawing addiction. My awful bed-fellow relationships with addicts since decomposed and liquified into death certificates and/or now imprisoned into the dungeons of Pray Sar. Relational miscarriages with Thea and my estranged wife. My wife's desertion to the States. The loss of my daughter. My failure to simply *exist*. After taking in his question, my spirits took immediate flight at the possibility of alleviating myself from the drudgery of Phnom Penh, and from the mundane process that the simple act of my holotropic breathing had become.

"I'll fly!" I answered without hesitation, without caution, unknowingly hurling myself deeper into the cogs of disorientation and the high gears of random chance.

My sudden response caught him off-guard. Big Ike did a doubletake, paused at the door. "You? Really?"

"Sure, why the fuck not?" He stared hard at me, wanting more, so I extended my resume. "I got no job. No obligations. I'm already well travelled. Been to over thirty countries. I know the ropes of the trade. I think I'd do very well at that sort of thing."

With one last glance at Little Mike laying in his bed spiraling through oblivion, Big Ike gave a nod and assured me, "I'll be in touch. And tell Little Mike to take care." Big Ike parted with a wink. "That heroin's a killer."

The following week was spent curled up with Lyda and getting used to having another warm body in the house. In the beginning she served as a healer of sorts, gradually pulling me away from my pain over Thea. With Thea, it had been all about the sex. Lyda seemed to only have two fundamental interests that I could glean. Her first and foremost passion was smoking ice. Her appetite for the drug impressively rivaled my own. Her ability to stay awake for three, four, five days on end allowed me company, compatible to my own extended and unpredictable hours. She seldom wore clothes; completely comfortable walking around naked, slicing vegetables while watching television, sleeping, gaming on my iPad, watching fist-fucking porn, chatting with her sister without wearing so much as a stitch. The only time she displayed an inkling of reticence was when a customer would show up; and even then, she didn't seem to have any real filter to her modesty. Only after prompting her to the customer's arrival, would she then disappear into the bedroom with a reluctant sigh and quietly close the door. My capability for lust had all but been extinguished long ago, murdered by my constant ingestion of ice. And being *Srey Kouc,* a broken girl, Lyda's libido proved equally annihilated. Her gorgeous naked presence was not a matter of sexual provocation in any way. But she was certainly fun to look at. And I of course, in my constant state of ice-induced, euphoric egoism, had elevated myself to the *Jesus* level. I was indeed, her Savior. And so long as I kept the glass loaded full, she responded perfectly laconic, dutifully endearing, half dead to any will. Ours was a sick and symbiotic relationship that found its nourishment through indulgence, indifference and the occasional sexual tryst. Lyda and I shared an intense interest in escape; fascinated with the role that death might play in such a game.

Second to Lyda's insatiable habit was her insistence on maintaining her anonymity. One random morning, while lounging in bed smoking our way into dawn, I listened while she spent the better part of an hour chatting whimsically in Khmer with her sister on the phone. When she hung up, I simply inquired, "How's your sister, Da?"

She shot up and out of bed with the sheets twisted around her waist, her hair gnarled, eyes black, breasts swaying lusciously like a Caligulaesque goddess. "Why you ask me like dat?" She snapped. "Huh? Why you ask about my family?" Exiting the bedroom, her fingers found an empty wine bottle on the nightstand. She hurled it just over my head, shattering into the wall in a million pieces. Inquiries, curious references, even references to my own family were strictly prohibited.

Thea had lured me into her family as an active participant. And I seized on her potential familial ties to replace the ties to Li and my daughter that I'd thoughtlessly began to obliterate. Da's concepts of family were abstract, at best, and induced a profound and violent reaction; a topic I quickly learned to avoid.

Big Ike's call came a week after our meeting at Little Mike's. He had spoken with his Nigerian boss, and the guy wanted to meet me. The appointment was set for a Sunday afternoon at a restaurant across town near the Vietnamese Friendship Monument in Hun Sen Park. I was to meet Big Ike at the Monument at 1:00. "Make sure you're on time." He urged. "The boss will wait for no one!" A job interview with a drug importer/exporter provides much the same anxieties as say, an interview with a legit employer. I had always been very good at interviews, but my mental prep for this one indicated my entry into a new and unknown world.

The entire interview process for this type of employment seemed completely and utterly bizarre. I couldn't imagine what questions were relevant to engaging in this type of work. So I simply decided to fire up the pipe, show up as high as possible and hope for the best. Lyda certainly got a chuckle out of it. Lying in bed, she eyed me with curiosity as I spent some moments selecting clothes. Setting aside her endless game of Candy Crush Fruit, she rolled over in bed and demanded, "Where you go?"

Loading the glass with a quarter G rock, I let her in on my recent meeting with Big Ike, the opportunity to meet his boss and what it all entailed. After listening intently, she exhaled through a disgusted sigh and simply observed, "You not get any job, Aaron. You sell drugs. You smoke. Nothing good comes for you."

At first, I was startled by Lyda's abrasive affect. And then, easily discovered my perfect semblance with it. I loved her negativity. It was pure. Naked. Stripped to the bone. Her penchant for staying indoors locked away from the world smoking for days on end with no ambition and anticipation for anything charmed me to no end. She expected nothing. No expectation to perform. No pressure to accomplish. Lyda's evaluation of herself and of me allowed me a barren landscape to comfortably exist in.

Lyda was nothing. She assured me I was nothing. She possessed the strength to label us both as nothing. We found strength to smile into nothingness, together. Human deterioration at its finest. Nothing left to do but remain safely ensconced to explore the slow process of moral and physical disintegration. In a matter of days, we successfully created a functional dynamic of co-existence centered on a total withdrawal from societal norms, loyal to nothing but our raging addictions and our acceleration towards achieving pure and justified apathy through our mutual hurt, unforgiveness and loathing for everything around us. We welcomed nothing. We expected nothing, but exerted our constant and selfish demand for everything.

Rolling up on the Vietnamese Friendship Monument, Big Ike gave me a coy nod and flicked his cigarette hard onto the pavement. Walking slow, he disappeared into the restaurant. Minutes later I entered and was led by the maître d' to the table where Big Ike sat in the darkest corner, away from the other patrons. The place was upscale, with fine linen draping the tables along with a casual table set. Big Ike sat fidgety, gnawing the insides of his cheeks, casting glances around the room, adjusting the silverware. I sat across from him completely calm, on an entirely different planet and eyed him with sympathetic concern. "Bro," I whispered, "you OK?"

He gave a quick nod, his eyes dashing around the room in an obvious state of OD paranoia. "Yeah," he whispered, glancing at the door and wiping his brow. "Boss will come soon."

Big Ike and I were equally jacked-up, but his squirminess and inability to successfully masquerade alerted me that I was sitting *not* with the consummate professional that I had perceived, but rather, a two-bit mid-level pusher. This was concerning to me. I sat poised, sipping water, and began perusing the menu while he sat shifting in his chair, itching his head and face while repeatedly adjusting the silverware. "Relax, Bro," I soothed. "Why you so uppity?"

Before he could re-join, a gigantic black man entered through the front door. Shaking hands with the maître d', the man scanned the small room and spotted Big Ike. Standing well over six feet and carrying two hundred fifty pounds, he made his way slowly through the table maze like an ox negotiating a china shop. I stood as he approached, taking control. Big Ike awkwardly followed my formality. Before Big Ike could speak, I presented my name with an eye-to-eye introduction and a firm handshake. Stan flashed a polite smile, gave a half-hearted nod to Big Ike, then motioned for us to sit. He and Big Ike took their seats across from me, interview style. "Thank you both for agreeing to meet," I said. "I'm grateful for your time."

"Yes, I normally reserve Sundays for my church activities. I've just come from church now, in fact. I normally stay for the afternoon's social activities, but when Ike told me about your interest in our business, I thought I'd come say hello."

A well-dressed church-going Nigerian businessman taking time out of his Sunday to discuss international drug smuggling. It was a curveball. I kept my eye intently on the pitch and swung. "How is the music at your church? Do you have a solid worship team?" I asked. "The most important part of the corporate church experience for me has always been the worship. My heart is sensitive to music."

Stan gave a knowing nod. "Yes. I agree. The music is quite good. But for me, I enjoy the social aspect. I usually stay after the morning service and volunteer with coordinating the afternoon social group activities. The community outreach programs... the children's Bible studies, things of that nature. But yes, the music is essential."

"I enjoy contemporary Christian music as well as secular. I collect all genres. I've amassed a wonderful collection of Fela Kuti." To this mention of his roots, his brow raised in approval. "Do you miss your homeland, Stan? And if you don't mind me asking, how long have you been in Cambodia?"

Dodging the questions entirely, he answered, "Cambodia has become my home away from home." He motioned to the menus. "Have you guys figured out what you'll be having? Please, order anything you want. It's my treat." With a glance at his watch, he added, "I hope you'll forgive me, but I don't have time to dine with you today. I have another appointment soon and I must be going." Big Ike and I dutifully reached for the menu's and began scanning. Stan then motioned for the waitress and handed her a credit card. "Before I go, tell me Aaron, what interest do you have in our business?"

Smiling at his invitation, I began, "I'm currently at an impasse here in Cambodia. At the moment, I have no professional or familial obligations. I'm available with a capable and professional enthusiasm. I've been all over the world—over thirty countries. Right now, I'm keeping afloat by small deals, you know, moving things around locally. I'm interested in travel, moving things around on a larger scale. Whatever capacity you think I'd work best at, I'm willing to explore."

After a long and expressionless stare across the table, Stan rubbed his nose and finally gave his approval. "Very well then. I'm sure we can find a place for you. Let me give you my number." He quickly produced a pen from his black blazer pocket, scrawled out his digits on a scrap of paper and slid it across the table. Big Ike, who'd remained completely mute through the entire conversation, shifted uncomfortably in his chair. Stan assured me with a wink, "I will call you within a week. But if you don't hear from me, don't be offended. Afterall, I'm very busy. If you don't hear from me, then give me a call and we can discuss things further."

Stan rose to his full height. I stood with him, offering a collusive smile. "Thank you, Stan, for your time and consideration. I look forward to hearing from you."

He clasped my hand, and within his giant palm I felt the fold of a tiny piece of paper. He gave a quick slap on Big Ike's shoulder, then retraced his slow path back through the restaurant and made his graceful exit.

I raced through the lazy Sunday afternoon traffic back to the flat, burning with anticipation. I found Lyda reclined just as I'd left her, naked and coiled wide-eyed on the couch and purring like a kitten with the pipe half emptied. In my short absence, she'd uncorked a bottle of red and had drained a third of it. She greeted me with a delicious smack on the lips, content in her minimal luxuries. Ducking into the bedroom, I fished out the folded piece of paper that Stan had dashed me at the restaurant. A crisp, clean $100 bill. Slam dunk! In one fell swoop and at the very least, I'd connected with a new supplier, eliminating Big Ike's intermediary services entirely.

Chapter Eight

Phnom Penh
December 2013

The following week came with crushing news. On the morning of 17 December, with Lyda sleeping soundly, I sat up in bed and powered up the laptop. The court had reversed their decision and sentenced Ricky to ten years for the murder of John Connell. The posting stated that Ricky and his lawyer would file their appeal. With one hand on the mouse and the other gently caressing Lyda's thigh, an unidentified call came in. "Hello, this is Aaron."

A pause, then a deep hushed voice. "This is Stan."

"Good morning Stan. Thanks for your call. What can I do for you?"

"I'd like you to clear your schedule for next week, the afternoon of the 22nd through the afternoon of the 23rd. Are you available?"

"If its work related then yes, I'm available."

"Do you know the Frangipani Hotel near the Russian Market?" I didn't know the place but assured him I'd find it. "Fine. Aaron, do you have a credit card?"

"Yes."

"Please book a room for two people. You and Ike will be staying there for a night. You'll be checking in at noon on the 22nd and checking out at noon on the 23rd." As Stan spoke, my heart pummelled into my shoes. I had very little cash on hand. I knew I had no ability for a cash advance and wasn't sure my available credit would cover the rooms. My first assignment for the organization and I didn't want to fail in any way. He continued, "When I arrive at the hotel to meet you, I will reimburse you in cash for your credit card charge. Do you have any questions?"

A hundred questions were jumping off my tongue, yet I wanted to appear facile, spontaneous, with no hesitation and capable of anything. "No, Stan. Perfectly clear. Anything else I can do for you?"

"Thank you, no. Please call me if you run into any complications."

I immediately looked up the Frangapini Hotel online to check out the cost of the rooms. $138 for two adults, one night. I then checked my credit card balance. My last payment for a paltry $306 had been received on the 4th. I threw into a jig around the room to learn that even though I still owed a balance of upwards to $5,000, I still had enough credit to cover the room with some play cash left over for the month. My comprehension of financial reality had completely evaporated into my lust for smoke. Owing five grand, while maxing the card and having no idea how I'd make the next minimum payment simply didn't compute as long as I still had rocks in my pocket.

On the morning of the 22nd Lyda and I lay nursing the last dying hours of a daredevil three-day binge. Added to our usual trail of charred foils, overflowing ashtrays, broken glass pipes and collection of spent lighters lay three empty bottles of cheap booze that we'd absently added into the mix. A bottle of red, a bottle of white, and a bottle of Baily's Irish Crème that we'd spilled into a glorious round of White Russians to tip us along to breaking point. Lyda was incommunicado, slurring words, swaying from room to room with all the grace of a rhinoceros. "Why you keep me here? Huh? You think I not go out? I stay here for a month and not go anywhere! You not take me anywhere! You not give me money! You no good for me!"

It was true, I hadn't given her any cash. But I had supplied her with free room, all the food she could eat, and a constantly full pipe which she'd been sucking on to the tune of a forty dollar a day habit. "Two weeks, Da. You've been here two weeks." I corrected. "You are free to come and go as you please."

"So, you want me to go?" She hissed. "You want me go fuck another man?"

"Da. You're trippin." It was 10:00. I had two hours before checking into the Frangapini to meet Big Ike and Stan. When I left, I wanted Da in bed and asleep so I wouldn't have to worry about her while I was away doing business with my new employer. I fished out two 10 mg tabs of valium from my backpack and placed them in front of her. "Time to cool down, Da. Take those and go to sleep with me. I'm tired. You're tired. C'mon pretty girl. Come to sleep." I tried to wind her down, but she had none of it. Instead, amping up the drama to a notch of insanity I had no desire or endurance for. Calling white black, and black white, she began marauding around the flat completely out of her head, reaching her apex of terrifying ice delirium. She staggered down the hall to the bathroom, supporting herself against the wall while she stripped off her bra and panties and fumbled for the shower. She was too wasted to stand. After aiming the water stream, she perched herself on the toilet and began lathering up her hair with shampoo. Da's pure will was stronger than any I'd ever had to deal with before. She made Thea look like a schoolgirl. Da, balancing herself on the toilet with shampoo running down her face and over her tiny body, she appeared so pathetic that I had to remove myself so she wouldn't see me grinning.

Ten minutes later she appeared wrapped in a towel. She began setting up her going out prep station. From her enormous orange purse came various jars and bottles of this and that, a curling iron, eye liner, cover-up, bronzer, a small cellophane fold encasing fake eye lashes, lipstick and a hundred other accessories. All this she attempted to arrange on the table. She kept dropping items, knocking things to the floor.

Tip-toeing through her items and trying to avoid her sensitive triggers was like negotiating a mine field. I took a seat next to her, reached under the couch to retrieve her mascara, placed it lightly on the table. "Da, it's ten o'clock on Sunday morning. Where are you going?"

"Away from you!" She spat.

She had no money, no ice, no place to go that I knew of. She was operating in the overloaded throes of a seventy-two hour booze and ice binge, coming down, brain frazzled and exhausted. "Why do you want to leave me, Da? Haven't I given you everything you need?"

"You no good for me, Aaron. I need to work!"

She knew where to insert the dagger. Pragmatically, she was absolutely correct. Living with a drug dealer wasn't good for her at all. She was an addict. I was an addict. Two addicts living together; a sure recipe for disaster. This was a very real and true perception, so of course, I ignored it completely.

"Lyda, I understand what you're saying and feeling. But please don't go right now. If you leave right now it will be difficult. You don't even have money for a moto. Please go to sleep, and then when you wake up, you'll feel much better. You'll be more organized. And then I can help you move to a guesthouse if you really want to leave."

Hearing this reality check brought her to a pause. She collapsed back into the couch, closed her eyes, sat small, fumbling with a bottle of blood red nail polish. I took her by her hand, led her into the bedroom. She disappeared into the sheets with a moan. I shut the lights, closed the door.

The bathroom was trashed when I went into shower. Water was still streaming. The floor was full of suds boiling up from the shampoo bottle she'd left toppled on the tile. Three towels lay soaked on the floor, one draped over the rim of the toilet half submerged in the bowl. Two new bars of soap lay melting next to their crumpled paper wrappings. Apparently, she'd gotten the munchies while showering, evidenced by a water trail extending from the bathroom into the kitchen to the fridge. She'd left a watermelon rind discarded on the kitchen floor. After a quick clean up I showered, dressed, kissed her good-bye, then made my way ten minutes through the lazy Sunday traffic. I checked into the Frangipani just minutes before noon.

The hotel was a breath of fresh air, a notch up from the dumps I sometimes slummed in around town. A bellboy saw me up to a seventh floor room, opened the curtains to a good view of *Tuol Tom Pong* and the outlying city. After a quick orientation of turning on the lights, the TV and showing me the mini bar, he made a gracious exit carrying my two-dollar tip. The room held two double beds facing a large flat screen TV, fresh linens, and all the necessary provisions. It reminded me of being back in the States. I quickly muted the TV, closed the curtains, packed a large glass. Once refreshed, I sent a text to both Stan and Big Ike letting them know I'd arrived. Unpacking my overnight bag, I made myself comfortable on the bed furthest from the window and proceeded to set up camp; laptop on the nightstand, surrounded by my pipe, ice stash, ash tray and lighter aligned neatly and ready for consumption. For the next two hours I blazed continuously, firing off a few overdue emails. One to my parents giving them a general sugar-coated update, and one to Li, asking about our daughter and hinting at how much I hated her for abducting her back to the States.

It wasn't until after 4:30 that a text chimed in from Stan. <Glad you are there. Is Ike there with you?>

Just as my fingers were typing the reply, Big Ike keyed in and came tumbling into the room. With little more than a grunt for a greeting, he began unloading a large backpack, situating his camp on the other bed. <Yes, he is here. When can we expect to see you?>

"Hey Bro! Good to see you." I crossed the room to shake his hand. He grasped it with no eye contact and disappeared into the bathroom. The room was instantaneously filled with the tension of having to cohabitate for the next nineteen hours with my supposed new co-worker who apparently held very little interest in getting to know me. I found him standoffish, arrogant, perhaps disgruntled that I'd been taken into the fold and therefore no longer had use of his services.

Big Ike emerged from the bathroom minutes later wrapped in a white towel, steam from the shower billowing into the room. He dressed quickly into black sweats and a white T-shirt. "Let's order up some food! It's all paid for by the way. Stan allows us an unlimited food bill." Tossing the menu onto my bed, he moved to the phone. "I'm gonna get the steak and fries. What do you want?"

"Thanks Ike. Not that hungry. Maybe later. What time is Stan supposed to arrive? And can you give me any clue about what I should expect when he gets here?"

Big Ike dismissed my questions with an impatient wave. "Yes. This is room 707. I'd like to order the steak and fries..." Hanging up the phone, he answered, "I have no idea when Stan's coming. He shows up when he shows up. And as far as what he wants of you, I've no idea on that one either. I simply follow orders. Stan told me to be here, so I'm here. Until he shows up, we're supposed to wait here. Period."

Big Ike commenced to packing up a huge glass and over the next half hour we maneuvered through some interesting small talk. He'd been employed with the cartel for quite a while, traveling in and around S. Asia. He referenced his usual bus route from Phnom Penh to Saigon and mentioned an occasional flight to Sydney. Offering me his glass, he proclaimed, "Sydney's hot! You get popped in Sydney and it's bye-bye baby."

"What's your usual method of carry?" I asked.

"Well, I've pretty much done it all. Body carry—which I refuse to do anymore. Too risky with all the pat downs. Luggage. Also risky, but a bit safer than the body carry. With luggage, all you really need to worry about are the K-9's. The packers are professional and there ain't much of a chance of the load getting picked up by the X-ray. It's the damn K-9's you gotta worry about. And then there's swallow."

"Swallow?"

"Straight down the gullet, my friend. Walking through the entire trip with your belly full of product. It's the only way I agree to work anymore. Other ways are too risky. Especially in Sydney. *Kingsford Smith* ain't your two-runway airport that you'll find in Laos or Myanmar. It's developed! With the latest in surveillance, X-rays, and whatever other shit they've been working on. You can cross the border into fucking Saigon carrying the shit in your hand, or fly into Vientaine or Yangon no problem. Sydney's a different animal all-together."

"How do you manage the pressure?" I asked. "Any rituals you do to reduce anxiety or paranoia?"

"I have no anxiety. Paranoia is for babies. Over the years, I've learned to train my outward appearance to mask the reality of what I'm doing. Before I got into the muling, I used to work for a mining company up in Laos. MMG. MMG mines copper, and before they dig, they have to make sure the land's all cleared of land mines left over from the war. Millions of landmines still up there, all over the fucking place."

He took another hit and continued. "Three little girls and a boy, hands joined, walking through the morning decide to take a short cut through an untamed rice paddy on their way to school. Random explosion. Bodies ripped apart and little arms and legs thrown up in the air in nine different directions. I used to go into the field as part of the de-mining team. Find those little arms and femurs and tibias left littered in the furrows of the rice paddies, gather them into a bag and take them back to the HQ. I've had my face right up into the mines, dismantling them with my bare hands. Lots of UXO's all over the place up there. That's where I learned my focus. *My trance.* I figured, if I could go crawling into a field on my hands and knees with my face staring into my very death, I sure as shit could go walking through an airport with my belly full of ice."

"Sounds intense." I answered. "How much product can you manage in the belly? I mean, when compared to luggage?"

"You can carry much more in luggage. Multiple kilos. But like I said, way risky! My last trip I managed exactly one hundred and fifty bullets. I've never heard of anyone doing more than one twenty-five." I was amazed. Truly. As I was struggling to do the math in my head, Big Ike did it for me. "My record load equals eight Big Mac's. As far as carrying in the belly, I'm the champ! None better than me." Firing up his laptop and plugging in his earphones, he disappeared into his own world and dismissed me altogether.

Big Ike's nightstand was a mirror image of mine: laptop, a big pouch of crystals and all the necessary paraphernalia. Once his food order came and he devoured it, we sat encamped in our respective sites, each messing around on our laptops, smoking, waiting for Stan to arrive. Ike was content while I was an absolute wreck.

I kept thinking of Lyda back at the house, wondering if she'd woken and made good on her motivation to leave. In the two weeks she'd been shacking with me I'd grown quite fond of her, *possessive* even. More fucking madness. In a sudden panic it dawned on me that I had come to *need* her. Subconsciously I knew that I'd dipped below the waves yet again, and needed a buoy—something to reach for. Something to cling to. The thought of her going back out on the streets made my stomach turn. Her phone was in the pawn shop and I had no way of reaching her.

By 9:40 I was climbing the walls. Still no Stan. I'd been in the room nearly ten hours with absolutely nothing accomplished. I'd been smoking for three days straight, hadn't eaten, and bemoaned being tethered inside a room with a guy I barely knew. I couldn't stop perseverating about Lyda. Was she still at the house? Asleep? Had she left in pursuit of making money the only way she knew how? The thought of her walking the streets stalking her next John or drinking with some fat slob down at GSM made my skin crawl. I glanced over at Big Ike. *Until he shows up, we're supposed to wait here. Not go anywhere.* I waved to get his attention. "Yeah, Buddy, what's up?"

147

"Ike, any idea when Stan's going to show?"

"Nope. Not a clue. Could be ten minutes, could be ten hours. Like I told you before, Boss runs on his own Nigerian clock. His game. His time. Nothin' we can do but stay put."

"Well, if it's Okay with you, I'm gonna run back to my place for a few seconds. There's some shit I gotta pick up."

"Suit yourself. Just make it quick. If Boss shows up while you're gone, I'll make some shit up, like you went to the store or something. But if I were you, I'd hustle. Don't fuck up your first gig if you know what I mean."

Wisdom. I skipped the elevator and took the stairs three at a time. Ripped through the narrow *Tuol Tom Pong* streets then opened wide up once I reached the Dyke road. Riding like a complete idiot through the slow traffic, I made it back to the house in seven minutes. Parking the moto, I raced up the stairs and paused a moment to peek through the door's window. All lights were off. I inserted the key and crept in with the stealth of a thief. I barely made out the lump of Lyda's tiny body still curled under the sheets. So intense was the relief that it dawned on me just how deep she had hooked me. Grabbing a few beers from the fridge, I clicked the door closed, then raced through the streets with my hair on fire back to the hotel. I keyed into the room at 10:08. The entire trip had taken me eighteen minutes. Handing a beer to Ike, I stationed myself back into my camp, nursing a cold one between tokes on the glass. I managed to find a spliced version of Jeremiah Johnson on YouTube and snuggled in to stall the time 'til Stan's arrival.

A few minutes to 1:00, the knock finally came. Big Ike muted the TV, nodded to the door. I answered it. Stan, followed by another stoic Nigerian, entered the room. Their sudden arrival swallowed the room into a cavernous realm of uncertain business. Big Ike stood. The four of us shook hands and waded through awkward greetings. Stan introduced his partner as "Sand," standing a head taller than me, dressed entirely in black with a red beret tilted on his head. Sand took a moment to drag the nightstand to the center of the room. We all took our places around the tiny table.

Stan took center stage and thanked us all for coming. "Unfortunately gentlemen, I haven't a lot of time." Glancing at mine and Ike's litter of ice and paraphernalia, he added, "As much as I'd like to stay for the party…" Reaching into the inside pocket of his black blazer, he dove directly into the business. A small sandwich baggie filled with what appeared to be about fifteen white suppositories landed on the table. "These are what we call bullets, Aaron." As Stan spoke, Big Ike took the opportunity to open the baggie and spill the contents onto the table. "Given all the hassles recently surfaced with airport security, this has become our preferred method of transport. We used to simply pack false bottomed suitcases. But recently, we've experienced some unfortunate events, so we've resulted into carrying with the bullet method. The process is simple. Prior to the flight, I will meet with you, and bring the product in the form of bullets." He gave a slight nod to Big Ike. "As Ike can tell you, I will sit with you through the entire swallowing process. Sometimes it takes a few hours. Sometimes more, depending on your ability and ease at swallowing. Big Ike here is the current champ." At this compliment, Big Ike straightened himself, swelling with pride.

Without prompting, I quickly selected a random pellet. I stood, popped the bullet into my mouth. The hard object hit the back of my throat and my gag reflex kicked in. I wretched, launching the bullet out of my mouth and onto the floor in a display of vomitous drool. Wiping saliva from my hot face, I moved quickly to the bathroom and washed the tangy acidic flavor from my mouth.

When I was again seated, Stan sympathetically explained, "It's a slow process, Aaron. You're cool. No hurry here. Take it slow." Over the next ten minutes, I tried again and again, regurgitating over and over. After my eighth failed attempt, Stan motioned for Big Ike to step in. "What do you think, Ike? Got any pointers?"

Big Ike stood to his full height, took a bullet and role-played with all the bravado of an aficionado. "It's all about relaxing, really. Mentally convincing yourself to do something that your physical self is denying. Head back. Throat relaxed. Place the object directly onto the back of your tongue. Don't swim it around. Just drop it as far back as it can go and swallow at the same time." With the ease of swallowing an entire egg, the bullet disappeared down his throat. "Just like that."

I tried a few more times, then collapsed, defeated and embarrassed onto the bed. "I can't seem to do it. The moment it hits the back of my throat it just comes up again. Is there any way to make the bullets smaller?"

Stan shook his head. "Do you like ice cream, Aaron?"

"Ice cream? Sure, why not?" I answered.

Stan turned his attention to Sand who sat with perfect poise in the corner, hands on knees, silent, chiseled into his chair like some dark, gigantic Egyptian Ramses, observing everything without expression. "Sand, please go to the nearest store… the gas station on the corner of Monivong and Mao Tse Tung. Bring back some ice cream."

Sand gave a nod, rose, made his silent exit. He returned half hour later with a pint of Ben and Jerry's along with a wooden spoon and a thoughtful napkin. And while the flavor and the lubricant of the ice cream seemed to make the process more palatable, the result was the same. Me running back and forth from the toilet blowing chunks of *Cherry Garcia*. Walking back into the room, my face red and hot, I sat down at the table with Big Ike and Stan. "I'm sorry to disappoint, Mr. S. Sorry to have wasted your time. Is there any other position within the organization that I might be helpful with? I got nothing going on right now worth mentioning. And I'm fully available whenever and to whatever capacity I can serve."

Stan looked me in the eye with an understanding smile on his face. "You have *not* wasted my time, Aaron. On the contrary; I can see you are dedicated, interested and willing. I think there are

150

other ways we can use you. Most definitely. Let me make some calls." Mr. S. stood, shook hands with Ike and me, then moved for the door. Sand gave us each a nod and followed. "Oh, I almost forgot..." Before making his exit, Mr. S. turned while reaching into his pocket. "How much did you charge onto your credit card for the room?"

"A hundred and thirty-eight." I answered.

Mr. S. peeled off and passed me three fifties. I fumbled for his change. "No need, Aaron. I appreciate your time and participation. While we didn't see the results we had hoped for, this was a good learning experience. And we'll take this experience and make it work for everyone's benefit. I will contact you again shortly. Please be ready to work when I call. There's work to be done soon in S. America. Brazil, to be precise. Perhaps as early as next month. I'll call as soon as I've outlined the specifics. You'll be hearing from me in the first week of the New Year."

I stalled a few minutes after Stan and Sand's departure before leaving the hotel and racing back to the flat. Taking the steps two at a time, I keyed into the flat and noticed the bedroom light left on. Lyda was gone, her only trace evidenced by a few articles of clothing left strewn over the bed. A strong scent of perfume lingered sickly in the room. Back down the stairs two at a time I blazed to GSM, parked, and began casing the bars and the fish game rooms. 3:15 am on a Monday morning, the place was near deserted. Working girls were everywhere, strolling the empty bars for anything they could find. No one had seen her. I ran over to the pawn shop and asked the clerk if Lyda had been there to retrieve her phone. He shook his head. Over the next hour I raced around like a complete idiot to all her usual haunts. The Walkabout was empty. G Pub, Pontoon, the Swiss Bar all vacant.

Boiling with paranoia and my tormented incapacity to be present with myself, I straddled the moto and made my way back to the flat. Streets empty, shadows and urchins and rats and small campfires whirring by in my peripheral, I raced blindly through red lights, intersections and stop signs at full suicidal abandon with no caution or care and fueled by a blood lust to suddenly end it all. It was all rather sickening. My will to *possess* something—anything. It sprouted like a poison weed growing from toxic loam.

The glow of a sick sun rose into the low hovering clouds creating blurred edges around the cement buildings defining the waking city. Over the next countless hollow hours, I made numerous trips back and forth from the flat to GSM, smoking like a fiend, racing through the industrial maze like a rabid rat scurrying only to meet dead ends. My crazed pursuit of Lyda ended on my bedroom floor, curling into my insanity with one hand holding the pipe and the other grasping the handle of her curling iron.

The empty house swallowed me whole. After locking the door and pulling the shades I showered, tilting my open mouth to the cold stream swallowing enormous doses of much needed hydration. Brushing my teeth, I glanced in the mirror and noticed another boil forming under the hairs of my left eyebrow. I fingered it tenderly, intrigued by the stabbing pain. Sitting naked on the couch, I wrapped myself deep in the silence. Thoughts of Lyda somewhere in the city fucking for her living were too treacherous to contemplate. I dismissed them.

Equally treacherous were thoughts of my daughter somewhere in California soon to wake to open her Christmas presents, so I dismissed these as well, enjoying the last pulls on a final cigarette before walking down the hall to the bedroom. Crawling slow into the bed, it felt like I was laying down into a small pond of quicksand, immediately enfolded and sinking deep into a fluid syrupy void. How long had I been awake? I vaguely recalled last waking a few days before meeting with Ike and Mr. S at the hotel on the 23rd. Five, maybe six days? Mental snapshots, recollections and horrors and frustrations and worries of the past week eventually slowed to a standstill. Memories morphed to blurs. Empty Christmas. Year ending. Grasping at the kite tails of last-minute epiphanies to contemplate... perhaps... tomorrow...

Chapter Nine

Phnom Penh, Bangkok
January - February 2014

January was a long and wasted reminder that nothing had changed. I continued to scan and totally ignore the content of the email pleas that arrived from my parents asking me to return to the States. Updates from Li concerning our daughter continued to fan the fire of my disdain towards life in general. The calamities of 2013 had simply rolled over into the New Year. The same addictions, the same destructive patterns, the insane relational issues with Lyda, the same day to day routine of dealing around the city and hustling for small cash.

Lyda was climbing the walls as ever, smoking like a chimney as long as I kept the fire lit. Living with her was a no-win situation. She devoured my profits as fast as I could make them. Sex was good but came with the steep price of trying to keep her domesticated. She was a svelte and cunning panther, blending in the shadows from room to room with an ever-present threat in her eyes. She was silent, at best, provided she was satiated. But the moment she intuited that I wasn't going to be able to keep her fed her eyes would dull over and her movements would begin threatening the impending attack.

The first week of January came and went without Stan's promised call. Sales, cash and product was dwindling. Every time I'd meet him for a pick-up, he'd simply wave me off. "Soon, Aaron. Please be patient."

"Mr. S., please understand, I'm right at the edge here. I must work! Half of my customers have traveled for the holidays and won't be back until mid-month. Your good price on the G's is keeping me afloat, but barely. I really need to go."

"Soon, Aaron. Just a few more days." It wasn't until the third week in January when Stan's call finally came.

"I've been in contact with my associates in São Paulo. You'll be traveling there sometime in February. First you must fly to Bangkok to obtain your Brazilian visa." Sitting across from Stan in a crowded lunch hour at the Pizza Company, I assumed my best poker face. I didn't want to seem too anxious, or too grateful.

"Fine. I appreciate this opportunity. I look forward to the travel, getting out of Phnom Penh, my routine here. I'm ready for a new challenge. I have every confidence the assignment will be successful."

Mr. S. took a bite of his chicken fettuccini alfredo and eyed me hard as he chewed. I returned his stare with a blank, business-like expression, waiting for him to swallow and speak. He washed the mouthful down with a dainty swig of mineral water. "Tell me Aaron, is your house in order?"

It was a peculiar question, immediately reminding me of the amazing Dottie People's gospel jam. I stuttered all over my answer. "Uh, my house in order? Um, yes, I suppose so." He stared straight through my smokescreen. "I guess it depends on what you mean about *in order.*" The more I stuttered on, the deeper I dug my grave. "Listen, Mr. S. If you want the truth, my house is in total disarray. With nearly all my finances sucked away because of bad investments, and with nearly all my customers away for the Christmas and New Year's holidays, I'm in a serious money crunch. My utilities are paid, and I don't owe anyone anything, but I'm facing an outstanding credit card bill and I haven't paid January's rent yet. That's why I really need this gig. I *need* this work. And I'm ready to do whatever the job entails, without question."

Mr. S. sat silent, nodding thoughtfully. "I hear you are living with a reckless girl. Is this true?"

154

Mr. S. had been doing his homework. His statement set me back a bit. "Yeah, I am living with a girl. She's pretty wild. Like's to smoke a lot. Sometimes can't handle herself when she gets too high. Why do you ask?"

"Because a girl like this could have a negative effect on you and your state of mind. When I send you into the field on a job, you shall have no distractions. I need you totally focused on the task at hand. Not worrying about your domestic issues back here in Phnom Penh. Not worrying about anything. Worry directly interferes with focus. Do you understand what I'm saying?"

"If it's any consolation, Mr. S., my girl won't be staying in my place when I'm gone. Whenever I leave town, I lock the place up, leave her with some money to live on her own until I return."

He absorbed this information like a statue. No reaction whatsoever. He summoned our waitress, had the remains of his meal boxed up while I swallowed the last bites of my pizza. I followed him out to the parking lot and stood quiet while he unlocked the door to his Escalade. "Thank you for meeting with me today, Aaron. I enjoyed your company." He climbed into the seat and brought the engine to a purr.

"Thanks for lunch. I enjoyed your company as well." I stood feeling unsure, like I'd failed the interview and fell short of his expectations. "Mr. S. Please let me know when you are ready to move forward. I'm ready."

With a grin and warm handshake, he assuaged my anxiety. "By the end of the day today I will send you your itinerary to Bangkok. You will be flying in a few days to obtain the Brazilian visa." He left me with a parting shot. "Get your house in order, Aaron. Seriously."

The house was silent, save for the faint knocking sound of glass hitting against tin. I walked down the hall into the large family room, windows shut against the day and blinds drawn tight to the blazing sun. Lyda sat stiff on the couch, her naked back to me, emptying the ashes of a pipe into the ashtray. She hadn't heard me come in. I stood still, watching her select crystals off the glass tabletop, packing up a new glass. Her hands were shaking. The gram I'd left her with was nearly half gone. In the hour I'd been away meeting with Mr. S., she'd devoured what would have taken me half a day to consume. She spotted me out of her peripheral, turned, gave a quick nod, then set her attention back to the task at hand. I took a seat next to her, watched her lay the flame and suck greedily at the glass. Exhaling an enormous plume into the room, she quickly passed the glass to me, then collapsed back onto the couch, pulling a pillow over her naked breasts. "Where you go?" She hissed. "I wake up and you not here? You go to fuck someone, huh? You think I not know?"

"Good morning, lovely Lyda," I answered sweetly after taking a hit. "I hope you slept well." I moved to kiss her. She pulled away. Her accusation packed more irony than I could process. I'd been out setting up the gig with Stan with the sole purpose of providing for her so she wouldn't have to continue prostituting herself, only to come home to her accusing me of infidelity. I passed the glass back to her and left the room with a groan.

Pouring a tall glass of Coke in the kitchen, I heard her bare feet marching down the hall. Swerving past me to the utensil drawer, she opened it and grasped the butcher knife. Making her retreat down the hall, I heard the bedroom door slam and lock. Following her, I knocked on the door. No answer. Putting my ear to the door, I could hear a peculiar sound that I couldn't quite identify. I hurried to the front room where just moments before Lyda and I had been smoking together on the couch. I stood, separated from the bedroom by a large sliding glass window. Lyda had locked the window, and had pulled back the curtain, affording me a wide cinematic view of her activities. I stood transfixed, aghast, as if watching a horror film, witnessing her maniacally swing and slash the butcher knife into my hanging wardrobe, rendering all my clothes: T-shirts, pants, dress shirts, sweaters into ribbons of lacerated material littering the bed. I pounded my fists against the glass. My frantic reaction only accelerated her tiny wrist slicing the large blade through the air with more enthusiasm, sending the remaining dangling shreds of fabric floating to the floor. She turned to face me, her lips pulled back revealing a horrible, ecstatic grin, her hair sticking to her sweaty face in a portrait of demented rapture. My horror fueled her hilarity. My frustration, her orgasm.

Turning my back on her tantrum with complete resign and with the hope of diffusing the situation, I took a calm seat on the couch, picked up the glass she had left and laid a long flame to a succulent inhale. Minutes later, I heard the bedroom door creak open. Her feet pattering down the hall with all the anticipation of a guilty child, gleeful in her dirty pleasure. She placed the knife gently on the table and held out her hand to receive the pipe. I placed it into her shaking hands. "What's up with you, Da? Why you destroy all my clothes? What the fuck is wrong with you?"

With an instantaneous Jekyll and Hyde transformation she curled next to me on the couch and put the glass to her lips. "You think I stupid?" She sighed through her exhale. "You think I not know where you go?"

"When I leave here Da, I go to work! And when I go to work, I don't have to fuck." It was a slicing blow. The second the words dropped, I regretted speaking them. She gave a slight wince, nearly indecipherable, but I caught it. She accepted the cut like it was nothing, staring stone-like into the room. Moments later, she stood, walked back down the hall and shut the bedroom door softly. When I walked in the room was pitch black. The light from the hall showed my clothes littering the floor in tatters and ribbons. I stepped through the carnage, slid into the bed and pressed against her warm skin. After feeding her a handful of Valium, we laid in silence for more than a half hour, my arms wrapped around her tightly, kissing her neck and her hair. "Da?" I finally whispered. "I had a meeting this morning with my boss. In a few days I'm going away. To work out of the country. I'll be gone a few days. A short trip."

"Mmmm."

"Da, when I go you can't stay here at the house. The house owner won't allow it. You know?"

"Mmmm."

"When I leave, I'll give you some smoke. Give you some small money so you can stay in a guesthouse and pay for food while I'm gone."

"Mmmm."

"Da, the next time you destroy something in this house I will put you out and never let you back in. *Never.* You understand me?"

"Mmmm."

I lay listening to the sound of her breathing deepen. As she fell asleep, I held her tighter, absorbing the sudden twitches in her arms and legs. Body tremors, like Thea had. Shaking anxiety symptoms typical of addicts and women abused. Matching my breathing with her own, I eventually was able to release myself into her, and let go.

Waking from an eighteen-hour crash, I groped through the dark relieved to caress the curve of her hip. In the front room I fired up the laptop to check email. Li had sent a short message proposing a handful of places she'd agree to move to if I were to return to the States. She also sent two videos. In the first video, I watched my daughter learning to ride her two-wheeler without training wheels. The second video showed my daughter standing onstage along with a bunch of other kids belting out Christmas Carols from the tops of their lungs. I replayed the clips ten or twelve times, smiling over her as if she were right in front of me, wanting to reach into the screen and pull her close. Tears burning my eyes.

I'd left and divorced the States seven years ago for all the right reasons; reasons that the government would have condemned as treasonous, finally turning my back on America's repeated violations on the world community that had been committed over and over and over covering countless saeculum. I simply had no intention of returning. And even if I did, Florida? Home of sunshine and AARP cards and pink flamingo lawn ornaments and the nation's largest geriatric population? I knew no one in Florida, but Li had her sister there. Selfish motives. The Bay area? Simply too expensive. And Phoenix? Nudged right up next to Florida on the political spectrum, and outnumbering Florida only in the number of registered golf carts. While I loved my parents and appreciated Li's extended olive branch to actually ponder relocating near my family, the very thought made me want to wretch. And where did Australia play into the picture? Li and I knew no one there. And the same with N. Ireland? Had no ties there and no acquaintances. Li's last suggestion: Singapore. She had friends there and I knew no one. Another one of her stagnant, selfish tadpole ponds.

Smoking myself into a quick physical acceleration, I set the pipe gently down on the table, walked back into the bedroom, threw the sheets aside and proceeded to give Lyda's semi-conscious, inert body a short and hard and angry fuck. Tucking her back in, I stormed into the kitchen and put a pot of tea to boil. I thought of Li, snug away in her sterile, laconic Los Altos suburb where she most likely sat spewing falsehoods and skewed truths into the innocent ears of my abducted daughter. Li's proposed itinerary made my mind simmer to boiling point. Truth be told, she could have proposed that she and I and our daughter all float up, hands joined in Angelic chorus, to live in our celestially prepared Heavenly mansions, and I still would have spat at her and told her to go to Hell.

On February 4th, after kissing Lyda goodbye on the corner of Monivong and Kampuchea Krom, and placing $200 into her eager hand, I hopped off the moto-taxi and hailed a cab that delivered me to the airport through the stifling traffic. The early flight to Bangkok was an easy fifty-minute snooze. After checking into a four-star I crushed up some lines on the glass table, straightened out, then walked two blocks to the Embassy to file my application. Routine paperwork, a short interview. I returned the following day and retrieved my passport along with the visa. No hassle. Back in the room I launched into a fierce non-stop smoking session that devoured the rest of my gram and sent me crawling the walls throughout the afternoon and wandering aimlessly the streets into the wee hours until I melted into lovely unconsciousness just as the sun began its gruesome orange, ominous rise.

4:32 PM. Woke with my tongue swollen like a dry caterpillar trying to squirm out of its cocoon. Skin crawling out of the sheets in a dry sweat. Heartburn raping my esophagus. Tears leaking out of my eyes like sleeping sorrow searching for an earlier, happier day. I fumbled my way through the dark, stumbled into the bathroom, winced under the lashing light and wretched acid and bile and blood into the bowl and into another typical day. Stood in the pitch-black bathroom, the frigid water pouring over my head. A lovely sensation on my hot skin. I craved cold. Demanded the dark. Sought nothing but silent still-frames. Ached for everything *anti-life*. Ice gone, I dove head-first into the throes of severe withdrawal.

Negotiating the hotel lobby demanded focus. Walk straight. Get to the door. Too many sounds. People. Too much motion. Light. The activity on the street was overwhelming and unbearable. The sidewalk stretched endless; a wobbly footbridge stretched like a tightrope between two impossible distances. Steaming traffic, dense passersby, cruel bustle, cursed life. Placing my hand on the door of *Everything*, I entered the restaurant and what I saw snapped my brain, ushering me quickly and directly into complete insanity.

In the very center of the crowded room, Thea sat at a table for two. She was dressed to the nines in an all-black loose-fitting pantsuit, perfect posture, hair curled, all dolled up with a subtle mask of make-up and perfectly piercing eyes that sliced me to my core. Upon my entrance, our eyes locked. Mutually stunned. No comprehension. My appearance to her and her presence to me entirely out of context, neurons misfiring, complete brain scramble. Instead of placing the bite into her mouth, her fork fell onto her plate with a clatter. Ashen face, she mumbled something to her companion and delicately wiped her mouth with downcast eyes. I floated past her table like a phantom, vaporized in horror. My arm brushed her shoulder. Unreal contact. I moved to the counter and picked up a menu. No recollection to what I ordered. Simply pointed to random pictures on the menu. A vague apparition of a person took my order, smiled, mumbled something in Thai. Walls closing in, I wandered suffocating back through the room, past Thea, my arm brushing again against her shoulder to make sure she was real. Out the door, filling my lungs with a renewal of breath. Staggered into the street and took a hard seat on the pavement across the street from the restaurant.

Collapsed on the pavement, literally, like a common vagrant, knees buckled, zero stamina. From my pavement perspective I tried to make sense of the image. Thea in Thailand, sitting across the street in a small restaurant called *Everything*. I watched her small image through the window. A first-hand real-life incubus. No filter of a silver screen to separate unreal from reality. It was happening. Thea in Bangkok. In a restaurant. With a client. Nightmare in real time. My stomach churned. Not from hunger but rather from a violent nausea. I sat on the pavement for ten, maybe fifteen minutes waiting for my order, waiting to go back inside to pick up the food, to see her again up close, all prettied up and sitting with her John. *Everything* a horror-show.

When I entered, she kept her eyes glued to her plate. Not eating, just sitting silently with her head bowed as if in prayer. I paid for the order, received the bag and left as quickly as I'd entered. Out on the sidewalk, I stood just to the left of the window, out of view. I took the vantage point to watch her through the window.

My sudden appearance had clearly affected her. She sat frail, frozen. Her usual charm ripped to shreds. Her casual animation gutted, replaced by a dilapidated posture and a mask of consternation. I could tell she was trying to recover, for the sake of her John. He was a large Anglo man, not fat but rotund *American* style in his fifties dressed in jeans and a casual black blazer draped over his broad shoulders. Not handsome in any way; absent of any outstanding physical characteristics. He sat across from her, shoveling the last remaining forkfuls of food into his mouth and flipping through messages on his phone, completely unaware of what had just transpired.

I stood, transfixed, observing every subtlety, every interaction between the two of them; him pre-occupied with his phone, her sitting dutifully allegiant and obedient to his whims. At one point he passed her his phone to show her something. She gave the image a quick glance, returned the phone with a nod and a fake smile, then returned to her posture of polite submission. The man then left the table to settle the bill at the counter, leaving Thea alone at the table where she sat frozen, staring at the remains of food on her uncleared plate. When the man returned, she stood and followed him to the door. I made myself small in the alcove. The man exited onto the street, not even bothering to hold the door for Thea. He passed me, Thea following a few steps behind. I followed them both. After half a block I found my voice and spoke. "Thea." She stopped, turned and faced me.

"Uh, hi." She met my eye and then quickly looked away.

"Hi. How are you? It's good to see you. What are you doing in Bangkok?" By this time, her John had realized her absence and had turned to find her. He saw the two of us speaking and retraced his steps.

"I'm just here with a friend." She stammered. She offered no eye contact, shifting uncomfortably.

"How long are you here for?"

Her John had joined us, standing three-quarters behind Thea. "I leave tomorrow morning. Back to Phnom Penh." She whispered.

"Hey what's going on, Sara? You know this guy?" He puffed out his chest and eyed me with scathing suspicion.

Thea collapsed, answered with a shake of her head, turned and walked away, leaving me standing face to face with her John. He was much larger than I had originally perceived, standing a half head taller than me. I stared at him with disdain, rage boiling, wanting to decapitate the smirk off his shoulders. After a few uncomfortable and silent seconds, he dismissed me with a shake of his head and followed after Thea. I watched them turn the corner and then raced down the street to the point of their vanishing. Peering around the corner I continued to keep pace, following them straight to the very hotel where I was staying. They gained the stairs, entered the lobby. The man paused at the front desk and chatted with the clerk for half a minute, then Thea followed him to the elevators where they waited for the lift and then disappeared.

I greeted the girl behind the counter. "*Sawadee ka.*" She returned my greeting with a slight bow and smile. "I'm staying in room 506. The man and the woman who were just here are friends of mine, but I don't know their room number. Can you please tell me what room they are in?"

The girl demurred. "I'm sorry, but I cannot give that information."

"I understand," I offered, gnawing my tongue. "Will you please call them and tell them I'm here? My name is Aaron."

The girl picked up the phone and tapped her delicately painted fingernails onto the number pad. 606. After a few rings she spoke. "Yes, you have a visitor. Mister Aaron is here to see you." She nodded through the return, then placed the phone back in its cradle. "I'm sorry Mr. Aaron, but they are not accepting visitors at this time." Nodding through my torture, I thanked her and then took the lift to my room.

The John answered on the third ring. "Hi, I'm calling for Thea. May I speak with her please." There was a long wrestling sound of the phone passing, and then Thea's uncertain voice spilled into my ear. "Thea, it's me. I know you are in a difficult position right now. But I want to see you. I need to see you. Please meet me down in the lobby so I can see you. I'm not mad. I just need to see you. Please meet-"

"-I can't see you now. I'm sorry." Click.

I hit redial and counted the ring tone until the call eventually went to voice mail. Hanging up the receiver I collapsed and curled onto the floor, lay in the dark tearing at my hair, repressing the urge to scream. Mental violence nearing its horrid apex. I had truly won the lottery from Hell. Out of the 86,687 hotel rooms registered with Bangkok's Department of Tourism, Thea and her John were staying in the room directly above my own.

I walked down the long silent hall and found the door to the stairs. I ascended the one flight to the sixth floor and approached 606 like a deranged madman. Leaning against the wall, I endured a thousand deaths while staring at the *Do Not Disturb* placard left dangling on the knob. Do Not Disturb what? Do Not Knock? Do Not Smash Through the Door and Rescue Your Estranged Fiancée from the Horrors of S.E. Asian Poverty and Prostitution? Instead of knocking, I fell like a feather against the door with my ear pressed against it, straining to hear a sound. *Any sound.* Any inclination or hint as to what was happening on the other side of the veil. Nothing. No sound of television, or radio, or hair dryer or laughter or crying. Nothing. It was the sound of Thea on the other side of the door, emerging from the shower wrapped in a white towel, moving through the candle lit room with her rotund John memorizing how the tiny flames danced over her bronze flesh in subtle shadow. The sound of Thea receiving clumsy and eager kisses on her arms and legs synchronized perfectly with her silent tears. The notes rose and fell in my ears, performed by a laughing imp pounding out minor keys, head thrown back howling reckless and infantile spurts of foul smelling and tearful pornographic din.

Very little left. Thea remained as an image of a discarded corpse, what left of her life trickling out from between her legs staining crisply starched hotel sheets in Bangkok. Little left of me. A pathetic and desperate stick figure leaning like a scarecrow against the barren fields of sobriety and rationale. Taking the stairs back down to my room I wilfully dismissed all horrific thoughts from my head and replaced them with the reality that in less than sixteen hours I'd be snug back in my room in Phnom Penh lying next to Lyda with an unlimited supply of ice and escape at my disposal.

I stepped onto the balcony and stared over the city.

When all seems lost, suicidal ideations can always be seen shimmering like freshly realized pearls singing peculiar songs on the bottom of the ever-shifting sea floor.

Chapter Ten

Phnom Penh, São Paulo
February 2014

Stan slid into the seat across from me with all his cool and calculation. "I trust everything went as planned in Bangkok?"

"No problems at all. No complications. I have the Brazilian visa stamped into my passport. It's a handsome stamp. Takes up an entire page. It's good to see you, Mr. S. How've you been?"

"Busy. Very busy these days setting up everything for your trip."

He withdrew an envelope from the inside pocket of his blazer and slid it across the table. The itinerary was rough. Departing Phnom Penh in the afternoon, routing through Ho Chi Minh on a nine-and a half hour flight to Qatar. A thirteen-hour layover in Doha. Then departing Qatar for the fifteen-hour flight on to São Paulo. Stan returned to the table just as my meal arrived. I started in on it as giddy as a kid experiencing his first pizza party.

"It all looks good, Mr. S." I spoke banal, disguising my euphoria over finally having something in writing. *Official* work. No more running around the city weighing out bullshit hoons and half G's and living hand to mouth. This was the real gig. The big time. International transport. A soon to be significant payday. "Leaving on the 13th!"

I devoured my lunch while Stan went through a pragmatic checklist of the trip. The hotel would be directly in the city center, paid for in full. Once checked into the hotel, the operatives on the ground would pay me a visit and outfit me with a burner phone to keep me in comms with both local updates and updates from Cambodia. I'd be given a healthy daily cash per diem. My return ticket had me landing back in Phnom Penh on the 26th—the entire gig lasting less than two weeks. An all-expense paid trip to the coolest city in S. America that came with a healthy paycheck to boot! "Relax while you're there. Get out and enjoy the city. Enjoy, but don't go crazy. Always remember, you are there for a purpose. A single job. A very important job. A job that will demand your absolute and one hundred percent focus. Especially on the day you travel. Do you have any questions?" Stan penetrated me as I took down the last nibbles of crust.

Several questions swam through my head. Obvious questions that should have been asked. What exactly am I carrying? What's the weight? What's the penalty for getting pinched? Have you ever lost one of your mules to an arrest? How hot is the airport in São Paulo? When will I get paid? If I do happen to get nipped, who do I call? Does your organization provide the costs to cover a lawyer? If I go to prison, do you support me through my incarceration? Instead of launching the grand inquiry, I asked nothing. Content to swim adrift in a sea of pure apathy and reckless chance. "Not at this time, Mr. S., but I'm sure once I'm in the field some questions will arise."

Stan nodded his approval. Sliding his Coke aside, his large palms hit the table like slabs of raw meat. He looked me square in the eye. "Aaron, I need you to understand some things regarding your upcoming mission. Please listen closely." I gave him my full and undivided attention. "When you are in the field, you will have a lot of down time. I hope you fill this time with rest and relaxation away from all your worries here in Phnom Penh. Away from your worries about paying your rent and your bills. Away from your crazy girlfriend. I hope you use your time in São Paulo to center yourself as you prepare for the job at hand."

"Absolutely, Mr. S. I'm burnt out here in Phnom Penh, need a break from Cambodia big time, away from the day-to-day worry-"

167

He raised a fat hand and silenced me. "-Aaron, I know you are using a lot. And I hear crazy stories around town about this girl you're shacked up with. Before you leave town, I need you to have your house in order. Remember when we discussed this in out last meeting?"

"Yeah, Mr. S. I sure do."

He lowered his voice to a whisper and held me with a terribly intense stare. "You need to understand, Aaron, when you are in the field you will have a very different perspective than the perspective I will have back here. My perspective here will be large. From my command center here, I see everything. Your perspective in the field is important, but it is also narrow. You must always keep in mind that the picture I see is the larger picture. From where I sit, I see all. Everything. It's your job to maintain focus. But it's my job to focus on many things. I focus on you and your movements. I focus on the other people there on the ground. I focus on coordinating movements so that everything comes together. Do you understand what I'm telling you?"

I took a deep breath and nodded my assurance. "Yes, Mr. S, I do. I really do."

"Above all, there is one single thing that you must always maintain. Do you know what that one thing is, Aaron?"

It was a typical set up question. Stan had the answer in his mind, and I had no way of reading it. Instead of attempting a failed answer, I acquiesced to his playing God. "Tell me, Mr. S."

"Trust." He stated simply. "Above all else, when you are in the field, no matter what is happening, you must *always* trust me. Remember, I see the bigger picture. Sometimes when you are operating in the field, things may seem a bit confusing for you, perhaps even frustrating. These experiences are normal when you are working halfway around the world with team members that you aren't used to operating with. But no matter what happens, you must *always* trust. Trust *me*. And do *exactly* as *I* instruct."

Back at the flat I fired up the laptop. An email from my dad went on and on about his concern of my falling away from the

168

family and falling away from God. "We talk about you every day and although it seems God is not a part of your life right now, we both spend a portion of each of our mornings in communication with him concerning you… Know we are in your corner and ready to help as we can, here to encourage you, pray for you, cry for you and eventually get you transported back to the States so your daughter can once again know who her Papa is."

I read his words while nursing the glass like a synthetic tit. I pictured my mother sitting in her prayer room halfway around the world wiping tears from her ashen face. The image meant little. I had been weaned. Somewhere along the rough road, a certain and pure apathy had come to devour the love bond between mother and child. Between child and father. And certainly, between child and my invisible God who served as the creator and overseer of all things destroyed.

A few minutes after midnight Lyda showed up hurling small pebbles against the window. She went straight to the fridge and selected two hard boiled eggs and a left-over chicken leg. She looked like shit. Unkempt and disheveled. After her shower she collapsed naked and glistening onto the bed explaining how she'd tripled the money I had given her, and how she had taken her winnings to the fish arcade and lost it all. She asked about my up-coming gig in São Paulo. I described the job in abstract. "It's a good job, Da. I'll be paid well. When I come back, we'll have nothing to worry about."

She took another hit of the glass, curled into the sheets and cackled like a fiend. "You always say that. When you have money? Huh? You have nothing! You not give me anything!" Both of us electrified by the potent ice that Stan had provided, I took her by the hips and silenced her typical rants and hurtful insults with aggressive kisses. Angry forgiveness. The two of us collapsing into the messy aftermath like spasmodic jellyfish writhing through final electrical and lethal discharge.

On the eve of my departure, I met with Mr. S. on a bench in Hun Sen Park under the shadow of the Independence Monument where I used to take my daughter to play. He handed me an envelope that I quickly slid into my backpack. "There's five hundred there. Plenty to get you to where you're going and sustain you for the first week or so. I will send you more as needed via Western Union."

"Thank you, Mr. S. Everything is in order on my end. Bills are paid at the house."

He raised his eyes in a pejorative slant. "So, your house is finally in order?"

"As much as it can be for the moment. I'm still having difficulties with her. But while I'm gone, she won't be at the house. She'll be taken care of." After a short silence I explained, "It's hard dating a Khmer girl, Mr. S. Fucking hard. They're all poor. All desperate. And all crazy to the extent that there isn't anything they won't do to ensure their survival."

Stan already knew the local scene. He nodded and dismissed me. He had no patience for my personal details. "Well Aaron, if you don't have any other questions then I'll be on my way. Please send me a text when you are boarding the plane tomorrow and send me a text when you arrive. Once you arrive, my operatives on the ground will come and give you what you need."

A few hours before my departure with bags packed, Lyda and I sat on the couch swiftly packing and blowing through glass after glass, smoking ourselves into a frenzy. Me amping myself up to deal with the airport check-in and customs and all the tedious travel procedures. When it was time to go, I presented her budget.

I had thoughtfully rationed cash into three separate envelopes. I had labeled the first *Guesthouse*, the second, *Food*, and the third contained a plastic baggie filled with 1.5 G's of choice crystals. Thirty seconds into explaining the budget to her, she impatiently ripped open the envelopes, wadded up the cash and the ice and stuffed it all into her purse. "Why you talk so much, huh? You think I stupid? You think I not know how to live without you?" It was the worst thing she could have said. I knew then deep down that within the week she'd be turning herself out on the street, bringing all my worst fears to fruition.

I parted ways with Da on my way to the airport near GSM, leaving her standing on the street with nothing but her purse and a small plastic bag filled with a few clothes items and her personals. She graced me with a few seconds of full eye contact, kissed me on the lips and thanked me. I watched her go, my stomach churning into knots. She gave a backwards glance and a small wave before disappearing around the corner.

The flight to Ho Chi Minh was a quick forty-five minute jaunt, flying low over the muddy scrublands of Eastern Cambodia. A dozen more passengers straggled on, then the plane doubled back and headed West towards the U.A.E. It wasn't until the pilot encouraged everyone to take a glance out of the left side of the plane in order catch a sunset glimpse of Angkor Wat that my waning high demand a re-fuel. Somewhere over Thailand I locked myself in the toilet, pulled the rolled and greased up baggie from my rectum and inhaled a gigantic refresher to stave off the horrible tremens I felt coming on. Back in my seat, I commenced to guzzling nine Heinekens in order to calm down to the point of curling into a lovely black-out.

Landing in São Paulo on the 15th of February, I took a cab into the city and checked into Hotel Braston. I immediately dug my stash out of my ass and enjoyed a wonderfully overdue re-fuel. Once again zany, I set out to explore the city. The Braston was a three-star situated in the financial center's chic part of town. Upscale restaurants were filled to capacity. Excited crowds queued outside neon theatres. Tall, handsome men with manicured eyebrows and goatees hailed cabs with stiff, confidant arms. Alluring ladies, sharply dressed, browsed the import grocery stores. Wandering the streets, I could feel the energy and whir of a city alive. Adequately stoned, I fell into place with the natural rhythms of the nocturne concrete, browsing storefronts, experiencing a tidal wave of renewal away from the suffocating sleaze of Phnom Penh; a spiritual revival of sorts to my pathetic and mundane existence. For the first time in many, many moths my eyes were alive, absorbing the wild array of actual people deliberately *doing life* with confidence. São Paulo left me feeling small, scurrying around its enormity, trying with a hint of desperation to integrate back into the world I had long ago abandoned.

After a week at the Braston I'd run out of cash. My litany of emails pleading with Stan to send more money went unanswered. When Stan's call finally came, he spoke in his usual Nigerian staccato monotone. "A delay... am straightening everything out... don't worry... staff there will contact you soon... Tomorrow I will send another $300... move hotels down the street to Novotel Jaragua. I have made a reservation for you there..." I began scolding him for his indifference and the line went dead.

A half-eaten tuna sandwich and salad plate set on top of the TV alongside a half-drained two litre of Coke. I tried re-tracing back into my blackout to recall when or how the food had arrived and found no recollection. Sitting on the floor I devoured the remains.

The Novotel Jaragua was indeed just down the block from the Braston. After picking up Stan's cash from Western Union, I checked in to room 2519. A four-star gig. Excellent central location. And my twenty-fifth story room offered a gigantic view of the twinkling skyline. Settling into the room, I called Lyda.

"Aaron darling, how you? Oh, I miss you too much. You back in Phnom Penh?" Her far away voice was small and sweet. I explained the situation as best I could.

After a long pause, her tirade began. "Ohhhh Aaron, now you make big problem for me. I no money. I have to pay guesthouse. You say you come back today but you not come back? How I pay guesthouse, huh? Why you lie me? Why you make me live like a dog?" Two sentences into my encouraging retort, the line went dead. Whether it was the international phone connection fuzzing out, or her furious thumb punching disconnect, I had no idea.

Stan had no interest. Lyda had no tolerance. I sat quiet and still, alone in some random hotel room halfway around the world. Delayed and kept waiting in the dark for unknown reasons. No real-time comms with Stan. Credit card frozen. Lyda anticipating my arrival that wouldn't happen, resulting in her once again hitting the streets prowling for customers in order to support herself.

After three days at the Novotel Jaragua, with no comms from Stan and with nothing left to lose I wandered down to the corner liquor store. I had $50 left to my name and spent $30 of it on two handsome bottles of Argentinian Malbec. Back in the room I set up camp on the bed, smoking cigarettes and getting bleary-eyed. Staring out over the city, dawn shyly presented herself between São Paulo's majestic skyscrapers. An email came in from Stan. "Sorry but I am writing to inform you that you will move again. On the 28th you will check into the Capital GC Hoteis and out on the 7th. I will send money soon. Do have a good day." Popping the last of my valium, I curled away from the screen and nuzzled into the sheets, back snug into the sincere apathy I had grown to know and love.

Checking into the Capital GC Hoteis, my ten-day sojourn in Brazil stretched into its third week. With little money and no hope in Stan's operation, I bought yet another bottle of Malbec and decided to walk off my frustrations. In my ambitious wanderings, guzzling wine, I managed to get lost and spent the dusk trying to find my way back to the hotel. It wasn't a horrible disorientation. Two specific songs were programmed on repeat into my MP3 player. The first was Metallica's *Nothing Else Matters*: A gorgeous composition I adopted as an anthemic *sermon* of sorts, allowing me to validate my current mission. *"Forever trust in who you are, and nothing else matters."* It was a sort of poignant psyche-up song. I was a mule, poised to shatter all international law and all-accepted societal mores. I didn't care about anything, and nothing else mattered. The second song, *Fuck You [An Ode To No One]* by Smashing Pumpkins was played full tilt, filling my head with a heart pounding and ear-splitting rapture of all things loathed. The song sucked me into a vacuum of pure and authentic rage. Images of my ex-wife destroying my life with my daughter; echoes of my very own family denying my requests for sympathy and financial assistance; Thea scrambling my efforts to redeem my understanding and future participation with love. With my feet falling hard and lost on foreign concrete, the image of Li weeping through the divorce brought warmth to my heart. I role-played the look on my parent's faces when they would finally be informed of their son's untimely death in some far away country under alarming and deplorable circumstances. Coughing up a large glob of phlegm and launching it onto the sidewalk, I imagined Thea, naked and crushed under some fat Euro-slob thrusting painfully away at her exploited and exhausted body. Everything I once held holy had melted into an iconic pile of pungent and steaming bullshit. In the end, I had created an ornate and elaborate mosaic of alienation, excommunication and self-rape that filled me with an orgasmic aesthetic. Wandering aimlessly the streets of São Paulo, I took mental hold of everything and simply flushed it all away. And in the end, there was nothing and no one left standing but me.

The phone rang at noon. I answered with a vicious hangover and a dry mouth that felt like a wadded up dirty sock. It was reception, summoning me to the desk. Wrestling into clothes and smoothing down my hair, I approached the desk with the best smile I could muster. A smile that wasn't returned. They wanted money, of course. Money Stan was responsible for sending, and hadn't. I assured them the payment was on the way, explaining the delay was due to the time difference between São Paulo and S. Asia. I assured them my supervisor would send the cash within hours, then marched back up to the room, locked the door. Sick and tired of being forced into living day to day like a beggar, I took the gloves off and sent Stan a lengthy email, giving best effort to balance my fury with respect. Stan never replied. The money never came. His men on the ground never showed up with the package.

Another in the Fire

Wednesday, March 5th. Precisely noon. I knew from the sound of the knock on the door that it was either cops or reception. I answered the door to the cute receptionist flanked by two bully security monsters dressed in tight fitting suits. "Mr. Reed, your stay here at Hotel Capital GC Hoteis has expired. Please gather your personal items and leave the hotel." Homeless. Penniless. I needed food. Water. Cigarettes. Fingering the last of my $12 dollars, I stood poised in the rain and hailed a cab to the airport.

GRU airport was in respective disarray. Terminal 3, where I would spend the next forty-eight hours, was undergoing a massive renovation in preparation for the FIFA World Cup slated to begin in June. With the many roped off corridors, make-shift barriers and hallways re-routed to accommodate the construction, there were plenty of obscure spaces, vacated areas and unassuming cubby holes. One corridor had been sectioned off by pylons. Stepping over the rope, I walked quickly away from the crowds and set my pack down on the floor behind an enormous piece of sheetrock. Hidden away from the masses, I quickly set up my transient camp. My remaining clothes articles served as a mattress. My wadded-up sweatpants became my pillow. The remaining wedge of a two-day old sandwich offered the only nutrition I had. And the last swallows of red in the bottle I had grabbed during my eviction from the Hotel Capital provided just enough sedative to ease me to sleep with a sly smirk on my face. Homeless, living at the airport.

Ravenous. I walked slow through the terminal past the maze of restaurants and bars eyeing businessmen sipping tall beers, travelers devouring meals, and a father delicately cutting up a slice of pizza for his delightfully humming daughter. At one point, while hovering over the food court, I noticed a professional looking businesswoman assemble her belongings and rush off to her boarding call, leaving her half-eaten burrito on the table. In the same moment I moved to take my place, a bus boy came by scooping up the half-finished meal and tossing it into the trash bin.

175

Back in my secluded homeless camp, I spent the late morning trying to dip into sleep, but the constant and repetitive boarding call announcements kept me alert to the dire circumstances of my vagrancy and unrelenting hunger pangs. Once again securing my pack under the row of chairs, I wandered my way through the terminal and found the marquee, a map of the airport. I traced my orientation, mapped out the direction to the Airport Clinic, and minutes later, presented myself as the sick and faint passenger in transit that I had become.

The clinic was small, but impeccably clean. A chubby nurse dressed in immaculate white wrote down my info as best she could. We both struggled, wading our way through the language barrier with a flirtatious exchange of giggles. I was admitted onto a small gurney with an amount of care that, after being bashed and beaten around the city for the past three weeks, I had no idea how to absorb. The nurse doted on me like some charming grandmother. She slid the IV delicately into my arm, fluffed my pillow, then set an entire box of sugar cookies into my lap along with a bottle of OJ. For the next three hours I feigned illness, munching on cookies, dipping in and out of sleep. Finally, with color restored to my cheeks, the nurse told me it was time to go.

The plane's descent into Doha slapped me awake. Shaking off a lingering beer buzz, I raced down the aisle to the restroom where I shaved, took a sink sponge bath and realized with terror that I was flat broke; no cash on hand to pay for my Cambodian visa upon landing back in Phnom Penh. I had a nine-hour layover to figure it out. After mechanically answering the customs agent's robotic questions, I exited the airport.

I stood alone watching cars pulling into the concourse to receive their friends, family members and loved ones. I begged two cigarettes off passersby and smoked them in succession down to the filter. Then I begged a third. After satiating the eternal nicotine crave, I moved onto my next task: Finding money.

Upon arriving in Phnom Penh, I needed $20 to pay for the *Visa Upon Landing*. Sucking down the last few hits of a smoke, I noticed a large group of handsome, athletic types huddled together on the sidewalk with designer garment bags slung over their shoulders. I approached the tallest man and drew his attention with confidant posture and piercing eye contact. "Pardon me, Sir. Do you speak English? May I speak with you for a moment?" I spilled out my story. Robbed in São Paulo. (Not entirely a lie, considering the way Stan had robbed me of all dignity and opportunity.) No family to contact. (True.) Stripped of all credit cards, resources and no credit on my phone to contact friends. (Also, entirely true.) My report was detailed with my recent horrors, and concise about having to purchase my visa upon landing once in Phnom Penh. I spoke not with any pathetic whine, but rather, with an alarmed dignity aimed at drawing the man's collaborative sympathies. The man listened intently. When I finished my three-minute tale of woe, he immediately turned to his colleagues, summoned their attention and began speaking in rapid Arabic. Following his short speech, all in the assembly began fishing in their pockets passing around coins and bills which eventually fell into the hands of the tall guy. He turned to me, and with a kind smile, dumped the entire load into my hands. Coins and bills falling to the ground, it was more than I could hold. "Sir, I cannot thank you enough." Turning to the group, I began making my way through the entire crowd, shaking the hands of each and every guy, bowing politely, exchanging shoulder-slaps. Once I'd made the round, I returned full circle to the man in charge. "Wow! I am most grateful for your kindness, Sir. Sincerely!" The man shrugged it all off. "If you don't mind me asking, who are you guys? Are you a business group, or a company travelling together?"

"We are the Qatar National Football Team. We just finished our match with Bahrain and now we are all travelling back to our homes."

"Ahh. Did you win the match?" I asked.

"It was a tie. Zero – zero."

"Well, I certainly wish you all the best in your season. And thanks so much for helping me out. I will never forget this."

At the airport currency exchange, I pushed all the money through the slot. A minute later, the teller counted out USD $57 and change. Pocketing the most money I had seen in nearly a week, I sought out the nearest airport pizza joint and ordered two slices and a large Coke. Seven hours to departure, I sought out my gate and settled into a makeshift camp on the floor. Belly full, and all worries about landing in Phnom Penh quenched, I settled in for a nap.

Contemplating my first trip to São Paulo proved an exercise in reliving an unbridled experiential mental torture: Squatting on floors of random hotel rooms reminded me of how far I had strayed from home. Wandering foreign streets yearning for familiarity and finding none. Sucking down the very last granules of meth dust with the intent of finding sobriety resulting in nothing but near alcohol drownings and fits of rage. Reliant on a disorganized, dirty and dishonest Nigerian on the other side of the world for my daily bread and peace of mind. Hoping for the delivery of the package that never came. In retrospect, the lessons to be learned were endless: a prodigal son retracing his life back to forgiveness and familial love. A turn from all things frantic, to once again feel the warm embrace of my daughter's small arms wrapping around my shoulders. A divorce from all things uncertain and reckless, recommitting to a life of predictability and comfort. And in the end, I learned absolutely nothing, save how to survive.

Phnom Penh welcomed my return on Saturday, the 8th of March. Wheels touched down in a cloud of burning rubber meeting hot asphalt. I cleared customs, immigration and raced face-first back into the hell I'd left just three weeks prior. I carried nothing but my ever-present lust for a quick ice score, a blood-thirsty vengeance for Stan, and a burning lust to once again inhale the scent of Lyda's freshly bathed shoulder.

Chapter Eleven

Phnom Penh, Saigon, Bangkok
March 8 - June 10, 2014

I bee-lined to Rumpelstiltskin Mike's with the intention of ingesting anything and everything he might have on hand. And then ordering or finding more. He answered the door in typical fashion, white hair wild and beard unkempt, swimming in an oversized shirt with a towel wrapped sarong style around his bony waist.

"Ahhh, Aaron. I was wondering what happened to you." He creaked. "Good to see you. Come on in. Lock it behind you."

Pleasantries aside, we got straight down to business. "Mike, I'm fresh back in town from overseas and I got nothing. Came straight here from the airport."

He gestured to his half-spent foil and a small pack of black tar situated on his nightstand. "Help yourself. Picked that up this morning from Gabby. Cut to shit, but not too bad. Gets you high."

"Gabby?"

"Yeah. You don't know Gabby?" I shook my head. Mike wrinkled his brow. "I'm surprised you two haven't crossed paths. Guy from Belgium, I think. Runs in your circle. Been here a long time. Friends with Danny."

I'd heard Danny's name dropped many times before but had never heard Gabby's. Danny, better known as "Double-D" was the stuff of legend in The Penh—one of the original ex-pat dealers who'd made a name for himself in the import/export cocaine business. I knew people who knew Danny, but I'd never had a reason to seek him out. He had a reputation as something of a psychopath. "Nope. Never had a reason to meet Danny and certainly none of his side-kicks."

"Ah, you're probably better off. Danny's a bit of a nut." Mike shrugged and added, "And Gabby's a bit out there too."

Eyeing the H on the table, the thought of taking a sample made me tired. "So, hey Mike, I was hoping for a pick-me-up. I got a lot to do. Gotta hit the ground running, you know what I mean?"

"Yeah, yeah, yeah." He sighed, pulled out the nightstand drawer and handed me a hoon.

Over the next half hour Mike and I burned; me chatting incessantly and him taking in all the details of my São Paulo catastrophe. My story left him shaking his head. "Damn dirty fuckers." He exhaled hard. "I thought you were running for the Khmers. What made you start running for the Nigerians?"

"Lower cost on product. Your boy Big Ike was the one who introduced me."

"Yeah, but it sounds like now you're footing the cost for peace of mind." He quipped. "In this business Aaron, you must always figure in the cost of your peace of mind. And that's not an invisible cost either. That one goes right into the ledger—cost for your peace of mind. Back in the 70's me and my partners made a million dollars muling shit between Miami and Seattle. Now granted, this was way before all the 9-11 security. But still, it was a very tight and successful operation. And there was one single reason we were so successful. *Peace of mind.* There was a total of six of us. And each guy had a separate job to do. I was a runner. And every time I went on a run..." I listened intently as the sage recounted his youthful heyday with a smirk on his face and a twinkle in his eyes. It was only a matter of days that I'd have to face off with Stan, and I found Little Mike's advice quite compelling—good fuel for the impending salvo.

I thanked him for the blast and promised him a quick reimbursement. After three weeks off the ice, my head was finally straightened out. Halfway out the door I leaned back in and asked, "Mike, you seen Lyda recently?"

Loading another foil, he mumbled, "Yeah, she's around. Saw her the other night at GSM chatting up some guy. She looked pretty wasted. She'll be glad you're back."

With Mike's departing words burning into my ears, I hopped on the back of the nearest moto and made a slow crawl through GSM. It didn't take long to spot her. She was sitting with some guy at one of the patio tables outside Mei Lin's Bar drinking a beer. I motioned the driver to pull over and approached the table. "Hey Da. I'm back. Let's go."

Seeing me, she stood quickly, gave me a soft hug, then stood for an awkward moment between me and her John before reaching for her purse.

Her company, some chubby guy with an untrimmed moustache wearing an I ♥ Cambodia T-shirt, stared at me incredulously and threw out his hands. "Hey buddy, do you mind? I'm trying to enjoy a beer and some conversation with the lady."

"Fuck off." I hissed, taking Lyda's hand.

Back on the moto, I sat wedged between Lyda and the driver. Once again feeling her familiar body pressed up against me, I melted as she wrapped her thin arms around my waist and rested her chin on my shoulder. "Oh, Aaron I glad you back. I missed you too much!" And just like that, I found myself willfully bound back into the throes of my self-inflicted destruction.

Next task was to track down Mighty. With wind whipping, I yelled into the phone. "Mighty? Yeah, I'm back. You home? Yeah, I'm coming over... be there in five!"

Mighty met me on the street in front of his building. "Hey man, I'm just heading out. Damn, I'm glad you're back. I've been taking G's at a 20% mark-up! You gonna score today? Cuz I could sure use a re-up. Hi Da." Lyda gave a half nod, then wandered a stones-throw away to a vendor selling food in the alley. "Everything go okay for you in Brazil?"

"Brazil was a total cluster-fuck. Bro, I need some help so I can straighten things out over the next few days.

"Sure, whatever you want. Cash? Product?"

"Both."

Within seconds, Lyda and I were back on the moto, my pockets full of two G's and enough cash to see me through the current crisis. Considering all the mess that was São Paulo, I was plagued with a strong suspicion that Stan was casing out my place and I had no intention of being ambushed. After picking up clothes and some essentials from the flat, Lyda and I checked into the Lucky 2 guesthouse. I needed the central city location over the next few days to get my shit together. Once safe within the confines of our rented room, Lyda and I spent the rest of the day and evening smoking and sharing updates on everything that had transpired. Around midnight, Lyda announced that she hadn't eaten in days. She dressed. I gave her a handful of dollars and she ventured out to score some food at nearby Orussey Market. I took the downtime to check email. Sure enough, a message from Stan.

To: Mresnick474@gmail.com
From: Chatstan@hotmail.com
Date: 8 March 2014, 15:24

Hope your flight was good. Thanks for wasting my money on your worthless decision. It is a cheap way to hide a weakness. Your ticket cost is over 4000usd and I will be waiting to be repaid in full. I hate liars and cheaters.

Stan's words threw me into a rage. After manipulating me nail-biting around São Paulo for three weeks, pleading with hotel receptions, going days without food, delaying the pick-up that never came, dumping me onto the street via an embarrassing eviction, rendering me homeless at the airport culminating into a situation of begging my survival from the Doha National Football team, and he had the gall to hold me accountable? And further, asking me for financial reimbursement to mend his investment loss? Normally, under confrontational situations, I would immediately assume the posture of a bitch willing to be screwed. But this one was so preposterous that, with a certain pause, I discovered a renewed vigor—a certain calm withdrawal over the situation. Instead of firing off a spontaneous and reactionary retort, I collapsed onto the bed, fired up the glass and enjoyed a peculiar lethargy to the very urgent situation. Reclining comfortably and naked on the bed, I sucked on the glass, waiting for Lyda's return. Whimsical thoughts returned to Stan. A handsome man poised as a charismatic player in the S.E. Asian drug trade; well versed in colloquial vignettes and other tales of cute and fascinating entertainment. Epiphany suddenly revealed Stan as he was: A pseudo drug patron running a completely disorganized operation who took a sick pleasure in manipulating others while assuming zero accountability in his disastrous supervision.

I wanted to spit in his face. Another part of me recognized Stan, like myself, as just another pathetic player in the miserable game, which left me with an overwhelming pity and urge to forgive him. Most of all, I needed his drugs and his cheap prices. I needed G's and I needed them now. This required our continued relationship. As much as I despised him for screwing me in Brazil, I was hoping for a potential healing which would keep the door open for future business. Yes, I was pissed about everything he'd done. But my love for drugs and my chains to addiction proved far stronger than any disdain I held.

Pondering these things, I noticed Lyda's purse laying on the floor. Ever suspicious of her behaviors, I peeked inside and discovered her phone. I quickly went to her texts and began scrolling through her recent messages. My every fear was immediately made very real with a punch of reality I wasn't prepared for.

Most texts were to and from Da's sister, whose number I recognized. There were also a few volleys between Lyda and her longtime friend, Peter, a good guy whom I had met on a few occasions. And then…

(+66) 866 681 896 7:12 PM <I miss you. Did you find out if you are pregnant? Craig.>

I Googled the +66 country code. The text had come from Thailand, and more than likely from some ex-pat who had recently visited Phnom Penh.

0973304109 6:45 AM <Lovely Lida, I wanna fuck you too.>

Switching to her phone log I saw she'd exchanged several phone calls with this number. I called the number from my phone and some elderly sounding guy with a European accent answered. I hung up.

017703711 9:49 AM <Boom boom today?>

I was able to trace the number to a local business, Madison Capital, located on Sothearos, a street across town close to GSM. Whoever placed the call was certainly one of Da's regulars.

I wasn't angry. Just nauseous and utterly defeated. I replaced her phone, curled back on the bed and tried hard to endure the torture. I knew on a sub-conscious level that my torture was self-inflicted. What had I expected to see? I was shacked up and falling in love with a prostitute. And my very best efforts to provide for her and keep her off the streets had fallen painfully short. If anything, the discovery of the texts drew me further into the depths of empathy for her, and self-loathing for myself. I hated myself for failing her, and she hated me even more. When she returned from the market with food, I said nothing, the two of us continuing happily on with our suicidal charade. *Hate*: The filthy bastard child of fear and misunderstanding ran rampant and seemed to be everywhere.

When Stan and I finally agreed to meet for our heavy-weight boxing match, I'd rehearsed my lines well. At our usual haunt at the Pizza Co. after faking through pleasantries, the fight began. It was Stan who came out swinging first. "You've been back for five days. You've been dodging me?"

"Dodging you? Why should I be dodging you? It's you who should be dodging me! Your disorganized Op left me homeless in São Paulo! No food! No cash! Left begging on the streets in order to get back here in one piece."

Stan greeted this with a grunt. "Yes, the mission ran into unforeseen difficulties that put you into difficult situations. But you should have stayed and worked through them. Instead, you collapsed and under pressure from your girlfriend, you used your pre-arranged return ticket as a deadline to abandon the mission. A man of vision and integrity would have stayed. Your vision was short-sighted." Stan sipped his water and excused himself from the table to receive an incoming call.

When he returned, I offered my retort. "Mr. S. First of all, my girlfriend had nothing to do with my return. Second, I was screwed from the very beginning. Your friends on the ground failed to equip me with a proper phone and SIM card. I never had real time comms with you. Further, your lack of financial support left me unable to eat for days on end, and eventually left me homeless. I was evicted from the last hotel. Do you have any idea how humiliating that was? How can you justify this type of operation? *You* dropped the ball, Mr. S. Not me! It was *your* lack of provision and *your* lack of ability to communicate that resulted in the failure of the mission."

Stan stared hard across the table. I stared back. Nearing the precipice of being crushed under the weighted silence, it was Stan who blinked first. "Well, none of this dismisses the fact that I'm out $4,000. Not to mention there's still a pot of gold back there waiting to be brought here to me. How do you intend to solve these issues?"

"Let's use this opportunity to re-group." I offered. "I didn't return with the thought of abandoning the project. I came back to meet and discuss. As far as your financial loss to date, that's your problem. Can't and won't help you there." Stan's bottom lip quivered and his eyes bulged. I quickly assuaged his anger. "You need your package just as much as I need the payday. So, let's examine what went wrong and begin planning my return trip."

After politely punching each other's teeth out, we shook hands and agreed on a stalemate. Most important to me was his parting gesture on the sidewalk in front of the restaurant: a baggie of ice bursting at the seams. "Take this. Get back on your feet. When you need more, let me know. I appreciate your willingness to return to complete the unfinished job. I will make arrangements and keep you informed."

March into April proved a continuum of Lyda and I smoking, fucking and fighting the blood lust tension between staying high with one foot in the street. The landlord was constantly knocking for the rent. In turn, I constantly plagued Stan with demands for more work. He continued to delay, slipping me just enough product to keep our pipe full and food on the table. Barely.

"Why you so stupid, huh? Your boss make you go to another country for work and you stay away one month. You leave me here. I live like a dog. And when you come back, you have nothing! Your boss not pay you. We not have any money. Why you so stupid, huh?" I was counting out my last remaining Riel notes on the bed, listening to Lyda emptying herself of her very last fragments of patience. I knew that with one phone call she could leave, take a five-minute moto ride and earn more in a single hour than I was currently turning in a day. The tension in the house was thick and constant, hanging over us both. Something had to give. Just when it felt like everything was about to explode, Stan's call came in.

Back at the Pizza Co., Stan explained the gig. "While we're waiting for the people in Brazil, there is another job that I think you are well suited for. It doesn't involve picking up or delivering packages. It involves bank accounts. You see, Aaron, our organization involves many different types of business. We have clients all over the world, and a lot of money is involved. And we need a way to channel and move the cash. We wish to open some accounts in S. Asia and our interests are currently in Vietnam. The job is simple and only involves a quick overnight to Saigon. We will provide you with a passport. You simply take the passport and open up a standard USD savings account."

"That's it?"

Stan nodded. "You do have a current passport photo?"

"Of course." I answered.

Stan continued. "If you agree, then I will send your photo to Bangkok and have our people there begin preparing the passport. The passport will show your photo, but all the info—your name, everything will be falsified. It should arrive here in a week. Once it arrives, you'll obtain an entry visa from the Vietnamese Embassy, hop a bus to Saigon, meet with our people there and they will show you what to do and how to do it."

"What's the compensation for this type of job?" I asked.

"Once the account is open, we will wait for our clients to make a deposit. Once the deposit is made, you are paid 12% of whatever the deposit might be."

"C'mon Mr. S., give me a general idea of what we're looking at here. I mean, a deposit of fifty bucks would be a laughing matter. Not interested in getting popped over small cash. Obviously not worth the risk."

"Our clients don't operate on that level. A general ballpark deposit is typically between $5,000 and up to $20,000."

"What's the usual wait time for a deposit after the account has been opened?"

Stan shrugged. "Hard to say. Could be a day, could be a month? Once the account is opened, we put the word out and then it's up to our clients. You have absolute job security over the account, because once the account is opened, you are the only one who can make the withdrawal. It's your photo in the passport, but all your information in the passport is under an alias."

I'd taken the Phnom Penh to Saigon bus many times before. It was a quick six-hour jaunt, allowing an hour to cross the border. Several bus companies ran the 230 km route, departing Phnom

Penh on the hour. Late morning, 29 April and after kissing Lyda goodbye, I paid for my $13 ticket and hopped on the Mekong Express. Three hours later I arrived at the dusty and pathetic border town of Bavet. Passport stamped, I then journeyed on and arrived in Saigon just as the afternoon rush hour was thickening in the *Phạm Ngũ Lão* district. I checked into Thanh Thuong Guesthouse—my favorite budget hole in the wall situated down a narrow alley just a stone's throw from the backpacker mayhem on *Bùi Viện* Street.

Un-taping the half-G baggie from between my ass cheeks, I settled in for a good refresher, showered, then called the number Stan had provided. The local contact, "Lucky," spoke perfect English and agreed to meet me at Boston Sport's Bar. I showed up early, ordered a beer and took it on the street patio with the hope of spotting Lucky as he approached. 6:00 on the dot, a Cuba Gooding Jr. look-alike strode up the street, spotted me and greeted me with a warm handshake. Lucky was a *yes* man. Said *yes* to everything. After ordering a Vodka and Cran we waded through some enjoyable small talk before moving inside. Lucky selected the smallest booth in the darkest corner of the empty place and there we got down to business.

Lucky pulled a FedEx envelope from his man purse, reached inside and slid a passport onto the table. A Spanish passport, and on the ID page was my picture. Directly to the right of my photo was my new name: Xavier Sagrera Rejes. I was from Barcelona, and next month I'd be celebrating my thirty-ninth birthday. The subsequent pages revealed that I had recently traveled to Rome before globe-trotting on to America. According to the exit and entry stamps, I had touched down in JFK and enjoyed three days in New York before flying on to Vietnam. The exit and entry dates were concise and the overall aesthetic and feel of the passport was flawless. Perfect and bizarre in every way.

"This is amazing." I mumbled.

"Our people in Bangkok really know what they're doing." Lucky answered.

"Does this passport get me through borders?"

"No. It's not officially registered with International Customs or INTERPOL. It can only be used as an unofficial document. For example, you can use it for renting a car or a motor-scooter. You can use it as an unofficial ID like when you're booking a hotel room. And it works for opening bank accounts."

Lucky passed me another document. It was a rental agreement. Xavier Sagrera Rejes was currently living at Water Garden Apartments #E1063, Nguyen Van Linh Pkwy, Tan Phong Ward, District 7, HCMC, VN, and my current phone number was 01325554216.

As I examined the info, Lucky encouraged, "Yes! That's exactly what you need to do. Study that shit until you know it perfectly. *All* the passport info. *Every* detail of the rental agreement. You need to be able to recite *everything* directly out of your head. So, if the bank asks you anything, you can just speak it like it's perfect and absolutely real. You are a Spanish national. You need to be able to speak about living in Spain, growing up in Spain, your experiences about living in Spain. Even the experiences of your family. And you need to have an answer when they ask you why you've relocated to Vietnam. What work are you involved in? How long do plan on staying? Study! Study! Study! This is your new identity, and you need to become that person, *be* that person. If the bank people ask you *anything*, you need to be prepared with your quick and natural answer."

It was a tall order. I was fascinated and enthralled with the whole concept. I loved the challenge. Anticipated the risk as pure adrenaline. "What bank should I open the account with?"

"Yes! Tomorrow we'll meet again—move around the city and check things out."

I spent the evening pacing the tiny cubicle, memorizing, elaborating, embellishing. Into the wee hours, I *became* Xavier Sagrera Rejes, comfortably reciting into the air my biography between constant hits off the foil. By early dawn, just as the hum of the small neighborhood began spilling its exotic sounds through my window, I was able to greet the day staring into the mirror with all the facial twitches, hand gestures and slight nuances of my new identity. I'd gone well and far beyond a mere name, address and phone number. Per Lucky's instruction, I'd *become* Mr. Rejes; fluent, handsome and in need of a USD savings account. *By the way, would you like to hear about my recent experiences in Rome? Please, let me tell you about my daughter losing her first tooth, and how I slipped a coin under her pillow, adopting the American tradition of the magical tooth fairy. My daughter is fascinated with American culture.*

Lucky and I re-joined for breakfast. He'd cased out a bank just a few blocks from the hotel. Rock solid, dressed in my Khaki's, a white button-down dress shirt and a sharp tie, I entered a Sacombank Bank just as the doors opened. I could see Lucky through the window stationed across the street on a bench sipping coffee. Poised, kind eye contact, voice smooth as butter, I presented my docs, answered all questions, then signed the papers. Fifteen minutes later I walked out with my new Sacombank Savings Passbook. I crossed the street, walked nonchalantly past Lucky and entered the park. Lucky followed. When we were out of sight from the bank, I turned and beamed at him. I was rushing with full tilt adrenaline, riding the redline. In that moment, with all senses in full bloom, I felt electrified and vibrantly alive. I felt... *successful*, for the first time since I could remember.

Walking back to the hotel twelve feet tall, I recited all the details to Lucky. It was nearing 10:00 when we returned to our breakfast joint and began ordering beers. By noon, I had a good buzz on. Calculating my return trip to Phnom Penh, if I caught the one o'clock, I'd be back to see Lyda by early evening.

Lucky shot me a surprised glance. "Bro, you can't go just yet. We got more work to do."

"More work?"

"Yes! Stan called while you were in the bank. Three more passports will arrive tomorrow, FedEx." As incentive, Lucky slid two hundo's across the table. "Stan sent this to cover your extra days."

The *turn-around* trip had suddenly evaporated into another mist of disappointment for Lyda. My promised return, from her perspective, now just another lie. Back in the room, I called her and managed to sputter out about twenty seconds of explaining before she hung up.

The following day, Lucky and I were back in our secluded booth at Boston's examining the three newly arrived passports. Like the first one, they were all flawless, with perfectly coinciding entry and exit visas from multiple countries. I also received three new lease agreements for various apartments around town. For fear of confusing my memorized biographies, I elected to only focus on one account at a time—opening one account per day.

On Friday the 2nd of May, Guilherme Diego Silva, an elementary educational consultant from Portugal walked into the ACB Bank in Zone 9 and with finesse, opened a USD account. Over the weekend, I morphed into Rafael Afonso Costa, a freelance writer also from Portugal, compiling information for a series of articles on the exotic fruits of S. Asia; and by late Monday morning, I'd collected my third passbook. Monday evening into Tuesday morning, I'd moved on to Belgium, becoming Mathis Enzo Peeters, an entrepreneurial ambassador of gastronomy introducing the tantalizing Belgium waffle to the restaurants in and around Saigon.

On Wednesday the 7th, after being gone for nine days, my bus rolled back into The Penh with the mid-day sun blazing down on Central Market. My first call was to Stan. He agreed to meet me the following day.

"Four accounts successfully opened in a week. It was cool. No problem. I enjoyed the work."

Stan sat across from me picking at his Spaghetti Carbonara, scrolling the messages on his phone. "You did very well, Aaron. I have already given the report to our HQ in Bangkok. They are pleased with your work."

"So, when does my payday come?"

Stan stared at me from across the table, gave a slight shrug, then focused back in on his phone, his fat finger scrolling texts. "HQ has alerted our clients of the accounts. You will be paid according to our agreement. I will let you know as soon as a deposit is made. Then you will receive your commission. Twelve percent, as previously agreed."

A brief, albeit tense silence followed. Staring Stan in the eye, I shattered the vacancy. "Listen, Stan. I'm handing you and the organization a solid week's worth of very successful work. You know I'm flat broke. My girl calls me stupid every day because I'm doing all this work and I have nothing to show for it. C'mon Bro, throw me a bone here."

"I will continue to give you product, knocking off $3 per G. That should be enough to sustain you until your big payday."

The following four days had me licking Lyda's wounds; making continuous promises of future wealth and ease. She despised me. And were it not for the constant flow of ice filling our glass and the scant cash I handed her to shop at the market, she'd have thought nothing of spitting in my face and finally throwing me to the dogs.

Six days after my first trip to Saigon, on the 13th, I was back on the bus. Once settled back into my usual haunt, I went to meet Lucky to obtain the new passport. I noticed a pattern developing. I was receiving a $100 per diem to finance each account I opened. If I budgeted and starved myself, I could pocket about fifty bucks. So, after opening the fifth account early morning on the 14th, I hightailed it back to Phnom Penh with nearly $45 in my pocket with the hope of showing Lyda some fruit, no matter how scant. As predicted, she threw her nose up when I showed her the cash. "Hmph! You go working in Vietnam for one day and come back with that? I not stay with you anymore. No, maybe tomorrow I leave. No man make me live like this!"

The next morning, hopping the Mekong Express' first departure, I was back in Saigon at noon. After meeting Lucky and opening the sixth account, I high tailed it to the border in a taxi, then hoped a bus back to Phnom Penh, hoping she'd still be there. I collapsed into the bed after the murderous fourteen-hour turn-around trip offering Lyda another $50.

Her continuous scorn permeated the flat like an invisible electrical storm; immeasurable fields of horrible energy crackling with cataclysmic discharge. Her abuse was constant, as was her unspoken threat to walk out the door any minute and into the arms of a better paying John. Ice was her only desire, and money her only love. And my efforts to supply her with both always fell short. That night she asked me for money to go to the market. I rationed her a $10. She didn't return. Over the next two weeks the silence of the house unraveled my brain like a distended sausage on a cutting board and spread through my stomach like a hollow cancer. The more I tried to forget the pain, the more I paced and smoked. And the more I wandered the empty halls of the flat, or sat in its dark rooms pondering bleakness, the more I focused on her absence.

The hollowness of everything, the utter emptiness continued its gnawing. Days we're spent locked down climbing the walls with blinds drawn. Nights were spent wandering around GSM, perusing the fish game arcades, or stalking 104 and the other girlie bar streets hoping for a glimpse of Da while peddling my shit as demand required. Several times I brought my working girl friends back to the place.

My flat was a revolving door. The endless parade of women who came and went were radiant in their beauty, precious in their sorrow, each possessing their own reckless and ancient resilience. Though markedly different and each with their own charms, they all held one thing in common: a peculiar fascination and curiosity surrounding my impotence. "Why you no boom-boom?" They'd ask, turning their faces to the window, taking me into their tender hands. How could I... Where would I begin to explain everything? My wife's desertion? My daughter growing up in the States without her father? Alienation from family and friends? My addiction, and its constant devouring? What words or expressions begin to

193

illustrate the bottomless chasm one finds himself drowning in after the methodical and merciless removal of one's soul?

In the vacuum of all things sacred and real, sex assumed the image and function of a silly cartoon. My cares and pursuits for relational comforts had dissolved into a slow flowing stream clogged with the corrosive plasticity of half-truths and stagnant whirlpools of deliberate and cunning deception. My concept of love had disintegrated into an unobtainable abstract; nothing more than an endless display of evaporating rainbows, formed from tears trailing down the cheeks of everyone I once cared for, now all left behind.

A glimmer of hope came on the morning of June 7th. Stan's voice was ever-present banal, but held a hint of rare encouragement. "I have a job for you."

"Another account?"

"No, this is different. You leave tomorrow. You will meet me at 4:00 AM at the Smile Mart, Orussey Market. Do you know the mart? Pack your backpack full of clothes, so you appear like a backpacker from the States on a long tour through Asia."

"How long will I be gone?"

"Two, three days at most."

"Where?"

"Bangkok."

I spent the day washing clothes, sorting and preparing. I still felt mule-kicked over Da's vanishing act, yet her absence allowed me to enjoy the rarity of having the place to myself, free from drama, tension, violence. I spent the evening leisurely packing and keeping my pipe constantly ablaze to the hypnotic rhythms of Ali Farka Touré. After midnight, my cell rang for a few local deliveries near Orussey Market. Shouldering my backpack for the trip, I locked the house and checked into one of the new hotels that had sprouted up around *Psar Themei* with my new, fake Portuguese passport. After dropping the order, I spotted an old friend, Any Chea on the street. She'd just escaped from spending 24 hours with some John. She was tired and haggard. Any was 27 and had worked the streets her entire adult life, occasionally traveling to Thailand with certain clients she knew and trusted. I liked her too much to sleep with her. I loved her contagious smile and silly personality, so I took her back to the hotel to clean up and relax. We took turns showering, ordered room service, and spent the night smoking, posing for silly photos taken with my iPad, laughing and watching TV. At 3:40 I hugged Any good-bye and set off to meet Stan.

I enjoyed this forbidden time of day with the streets around the market vacant and dark and decorated with little lamps hanging from the 24-hour food carts. A few dilapidated trucks, having arrived from the countryside were unloading flowers, fruits and produce. Rats scurried, making off with food scraps. Clusters of faceless vagrants huddled around small campfires smoking with debris and smoldering trash. The pre-dawn ambiance was peaceful. My wide eyes scanned the spacious streets. My empty head, fueled with precise amphetamine clarity greeted the absent day, entertaining all possibilities.

I spotted Stan's black Escalade idling in the shadows and slid into the back seat. The sound of classical strings leaked from the radio. Mr. S. eyed me for a moment in the rear-view, greeted me formally, then handed me a package over his shoulder. I switched on the dome light. It was filled with knick-knacks and cheap souvenirs, little statues of Buddha, Khmer scarves, a miniature model of Angkor Wat. He then handed back a second package wrapped tightly in newspaper, secured with twine. From the heft of it, I estimated its weight at approximately two and a half kilos.

"Take half the stuff out of your backpack," he instructed. "Put the second package in first, and then put the first package of souvenirs on top of it. Then pile all your clothes on top of the packages." I did as I was told to the soundtrack of Mahler's strings. Once the pack was situated, Mr. S. pointed across the street to another car idling. "See that maroon Toyota Camry?" Without waiting for my answer, he continued, "That taxi will take you straight to Battambang... about four hours, and then onto Poipet.

At Poipet, you'll walk across the border. Once you're in Thailand, buy a new SIM card and send me a text. Then find the microbus leaving *Aranyaprathet* going to Bangkok. You'll arrive in Bangkok this evening around five or so. Any questions?"

"Yes. I sent you an email about four hours ago. Did you read it?"

"I have not. I've been away from the house since yesterday getting everything together for your trip. What did your email say?"

"Please read it, Mr. S. It details some suggestions so you and I don't end up in a situation like my last trip to Brazil."

"I will read it, later today once I am back at home."

"Is the taxi already paid for? What about expenses?"

Over his shoulder came a white legal sized envelope. "The taxi, along with your room in Bangkok is paid for. Here's an additional $150 for food and miscellaneous expenses. The hotel address is in the envelope with your cash." As I was fumbling with the cash and reading the hotel info, he continued. "Relax tonight. I'll forward your number in Bangkok to the contact and he will call you tomorrow. He'll come to the hotel, pick up the package, and once the package is delivered, you can come back to Phnom Penh the following day…" He checked his watch, "…on the 10th."

"Will I receive anything from your guy when he picks up the package?"

"No. Just give him the package, it'll be very quick. You'll be compensated once you meet me back here. You'll receive your wages then. You're only going to be gone for two days. You'll return the day after tomorrow."

I shouldered my pack and opened the door. So much for the fat expense account, the glamorous life of a drug smuggler. And I didn't really care that he was pinning me down so hard on the expenses. I had a half gram in my pocket for the road and another quarter taped in my ass crack for indulging once over the border… plenty to get me through the next 24 hours.

196

The taxi from The Penh to the border was wide-eyed and uneventful. Rolling into Poipet just before nine, the June sun pounded the dusty streets of the shitty town with all its relentless fury. I'd heard Khmers and foreigners alike refer to the border town of Poipet as *the armpit of Cambodia*. An early monsoon had swept through the night before leaving the entire town swirling in mud. The main street was little more than a two-track mud bath with mud-splattered vehicles trudging along. The floors of the stores, squat buildings and dilapidated houses plastered with mud. People's clothes, faces and arms were caked with it. Children romped and played in it. Everything hot and filthy.

The cab dropped me at the roundabout in the shadow of towering casinos saddling both sides of the immigration checkpoints on the Thai/Cambodian border. Heckling shopkeepers, lazy whores, aggressive taxi drivers, crazed paint-huffers, widows unravelling in homespun gossamer with suckling infants dangling from their sagging breasts, cripples scooting along on skateboards and holy beggars scurried to and fro like an army of ants all blindly carrying out their necessary duties.

Immigration checkpoints. They're all the same. The mechanical robots who run them are merely cogs turning the earth's bureaucratic machinery. Generally, they care more about their lunch break than they do about who you are, what you're up to, why you're there, or when or where you've been. This reigns especially true in the checkpoints between third world regions. Thailand now ranks among the world's progressive countries, but Cambodia still has a ways to go. At the Poipet crossing there were no retinal scans, no agents wearing body cams, no hand imaging or facial recognition. And with a frontier border crossing like Poipet, the immigration official's potential for sharp observations and/or acute perceptions were mirrored in the way their K-9 Shepherds made the most of their duties by lazing away in the sun.

10:00 AM, Sunday. Perfect timing. All the early morning Euro-trash trust-fund backpackers on the bus from Siem Reap had already passed through, and the busses from Phnom Penh weren't due 'til mid-afternoon. Movement in the large room was sparse. Industrial sized standing fans hummed and circulated the tired, stale air. Only three of the fifteen turn styles were open. I took my place in the queue behind a fat Thai businessman dressed in a disheveled pinstripe suit who most likely had spent the night dumping his Bhat into the local casinos. He passed quickly, and the Immigration Official gave me a wave. Approaching the counter, I rehearsed my protocols.

The Agent nods. *Always return the nod with kind eye contact and a half smile. Take a second to secure your backpack up against your leg like you're an aware, responsible and organized traveler.* As you're doing this, the Agent fills the brief time lapse by asking you for your passport. *In one fluid motion reach and slip your passport from your back pocket and place it squarely on the counter.* The Agent then begins flipping through the pages, punching his keyboard, catching glimpses of info that appear on his monitor. This is the Interpol check and could take between 30 seconds and 1.5 minutes. Anything over 1.5 initiates a slight cause for worry, but no matter what happens, always… *Maintain erect posture with fingers laced and placed directly in front of you on the counter. Keep eyes focused, blankly alternating between the Agents tie knot, name badge and other random objects arrayed around his workstation. The coffee mug with broken handle filled with ink pens. Wireless IP camera. Always offering a half smile, ignoring the fact that just 20 minutes prior you inhaled a gargantuan line of meth resulting in your face melting into a paper maché mask, your lips pulled back freakishly over your teeth and your eyes bulging out of your head like two tambourines pounding out cryptic celestial rhythms. Never glance at the cameras in the sky and remind yourself at all times that no one… no one… has any idea of what you're up to. Not even the Thai/Cambodian Immigration Agent whose studying your face while stamping your passport and sliding it back to you over the counter while welcoming you into The Royal Kingdom.*

With a kind and grateful nod, I proceeded calmly to the X-ray machine. With my pack on the conveyor, I sauntered through the metal detector, shouldered my pack once again and walked into Thailand. Immediately leaving the Immigration building, I was greeted by a sign that announced, "*Welcome to Thailand.*" A few paces beyond that another sign announced, "*Death for Drug Traffickers.*"

Aranyaprathet presents itself in direct contrast with chaotic, mud-splattered, Poipet. The streets are easy to follow and buildings are presentably clean. The heat of the day was in full force as I trudged the quarter mile to the bus station where micro-busses departed for Bangkok on the half hour. With my pack into the rear of the micro-bus, I took my seat in the rear bench where I could keep a good eye on it, then settled in for the five and a half-hour roll to Bangkok.

Three weeks earlier, the political climate in Thailand had collapsed into turmoil when the Royal Thai Armed Forces had led a *coup d'état* against the government. In the throes of political crisis, the military had established a junta to govern the nation. Rolling into the gigantic metropolis, the current unrest was alarmingly evident by the lack of traffic. Stoic soldiers lined the streets with machine guns. Police barricades blocked access to all the main thoroughfares. A curfew had been imposed, leaving public activity sparse and at a minimum.

After snaking through a series of secondary roads, my taxi delivered me to my hotel. The curfew, coupled with my apathy to explore the city resulted in my most welcomed and self-imposed seclusion. My first 24 hours in Bangkok was spent barricaded in the room, content, with my only focus on the pipe. The following afternoon, when the phone rang, I showered, ventured out for hot dogs at the nearest 7-11, then waited for the arrival of Stan's associate.

A non-descript Nigerian entered the room and dutifully welcomed me to Thailand.

"Thanks," I mumbled. "I've been here a dozen times before."

I fished out Stan's package and placed it on the bed. The man unwrapped the twine, looked inside, then slid the parcel into his small backpack. "I will let your supervisor in Cambodia know I have received the gift."

I wasn't falling for his evasive scam. "Why don't we just call him right now while we're both here in the room?" I suggested.

The guy nodded, took a seat on the bed and called Stan. The man spoke with Stan in Nigerian Pidgin English. After a minute of trying to decipher the gibberish, I motioned for the phone. "Stan? Yeah, I just did the drop. All is well. I'm coming back tomorrow on the first bus... yeah, I'll call when I arrive." The drop lasted an entire three minutes.

The trip back to The Penh ran like clockwork. Rolling into *Phsar Thmei*, I took a moto-taxi back to the flat, blazed up, then phoned Stan. "I got word from the people in Bangkok. The mission was successful," Stan announced. "Congratulations." He handed me an envelope.

Sitting there on the bench, I coyly fingered out twenty, hundred-dollar bills—the most money I had seen in two years. "It was easy. No problems. When's the next gig?"

Stan thought for a moment. "In three weeks, more or less, you will return to Brazil..." After a long pause, he couldn't resist adding the dig. "...to complete the job you left unfinished."

"Oh yeah, I remember. That was the one where profound administrative errors and fuck-ups left me homeless on the streets of S. America."

Touché. Stan took the jab with a patient sigh, and we agreed to leave it at that.

With my newly found wealth, I asked for a sizeable re-up of twenty G's. An hour later, back in the flat unpacking and de-compressing from the trip, one of Stan's couriers called and met me on the street, handing me a bulk package of beautiful and glistening ice. The rush was gigantic beyond description. In a matter of three days, I'd transformed from a Phnom Penh street vagrant into a respectable Prince of the Kingdom. Elevating myself into an ice-induced orgasm, I launched into the night with the single intention of finding Da.

Our reunion proved effortless. It was as if the girl could *smell* the money. I hadn't walked two steps back into the filth of GSM before we collided face to face on the street in front of the Swiss Bar. Before the Thailand gig, financially and emotionally spent, I had passed weeks wandering the streets looking for her, asking everyone about her, trying to track her down. And now, having found my feet again, she was instantaneously there.

She appeared tired, walking with a slight bend in her normally rigid posture. Gorgeous in her furious stare. A bit haggard, without make-up; her hair falling uncombed around her shoulders. After hemming and hawing through awkward space, she finally turned coquettish eyes and asked directly, "Did you miss me?"

"Always." I returned the question, bracing myself for the injurious blow.

"Mmm... maybe a little." Like an ouroboros with a flickering tongue swallowing its own tail, we locked eyes. We exchanged tired smiles, agreeing to continue devouring each other on our uncharted field of treachery. I took her by the arm and led the way.

The trick with Da was to walk the line and negotiate her razor-sharp perceptions: Assuring her that I had means, and at the same time, convincing her that I was still falling short from providing her with stability. If she knew I had cash, she bled me. And if she suspected me of indigence, she simply left. *Stability* was the very thing she desired most of all—and the very thing I lacked. Brief glimpses of stability kept her by my side, albeit furious, but by my side, nonetheless. And it was the ever-present concept and image of *stability* that kept me continuously digging through the trenches—not only to fulfill her desires, but to also convince myself that I wasn't a complete and total failure. Stability was the final inroad to Lyda's potential happiness; and the one singular component that would elevate me to a self-respective platform. I always fell short. Always seemed to run a good race, always collapsing at the finish line.

I flashed a hundred. She took my arm and together we strolled proudly through the filth and desperation of GSM to the nearest fish game arcades. She spent the next hour going up, then eventually going down to the expected and total broke loss.

We parked ourselves in the Swiss Bar, ordering three rounds before running out of things to discuss.

She finally asked, "You have smoke?"

We checked into a tiny room, showered, then dimmed the light and smoked a few stones together on the thin, tattered mattress. I wanted to avoid our typical smoke marathon in order to keep her in the dark of just how much product I was sitting on. In the thick of some timeless hour, I lay watching Lyda scraping the glass in the glow of the muted television and drifted off to sleep. Centuries later I woke in utter darkness, haze and drear, reaching for her and grasping nothing. Peering through the glum, I caught the image of her silhouette standing at the small window against the first hints of dawn. She stood still, frail, naked, like a weeping widow with fingers interlaced, or a devout nun with ears perked to the sound of a funeral drum. I moved behind her and gathered her into my arms. She allowed me to hold her for a tender minute.

"Do you see the tree?" She whispered.

"Yes."

"Do you see little yellow flower?"

"Yes."

"Do you see little yellow flower touching the tree?"

Her hand curled into mine like a leaf. She led me like a stray dog to the bed. Laying in the dark, mine was a painful howl, while hers was more of a stoic, silent cry.

My spot for street deals, Boeung Kak, Phnom Penh

Thea, Youngbin, and her niece

Sana and her children, Boeung Kak, Phnom Penh

Smoking session in an abandoned building, Phnom Penh

Street party on Augusta Blvd, São Paulo

Lyda checking on her sparrows

Little Khmer wooden house with my landlord, Mr. Hua and my friend, Kanya

Khmer house hallway, rear to front, before and after renovations

La Modelo Prison, Bogotá

Sharing my story in the little prison church with Edgar translating

Freedom! Feliz Navidad, 2018. Celebrating Christmas with Luis Gonzalo Peña Rodriguez, Olga Lucia Perdomo, Alba Liz, and Jose Cruz

Chapter Twelve

Phnom Penh, Itaquaquecetuba, Brazil
July 13 - August 10, 2014

On the eve of my second departure to Brazil, Stan and I held our usual meet. The itinerary was absolute Hell, routing through Kuala Lumpur, Tokyo, a layover in NYC, then onto another connection in Atlanta before finally arriving in São Paulo two days later. "Where's the return info?" I asked. "I need return info, Stan. I'm not going back there without return info."

He looked me in the eye directly. "Do not worry. You will not be there as long as last time. Ten days… two weeks maximum. My associates assure me that the package is nearly ready." He continued. "I lost a lot of investment cash on your last trip. Believe me, I do not want you there any longer than is necessary. And because of this, you will not be staying in the city this time. My operatives have arranged a smaller hotel for you in one of the outlying suburbs. Cheaper than the previous accommodations. I'm sure you will find it satisfactory. If not, simply let me know and I will move you."

"What about cash for per diem?" I asked. He handed me an envelope and I counted the cash. "Five hundred?"

"That is plenty to get you there and checked in safely. Once you need more, simply notify me and I will send what is necessary to keep you secured."

"Stan, forgive me. But let's examine this for just a second. No return ticket. No prescribed date for the pick-up. No assurance on an exact return. Limited funds. I'm sorry, but how is this any different from the last failed mission? This has all the earmarks of another stressful trip. And what about that email I sent you about all the insight and advice my friend Mike shared with me. You never gave me any feedback on that info. Whenever *he* went into the field, it was his supervisor's sole responsibility to keep him without worry and totally provided for. And it seems every time I go into the field there's nothing but ambiguity, fear and question marks."

"Yes. We both learned a lot from that last trip. We now know what not to do, yes?"

It was a dodge. The way he pluralized me into the last mission's failure made me simmer. It had been his fuck-up. Not mine. His *we's* should have been *I's*.

"Were you not provided for on the Bangkok run?" He challenged.

"Big difference between Bangkok and Brazil, Mr. S! I know people in Thailand. Everyone speaks English. Thailand is our backyard. Brazil is halfway around the world, and you know I have no resources there." After a short silence, I added, "Let me be perfectly clear, Stan. If at any point on this mission I am begging to pay rent or without food provisions, I will go directly to the airport and fly back. I have cash resources this time that I didn't have on the first trip. I'll simply purchase a return ticket, fly back and hand you the bill. I will not be forced to endure what I did the last time around."

"Fair enough." He nodded. I was bluffing and he clearly knew it, given the fact that I was already into him a grand for his last ice front. "And when you return successfully, you'll be compensated as we agreed, minus what you now currently owe." He was raising me on the play and there was nothing I could do. Stan owned me, and this gave him complete leverage to do as he pleased. There was nothing for me to do but bend over and hope for the best.

The following day on the way to the airport I checked Lyda into one of our usual guesthouses, paid a weeks-worth of rent, left her with a gram and a $150 to tide her over until my return. Letting go of her was simply releasing her back into the horrors of her desperate existence. I hated myself for not being able to keep and protect her. But not being able to keep or protect myself left me little room or wherewithal to care for others.

Once in the air, frequent trips into the tiny airplane toilet in order to blaze lines kept me buzzing through my first ten hours of connections through KL and Tokyo. Departing Narita, I decided to dry out, downed a bunch of beer and settled in for the long thirteen-hour haul to New York. Nearing America's mainland, I was finally able to mellow out and get some zzz's, sleeping six solid hours before landing at JFK.

Being back in the States was a complete and utter horror show. Once welcomed by Homeland Security, I spilled into the terminal and began wandering around killing time before my departure to Atlanta. The mom-and-pop food stalls selling dim sum common in the Asian airports had been replaced by McDonald's, Burger King, KFC. Everyone appeared obese. I was left reeling when the curt cashier at the Duty Free rang up a pack of Marlboros at $17.50!

I landed at GRU thoroughly wasted from the forty-eight-hour journey and stunned to silence when asked by the Immigration Agent my purpose for coming to Brazil. I mumbled something about wanting to explore the natural wetlands of the ecosystem of the nature lodges exploring the flora and fauna of native *blah blah blah*.

After a lengthy stare of burning suspicion, the frowning Señorita stamped my passport. "Welcome to Brazil."

I approached a yellow cab and climbed in. "Itaquaquecetuba, por favor." I stammered.

The cabbie eyed me with concern. *Why is this crazy Gringo going there?*

Compared to the grandiosity of São Paulo, Itaquaquecetuba presented itself as a dusty, one horse town saddled with a weary ambiance. Its narrow streets and dilapidated stores reminded me of the desperate decay of border-town Nogalas, Mexico. After circling the streets and searching for the address, the patient cabbie eventually pulled to a stop in front of a two-story structure situated on a narrow strip of dirt road. I shouldered my pack and walked into reception. A small army of construction workers dressed in mud-caked coveralls filled the small lobby, chowing down on chorizos, arepas and filling small plastic cups from a coffee station. Knocking on the bullet-proof glass, I aroused the chubby *matrona* from the depths of her afternoon siesta.

Room 2 was a statement of rudimentary functionality. Stepping into the cubicle, with its small wooden bed frame enduring the sagging mattress, the ancient wooden nightstand and the filthy antiquated bathroom felt like stepping back into the shit-hole rooms that Lyda and I often found ourselves dying in. Dropping my pack, I tried connecting to the motel's Wi-Fi. No connection. Enduring a hopeless folly of miscommunication with the chubby and loveable *matrona*, I returned to the room and grinned into the fact that Stan had indeed arranged for me an absolute crap-hole. And on some masochistic level, I appreciated it. I integrated naturally with the organic poverty of it all. Felt at home in the grit. Settling into the dark and uncertain, I sent a quick text to Stan letting him know I'd arrived.

Stan's boy rang at noon several days later. I met him on the street in front of the motel. Extending my hand, I introduced myself. The tiny Nigerian man with beady eyes and a scruffy beard gave no response. We walked in silence half a block to a small coffee shop. He ordered two beers. His two-word responses clued me in to his wanting to ensure his anonymity. I was cool with it. He handed me a SIM card. He scrawled out his phone number, barely legible, on a napkin. "Only call me in emergencies. All your communication should be through Stan. You want to change hotels? Move down the block to... Stan will send you money on Monday."

"I'm nearly out of cash. I'll have just enough to pay to move my room. How am I supposed to eat for the next four days?"

The man shrugged. "I do as I am told. As I said, Stan will send money on Monday." The man's phone rang. He took the call in a hushed voice and spoke for a minute. "That was my wife. I must go now. I am sure I will see you again soon." And with that he slid from his chair and out the door, leaving me to pay the bill.

Taking the man's word that a cash re-up from Stan was only three days away, I moved down the block to a new motel. Walking into my new room, I at once saw it was no better than the place I'd just come from. Same barren room, bed hardly bigger than a child's crib wedged into a cold corner, cracked mirror in the bathroom, no hot water, no English-speaking staff, a retired bedsheet now serving as the window shade soiled with unidentifiable stains. It did, however, afford me a direct internet connection which was a marked and significant improvement. Over the next twenty hours Stan and I engaged in a rapid and wearisome email exchange reminiscent of all the frustrations of the first trip. Me begging for money, instructions and support; Stan evading, pacifying with empty promises, tension festering like an open sore.

The following twenty-four hours saw no less than a banter of nineteen emails volleyed back and forth between me and Stan. Stan evading and constantly putting me off with admonishments to relax. Under normal circumstances, say, back in The Penh, I would have been fine being down to my last dollars. I had connections there, a secure place, friends willing to credit product and lend cash on the front. Halfway around the world in Itaquaquecetuba, my life and my entire world had been reduced to a complete alienation from all things familiar, crouching in a dirty, cold cubicle with a few dollars left in my pocket, a half-eaten tin of tuna on the desk and without even possessing a return ticket. No glass to suck on. No bottle to crawl into. Naked. Reduced to an infantile state with no access to a caregiver. Stan wanted me to relax, and all I could do was climb the walls.

Saturday, 19 July, my phone rang at sunrise. "I am Stan's friend. Come now to the entrance of the train station."

I walked up to the ticket booth and spotted a Nigerian guy standing near the turnstile smoking a cigarette—not the same guy I'd met at the coffee shop. He was younger, tall, skinny, all decked out in the latest hip-hop street gear. I approached him with a smile and a nod. He dismissed my friendly advance with a flip of his hand and a smack of his lips. "Here, take this." He handed me a small plastic baggie which I shoved into my pocket. Before I could thank him, he narrowed me with cold eyes and asked, "Why you make so many problems, huh? I work in the city and now I have to come all the way out here and take care of you? No one before make problem like you!" The guy was a complete jerk. With that parting shot he turned and walked briskly back to the platform. Back in the room, I counted out the cash—250 in local currency––about $66 USD. Luxurious in my newly found wealth, I paid reception up for the next three days then hit the town with the remaining change. Two days later, with all the pizza chowed and all the beer drank, I set out to beg for cigarettes on the street.

My furious and desperate footfalls led me three kilometers where the sidewalk suddenly turned from uneven pavement to a curious pattern of crumbling cobblestone. I paused in front of *Igreja de Nossa Senhora da Ajuda*; a simple but pretty church. Built in an intimidating gothic aesthetic, the steeple cast its patient shadow over my aimless wandering. Lingering in front of the steps, I lit a smoke. The church, and my arrival in front of it culminated in a sudden and mystic effect that rendered me completely and utterly humbled. With my feet feeling like lead, I started shyly up the stairs and through the door.

Late Monday afternoon, the basilica was near deserted with only a few parishioners scattered throughout the cavernous sanctuary. I discerned from the small marquee that 7:30 Monday night mass was soon to begin. I took a seat in an empty row and closed my eyes. The sound of emptiness was profound and divine. A faint scent of candles and incense enveloped me in melancholic elegance. Overwhelmed at the stillness, I felt a lump growing in my throat and the sudden threat of tears. Behind the pulpit hung the traditional and gigantic image of Christ on the cross. I evaluated the art without pondering the image. Cheap plastic. The blood could have used a deeper pigment of red. Not enough agony. The surrounding angels had been sculpted in that absurd cherubic style of babies bearing grown men's faces. The whole aesthetic appeared cartoonish.

A figure suddenly appeared and sat next to me. I was irked, with my personal space invaded and my intimate moment with my plastic Jesus shattered. *The entire place near empty and they sit directly next to me?* I eyed the person in my peripheral. Small, frail. Either a child or a woman. *"Desculpe. Eu não quero te incomodar. Mas você está bem?"*

I turned and looked into the kindest eyes. The woman pierced me with a genuine and unnerving stare. Her brown skin was weathered, eyes wrinkled and slightly sad at the corners, her ebony hair streaked with grey, gnarled and unkempt, held back by a flowered hair pin in the shape of a blood red mariposa. Her age was indeterminable. She could easily have been sixty or a hundred and twenty.

"Senhora, sinto muito, mas não falo português. I am a foreigner. I do not speak Portuguese."

The woman smiled. After tenderly patting my hand, she stood and wandered away. So tiny. Her full posture was only slightly taller than when she was seated. She approached a door built into the church wall I hadn't noticed before. Knocked. The door opened and she disappeared. A minute later, the woman came out followed by a younger man dressed in a long sleeve white dress shirt tucked smartly into jeans. The two of them approached and took places in the pew directly in front of me. The woman spoke softly in Portuguese while the man listened and nodded. After her short blurb, the man looked at me and spoke through a smile.

"I sorry my English bad. I will try." I introduced myself and nodded for him to continue. "I am Father Mateus. This is Senhora Xoana. She want to say that… she…" I kept nodding, smiling fake through his stammered translation, eyeing the door, negotiating my swift but polite exit. "…Senhora Xoana want to know why you so sad?"

The question left me stunned. Pierced into my core like a burning dagger, unravelling me at the seams. A precise and accurate spiritual circumcision, revealing my corroded heart. I recovered as quickly as I could, wiping burning tears and running snot with my sleeve. Sister Xoana's simple question was a loud knock on the door I'd kept locked for so long; a door I was nowhere near willing to open. Despite sensing a sincere and tender movement of the Spirit, I quickly buried it under heaps of bullshit; spewing forth a gushing quagmire of authentic lies in broken English churned together with sugar-coated half-truths and all in the name of pathetic spiritual pathos.

I am here working. I've been abandoned by my employer. I have no return ticket to… I have no money. Destitute. I left God long ago… He no longer knows me. I am frightened.

My emotive confession sent Father Mateus and Sister Xoana huddling into a hushed exchange of concern. "We pray for you?" The question was rhetorical, as hands were suddenly laid upon my shoulders. After a quick prayer in Portuguese, Father Mateus excused himself and re-entered his vestibule while Sister Xoana remained rubbing my hands. I sat with her in complete silence, with no strength to look into her eyes. Father Mateus returned moments later and handed me an envelope. "Take this. It is what we can do for helping." I received the envelope with a bashful glance of pure gratitude. After enduring a lengthy silence, I thanked them both each with a hug and then made for the door.

Walking back to the room I pulled the cash out of the envelope and counted out the loot. Fifty Brazilian Reals, about USD $13.50. Dodging into the supermarket I loaded up on two 40's of Bud, a mini pack of smokes, three cans of tuna and a loaf of bread. Back in the room I made a sandwich and enjoyed a few smokes for dessert. Draining the second 40 ouncer, I slipped into a long sleep while fending off all pinions of guilty conscience.

Another in the Fire

I woke coiled in a fetal position in the cold sheets. I showered and dressed for the first time in three days and stepped out into the impending night. My steps were aimless, wandering down to the stagnant lake, then over to the train depot where I sat listless watching patrons climbing wearily on and off the train purchasing small platefuls of *papas fritas* from a scowling vendor. I angled over to the church where days before, Father Mateus and Sister Xoana had plagued me with their kindness. It was near mass. I didn't want anyone to think I'd returned for another handout. Pulling my hoodie over my head, I slithered into the last pew.

I scanned the sparse assembly and spotted Sister Xoana seated near the front. I recognized the unkempt hair drawn up by her blood red butterfly hairclip. Father Mateus walked solemnly to the pulpit, raised his arms and proceeded into his Order.

After six minutes, just when I felt like blowing the boredom out of my brains, Father Mateus stepped aside and a comely pubescent girl in pigtails appeared side stage and eased into an a cappella rendition of *Agnus Dei*. With her small face tilted to Heaven, she sang horribly off-key, with all the passion and radiance of a divinely appointed angel. It was one of the best and most memorable performances I had ever witnessed. When she finished, she offered a small bow as I made my quick exit to the ovation of robotic applause.

If a person's soul has a head, the young girl's voice had decapitated mine with guillotine precision. My body stumbled out the side door rectory and wandered the streets. My indigent and homeless soul was left swirling aimless through the cosmos with tears welling up from my heart, overflowing my jagged neck and spilling over my body in a hideous stinging baptism of boiling holy water.

The magic call finally came on the morning of Thursday, 7 August. "I'm at the train station. Come now." The tall, rude asshole all decked out in his hip-hop gear stood with the shorter, distractible man. The short guy was holding a nondescript grocery bag by the handles. They began walking. I followed. After a few

217

blocks they ducked into a small coffee shop. Seconds later I entered and joined them at their table. Three coffees were ordered. The bag was placed under the table near my feet. "Everything is in the bag. Package. Cash. Return ticket." Coffees drained inside two minutes; we made our exit. The two men turned and walked back in the direction of the station. I returned to the room.

With my heart thumping, I locked the door, checked the street and drew the blinds. Onto the bed tumbled twelve bottles of Shea Moisture African Black Soap Deep Cleansing Shampoo. Each bottle was marked weighing 13 fluid ounces. Hefting each one, I knew that the weight was far more than a mere thirteen ounces—the total weight of the load impossible to guess. Checking the street once again, and making sure the door was secure, I returned my attention to the contents on the bed. The first envelope held cash. The second presented my return flight, departing the following day.

The chubby *matrona* and her staff bid me good luck through fake smiles. For three and a half weeks I'd given them nothing but grief. They were happy to see me go. Traffic moved easily along the autopista and the cabbie delivered me to the airport without incident. I was the first in line to check in. The faceless agent processed my info and handed me boarding passes for my connections in Abu Dhabi and Kuala Lumpur. Luggage was checked all the way to Siem Reap, my final destination. Returning her suspicious frown with a weary smile, I cast a last glance at my rolly as the conveyor belt carried it away. No turning back now.

The three hours before my flight were spent strolling the terminal with my best game-on expression. Cops were everywhere. I'd never noticed so many airport police in all my travels. The Civil Police, dressed in their yellow vests, eyeing me with dead expressions. Federal Police dressed in their camo, restraining their lunging German Shepherds on taut leashes. Not to mention the Military Police decked out head to toe in full commando garb, eyeing me with pure suspicion. And of course, there were the undercovers, the legions of plain-clothed pigs lurking in the shadows, poised perfectly in the restaurant lines, casually socializing while paying for fruit smoothies or perusing small toiletry items at the duty-free. Cops were everywhere, eyeing me with pure disdain. Greeting each and every one of them with a placid smile, I took my seat at the gate. I thought of Stan's instructions to call and assure him I'd arrived. Fuck him. Make him sweat it out.

Good afternoon passengers. This is the pre-boarding announcement for flight EY 4399. We are now inviting those passengers with small children, and any passengers requiring special assistance to begin boarding at this time. Please have your boarding pass and identification ready. Regular boarding will begin in approximately ten minutes time. Thank you.

I filed into line. The lady at ticketing examined my passport and boarding pass. Setting foot on the plane, I immediately found my seat. 45G, an aisle seat in the first row of Economy Class. An aisle seat was better than a middle, but not as good as a window. Buckled in and secure, I fished out the complimentary goodie-bag. With pure intentions of annihilating everything around me I secured the ear plugs, strapped on the eye shades and centered into an absolute absence of reality. Heart pounding.

The make it or break it stretch. I knew if my bag had been sniffed out, flagged, inspected and discovered, this would be the time they'd come for me. I tried to appear calm. My jaw taut, gritting teeth. I was sweating uncontrollably, and my heart felt like it was going to explode. Fifteen minutes... the sightless and soundless ambiance of passengers boarding, shuffling for seats, re-arranging carry-ons, politely negotiating space and fretting time... When the activity died down, I took off the eye shades and surveyed the plane. Four rows back I spotted a window seat. I gathered my things and quietly slipped back to 49K. From my new location I had a clear view of the plane door. The constant stream of passengers had tapered off to a few stragglers. I fixed a permanent stare on the door, waiting for the Police to appear.

Ladies and gentlemen, welcome on-board Etihad Airways flight EY 4399 with service from São Paulo to Abu Dhabi. Final checks are being completed and the captain will order for the doors of the aircraft to close in approximately five minutes time.

As the second hand swept past the exact scheduled time of the departure, the doors remained open. Breath deep. Everything's cool. Five minutes later, another announcement. *Ladies and Gentlemen, will passenger Flemming Dich Lund please identify yourself to the flight attendants? Passenger Flemming Dich Lund, please come to the attendant's station located in front of the first section of economy class seating. Thank you.*

Ten minutes past scheduled departure time, and my eyes were bulging out of my skull, transfixed on the open door. *Ladies and gentlemen, as you can see, we are experiencing a slight delay in our departure. The delay is due to a slight complication with off-boarding baggage. This delay will be brief, and we expect to be underway here in a matter of minutes. Thank you for your patience.*

It was a ruse. Why would an issue with off-boarding luggage be the cause for the door of the plane to remain open?

Fifteen minutes past the scheduled departure, they finally appeared. Two *Policia Federal* walked onto the plane and were met with a cluster of flight attendants. The chief attendant then presented the officers with a clipboard of paperwork which I guessed to be the Passenger Manifest. After a moment of discussion, the entourage then gathered in the aisle *directly* next to my originally assigned seat, 45G. Standing next to my deserted seat, the discussion continued with the cops flipping through the attendant's paperwork.

The cops turned their attention to the man seated in 45F; the guy I'd originally been sitting next to. After a minute of dialogue, the man stood, placed his hands behind his back and was led in cuffs off the plane without incident. Another mule, who had just so happened to have been seated next to me, taken down. The plane door closed. *Ladies and gentlemen, we apologize for the delay. The complications have been cleared up and we are currently third in line for take-off. Just a reminder, illegal substances are not allowed on the flight. If you are suspected or found to be carrying, you will be dealt with by the local authorities.*

Stand by... We are expected to be in the air in approximately seven minutes. We ask that you please fasten your seatbelts... Feeling a small and sudden bump, I watched the tarmac as the plane began rolling in reverse. Once in the air, I began drinking myself silly and managed nine beers before being cut off by the flight service.

Stan had routed me to land into Siem Reap—a strategic move. The tourist volume landing daily in Siem Reap was small when compared to an arrival in Phnom Penh. I was sure to endure far less scrutiny. Smart move on Stan's part.

I was a little on edge standing at the luggage carousel; but nowhere near the wreck I'd been back in São Paulo. When my little gold rolly finally spilled out and onto the conveyer, I nearly hit the ground. I let the bag roll by like it was poison. It had clearly been opened, evidenced by a large swath of duct tape wrapped around its middle. On its second pass I could see that one of the four wheels was missing, sawn off entirely by a saw blade. On its third pass I hesitated; petrified to touch it for fear of being tackled by a security mob. As it came around a fourth time, I went for it. Placing it on the ground I made for the exit, but quickly realized that wheeling it behind me was impossible. I had no other option but to carry it like an awkward bag of groceries.

Approaching customs, I appeared conspicuous and ridiculously awkward. Dropping the damaged rolly down on the ground like a sack of potatoes, I handed the agent my declaration card. The woman examined the form. Nothing to declare. She then glanced at my dead rolly. "It looks like your luggage was damaged in flight, Sir? Would you like to report the damage to the airline?"

I thanked her. Politely declined. Made for the exit. I could see the sunlit windows and doors to the street. Thirty yards. Taxis and tuk-tuks queued in the circular cul-de-sac. Ten yards. I walked brisk, waiting to be tackled by a team of angry security. I could see passengers standing on the street smoking cigarettes, negotiating transportation. Five yards. Through sliding doors and into the familiar sights, scents and sounds of Cambodia. I approached the nearest tuk-tuk, tossed the rolly into the cab and climbed in. As I balanced the damaged luggage between my legs, an old codger climbed in and turned to face me. *"Suostei mitt. Tae thngainih anak sokhasabbay cheate?"*

"Tow! Tow!" I barked. The old man shrugged and shifted into gear.

I lit a smoke and took down half of it in one drag, glancing back at the airport, wondering if I was being followed. With my paranoia at its peak, I directed the driver through a maze of streets, doubling back twice on the way to the guesthouse. Once inside the room, I threw the rolly onto the bed, ripped off the tape and examined the contents. Everything in its right place.

Chapter Thirteen

Phnom Penh, Saigon
August - November 2014

On Monday morning, August the 11th, in the dust of the Siem Reap bus station I watched three small near naked children wander through a maze of adult legs tugging on trousers and skirts. Round faces smeared with dirt. Hungry mouths in the shape of *O's*. Small wrists wiping runny noses. Wide eyes absorbing the callous functions of tourists paying paper money to go *somewhere*. Like the children, I was flat broke, but with well over a $100,000 U.S. dollars of pure product buried in my rolly. I couldn't recall the last time I felt so miserable.

Back in The Penh, I spotted Stan's Escalade slowly negotiating a parking spot under a shade tree halfway down the block. I hopped into the front passenger's seat and shook his hand. Stan's nerdy looking sidekick sat directly behind me. "Good to see you, Aaron. You remember my colleague, Sand?" He was the same guy I'd met eight months ago at the Frangapini when I had tried and failed to swallow the bullets. We exchanged knowing nods while I passed Stan the grocery bag. Stan passed it back to Sand. Handing me an envelope, Stan congratulated me. "For a job well done. This is half of your compensation, minus the thousand you owe me. You will receive the rest after the lab has verified the product."

"When?"

"I'm taking the product to the lab now. I will contact you this evening."

"Fine. But I need a re-up of ten G's, *like now*. Can you meet me tonight?"

Parting with Stan and Sand, I took the Dyke road directly over to the house. The house owners met me at the gate with glances of doubt and disdain. Their demeanor morphed into a renewed air of tolerance as we sat in their parlor and I counted out the back rent, along with another six bills to carry me through November.

Five hours later, Stan and I continued our dialogue in Hun Sen Park, on our usual bench under the shadow of the Independence Monument. Per usual, we ran the dance of wanting to rehash the glitches and frustrations of the recent job. But until I was paid in full, I decided wise to avoid the clash entirely. I had plenty of ammunition, but it wasn't the appropriate time to unleash the assault. Avoiding all questions that could lead to the inevitable confrontation, I kept things quick, focused on getting my hands on more supply and angling toward the second half of my pay day.

I scurried back to the Lucky 2 and presented Lyda with the wealth.

Patient lioness. She eyed the stack of bills with composed curiosity. "How much he give you?"

"Enough to pay our houseowner and buy more product to sell."

It was when I threw out the ten G pouch that she really started to purr. She reached for the bag and held it up to the light. My delivery earned me a single kiss. "Clear. Looks good. Let's try." I took out one of the largest rocks and handed it to her. She began preparing the glass.

We checked out of the Lucky 2 the next day and returned to the flat. Over the next two days, with lights dimmed and blinds drawn, we managed to swim through half the stash that Stan had given me; passing each other in the hall with barely a glance, circulating around the flat with all the grace and gorgeous madness of two Siamese fighting fish trapped in the same bowl.

An unrecognized call came in. "Hello, this is Aaron."

"Hi. This is Gabby."

A long silence ensued, permeated by the caller's arrogance and my saying nothing.

"Yes?"

"I was given your contact information by mutual acquaintances."

"Yeah. I know who you are. What can I do for you?"

"Are you free to meet?"

Gabby and I lived on the same side of town; the extreme southern fringe of the city near Wat *San Sam Kosal*. We agreed to meet at one of the random mini-marts on 271. Without a clue as to Gabby's intentions and with my paranoia at its height, I showed up late. Circling the block three times, I spotted a middle-aged man, fortyish, slim build, black short-cropped hair seated alone at the shop's outdoor table. Staking out the scene convinced me Gabby was solo and posed no threat. Joining him at the table, I sat silent, waiting for him to take the lead. I was annoyed. I only wanted to be back swimming in my fishbowl sucking the glass with Da. I didn't like meeting people. Especially other ex-pats.

"So, how long have you been in The Penh?" He asked in his peculiar Northern European accent.

I gave my short answer. "Where are you from?" I returned.

"Belgium."

Annoyed with the pleasantries, I cut direct to the chase. "So what's up, Gabby? Why did you call me?"

"Oh, nothing serious." He demurred. "Just a social meet. I've been hearing your name around town. I just wanted to put a face to the name."

We chatted superficial shop for the next few minutes, cautiously name dropping, finding common ground. In a hurry to return to Da, I angled to wrap things up. Parting with a handshake, it was then that Gabby threw me a line. "If you ever need a good price on whatever product, give me a call. I can beat whatever you're paying now."

On the ride back home, I replayed the meeting. I didn't like his face. His thick accent demanded too much head space. His close-cropped bristly hair and ears too large for his head reminded me of a narrow-faced weasel trying to squirm uninvited into my small but secure burrow. "*I can beat whatever you're paying now.*"

Lyda was as I'd left her. Naked on the couch, scraping the glass with an unraveled paper clip, smudging out resin onto a torn scrap of aluminum foil. Her natty hair fell forward, hiding her face. With all focus on her next inhale, she gave no acknowledgement to my return. I kissed the top of her head and plopped down another rock onto the table. She shot me a thankful glance, then loaded the glass, inhaled, passed me the pipe.

Stan met me in the park two days later and settled my payment. Curiosity eventually motivated me to connect with Gabby, and by the end of August I was pulling my supply between both Gabby and Stan. With plenty of supply flowing through the house, Lyda was content, even docile. And whenever I sensed her mood swing, I simply took her over to Naga and let her burn through a wad of $20's playing the slots. I sold my old moto and bought another—a newer Suzuki *Smash* which set me back about $500. It was a good season; cut short by Stan's rejuvenated focus on the Saigon accounts. I kept begging for another local run to Thailand. Afterall, this had proven a simple gig that had actually paid off, compared to the bank jobs that had yielded nothing but unpaid leg work. But Stan had none of it. He kept putting me off. "We're lining up another job in S. America. Or perhaps a weekend run to Taiwan. Just be patient. For now, we'll continue focusing on the work in Vietnam."

On 8 September, Aaron Reed spilled off the bus and checked back into the *Thanh Thuong* Guesthouse and the following day, Elgin Jules Janssens walked into Saigon Commercial Bank and opened a U.S. dollar account with his newly procured lease and Belgian Passport. Three weeks later I returned, this time as Lucas Dinis Pinto, from Lisbon, and opened another account at an ACB branch.

Back in The Penh, Lyda and I were inhaling the last trails of my São Paulo payday. She hated when I went off to Saigon on the extended day trips and returned with nothing.

Huddled into intense conversation at The Pizza Co., I spelled it out to Stan. "I'm done with the accounts, Stan. Not doing it anymore."

He eyed me with sheer displeasure from across the table. "And why is this?"

I'd just left the house moments ago where Lyda and I had spent the entire morning rifling non-stop through the last pile of crystals. I came to meet Stan on full adrenaline throttle, careless and verbose with a razor tongue. "Why do you think? Eight fucking accounts over the past four months and what have I gotten out of it? Absolutely nothing! Each time I go I risk my freedom. You keep stringing me along. '...Be patient... just wait... we are actively trying to sell the accounts to the clients... we'll sell one soon... blah, blah, blah...' I'm tired of hearing your empty promises. There's no fucking compensation in these jobs. If you were me, would you continue? I know the answer to that question!"

Stan chewed slow and thoughtful through his lunch special, taking time to swab his plate with carefully selected pieces of garlic bread. I hated the ease and comfort he always exuded, in direct contrast to my day-to-day frantic nightmare. "I think you have a narrow view of things, Aaron. You tend to view things in the short term, lacking focus on the long-term benefits. We are very close to selling the accounts. And when we do, you will be compensated per our agreement."

"Do I continuously need to remind you of the reality of my day-to-day existence? Don't get me wrong—I don't mean to sound like an ingrate. I *do* appreciate the work, but you gotta understand my frustration. Every time you send me on a job, I end up scraping myself through the gutter just to bring the mission to completion. You constantly keep me at the bare minimum, promising me everything, giving me little. I'm done, Mr. S. Not going to do it anymore. Until I see some results, please don't call me again."

Riding back to the flat, I was pleased by my sudden step-up to the plate and the way I'd swung for the fences. But whether I'd connected with the ball remained to be seen. Reality dictated that Stan was my only serious connection to viable income. And I had just lit a furious match to the bridge. The idea of returning to Lyda back at the flat with nothing to show for my efforts motivated my call to Gabby. I arranged for a pickup. He met me at Russian Market outside the KFC and passed me a G front.

Unlocking the door, I sensed a menacing air permeating through the rooms. The lioness was on the prowl. I found her poised over the cutting board in the kitchen, butcher knife in hand, slicing vegetables with an over-exaggerated effort. She turned to face me. "He pay you?"

"No. But I have some new smoke."

She followed me into the living room, selected a stone, handed it to me. Holding it to the light, I could see it was peculiarly clear. Dry. Excellent vertical lines. I licked it. Ultra-bitter. We began our endless ritual of crushing out the stone and preparing the glass. Gabby's product was *super-charged*; An anomalous inhalation that immediately launched both Da and me spiraling into uncharted territory. Far superior to anything I'd ever sampled. Zero to ninety in 3.7 seconds. We both jumped off the couch. I relocked the door, redrew the blinds and began frantically tidying the place. Lyda whirled into hurricane motion, paced down the hall and disappeared into the kitchen. I could hear her chopping vegetables with intense speed and fury. Minutes later she returned to the couch. Placing the butcher knife on the coffee table, she took another long pull on the glass, exhaled, then picked up the knife and pointed it at me.

"Why you not buy me a moto?"

Her question came straight out of left field. "What?"

She wiped the sweat from her face, then gathered up her hair and secured it with a scrunchie. "You not hear me? You have problem with your ears? I say why you not buy me a moto?"

It was an oddball question. She'd never mentioned ever wanting a moto. Before I could reason anything she added, "...or a new purse, or some new clothes, huh? You buy new moto for you but not me. Nothing for me, ever!"

I stood in the center of the room and stared blank at her. The thought of buying her a moto had actually crossed my mind. But the unspoken truth—and we both knew it—was that a moto in her hands would end up in the pawn shop the very next day and I'd eventually find her at Naga or in the fish games burning through the cash. A lesson I'd already learned from Thea. Gifting anything of worth to the girls of Phnom Penh was always a double-edged sword. If you didn't, then they'd crucify you, or just simply leave. And if you did, then their need or lust for cash would always quickly out-value the gift. The gift—be it jewelry, a moto, or tablet would end up being pawned and the cash spent before you'd even notice that the item was missing. Stuttering for a response, I offered meekly, "Da, you never mentioned anything about wanting a moto."

"You not think I want? *Tzzz!*" With each word, she stabbed the air with the knife. She took her third pull off the glass. I was still in orbit from the first.

Her face glistened with sweat. As she sucked on the pipe, a bead trickled down her face and hung on her chin before falling to the table. Her fury, coupled with her white-knuckled grip on the knife was unsettling. I moved in and reclined on the opposite end of the couch, trying to slow my heartbeat, hoping to de-escalate the tension. I spoke soothingly. "Da, listen-"

"-And why you not get paid from your boss, huh?" Launching herself from the couch, she stood in the center of the room, her gorgeous, angry, angelic eyes bulging, lips recessed in a rage exposing a crackbrained grin. "You go Vietnam two times last week and you not have money? You work for nothing? Stupid man! *Tzzz!*" I *hated* her *Tzzz*, her way of dismissing me as nothing more than a squirming maggot. Knife in hand, she stormed back down the hall. I followed.

"Da, listen!" I grabbed her arm. "I *did* get paid from the work in Brazil. Our rent is paid for this month. We have food. We have smoke. I take you to Naga and you burn through money faster than I can make it!"

She whirled. Her movement quicker than my comprehension. The knife sliced the hem of my shirt before being raised high in the air. Avoiding her downward slash, I collapsed onto the tile. Grabbing her ankles, I pulled hard. She hit the floor with a sickening thud. I threw my full weight on her maniacal writhing, wrapping my fingers around her thin wrist like a tourniquet. She released her grip and with a kick, I sent the knife sliding across the floor. Legs, arms entwined in a frenzied death dance, it was all sweat, wet whiplash hair and convulsion. Just when I had her pinned and inert, I felt her teeth puncture into my abdomen. The unreal and grainy tic of old fashioned 8mm suddenly took on a warm sticky and slippery hue of widescreen Technicolor. I pushed and kicked her away like a ragdoll. I stood and stared astonished at the blood running down my thigh. Lyda lay gasping, her thin bare legs jutting from her multi-colored sari wrenched up above her waist, exposing her panties. She looked up at me; her mouth and chin smeared with my blood.

The faint sound of pounding coming from another universe, I turned to see Mr. Sokhom, my landlord, standing at my door and staring at me through the glass. Stepping over Da's twisted body, I unlocked the door. The events that followed occurred in a vacuum of the unreal. I heard voices but didn't understand. Mr. Sokhom entered the hall flanked by his scowling wife. I disappeared quick down the hall into the living room and swiped up the evidence. Sokhom began wandering through the rooms voicing his disapproval of... everything. Lyda righted herself on the floor, then began screaming in Khmer as the wife helped her to her feet. Countless napkins and paper towels, used to swab up

230

our sins, accumulated in a bloody heap on the kitchen counter. As Lyda continued ranting in Khmer to the wife, I pulled Mr. Sokhom aside and began offering my English version of the events. His response surprised me. "Aaron, you know by now that *these kinds of girls* are nothing but trouble. If you don't give them everything they want, they will try to ruin you. Please get her out now. I don't want to see her here again. If I see her here again, I will ask you to move out." Everything was sorrow. Frantic. Pathetic. In the shadow of the frowning wife, Lyda and I scrambled to gather our immediate necessities.

I scooped up a pair of Da's jeans and a few of her shirts off the floor, then unhooked two of her dresses off the hangers. I then buried the stash, the glass, a wad of cash and passport into my pack under her clothes. Da stood small near the door, staring into nothing, with her orange purse draped over her shoulder. The houseowners stood next to her, patiently.

The wife filed out the door, pulling her husband along. Lyda followed. After locking the door, I began making my descent. The motion light was out. The four of us groped our way cautiously down the long concrete stairs spanning the height of three stories. We all heard the crack, like a large stick being stepped on and snapped in two.

Five steps ahead of me, Lyda collapsed and hit the stairs with a wail. Sokhom and his wife paused and turned. Coming up behind Da, I bent, grabbed her arm and tried to help her up. She collapsed again, grasping her ankle. I picked her up in a fireman's carry and eased down the remaining flights. Lyda leaned on me like a crutch as the houseowners examined her ankle. Weary of the night's drama, Sokhom recommended that I take her to the nearby Russian Hospital to get her checked out, then led his scowling wife back into their flat.

I helped Da into a tuk-tuk, gave the driver directions to Lucky 2 and followed them on the moto. Reaching the guesthouse, I helped her hobble into the lobby. The young boy at reception recognized us. Seeing Lyda's condition, he simply slid a key across the desk. I laid her on the bed and helped her slip out of her Sari as gently as possible. Her ankle had swelled to the size of a grapefruit. After drawing the blinds, dimming the lights and leaving her with the remote, I ran down to the Mini-Mart and bought a half kilo of ice, a couple of hotdogs and an assortment of ice creams and popsicles. Back in the room, I smashed the ice block into cubes, filled the waste bin to the brim and arrayed the ice creams and popsicles on the top. I then fashioned an ice-pack and placed it on her ankle. With a slight re-arrangement of the furniture, I had created a sort of comfortable hospice. Pleased with my work, I curled up next to her and cradled her head into my shoulder.

"You fucked up, Da." I whispered, like speaking tenderly to a child. "Mr. Sokhom told me he doesn't want you to come back to the house." She took this in silence, staring at the TV, flicking through channels. Her lack of response was a straight razor slipping slow over my heart, pulling me deeper into her, loving her for everything she was and more intensely for everything she wasn't. I took her hand and pulled her forearm to my lips, kissing gently the countless army of tiny self-inflicted scars running the length of her arm. She lay inert, lifeless, her eyes black as coal; the television glow illuminating her face with all the shadow and hue of a contemplative angel brimming with apathy.

The alien chime of my phone jolted me awake, piercing my mind like a shiny steel hook, pulling me once again to a horrific surface. I instantly recognized Chan's raspy voice. She wanted a hoon. She was waiting for me at GSM. She had news for me. "Come now."

Lyda swirled in the sheets, naked and slippery against my skin. "Who call you?"

I kissed her eye lids. "Shhhh. You sleep. I'll be back soon. Maybe an hour." Unraveling myself from the warm grip of her silence and back into the city was like diving headfirst into a cauldron of boiling fat. The boy at reception stood poised, offering me his best grin. I wanted to knock his teeth out. The lights on the street dug into my eyes like spikes. Urban machinery. Acres of backhoes churning into my reality, unapologetically invading my most protected and private sanctuaries. Emerging from the unreal recesses of Lyda and re-entering life reminded me how weary I'd become.

Chan met me outside the fish game arcade down from The Walkabout. After slipping her the bag and taking her cash, she pulled me into the bathroom in the rear of the arcade and treated me to a toke. "I saw Master Hout. He wants you to call him." She reached into her tight jeans and withdrew a crumpled slip of paper. "This is his new number."

"What's he want?"

"He not tell me anything."

"Let's call him now. I can't understand a thing he says, and you can translate." I dialed the number and handed Chan the phone.

After a minute of discussion, she hung up. "He want to see you at his house. We meet him now and he take us there. He want us at the *Tuol Kork* circle in fifteen minutes."

Tuol Kork was clear across town. It was already nearing 10:00. I hadn't seen Hout in months. The meet was likely to be a lengthy affair. But with Lyda secure back at Lucky 2, I knew she wasn't going anywhere with her injured ankle, and an evening with Hout and Chan could prove to be interesting. One thing was certain, there would be no shortage of drugs.

Chan and I rolled up to the *Tuol Kork* roundabout and did three laps before spotting Hout filling up his moto at the CalTex. Pulling into the station, I greeted him, then went in to pay for my fill-up while Hout and Chan chatted. As I was pumping gas, Chan explained that Hout had recently moved to a new place and was no longer living in his *Phsar Chas* tower. When I asked where his new house was, she simply replied, "Far."

We followed Hout's maniac speed out of the dizzy city traffic and onto a two-lane heading west. The urban sprawl quickly gave way to rice fields. The cloudless sky was peppered with a zillion pinholes, a dazzling array of gorgeous stars. The smell of cattle filled my nostrils. The warm rush of country air felt good on my skin. Dilapidated shack huts ran the length of the road, and here and there I caught the sight of the red-light lanterns hanging outside shanty brothels. After a good twenty minutes, Hout's speed slowed as the pavement gave way to a rough dirt road filled with gigantic craters. After a few kilometers, the road then narrowed to nothing more than a path winding its way through a small community of one room cabin-like houses and thatched-roofed wooden shacks. We were deep into Khmer country. Pure, authentic Cambodia.

We turned off the path, then had to walk our bikes a distance to where the path met its end. Hout's place was the last in a line of small structures and butted up against an expansive rice field that stretched away under the stars like an endless black ocean. Chan and I took seats on the floor mat while Hout turned on a small lamp, lit a few candles, then joined us cross-legged on the floor. The place consisted of just two rooms: The main meeting room, where we sat, doubled as the kitchen. A tiny bedroom was attached. If Hout had moved here with the intention of blending into perfect anonymity, he had chosen the right location. Nothing but space, silence and stars.

Per usual, Hout got right down to business. It felt like no time had passed since our last rendezvous. He tossed me his stash to examine, and I tossed him mine. Chan prepared the foil and the water pipe. Within minutes, the three of us were chatting away like wide-eyed, steroid-injected magpies. The recent score from Gabby was far superior to Hout's product. After a long dialogue with Chan, she turned to me and translated. "Master Hout wants to arrange a deal with you. He say your product is very good, *klang nah*! Very strong. He say he wants to buy big amount."

"How much does he want?" I asked.

Following another lengthy exchange, Chan answered. "He say a hundred grams." A large order indeed. As the middleman on the deal, bridging the gap between Gabby and Hout, I could jack the price and come away with an easy chunk of cash. Hiding my enthusiasm, I simply answered that I'd look into it.

The three of us smoked endlessly, chatting into the wee hours. The crow of a rooster prompted me to check the time. When Chan and I finally saddled back on the moto, the first hues of sun were bleeding into the sky. Chan and I rolled back into *Tuol Kork* just as the morning markets were opening. Dropping her back at the fish game, I thanked her with a quick hug and a free hoon. Back at Lucky 2, I keyed into the room as quietly as possible. In the dark I could see the vague outline of Lyda's body under the sheets. Still racing hard from the all-night session, I closed her away and headed back into the morning with uncommon conviction, intent on taking care of things.

I found Stan sitting in our usual booth, in his typical Jabba the Hutt posture; obese in his lethargy, posturing as if nothing in the world mattered. Bypassing my usual pleasantries, I refrained from ordering anything. I had no intention of sharing a meal. I was zooming—intent on gaining info—nothing more. I quickly discerned his usual ambiguity.

"What's up, Stan? You got anything for me? I need to work *now*. Thailand? The accounts?"

He was startled at my brevity. Frowning over his cheese sticks appetizer, he attempted to narrow me with his typical recrimination. "I can see you are in a hurry. Aren't you going to order anything?"

"I'll order next time when you have something productive to discuss. I'm tired of waiting, Stan. I'm outta here."

It was then he slapped down his Ace. "I received word there will be a deposit at the end of October."

"The end of October is next week." He nodded, like an all-knowing guru. I hated his arrogance and his refusal to expound on the information. "Details Stan! What are we looking at, exactly?"

"It will be sizable. Be ready. I will let you know. Do you need any product at the moment?"

Weary to death of his empty promises; tired of his endless lures, I spun around and gave best effort to sting him in the eye directly. "Sorry Stan. I'm picking up product elsewhere. And it's far superior to yours."

The brief meet with Stan had yielded nothing certain, but I did feel a sense of renewal at his mention of a potential deposit.

On the street I checked my messages. Nothing. I was feeling a slight come down and needed a blast. I decided to check in on Rumpelstiltskin Mike. Aside from enjoying his company, his location in Ice Alley was perfectly situated next to GSM, and at this time of day I knew I could always dish out a few hoons.

Mike's door was ajar. I peeked through the crack and called his name. Nothing. Pushing the door open, my heart hit the floor. I always carried the distant fear of Mike dying and my first thought was that the old guy had finally crossed the river. Coupled with his obvious infirmity, he was old, frail, maintained a miserable diet, not to mention his life-long marriage to the H. The room had clearly been vacated, left like a dark and empty tomb. Besides a collection of dust bunnies left swirling on the floor, a few papers, a broken pencil, a soiled pillowcase left crumpled in the corner, nothing remained. My spirit soared when I noticed that the light bulbs had been removed from their sockets. I knew then that Mike hadn't died. He'd moved. Now it was just a matter of tracking him down.

The girls of GSM were a treasure-trove of knowledge. They knew what was happening, who had the good drugs at any given moment, and they certainly knew where people were. Their transient lives were a flurry of enormous activity that spread like a web throughout the entire city. They all talked, passing info about their recent escapades, their experiences with their Johns—an

236

endless galaxial mind map offering the what, when, where, why and how. Their exchange was a constant twenty-four-hour electrical current that kept the industry alive. Their communication was not just a channel of juicy gossip, but also served as a means of protecting themselves. These girls were the *go-to* whenever you needed quick info. But their facts, figures and details always came at a price.

Cruising through the mall, I came upon a cluster of girls sipping soft drinks outside the Swiss Bar. I knew Srey Pheap through Chan and had dished hoons to her on many occasions. The girl sitting next to her I had partied with at Mike's just a few weeks before. She was small, wrapped in a tight miniskirt, braless under a skimpy halter top; thick black curls framing thin lips and a pouty nose protruding from her barely-legal face. She stared at me with perfect and stunning wide-eyed apathy, dripping sadness. Another broken girl. Some stupid pop song blared from the bar's speakers. None of the girls at GSM ever felt like dancing.

I joined their circle, bought a round of beers and started chatting. The girl I'd met at Mike's re-introduced herself as Pisey. She said Mike had recently moved from his house and was now living in some building over on Street 110.

"Where exactly?"

"*Jit Phsar Chas.*" Hout's old neighborhood. I knew it well.

"Will you take me there?" The promise of a short party made her more than willing.

Pisey directed me to park the moto just down from the ACE English school. After following her up and down 110 for a few minutes, she finally identified the building. It was an unassuming four story with a single entrance of narrow stairs that led up to the first floor. Into the heart of the windowless building, the stairs took a turn and continued winding spiral-like to the upper floors. On the second floor, Pisey paused at a random door. "This is it." I knocked.

Mike's familiar and frustrated voice came whining through the door. "Who the fuck is it?"

"It's me, Mike. Open up!"

"Aaron? Ahhh, I was hoping you'd figure it out. Hang on just a minute. Let me get decent."

A half minute later, the door creaked open. Mike eyed us with all the suspicion of a junkie. Once he'd verified our identities, the door opened just wide enough for me and Pisey to slip in. Mike's 'decent' was his small, bony body wrapped in a towel. "Sorry, I was just getting out of the shower... washing off the ointment that's helps me get rid of my parasites. Magical stuff, really. Just minutes after swabbing it on, the little fuckers come crawling right out of my skin!" Mike had explained this phenomenon to me before. He claimed to be infested with hookworms; legions of worms that had taken over his body, enjoying him as a host, constantly burrowing beneath and throughout his skin. I'd never actually witnessed a worm breaching the surface, but he insisted they were there, everywhere, constantly simmering. "How are you? Glad you came! Come in, come in. Can I brew you some tea?" Shifting his attention to Pisey, he welcomed her with a hug and a pat on the ass. "And you brought Pisey with you! And how are you, Cupcake? Always good to see you. Mmmm... delicious!"

The three of us settled on Mike's mattress laid out on the concrete floor. He produced his ever-present party tray littered with crumpled foils, an array of lighters, matches, along with squares of paper and small baggies smeared with all the samples of the black tar that he'd accumulated over the past twenty-four hours. "Help yourself. You got anything to share, Aaron?"

I handed Pisey a small baggie and she began preparing the bong. Mike continued his warm welcome. "Yeah, glad you found me. I moved last week. Found this place through Peter Gold. You know him?" The name sounded vaguely familiar, but I'd never met the man. Mike continued his lonely rant. "Yeah, I would have called you, but you know these days I don't have a phone. And I'm always glad to see you, Pisey." He reached over me and began fondling Pisey's breasts. She brushed his arm away.

Pisey and I set in on the ice while Mike reclined back on his pillow with his H. We enjoyed our usual catch-up. "It's a good building. Super quiet compared to living back in the alley. There's only six tenants here. Hey you know Hugh, don't you? He's down on the first floor." I'd known Hugh for a couple years; a common face in the scene; a near death casualty just waiting to happen. Jittery and paranoid as hell, he was a notorious ex-pat ice head who made ends meet by running two-bit scams and selling poor quality product all over GSM. "Rent's a bit cheaper here too." Mike continued. "Peter's an asshole though. A real top-notch prick!"

"This Peter guy owns the building?" I asked.

"No, but he acts like he does. Building's owned by some Khmer. Peter's from Britain. A true criminal. Been in The Penh for a year or so. Moved here from Thailand. He got run out of Pattaya for real estate fraud. His story is all over the internet. Check it out. He's apparently got warrants over there. He's just the rent collector for the house owner. And he's a real ball buster, lemme tell ya. Rent's due on the 5th and sure as shit, here comes Peter pounding down your door at 11:59 on the evening of the 4th. Yeah, a real ball-buster, that guy. He likes drugs, though. He knows that everyone in the building is an addict, but he's cool with it. As long as we all pay rent on time we're pretty much left alone." Exhaling a large and pungent plume into the air, Mike tried snuggling up to Pisey again, attempting to lay his head in her lap to enjoy his nod. She gave a grunt, lifted his head, gently lowered it to the floor, then scooted to the other side of the mattress. Pisey looked at me shyly and passed me the pipe.

When Mike came to I asked, "So how does a Brit ex-pat druggie international criminal on the run become a rent collector for a Khmer building owner?"

Mike sniggered, then mumbled, "Well, we *are* in The Penh, after-all. You'll have to ask him yourself, Aaron. You know me, I like to stay out of other people's business." Mike barely got the sentence out before nodding off again.

I was intrigued. Peter had a colorful resume and sounded like someone I'd like to meet. My phone rang. It was Mighty. "Hey man. Yeah, I can do that. Yeah, I'll come now. See you in ten." Cleaning up after ourselves, Pisey and I left the room quietly. Making our exit, we were met by a tallish blond haired older guy entering the building. He stopped directly in front of me, blocking our path, eyeing me up and down. "May I help you?" I asked.

"May I help *you*?" He answered. "This is my building." His tone was mimicking, sardonic. His lips pulled back over his teeth giving him a sneering grin. I'd learn later that this was no sneer at all, but simply the way his face naturally shaped his sincere, but most unfortunate smile. He looked like a maniacal Dutch boy aged well past his prime; a gentleman, perhaps, at one point in his life, now cut and jaded to a peculiar and menacing presence.

"Oh, you must be Peter." I held out my hand and he grasped it firmly, with good eye contact. "I'm Aaron. I know your tenants." Leaning into his ear, I added, "And I've got the killer ice. Give me a call sometime. Mike and Hugh have my phone number." And with that, Pisey and I left Peter staring after us as we made our way down the street back to the moto.

Dropping Pisey back at GSM, I rolled over to meet up with Mighty. I was anxious to show him the recent super score from Gabby. Minutes later, ensconced away in the back room of Mighty's fourth floor flat overlooking *Phsar Thmei*, I counted out five G's onto the scale as he counted out his cash. "Hey Mighty, you ever heard of a guy by the name of Peter Gold?"

At the mention of his name, Mighty nearly puked over our workstation. "Peter Gold! You know him? You seen him?"

"I met him for the first time about a half hour ago." I offered.

"You see that fucker again you be sure and tell him I'm looking for him. That grade-A piece of shit owes me serious cash and has been dodging me for over a month! I catch up to him and I'll peel his goddamned skinny face off. Peter Gold, humph! Fuckin' loser."

Riding back to the Lucky 2, I began feeling the first hints of the proverbial bleak weariness crawling. A familiar sensation, always presenting itself somewhere between the second or third day of sleeplessness. The subtle hallucinations I'd been enduring all day suddenly announced themselves in screaming sermons and unsolvable threats of mental turbulence. When this happened there were only two choices: either collapse appropriately or fill the glass with more fuel.

Slipping into bed, I tried to move as slow as possible so as not to wake Da. She curled into me, filling the room with the scent of sweaty sleep. "What time is it? What day?" She mumbled.

"Time to sleep."

Minutes later, her soft breathing morphed beautifully into a snoring purr. As she entered her nineteenth hour of sleep, I was trying to wind down my thirty-five hour marathon, giving best effort to slow my pounding heart and empty my head of all the clutter. Easing my breathing, I thought of all the billions of stiff and miserable 9-to-5'ers all over the world; the neck-tie choked CEO type pricks falling through their front doors, nodding to their wives, sitting down to their meals, then ending their days pushing their spouses and kids aside and nodding off in front of the TV. "Honey, not tonight... I had a rough day... The office is a killer this week... The accounts are nearly closed, and until then..."

In the past thirty-six hours I had arranged two meetings with Stan and had set up plans to finally close an account with the Vietnam gig. I'd met with a new supplier, picked up $500 worth of product and had managed to unload half of it to the tune of a 35% profit (the majority of which Lyda and I had ripped through at the fish arcade.) I'd survived an attempted murder from my insane girlfriend, narrowly avoiding an eviction from my landlord. I'd rode the emo waves of Lyda snapping her ankle, relocating her across town to a secure location and providing her with crutches. After that, I'd reconnected with my former supplier, Hout, and enjoyed a six-hour meeting where I'd managed to set up a future deal that could provide me with enough cash to pay for a half-year's rent. I had tracked down Rumpelstiltskin Mike and met up with Peter Gold, a new contact and potential slime ball customer. And I'd done this all on *three hours sleep*. Fuck the world and all its menial deadlines.

Lowering my skull into the curved space between Lyda's naked shoulder blades, I finally let myself dissolve. Swimming into a melted sea of crayons, I floated into the whirlpool of celestial nothingness, finding a rare and gentle awareness of myself and forgiveness for everything around me.

I spent the following week nestled away at the Lucky 2 nursing Da. When we finally woke two days after our eviction and her injury, I took her over to see Gloria at *Sokhapheap Thmey* Clinic. After a quick exam and x-rays, Gloria pronounced the injury was not a break after all, just a severe sprain. Handing us a spool of compression wrap and a bubble pack of Motrin IB, Lyda pressed Gloria for something harder. Gloria shook her head. "Not for you, Honey." Addressing us both with a hint of scolding, she added, "Prescription meds don't mix well with Amphetamines. You both would do well to take a breather." I took Gloria's caution with shame, turning three shades of red.

Two days after meeting Peter Gold, he called, greeting me in his fine Brit accent. "Hello, my boy! I'd like to see you today. Are you available?" I got a kick out of him greeting me as *his boy*. Funny shit. He gave me directions to a two story about a half block down from The Walkabout. After securing Da back in the room with lunch and a small rock, I rolled over to Peter's place.

He answered the door wearing nothing but a white, long sleeved dress shirt that extended down just past his black Speedo underwear. He led me the few steps through the kitchen and into his windowless bedroom. Lin sat cross-legged in the corner. I'd met Lin on several occasions, and now, she'd obviously fallen in with Peter. Her workstation consisted of a small scale, along with thirty or so small baggies of product arranged on the floor. She was busy constructing some sort of smoking apparatus. She greeted me with a scowl, then threw her focused attention back to her artistic endeavors.

"Take a seat my boy!" Peter patted the mattress, inviting me to join him on the bed. "And thanks for coming over. We're happy to have you." Over the next hour the three of us sat on the bed passing Lin's homemade bong, exchanging product while I sat thoroughly entertained listening to Peter reveal himself. He spoke charming Queen's English and held all the manners of an innocent alter-boy-turned-villain, divulging his sketchy history.

"Originally from Coventry. A desperate upbringing in a rather shit-hole town in the middle of England. Nothing for a lad to do there really except get into mischief as an order for entertainment. My Pap taught me how to steal. I made my first five hundred pounds at the age of ten when I managed to lift all the cash from the Church's Sunday collection. Ha-ha-ha."

I immediately fell in-step with Peter and Lin's insatiable rate of consumption. Enamored by his laconic narrations of his tragic childhood. I loved the way he varied his story telling with clever English colloquialisms, peppering his fairy tales with sudden and unexpected onslaughts of unrepentant horror. "...she was a lovely lass, really. Until one night, after a long pull at the pub, we returned bladdered, crooning away at the moon. After stuffing down some bubble and squeak, I pulled her to the bedroom. And it was there she left my bell-end stinging, so we spilled into a kerfuffle, romping this way and that until I lost the plot and ended up in the pad playing cards with the bobbies..." I sat on the bed next to Lin, exchanging the bong, completely absorbed in Peter's loquacious poetry.

"So Peter, what happened to you in Thailand?" I asked.

"Ahh, you heard about that?" He took a long pull, shrugged, and passed me the bong. "A mere trifle with the authorities in Pattaya. Nothing I couldn't run from. And so, I came here... about a year past. And I'm certainly glad I did! I met Lin shortly after arriving, and I've been smitten ever since." He moved in for a kiss and she smacked him away like a fly.

And so began my intense, albeit brief relationship with Peter and Lin. There was no profit in it. Peter and Lin had set themselves up with a good source. An old school operative doing a ten-year bid in Pray Sar (where Ricky now lived) was providing them product straight from the prison. With a simple phone call, they had their orders delivered directly to their door! No, it wasn't opportunity, or the lure of money that connected me to Peter and Lin, but rather, a common interest in everything contaminated and profane. Together, they comprised a fascinating duo of intellect, along with an insightful perspective into The Penh's urban filth. Lin was the Khmer local—the experienced and slithering brain, genius in all cultural functions, while Peter directed her with his Western perspectives and cunning. Together, with their contact inside the prison, they were enjoying a slick operation.

"I love crime, my boy!" he continued. "There's nothing else I've ever given my hand to. The only thing I've ever known." Peter ginned at me, his teeth as blonde and slimy as his hair. Peter was a truly repulsive individual. A true reprobate. I enjoyed his reckless approach and found semblance with his extreme and fatalistic projections. In contrast to my estranged parents who continued to pepper me with their weepy pleading phantasy emails of returning to the States, I adopted Peter as a solid and secure parental surrogate; An invaluable contributor to my moral decay.

I continued drawing killer product from Gabby and unloading it at a good profit. I'd mentioned Hout wanting to make a big purchase and asked Gabby if he could supply it. He asked me about the buyer. I didn't want to spill Hout's name, so I simply referred to him as a figure high up in the Khmer cartel, with means. Hearing this, Gabby shook his head and flat out dismissed the deal. "Sorry Aaron. I don't do business with Khmers."

In our dark room at the Lucky 2, Lyda's ankle continued to heal. I met with Peter and Lin regularly, enjoying the formation of a bizarre familial circle.

Late one evening, Lyda was hobbling around the room and asked me to take her out. The swelling and discoloration in her ankle had subsided, and she'd taken to the crutches rather well. "I can go. Now I okay."

Riding slow on the moto through the city with Lyda balanced on the back with her crutches, I pulled up to Peter and Lin's and carried Da up the stairs. Lin answered the door. Sharing a similar background, Da and Lin exchanged a casual, familiar glance and began speaking in Khmer. Lin led us to the bedroom. Peter was lying flat on his back looking peaceful as a corpse with his hands folded neatly on his chest. Next to him on the bed was a black book covered with lines and smears of white powder. After fluffing his pillow, Lin turned her nose to him and dismissed his with a glare of disgust. Lin and Da situated themselves on the floor around the bong; an enticing array of thin and naked limbs, like two praying mantises silently plotting their sexual devouring.

"Lin," I whispered, motioning to Peter. "He sleeping?"

"No, he not sleep!" She shouted. "He all fucked up on that white shit! That shit make him crazy!"

"Coke?" I asked.

"No coke!" She snapped. "Some other shit! I don't know!"

As I bent over to examine the powder, Peter began mumbling incoherently. A minute later, his eyes fluttered open. A wide smile spread slow over his face as he focused in on me. "Aaron, my boy! Thank you for coming."

"What's up, Peter? What are you trippin' on?"

"Ahh, a most lovely ride, indeed. Ketamine! I discovered a local pharmacy that sells me a 200 mg vial for $20." Peter and I spent the next half hour dipping in and out of the K-hole while Lin and Da devoured the rock I'd given them. When the K was all gone, the four of us assembled on the bed and continued passing the ice until sunrise.

A text from Stan came chiming in just after 8:00. <There will be a deposit today. Are you ready to work?> I responded that I most certainly was and prompted Lyda to ready herself to leave.

As Lin began crushing another rock, Peter inquired in his charming vernacular. "So, tell me my boy, exactly what kind of work are you involved in with these Nigerians?"

Over the next half hour, I griped out all the details: my frustrating history with Stan, my disastrous trips to Brazil, how Stan constantly kept me at the breadline, my eviction and brief homeless stint in São Paulo, my work opening the endless accounts in Saigon and Stan's continuous non-payment for my labours. Peter listened fascinated, without any interruption. When I'd finished laying it all out, he shook his head and stared deep into my eyes. "My boy... my boy... it certainly is a tedious industry we work in. And it's a credit driven industry at that! Always walking the fine line between extending the credit and expecting the payment. Once the credit is extended, you're locked in to wait for the payment. Payment is promised, but as you wait, the client wants more product or, in your case, more services. But if you cut them off, then you're cutting off the hand that feeds you. Ahh yes, the endless cycle. I know it well." After further thought he added, "And in your case, it sounds to me like this boss of yours has bled you well, left you completely knackered. Ahh, I feel your frustration..."

From the corner of the room, Lyda uncoiled and spat. "Aaron just stupid! He work for boss who not ever pay him. Stupid!"

Peter silenced her with a stern glare. Commenting on Lyda's quip, Peter sympathetically added, "And the Khmer's do not have this problem like we Westerners. They simply do not extend the credit. To them, we *are* stupid. Because they believe that if the cash is not in their hand-"

"-then it doesn't exist." I finished Peter's sentence and reached for the bong.

Peter nodded. "I understand your dilemma, my boy. I truly do. But where most would see this as a problem, I see this as a golden opportunity." Peter melted me with his twisted grin. "Indeed, a very good opportunity here..." With our heads bowed in whispers of criminal expertise, Peter and I began twisting together the scheme.

Dropping Da back at the Lucky 2, she started needling me. "So now you go back and work for free in Vietnam, huh? Leave me here alone? Stupid man!"

"Da, I'll be back tomorrow and this time I'll be bringing money. Quite a bit of it, actually."

"Yeah, you come back tomorrow or the next day like all the times before with nothing. Maybe I be here and maybe I won't." Her threat crushed me, and she knew it. The idea of her hitting the streets while I was away rattled me to no end. Pleading with her was futile. The only thing she responded to was cash and product. I left her with $20 and a nice sized rock, hoping it would be enough to keep her put until I returned.

I met with Stan to receive final instructions. Tuesday morning, Hun Sen park largely deserted, we convened on our usual bench. "The deposit will happen today or tomorrow. Pack your bags for two days." Stan glanced at his watch. "It's noon now..."

"If I go to the flat and pack now, I can be on the two o' clock bus. I'll get there around 8:00. Chill. Be there in the morning to pick up the money. I need cash for the trip." Stan fished out a fifty. I stared disapprovingly and shook my head. "Not doing this again, Stan. No way. I'll need at least a hundred for the next day's expenses."

"Not to worry, Aaron. Get on the bus. I'll be joining you in Saigon this evening. I must go into the provinces now to check on a few things, but once finished there, I will fly to Saigon to supervise the withdrawal. I anticipate arriving tonight or tomorrow morning at the latest. Once I arrive, I will take care of all expenses."

Keying into the front gate at the flat, Mr. Sokhom greeted me with a frown. He asked about Lyda. I told him she was healing, then rushed up the stairs and did a whirlwind pack. Shoving a large rock into my ass, I raced off to the *Phsar Thmei* bus station.

The ride to the border was typically blasé. I spent the hours replaying the dynamics of the scheme that Peter and I had hatched together. Stan's sudden detail that he'd be flying in to supervise the withdrawal certainly threw a wrench into the cogs. But I didn't sweat it much. Stan was a pathological liar. I knew this. And my faith in his words had come to equal my faith in God. Stan's credibility, much like God and his promises, simply didn't exist.

Rolling into Saigon, I checked into my usual hole-in-the-wall. Crouched in my cubicle, teetering on naked ankles, inviting collapse, I spent the night sucking down my stash, crawling the walls, counting the hours. In the silent and vacant stretches nursing the dawn, and with the Cure's *The Figurehead* playing on continuous repeat, I curled into the sheets, thudding my head against the wall. I had come to love my frightening stretches of self-loathing, and my secure refusal to heal.

As sunrise began slithering its tongue through the blinds, I showered, dressed and made myself presentable enough to venture into the world to purchase a breakfast of kebabs from a frowning vendor. I stood in line behind two drunk Americans. The one with wide shoulders and bushy eyebrows stood alarmingly tall, appearing like some anomalous Nephilim. His friend stood small, robust in the chest, like some paunchy sixth-year university student eternally stuck in the hilarious throes of college. The tall one loomed over me. "Hey Buddy, you seen any cheap pussy 'round here?"

I stared into his face. Incomprehensible. Before I could speak, his companion barked, "Yeah, we seen some hookers earlier but now they ain't around."

Making myself small, I moved to place my order. As I was waiting for the food, they whirled on me again. "Yo man! You look like you know the area. Where's the Asian street meat?"

The small frat boy echoed, "Goddamn, we wanna' fuck!"

I wanted to die. Back in the room, I swallowed my small meal whole. Taking down my last rock, I curled back into the sheets and continued thudding my head against the wall until the blessed blackout came.

Stan's text chimed in at noon. <I am sorry but no deposit at this time. Please return to Phnom Penh. Further instructions when you arrive.> With my last $15 I bought a ticket on the Mekong Express departing at 1:00, then headed back to The Penh with nothing to look forward to, save for another endless berating from Da.

Rolling into town and bypassing Lyda's abuse, I went directly to Peter's from the bus station. Lin was out, and Peter and I had the place to ourselves. I called Stan and put the phone on speaker so Peter could hear the conversation. "Stan, what happened?"

"So sorry Aaron, but I received word this morning that the deposit will be delayed exactly one week from now. I alerted you directly when I received the news. Are you back in the city?"

"Just arrived. So, once again you've sent me on a failed mission. You asked me to go, and I agreed. You sent me with just enough cash to pay for the bus and hotel and a meal. I disrupted my life based on your assurances and promises that never happened, and now I return with nothing. No compensation whatsoever for my willingness and time?"

Following a long pause, Stan finally answered, "You are free to find employment elsewhere, if you so choose."

My blood boiled. I wanted to reach through the phone and carve out his jugular. Peter met my eyes and shook his head. Avoiding the clash, I simply asked, "You're telling me the deposit will happen next week?"

"That is what I am told. And it will be sizeable."

"How much is sizeable?"

"That is all I can tell you for now."

I hung up on Stan, looked at Peter and shrugged. I then began spilling out endless vignettes of all the other times Stan had left me with my ass hanging in the wind with no cash, forcing me to beg for support, going days without food. Peter was a good listener, validating without antagonizing or fanning the flame, at times even playing Devil's advocate. Peter's insight held a certain wisdom of experience that in my brief tenure in crime, I had yet to glean.

The failed deposit had actually been a blessing of sorts, allowing Peter and me more time to solidify details. And over the next week he spoke with absolute assurance that his scheme would come off without a hitch. My biggest worry of course, was mine and Lyda's safety. "No worries there, my boy." Peter guaranteed. "Tomorrow I will call my point person in Bangkok and explain everything just as you've shared it with me. I'm certain he will agree that misdeeds have been done. And he'll be on alert for when the deposit actually happens."

"But the two thing I don't understand are this: First, what's your contact's motivation for helping out on this? And second, how will he be able to intervene if necessary?"

Peter melted my fears with his ever-present and all-knowing smile. "My friend in Thailand and I have a history that extends back many years. And it just so happens that he owes me a favor."

"And what about my second reservation? The *how* part?" I asked.

"My boy, you must understand where we are. S. Asia is not run by the Nigerians. It's run by the Thai's. Nothing happens in S. Asia without the Thais allowing it to happen. Rest easy, my boy. When I explain your situation, your protection will be granted."

When the deposit was finally made, Peter was there to soothe my increasing worries. "Calm down, my boy. Why don't you come over now and we can discuss the final details?"

"Stan's meeting me at the Vietnamese Embassy in the morning at 8:30. After I get the visa, I'll hop on the 10:00 Mekong Express. I'll reach the border around 1:00. Once over the border, I'll begin looking out the window for the first bank branch I can see. When I spot the bank, I'll get off the bus, walk in and make the withdrawal. Hopefully I can do this all before the bank closes. It's gonna be close."

Peter absorbed all this with a frown. "What's wrong?" I asked. "What are you thinking?"

"It all sounds fine. But how do you plan on getting back over the border?"

"What do you mean? I'll cross back over like I always do."

"Not with $15,000 in your pocket you won't."

In my excitement, I'd forgotten that crossing into Cambodia carrying anything over USD $10,000 needed to be declared.

"You can come with me." I suggested.

"Not with my expired visa I can't."

It took Peter and me fifteen minutes huddled over the bong and smoking furiously before we came up with the solution. Lin would accompany me on the trip. It was a risky endeavour, indeed.

The first task at hand was checking out of the Lucky 2 and stashing Lyda into some guesthouse across town. Too many people knew the Lucky 2 had become our default residence, and upon my return to The Penh, she and I needed to be completely and utterly off the map. I checked her into a room in an area of town we never frequented. I left her with food money, a small rock and under strict instruction that she remain at the guesthouse until my return later that evening. "I'll be back tonight. Make sure you are here. Understand?"

"What time you come?" She sighed.

"I'm not sure, not before 8:00 and not after 10:00. If I'm not here by 10:00, go to Peter's and wait for me there."

She took this all in with her typical nonchalance. Examining the rock on the table, she shrugged with her usual infuriating threat. "Maybe I be here and maybe-"

I glared hard into her eyes, like a parent to a child. "No, Da! No fucking around from you on this one! I'm picking up a lot of money. This time it's for real. If I get back tonight and you aren't here, then we are finished. Understand? You will never see me again!" She stared into my face, startled. It's the first time I ever laid down an ultimatum, and from the look of shock on her face, she wasn't quite sure how to respond.

After securing Da, I raced over to the flat. Slipping silently through the gate and past the houseowner, I packed my only presentable outfit that had survived Da's slashing: a crisp, white long sleeve button-down and a pair of (un-ironed) khaki slacks. From there, I raced through the morning traffic to the Vietnamese Embassy. Stan's Escalade sat double-parked and idling in front of the entrance. I slipped into the passenger's seat. "So, after all the waiting, this is finally happening?"

He gave his usual, arrogant, all-knowing nod. "The deposit had been made. Are you ready?" He handed me an envelope. "As you requested, $200. This will cover all expenses for your visa, the bus, hotel, meals, etc. If you are on the 10:00 bus, then you should be in Saigon between 3:00 and 4:00. Upon your arrival, contact Lucky immediately. He will go with you tomorrow to the bank to make the withdrawal. Once the money is secured and Lucky verifies the amount, you will be paid accordingly once you return to Phnom Penh."

"Fine, Stan. Clear on everything. But if I'm able to make the withdrawal today, why can't I just hop a taxi and return tonight? Why not just bring the cash back and deliver it to you personally?" Before he could think any further, I threw my final logs of ruse and trust onto the fire. "I mean, I like Lucky, and I know he's trusted. But in truth, my history with you is much deeper. If we're dealing with this kind of cash, I'd prefer delivering it back to you, directly into your hands. Face-to-face, without any middleman. Know what I mean?"

After a minute of reflection, he agreed. "Yes, I suppose that would be fine."

Receiving Stan's blessing, we parted ways. I entered the embassy, secured the visa then made my way over to meet Lin. She was waiting at the door with Peter hovering behind her. After a few last-minute bong blasts, Lin and I left Peter and arrived at the

Phsar Thmei station. The bus rolled out at 10:03 and arrived at the border a few minutes past 1:00.

The scene at Customs and Immigration was chill. Once Lin and I processed through, I dodged into the restroom, inhaled the rest of my stash, then changed into my *white-collar* clothes. Back on the bus, Lin and I continued our winding way through the suburbs of Saigon. Face plastered to the window with eyes peeled, I searched the commotive streets. Spotting the first ACB branch, I motioned to Lin and together we jumped off the bus.

The scene in the bank was unremarkable—a typical afternoon. Smiling tellers seated at their respective windows attending to the few customers. A single, armed security guard stood alert at the door. The actual size of the bank didn't feel right. It was a small branch, with only three tellers serving customers. Lin took a seat in the waiting area while I took my place in the queue. Fighting pure amphetamine adrenalin, I reminded myself to stand calm, negating all mental paranoia, thwarting all instincts to turn and run.

"Hello." *Offer pleasant eye contact.* "I'm sorry, but I do not speak Vietnamese." *Smile weakly.* "Do you speak English?" *Maintain posture while the teller wanders off to summon her supervisor.* "Thank you. I am sorry for the confusion." *Place fake passport, bank card and empty withdrawal slip onto the counter.* "There was a transfer made recently into my account. I would like to make a withdrawal, but I first need to verify the transfer and the amount." *Breathe. Calm heart rate. Focus.*

After a few clicks on the keyboard, the manager verified in excellent English, "Yes, the transfer was made three days ago and cleared yesterday. Would you like me to print the details?"

"Yes please. I'll be needing the paperwork for my records."

An eternity passed until the printer began doing its thing and the teller presented the docs. "Okay Mr. **Pinto**. Here is your transfer statement." With yellow highlighter in hand, she circled as she spoke. "This is the date of the transfer, and this is the date it cleared." Turning her attention to the second slip, she continued.

"This is your bank statement showing your current balance and amount available for withdrawal." After allowing me a moment to examine the docs she asked, "Will you be making a withdrawal today, Mr. Pinto?"

"Yes. I'd like to withdrawal the full amount but leave $25 in the account to keep it active. I'm expecting another transfer soon."

"Very well then. Just fill out your withdrawal slip, and we will begin processing right away. Mr. Pinto, we are just a satellite branch, and it's possible that we do not have all the cash in U.S. dollars. Would you accept a partial amount in Vietnamese Dong if we don't have the full dollar amount in our safe?"

I answered with a smile. "That won't be a problem." My hand was shaking like a leaf, and I had to write slow, pressing the tip of the pen hard to manage a legible print.

"Excuse me Mr. Pinto while I check to see what amount of U.S. currency we have on hand. I'll be with you again in a moment."

The manager moved into an office partitioned by a large glass window. She took a seat at a desk, picked up the phone and began talking.

So, this is the bust. I could feel sweat beads running from my arm pits and down my torso. *I've somehow tripped up. My fake signature hadn't matched up. Or maybe the account had been flagged when the bank cross-referenced my fake Portuguese passport and fingerprint with Customs and Immigration?*

I eyed the clock on the wall. Two minutes. Four minutes. The manager was parked in her chair chatting away—far too long to simply check the cash on hand. At one point she glanced blankly at me and then quickly looked away. She's calling security. The police will come storming through the doors at any moment. *Get the hell out while you still can.*

I measured the distance to the door. Took a long look at the security guard and decided I could take him if I needed to. *Go. Grab Lin and leave. Now.* While the oblivious teller clicked away on her keyboard, I excused myself and walked the few paces to the water cooler. Downing two little paper cups, I caught Lin's eye. I gave her a wink, then returned to the counter. Hanging up the phone, the manager made her way out of the adjoining office, met my eye and held up a finger as if indicating *one minute*, then disappeared down a hall. Three lifetimes later, she appeared carrying an armload of money.

With the manager and teller working in tandem, it took them a few minutes to run the cash through the automatic counter. Once the cash had been tallied, they ran it through again. The majority was in USD, lined up in fat stacks next to smaller stacks of VN Dong. "Is there anything else we can do for you, Mr. Pinto?" She smiled.

With all the fluffy charm and precise etiquette of a Cheshire cat, I thanked them both. I turned, took Lin by the hand, and disappeared out of the bank to the tune of $14,985 and change.

Lin and I jumped into a curb-side taxi and headed for the border. In the back seat I counted out and handed Lin $3,000— Peter's cut for his good criminal tutelage and the price for my protection. I sent Peter a text with the update.

<Done! We did it. Heading back to the border now. Just gave Lin your 20%. Text Lin now.>

Lin's phone chimed. She sent a text back verifying my payment. A few minutes later, Peter sent me a return text.

<Well done, my boy. Come directly to my place to celebrate.>

Rolling up to the border, I paid the taxi and then bought two lukewarm Cokes from a bedraggled vendor. Sitting in the grass between countries in no man's land, sipping the drinks with Lin, I sent a text to Stan from my Vietnamese SIM card.

+841673802146

<Stan. The withdrawal has been made. I have no intention of bringing you this cash. I am keeping this money to finally compensate myself for all the mistreatment you've inflicted upon me over the past many months. I am keeping this money to pay myself for all the work I have done for you that you never

255

paid me for. I am keeping this money for all the times you left me stranded on the other side of the world with no food, no communication, no support. I am keeping this money as reimbursement for your lack of appropriate supervision, leaving me hungry, evicted from my hotel and left homeless in São Paulo. I will contact you in a few days when I return to Cambodia. Please do not respond to this message. I am taking out this SIM card. And please do not respond to my Phnom Penh number. If you respond to any of my usual numbers, *I will not see your text*. I will contact you when I am ready to discuss things further. Do have a good day.>

Preparing to negotiate Customs and Immigration, I handed Lin another two-thousand. This left us both nothing to declare. Once over the border, we flagged a bus and settled into our seats. The rush of the entire day began to wane. I hadn't had a blast since draining my stash before walking into the bank. My only thought was to get back to the guesthouse. I wanted to lay all the cash onto the bed and see Da's expression. I wanted us to spend the night smoking and rushing triumphant around the city dumping dollars at Naga and the fish games, revelling in complete excess. Collecting the two-grand back from Lin, I then switched out my Vietnamese SIM for my usual number in Cambodia. As expected, Stan's response was waiting for me.

+855294669338

<I am not owing you… I am not your worker. Be careful the way u speak and what u say. Hope u realize what u are doing n return to your senses. But be assured that no one steals from me…. am waiting to hear how u intend to return the money before we can talk about future.>

I knew the road between Saigon and Phnom Penh like the back of my hand. All the busses coming from Saigon entered Phnom Penh via the slum community of *Khum Chbar Ampov* over

256

the Monivong Bridge. I knew if Stan and his crew were going to set up surveillance and try to pick me off, this is where they'd be. Reaching *Neak Lueng*, the bus lumbered its way onto the ferry, crossing over the river and into the desolate rice fields that nudged their polite amber sway all the way to the concrete high rises of outer Phnom Penh. Nearing the city, I shouldered my pack, walked up the aisle, slipped past Lin sleeping in her seat and asked the driver to stop. Perplexed, he brought the bus to a standstill in the middle of a desolate rice field. It was a surreal moment, standing there in the middle of nowhere, the dying sun sending fantastic hues swirling through low clouds threatening rare storms. Field workers, finished with their day's work, walked weary and slow in a short line along the road. Clothed in mud-caked rags, they filed past, carrying pickaxe's and hoes, nodding in sundry and sorrow.

I walked awhile with the peasants before flagging a taxi. Entering the city, I directed the cab to the guesthouse where I'd left Lyda waiting. She was there, lying barely visible under the sheets, the room illuminated by the muted glow of the television. I sat down next to her and ran my fingers through her hair. She mumbled incoherently, sat up and rubbed her eyes like a child waking to her day. "Ohhh Aaron, I wait for you long time." After holding her for a silent minute, she asked, "Your boss pay you?"

Laying there in the dark with Lyda's head in my lap, a sudden rush of exhaustion enveloped me like a leviathan from the depths, swallowing me whole. I wanted nothing but sleep. A sudden and random flashback shot through my mind of sitting back in the *Igreja de Nossa Senhora da Ajuda*, listening to the small girl singing her frail rendition of *Agnus Dei*. I craved nothing but a permanent vacation from all things chaotic. Away from Stan. Far from Mighty and Gabby and Peter and Master Hout and crazy women and desperation and plotting the next score. Silence from nagging landlords and unpaid rent. Relief from the constant suction of addiction and all the cancerous filth that trailed after it. I cried for sanctuary; an X-ray of my heart that for once, revealed cleanliness.

Chapter Fourteen

Phnom Penh
November 2014 - April 2015

It took a couple months to mop up the Nigerian predicament. My first days back in The Penh were spent sequestered away with Da in the guesthouse doing our usual and gloating over Stan's flood of desperate texts and pleading emails. For the first time since meeting Stan and joining the organization, I was in control. I wanted him to feel what I had felt all those times when he'd left me coiled and sweating in cold sheets, hungry, scared, and stranded with no resources on the other side of the world.

Perhaps this is also what Lyda had felt during all the times I had left her? Da and I had come into a rare season of wealth and ease. And though she remained docile for the moment, I continued to exert best effort to keeping her under my thumb.

After sleeping solid for two days, Lyda and I eventually emerged full swing back into the city, back into the debauchery, into the suck. She asked me to buy her a new purse and I did. She asked me to take her to Naga and place $300 on black, so I did (for a total loss.) Back in our room, she pinned me to the floor and explained (with alarming eloquence,) "I will know a man really love me when he give me one thousand dollars. I never have my own bank account before." That afternoon Da and I walked into Sacombank and I deposited all the remaining cash from the Saigon withdrawal, minus two grand into my account; keeping out a thousand for operating cash and another thousand which I handed over to Da. "We can open your account now Da, while we're here."

"No, I want to open my account at the FTB bank. That's the bank my mom has her account. Easy for me to give her money." Exiting the bank, I offered to go with her. "No," she answered, hailing a moto. "I go by myself. I have my papers. I see you back at the room."

Parting ways, I called Gabby, then rode clear across town to meet him. Seated outside a Llama Mart across from the Russian Hospital, I picked up another ten G's. I then continued to pepper him to be the supplier for the big deal I was trying to line up with Master Hout, assuaging his fears. "I've done business with him for a long time, Gabby. He wants a hundred grams. I trust this guy and he trusts me. As a matter of fact, I am the only person he has ever extended credit to. The only one! He's got the cash. He's just waiting for you to supply."

Gabby stared at the passing traffic, sipping his Coke, shaking his head. "Like I already said, I don't like doing business with Khmers. As a rule, I just don't do it. And I don't need to do it. I have a good client list now. All my clients are American or European. No Khmers and no Nigerians... as a rule."

"C'mon, Gabby," I kept prying, "Do this for me. He's willing to pay you five thousand for a hundred G's. I'll tell him the price is six and I can walk away with a grand as the middleman. It's a good score for everyone."

"I don't like it. I just don't like doing business with Khmers. In my experience, I've found them unpredictable. Let me think about it."

"Fair enough," I answered. At the very least, I had his ear.

After meeting with Gabby, I ran over to the flat and met with Mr. Sokhom. He sat stoic and expressionless as I counted out all the back rent along with a pre-payment for December. His affect was nothing but cold. "Are you still with your girlfriend?" He asked.

"I still see her sometimes around town."

259

He frowned. "Please leave her, Aaron. There are plenty of good girls to find in this city. I also want to ask you to begin preparing to leave. Your monthly rent payments are never on time, and things have not worked out the way I had hoped." I thanked Mr. Sokhom for his patience and assured him I'd begin looking for a new place. One more eviction didn't matter. Walking back into the flat, I lifted the blinds and opened the windows to circulate the stale air. After a quick shower I locked up and rolled over to the guesthouse to meet Da.

She wasn't there. A part of me had known something like this would happen. Living with Da was like living in a constant mantra of prayers, all which went unanswered. At midnight, with a sinking heart and donning my dunce cap, I set out to find her. After a fruitless pass through the fish games, I cruised through GSM asking any and all if they'd seen her. Parking at Naga, I spent an hour scouring the blackjack tables, the roulette wheels and the endless rows of slots. No Da. Checking out of the Lucky 2, I returned to the flat and resumed my normal operations, making deliveries around town and always on the lookout. Three days after handing her the thousand, I was sitting on the couch figuring finances from the Saigon gig when she called. "Hi." Her voice was small and tired.

"Hi."

"What you doing?"

"Waiting for you, Da." I answered, once again walking the fine line between coddling her and ripping her head off. "What do you think I'm doing?"

After a long thin vapor of silence, she creaked her apology. "I not have any money, Aaron. I sorry."

"Come back to the house. When you get here be very quiet. Call me from the moto driver's phone. I'll come down and pay him and then bring you in. But you must be very quiet. Mr. Sokhom does not want you here. Remember?"

She showed up just past four and did as she was told. After tiptoeing down the stairs and paying the moto guy I snuck her back into the flat with as little noise as possible.

Lyda's return typified the classic prodigal daughter homecoming. She looked horrible. She was in the same clothes I'd last seen her in. Her hair was frazzled. She appeared gaunt, as if she'd been eating from a pig trough. She avoided all eye contact, and once in the flat, made her way directly into the bathroom and closed the door. There was no discussion as to what she'd done with the money I'd given her. Every cent of the grand swallowed down the insatiable gullet of addiction. Any normal person would have reacted with rage. I had no rage left—only a residual urge to continue breathing, no matter how slight.

Da emerged naked, shivering and coughing from the steaming shower. I wrapped her into a towel and helped her to bed. Neither of us had any words. We moved together, slow and gentle. Brushing her hair and kissing her salty skin, I hovered over her like a priest, anointing her forehead and throat with gentle finger swabs of Vicks VapoRub, then cradling her into my best ceremony of absolution.

My evolution into a crisis junkie had come gradually: a metamorphosis I didn't seem to mind. All disappointments, failures and dreams dissolved over the past two years had rendered me in a peculiar and complacent stasis, ready and willing to re-define the concepts of both hope and horror. The two words had become one and the same, and I'd become numb and comfortable to use them interchangeably.

I held her light in my arms. Not as a weight, but as in *actual light*. I stared, transfixed on her radiant glow—the color of the rise and fall of her collar bones until her breathing slipped into REM. Once Da was asleep, I finally responded to Stan's litany of pleas. I was nervous. I was swimming in the deep end without a life jacket and needed a coach. I called Peter and arranged a breakfast at The Rising Sun. When I rolled up, he was seated on the patio sipping tea and reading the paper. He reached across the table and gave me a warm smile and a clap on the shoulder. "Congratulations my boy. You did it! Lin told me everything. And by the way, thank you for your prompt payment." The waitress arrived and took our orders.

After some small talk, I alerted Peter to the recent events. "Ever since I got back, Stan's emails have been relentless."

"Of course they have! What did you expect?"

"I expected it, but I haven't engaged with him at all. I'm not really sure what to say."

"Do you have your laptop?" After powering up and tapping into the Wi-Fi, Peter asked me to read him Stan's messages. After listening to Stan's admonishments, Peter gave a slight scoff. "Okay my boy, this is what you write back." Taking a dainty sip of tea, he dictated as I began typing. "Dear Stan, thank you sincerely for your concerns. If it is relief you are seeking from your current and unpleasant circumstances, then I suggest you go find your mother, lube up her buttocks and bugger her deep in her arse…"

I collapsed in the chair. "C'mon, Peter, a little professionalism here? This is serious. I can't write that."

"Oh, you most certainly can! And you most certainly should! It's hardball at this point, my boy. And this is how the game is played. And you're playing for keeps. You've taken the money, and now you need to stand behind your actions. Not a time for hemming and hawing like some little schoolgirl. No negotiations. That time is over. You've taken control of the situation, so control it!"

With our breakfasts delivered, we both started eating. "Peter, ever since I got back, I've been trying to lay as low as possible. Just me and Da staying out of sight. I've ceased all sales around the city and am only dealing with one main customer. I'm avoiding all unnecessary movement. And when I do go out, I avoid all the places where I think Stan may be. I'm scared they're after me."

Peter gave another snort. "That's the last thing that'll happen."

"How can you be so sure?"

Wiping his mouth, he stared across the table. "Because killers don't send pleading emails. They kill. And if this organization was serious, they'd have popped you in the first twenty-four hours of your return.

"But both Lyda and I have been pretty much off the map since I got back."

Peter shook his head at my naïveté. "My boy… my boy. You think they don't know where you live? Phnom Penh is a small city, and you've got a wide audience in this town. They could easily track you down if they wanted to. And if they intended to snuff you, it would've already happened." Peter dipped his toast into his tea and swabbed up the last smear of his eggs. "From the content of his emails, it's clear to me that Stan is nothing but a low-ranking prick within the larger organization who happens to be your boss. He's mistreated you. And you've finally stood up to him and taken what's yours. Now you've threatened to expose him to his associates and supervisors and he's running scared. He has no idea what to do."

Lyda's cold morphed into a flu and she carried a low-grade temperature over the following weeks. At the same time, the curious rash that had appeared on my left calf quickly spread to my shoulder, and then to my neck. Seemingly overnight, the rashes swelled into boils the size of dimes, and then increased to the size of quarters. The infection eventually began oozing yellow pus and blood and I had to cover the areas with gauze. In the evenings, while taking turns on the bong, I made Lyda tea, brushed her hair and applied her VapoRub. I then would lay down and allow her to bleed my sores. She held a peculiar and intense fascination doing this, squealing in delight when a particularly hard pinch produced an excessive amount of discharge. Bending over me with the intensity of a surgeon, applying unbearable pressure, she brought me to the threshold of my pain. "That's enough! Enough!"

"Whhoooo… that was a good one! A lot come out!" Puss oozing out of my body and out of my mind.

I put the word out I was looking for a new flat. It didn't take long to find one. Nik the Dick, one of my long-time customers was vacating his place—a two story walk up near GSM. The place came furnished. Da and I didn't own much anyway. Loading up our things into a tuk-tuk, we rolled up to our new flat on the afternoon of January 1st. New Year's Day. As Da set into unpacking what little belongings we had left, I made a jaunt across town and plunked down a $1,000 on a used Honda AX-1. My favorite bike.

Wrapping up the purchase, Gabby's number suddenly appeared on my phone. He wanted to meet. When I rolled up to the Russian Market, I spotted him sipping coffee at one of the outdoor cafes. I joined him, passed him some cash under the table. Back under the table he handed me my next pack of glee. I ordered a Coke. After passing a pleasant silence, he finally spoke. "I've been thinking about your deal with the Khmer... what's his name?"

"Hout. *Master* Hout. He's a crazy prick, but a straight shooter. He was my supplier before I started doing runs for the Nigerians... before I met you. Works on a strictly cash 'n carry basis. I'm known in the circle as *the only associate* he's ever given credit to. He trusts me implicitly."

After nodding on this for a moment, Gabby asked, "Yes, but do you trust *him?*"

The question caught me off guard. Hout had never screwed me on a deal. "I do. He's always been straight with me. Always good on his weight."

"Does he speak any English?"

"Not a word." I answered. "The deals we do have a language all their own. No English necessary. But if you want me to set up particulars around this deal, I have a girl who's a friend of both mine and Hout's who can provide good translation so we're all on the same page."

Gabby ordered a refill on his coffee and offered me a cigarette. We smoked in silence. After crushing the butts, Gabby eyed me across the table and spelled it out. "OK, here's the deal. A hundred G's delivered for a cash and carry payment of five thousand. Payable in hundreds, no denominations less than hundreds. I don't want to spend the evening counting out dollars. I'll bring one single package. Tell him to have his scale ready and I'll bring mine as well. I don't want a crowd. Just you and me, and he can have a witness there if he wants, but not a crowd. If we show up and he's got a house full of people there, I walk. Very important you tell him this. No crowd! I'm not looking to make friends here. This is a one-time gig. In and out quick. No more than ten minutes. Whatever you negotiate over the five is none of my business. Yours to keep."

I wanted to leap across the table and hug him. "I really appreciate this, Gabby. I'll make the arrangements." Lighting another smoke, I asked, "Where do you want this to go down?"

"We'll ride out to his house. I want to know where he lives in case anything goes wrong."

"Fair enough. I'll connect with him today and be in touch."

Parting ways on the street, Gabby was eyeing my new AX-1. "Nice bike."

"Thanks! I just picked it up an hour ago. Good machine. Strong enough engine, but small enough for maneuvering around the city."

"Yeah, I got an AX-1 back at the house." Straddling his vintage Buell he asked, "Did you buy that with the cash you took from the Nigerians?"

His question threw me to the pavement. I had no idea he had any insight or communicative connection with my recent goings-on. Word travelled fast in The Penh. "You know my former employers?"

"I know *of* them. Heard they've been fucking you around on jobs so you took 'em for some cash."

I didn't want Gabby anywhere near my other deals or privy to my movements. I cut the conversation short. "I'll make arrangements today for the deal. I'll be in touch."

265

I bee-lined over to GSM and found Chan standing on her long and shapely legs snaking up into a tight pair of blue jean shorts that sculpted her ass quite well, accentuated by a flimsy halter that she wore braless. Her face was painted with siren blush, evil lipstick and fake eyelashes rounding her out to a majestic, salacious perfection. She called Hout and arranged the Gabby deal. After slipping her a small rock for her services, I called Gabby to affirm plans.

The following week, Peter called and asked to meet. Seated at our usual gentleman's breakfast at The Rising Sun, he asked about Stan.

"Haven't heard anything from him since our last correspondence."

Peter gave a triumphant grin. "And you probably won't. Ever again. He's a loser and finally got what was coming to him." After a silent cigarette, Peter resumed. "So, my boy, now that you've taken what's yours and severed your relationships and ties with the Nigerians, where do you go from here?"

"I'm pulling product now from this guy, Gabby. I've set up a big deal between him and the Khmers for next week. Same old shit, I guess."

Peter stared hard at me. "Gabby? Short, dark hair, European? Friend of Double D's?"

"Yeah, that's the one."

He stared at me repulsed, like a disappointed father. "I'm sorry to hear that, my boy. Sorry to hear that, indeed."

"And why's that?"

"Double D... Gabby... that whole camp and everyone involved is nothing but trouble. One big crew of dope fiends and sex freaks. Double D calls Lin every few months and has her arrange sex parties for him and his friends. She has a difficult time finding girls to work. Apparently, they're into some real kinky shit. Complete and utter psychopaths. *Even I* don't do business with them!"

Dusk was gathering its slow possession over the city when I left Da with a nice rock and set out to meet Gabby. I loved the new AX-1. The way it tore through the city streets. I loved its compact design and capability. Perfect for the crowded streets of Phnom Penh—small enough to race around and large enough to exert raw power when needed. Gabby met me at a Llama Mart out on the Dyke road where Da and I had last been evicted. Rolling up to the mini-mart, I saw he'd arrived on his AX-1. Parking mine next to his, I took a seat at his table. The swirling charcoal skies darkened, and a thin drizzle began to fall. "Everything OK?" I asked.

"Yeah, fine."

Staring into the rain, I suggested a quick smoke. "Let's wait a few minutes. Maybe it'll slow up. It's a long ride." He shrugged and we both lit up. After a silent cigarette, Gabby flicked his butt to the ground and began fishing out his rain gear from his luggage box. I did the same.

Gabby's frustration was evident. He didn't want to be here. Once we were dressed, he mumbled, "Let's get this over with."

"OK. His place is directly west, a straight shot for about twenty-five, thirty minutes. The road's fine until about five minutes from his place the concrete turns to dirt. Potholes, so we'll go slow. I'll lead and take it slow 'cause of the rain. Road may be slick."

We made the trip without incident. When we arrived at the dirt trail that led to Hout's house, the path had been blocked with a row of large stones and sticks, a type of makeshift barricade. A bit odd, I thought. Instead of walking the bikes and parking at Hout's house, Gabby and I locked our wheels, chained the bikes together and left them at the entrance to the trail.

I led Gabby the three-minute walk to Hout's door. Knocked. A small, rotund Neanderthal Khmer answered and let us into the dark room with a grunt. Shirtless and shoeless, his belly flopped over his waist and his toenails were blackened with dirt. His shoulder tattoos were so poorly done that the ink had blurred into indecipherable black blobs. Walking through the small room, he held his head princely high, knocked on Hout's bedroom door, then took a seat on the floor examining the disemboweled parts of a small radio. He reminded me of a fourth-grade bully—the illiterate kid who took pleasure in cornering you and stealing your lunch money.

After hanging our dripping rain suits, Gabby and I stood uncomfortably until Master Hout emerged from his bedroom dressed in his military fatigues. He greeted me with his usual warm handshake and then turned to Gabby. Locking eyes, they both gave an obvious and reluctant start, mumbling a brief exchange in Khmer. Once we were all seated on the floor I leaned over and whispered to Gabby, "You guys know each other?"

"No, but we know *of* each other. We recognize each other from Prey Sar. We were in the joint together." That was the first I learned that either of them had been in lock-up before.

Unlike my previous visit with Chan, a cold atmosphere shrouded the room. No offer of tea, no cordiality, no ice breaking conversation. Master Hout smiled and held out his hands suggesting we get down to business. Gabby placed his small digital onto the floor. Reaching into his hip pouch, he withdrew a freezer bag filled with a hundred grams of crystals and placed it in front of Hout. Being the go-between, I opened the bag, selected a choice rock, placed it into the bowl of Hout's bong and lit the rock to a sizzle. Hout took a huge pull, then sat back with eyes closed, absorbing the rush. With a smile on his face, he passed the bong to Gabby. Gabby followed suit, then passed the bong to me. I in turn, offered it to Hout's silent friend who paused in his radio repair operation to take a long and satisfying suck. We all leaned in for a second hit.

The product was excellent, per Gabby's usual. Hout seemed satisfied. After a brief exchange in Khmer between Gabby and

Hout, we all lit cigarettes. I leaned over to Gabby. "What's up? Are we good?"

"Not sure. He likes it. Says its good. He wants it. But now he says we all have to ride back into town to show the product to one of his associates. He says his associate has the cash, and once he approves, then we'll seal the deal."

"Ride to where?"

"Back into the city… somewhere near *Phsar Chas*."

"That's his old neighborhood," I explained. "That's where he used to live before moving here."

Adjusting to the new plan and a bit befuddled, Gabby and I stood and began dressing back into our rain gear. Hout stood at the same time and in one fell swoop, scooped up the bag, disappeared into his bedroom and closed the door. Hout's thug, with his head bent low over his array of cogs and wires, plugged in a small device that resembled a dental tool that filled the room with an annoying hum and continued his operation on the radio.

After standing stupid for a few minutes waiting for the Master's return, Gabby finally eyed me with a piercing stare. "Where is he?"

"Not sure. Getting dressed for the ride?" I suggested.

Gabby reached up, pinched the bridge of his nose with his forefingers and sadly shook his head.

"He'll come in a minute," I assured.

Following the longest five minutes of my life, Gabby sighed, and ripped my eyes out with his silent glare.

"He's coming." I insisted, motioning to Hout's thug seated in the corner. "Ask his friend. Ask him what's up."

Gabby addressed the guy in Khmer. The idiot shook his head, clutching his small operating tool to his hip like some gun toting deputy. Acknowledging us with his silent grin, he walked to Hout's bedroom door and opened it. Gabby and I peered in and saw the room empty with the window left open. The thug, grinning and nodding, opened the front door and nodded for us to leave. The cool scent of rain filled the room. Gabby and I stood staring out at the continuous drizzle, absorbing the reality.

Sludging through the rain back to our bikes, I realized that Hout, in all his military splendor had commanded the shots, leaving Gabby and I standing like twin wooden soldiers with our thumbs firmly inserted in our ass. When we reached our bikes, two young Khmer sentries emerged from the darkness. Handsome and shirtless in the rain, their wet bronze bodies stood firm, each holding lead pipes in their hands, hovering over our every move.

"What's up with these guys?" I whispered.

"Hout's thugs more than likely, involved in the scam." Gabby returned. Gabby made a sharp turn toward the men, as if launching an assault. The men stood firm, glistening in the rain, flaunting their weapons into a better view. Gabby relented. "C'mon. Nothing left to do than get the fuck outta here."

I followed Gabby's taillight back to the city; the rain beading over my face shield like extraneous tear drops heading blindly into yet another relentless chapter of chaos and disorder. A peculiar sense of evaporation swallowed me whole, like racing through space and time with no mindful or spatial orientation. A piece of dust floating in a storm. A fragment of nothingness suspended in an unreal preoccupation of gradual decay.

Drizzle continued to fall. It was difficult to follow the road with my smeared vision. I was thankful when Gabby abruptly pulled over just shy of the city proper. We parked under the torn canopy of a small food stall and took seats across from each other. I sat speechless, staring at the bowl of soy sauce centered on the table. Nothing to say. Gabby ordered a coffee and graciously asked if I wanted one. In that moment, trying to make sense of what had happened at Hout's, I wanted nothing more than the earth to swallow me whole.

Coffee's delivered, Gabby took a delicate sip, then narrowed me across the table. "What happened back there, Aaron?"

"I have no fucking idea what happened back there, Gabby."

The food stall was tiny, lit by a single bulb. The table was small. Rainwater dripped through the umbrella. We sat through an unbearable silence. The only ones there. The cup of soy sauce centered on the table was surrounded with drips of black that had yet to be wiped up. Used napkins strewn across the dirty floor. The rain fell. Overhead, a million tiny mosquitos buzzed, colliding occasionally with the bug zapper. Insect corpses littered the plastic tablecloth. Gabby stared.

In my drug induced haze—in my refusal of reality—my only focus was getting back to the flat, into Lyda's warmth and into the pipe. I shook my head. "Don't worry, Gabby. It's just a miscommunication. I'll call him when I get home and ask him where he is. He'll most likely tell us to come back tomorrow for the payment. Everything's okay." Gabby's eyes were dark and full of nothing. "Gabby," I assured, "This is completely fucked up and unexpected and I understand what you must be feeling right now. But believe me, I will not let this go. I'll stay with you until this is all figured out."

Gabby ordered another silent coffee and absently paid the bill without tasting it. He stood abruptly and walked back into the rain to his bike. I followed. "You'll call him tonight?" He asked.

"The minute I get back home."

"And you'll tell him I'm waiting payment?"

"I'll arrange for us all to meet tomorrow. I'm sure everything's fine."

Gabby turned the key, pulled the throttle and gunned his bike into a furious roar. Speaking loud over the mechanical growl, he made himself clear. "You will take care of this! You were the middleman."

"Yeah, I'll sort it out. It's all cool…"

With no mental capacity to accurately absorb Gabby parting words, I waved him off with a weak smile. Climbing onto the AX-1 I rode to the flat. Collapsing back into the hallucinatory effects of Lyda's naked legs and arms, I was clueless to the severity of the situation. I had no accurate concept of Gabby's frothing at the mouth.

I called Hout throughout the night, but his phone was off. I called every hour on the hour the following day. Nothing. A call in the evening finally went through. Hout answered. Upon hearing my voice, he spoke terse for a few seconds in Khmer and hung up.

"Have you spoken with him?"

"I've been calling him non-stop on the hour. His phone is off." I neglected to let Gabby know that Hout had actually answered once, and then cut the call.

After an impossible silence, Gabby asked, "Should we go back out there and see if we can meet with him again?"

"That's what I want to do, but I don't know how we'd be received." I answered. "I keep thinking about those two thugs he had stationed near our bikes." After another pause, I added, "Hout carries a gun." This bit of information brought Gabby hunched over and wringing his hands. "Gabby, I want to make this right but I'm not sure how to go about it."

Gabby sat chain smoking one after the other, staring into the passing traffic, staring into space, occasionally digging into me with his menacing stare. His intensity was unbearable. I excused myself, entered the store and bought a Coke. Back at the table, and after many contemplative minutes he leaned into me and spoke in a hushed whisper. "You were the middle-man on this one, Aaron. And I'm holding you personally responsible."

"Gabby, really, I haven't seen him. What makes you think-"

"You know what I think?" Before I could answer, he continued. "I think you and Hout are working together. You were the mastermind on this scam. You set this all up to rip me off and you and Hout have gone on your merry ways with all my product. You ripped me off, Aaron. And I'm holding you personally responsible. A hundred G's selling at the price of five grand. And you owe me half!" He stared at me with his dead eyes, drumming his fingers on the table.

His words flooded over me in a dirty deluge, leaving me gasping for air, scrambling my brain trying to process the onslaught of my sudden drowning. "Gabby... what?" I stuttered. "What are you talking about? I had no idea Hout was-"

"-Oh yes you did. You set the whole fucking thing up. And now you owe me half! Half for my lost product. You understand me? Two thousand five hundred! You understand?"

"Yeah, I hear what you're saying. But I need to explain to you that you are completely wrong on this one, Gabby. *Completely* wrong. I would *never* have set up a deal to rip you off. I would *never* do that to anyone. That's *not* the way I do business. Everyone knows me in this town. Ask anyone!"

He stood abruptly. Crushed his cigarette. Mounted his bike. As he turned, I barely caught his last sentence spoken hushed and under his breath. "Two and a half grand, you will..." He rode off in a plume of noxious exhaust.

Falling back into an afternoon bed with Da, we spent the next countless weeks barely eating, burning through smoke, enjoying an occasional romp in the sheets, and throwing cash around like Monopoly money. Gabby continued his pursuit of Hout, and some sort of compensation from me via a continuous stream of erratic texts and menacing emails.

To: Mresnick474@gmail.com
From: Marc Gabriels Gaby6966@gmail.com
Date: Feb 17, 2015, 12:59 AM

Trying to buy time again... You have not addressed any of the issues nor answered any of my questions. I know you recently came into a lot of money so if you are not stupid you must have about 10k$. So why the fuck don't you want to pay? I don't remember anybody pissing me off as much as you. Pray you catch your next plane before I catch you. I understand you are clearly avoiding/running from me. That is ok. I will come see you... soon.

My reality with Gabby was truly frightening, and I did everything to distance my thoughts from his berserk and viscous bullying. I hated every interaction, every word of his misguided and misinformed rants. It was like trying to reason with an unpredictable lunatic; a bully on the playground. I continued to place random calls to Hout with no resolve.

Lyda and I continued our frivol days pulling at the Naga slots, stabbing away at the fish games, liquidating dollars at a reckless pace while throwing all cares to the stars. Nothing mattered. In our constant state of intoxication and sleep deprivation, the only thing sacred was our devotion to remain high as possible, supercharged, and completely unplugged to reality. Riding February into March, everything was confetti. Gabby's incessant and noisome texts eventually tapered off. For every hundred Da and I spent, there was another bill in savings. For every glass smoked, there were another thousand crystals waiting to be inhaled. Da was content—so I cared for nothing.

I hadn't heard anything from Stan since our last round of emails when I'd told him to go to Hell. I then began receiving emails from the man who had wired the cash to Stan. Whenever residual emails trickled in from the Nigerian predicament, I simply called Peter and resumed our gentlemen's breakfasts at The Rising Sun to seek his raw and twisted tutelage.

To: Mresnick474@gmail.com
From: Rcrinza@za.net
Date: 16 March 2015, 06:07

Hello Aaron,
My name is Richard, why i contacted you? there is my friend i have known him for long time and i trust for business. I transferred the money to the account bank 15,000 usd, and they told me that you are the person that open the account and you are the one who come and withdraw the money for them and they have been calling you and you have not come and bring out the

money to take your share and give them remaining to send to me so that i can do another transaction. So please i want to know the problem, why you haven't bring out money up till now? I have contacts all over the world. Believe me i will make you more richer in this business, once this transaction go successfully. Please return the $15,000.

Mr. Richard.

Peter frowned over his ham and eggs. "Where's this fellow emailing from?"

"Stan said the deposit came in from S. Africa."

Peter dropped his fork clattering onto the plate. "South Africa? South Africa! My boy, what are you fretting over? Can't you see what's going on here?"

Swabbing up the last of my eggs, I slide my plate aside, motioned for another tea refill and returned Peter's bravado with a blank stare. "Tell me, Peter. What's going on here?"

"Criminology 101. Simple and basic, my boy. You've fucked the organization, yes? Got all their panties in a bunch. Stan has all but disappeared. And now the guy who made the deposit is trying to re-coup his losses. Dismiss him!" Peter waved his hand. "In fact, if I were you, I wouldn't even respond. But if you want to continue your mamsy-pambsy polite exchange, simply explain to him what happened. Now c'mon, lets pay the bill and get back to the house. If you have the ice, I have a fresh batch of K waiting to share."

Later in the day and back in the flat I was on the couch with an ice pack on my head nursing a demonic K headache from Peter's and mine's late morning escapades. Lyda had just returned from the local market and was preparing something in the kitchen. I keyed up the laptop and spun off a return email to Richard, the invisible face in S. Africa. Peter had proved correct on one account: The "Nigerian Cartel" I'd been working with for the past year had turned out to be nothing more than a loose organization of low level criminals trying to eke out a living under a ruse of severe disorganization and fruitless intimidation. I never heard from Stan or Richard again.

Moving into the last week of March the temperatures suddenly soared, blistering the thermometer to a near hundred degrees. Lyda's rage equaled the rise. Her animal instinct sensed we were nearing the end of the party, and she fell into a thick and suspicious prowl. I still had about twenty G's hidden away, but with my contact severed with Stan and my relationship with Gabby on full strain, I started to worry. I decided to put a stop to sales for a spell until I could locate a new and reliable source for my supply.

With the Nigerians out of the way, Da and I once again began to circulate freely around town. One evening after blowing through a few twenties at the fish game, Da and I took a stroll through GSM. The Mall was in full swing with ex-pats drinking themselves silly, ogling the girls. Music blared. Swarms of girls, painted up and dressed in their skimpy best filled the place strutting their stuff, hoping for a score. Same weary faces, same redundant scene, everyone intent on celebrating unobtainable excess and killing themselves in the process. We took seats in the center of the chaos outside the Swiss Bar and ordered Cokes. Lyda asked for a fiver for some crab legs and off she went. A few of the girls stopped and asked for hoons. "Nothing for sale right now. Check in next week and I'll have something." Lyda returned with her snack and as she started munching, my heart sank as a text from Gabby chimed in.

<Where are you? I want to meet.>

<At GSM but not for long. Going home soon. What's up?> I answered.

<I too at GSM. Where are you? We meet now.>

I ordered Lyda a beer and told her to stay put. I then walked down the street to Katy Peri's Pizza, ordered my usual double cheese and shrooms, and took a seat. Two and a half weeks since I'd last seen Gabby, and when he walked up, I was floored with his enormous wave of negative energy. I offered my hand and he looked away, pretending not to see it. "What's up Gabby? Everything Okay?"

Jittery as Hell, he took a seat scanning the street with dark and flickering eyes—high as a satellite, but on what I couldn't tell. "No, everything is not *okay*." His pronunciation ringed of a loud and clear sarcastic mimic. Before I could begin to try and iron things out, he hissed across the table. "You seen him? You speak to him?"

"Hout? No, I continue to call him but he-"

"-Oh, I'm sure you've seen him." He stabbed me with his leaden eyes.

"Gabby, how are we going to solve this? I can't stand your violent texts and emails. How many times do I have to tell you that I had nothing to do with Hout ripping you off? I had no idea he was going to-"

"-You owe me money and you will pay. That's how we're going to solve this. You figure it out. Fucking pay me. And *you will pay me*, one way or the other." He shoved back from the table and disappeared into the foot traffic.

I returned to Lyda carrying my pizza, dizzy and spiraling. "C'mon Da, let's go home."

Back at the flat I devoured the pie, tucked Da into bed with a small rock to end the day, then situated myself on the couch and sent Gabby a text.

`<I don't know what to say. The deal with Hout was NOT a set up. No way. Why do you think this? I would NEVER do that to anyone. NEVER! My reputation speaks for itself.>`

Loading a glass, I spent the next hour smoking and waiting for his reply. Nothing. Nearing dawn, I wandered into the bedroom to find Lyda sprawled naked and masturbating on the bed. Her thin arm fell out of the sheets and pulled me in. It was Wednesday the 1st. A new month. April Fool's Day. Unable to rid my mind of Gabby's parting words, and with my hernia bulging from my groin, I laid next to Da in complete fear and turmoil. "You no have power?" She whispered.

"No Da. No power tonight." The last sound I heard was Da's sardonic laughter filling the room with her hideous scorn aimed at my impotence.

Waking late afternoon on Thursday the 2nd, I reached for the phone to check messages. One message from Mighty. Nothing from Gabby. The tension continued to simmer. Lyda appeared gorgeous lying next to me; pure in her nocturn drowse with her long black hair spilling over the pillow, savage in her temporary tranquility. I kissed her cheek. She coiled with a whimper. Dressed, I set out to meet Mighty at GSM.

GSM was dead. A few of the bars were opened and waiting for early customers, but overall, the place was a ghost town. I found Mighty seated at the Swiss Bar sipping a soft drink and scrolling through his texts. "What's up bro? Have a seat."

"Nothing happening, Mighty. Nothing at all." I thought to inform him of the recent developments. About settling up and severing ties with the Nigerians, and the whole Hout and Gaby debacle. "I had a falling out with my crew and I'm not drawing product from anyone at the moment. Things are tight. I've closed up shop until I can figure a new source."

"Damn, dude. Are you serious? I got calls coming in all regular like and I need a score. I was hoping for at least ten G's today. I thought you were pulling from Gabby?"

"Was. Now that's on the back burner also. Me and Gabby are in the process of sorting out a misunderstanding. Things are really fucked up, Mighty. Let me tell you what happened."

Mighty listened intently as I spilled out the whole Gabby and Master Hout debacle. My summation of the story left him ordering a morning beer and shaking his head. "Didn't I warn you not to get involved with that whole Gabby scene?"

"Yes, you did. And so did three other people."

"Bad crew. Gabby, Double D. Bad rep. And everything that goes with it. I've always avoided dealing with them as much as possible."

"Well, it's too late for me. I'm sucked in and sucked deep with no fucking idea what to do. He's leaning on me hard and I don't want to pay him for his loss. I mean, why should I? He's the one who went to the gig, laid his product out on the floor and allowed the buyer to walk out the door with it. True, I was the middleman, but I had no hand in any set up like Gabby thinks. No hand whatsoever! In the end, he's the one who allowed himself to get ripped off. And now he's holding me fifty percent accountable! No way. No fucking way am I paying him! What do you think, Mighty? What should I do? What would you do if you were me?"

After draining his beer and ordering a second, Mighty lent his wisdom. "It's a tough place to be, for sure. Gabby's a complete sociopath. You know this. So, when you deal with him you need to know you're not dealing with a rational or reasonable person. This is what makes it difficult. True, you were the middleman, and in all honesty, I think you do hold a part of the debt. But on the other hand, it was his decision to attend the meet and throw his product onto the floor. That part is clearly his fault. So, I think some kind of compromise needs to be agreed upon. Not sure what. But this is the way I think you both need to approach it."

"Fine. But therein lies the problem. Like you said, Gabby's a nut, and it's hard to deal with a guy who can't think straight. And that's where I find myself... dealing with a complete psycho."

Mighty licked the last of his beer and gathered his pack. "Well, whether you sort your shit with Gabby or not, let me know asap! I need supply and I need it now. If I don't hear from you in a week, I'm gonna have to go scrounging for new source. Feel me?"

"A week maybe. Two at most." I lied. "I can do you three G's right now but that's all I can leak." After some seconds, I added, "You can probably call Gabby directly if you're in a real pinch. I know you're already pulling your H from him. Why wouldn't he sell you the ice?"

Mighty shrugged. "He probably would, but like I said, I don't like dealing with him on any regular basis. The guy's clearly a nutter."

I lit a cigarette. Mighty and I sat staring into the slow afternoon traffic rolling down 51. A couple of tuk-tuk's parked with ex-pats trying to lure tired hookers into cheap deals. A few vendors setting up their carts in front of the Heart of Darkness Bar. Out of nowhere, a man suddenly appeared on a moto, slowed to a stop directly in front of the Swiss bar and parked about fifteen feet from where we sat. The man took off his helmet, turned and met me with a full-on stare. I froze. "Mighty," I spoke softly. "Keep your eyes directly on me. Don't look at the street."

He met me with a steady gaze. "I gotcha. What's up?"

"On the count of three, slowly stand with me and walk back towards the parking area. When we get to the corner of the Swiss Bar make a sharp left. Once we're out of view from the street we need to get the fuck outta here. Understand?"

"On your count."

"Three. Two. One. Now." We stood in unison, walked calm to the corridor and once out of sight, made a sprint about thirty yards through the mall and out onto the street near Pontoon Bar. "Go your own way, Mighty," I huffed out of breath. "You're Okay. But I need to disappear. I'll call you later to explain." Parting with Mighty, I continued my sprint down 172 and dodged into a maze of alleyways. Hailing the first moto I could flag, I directed him away from the mall, zig-zagging streets and peering over my shoulder all the way to Orussey market. Heart pumping, I jumped off and dodged into one of the countless food stalls, took an obstructed seat in the rear and disappeared behind the pages of a Khmer newspaper.

The man who had randomly pulled up on 51 and stared me down was Stan's sidekick, Sand. The handsome man from the Frangipani. The guy who'd always appeared silent and stoic in the back seat of Stan's Escalade. The man in the red beret. I'd taken the money. Told them all to go to Hell. And now the Nigerians were tracking me.

In absolute panic, I decided Da and I needed to hole back up for a while, only venturing out of the house for groceries, smokes and other necessities. For the next four days we sequestered away with nothing but our drugs and loneliness. I didn't mind at all. I welcomed it. Both Da and I had near mastered the process of escape. Her reasons for escape were more obvious than my own, but it pretty much resulted in the same thing. Countless disappointments. Immeasurable pain. Life films of the horror genre spinning endlessly on the undersides of our eye lids. So much easier to hate. The former presents itself as an impossible weight. Left with the choice between forgiveness and hate, we both had gravitated towards the latter.

The process of continual hating carried with it a simple and pure and incredible exhaustion. And the rivulets of this lethargy emptied into a peculiar pool of stagnant apathy. The most dangerous of all places. And so here we continued our struggle to breathe. And in perfect sync with our collapsible intrigues with life, we simply didn't care anymore.

Sunday morning. Emerging from a fifteen-hour sleep, I reached for the glass. I lay still, smoking, listening to the sparrows. In the last week, they had built a small nest in the nook just above our window jamb. I could hear Lyda shuffling around in the next room. The churn of the washing machine.

Properly stoned, I shuffled out and took a heavy seat on the couch. A beautiful morning, with the balcony door left wide open and vibrant sun spilling into the room. Da had taken time to tidy the place. The dishes were washed and put away. All clutter had been cleared. She had been to the market. A small army of vegetables were lined up on the kitchen counter, ready for her lunch prep. She'd even taken a moment to light a stick of incense. The aroma swirled through the room filling it with a rare sweetness. The place looked great, as if prepared for visitors. I gathered her into my arms and thanked her with a kiss. She looked at me with a peculiar smirk. "You know the birds in the window? They make eggs. Today I look into their little grass home and I see they have two eggs."

"Really? That's beautiful! Show me!"

I followed her into the bedroom. She situated a chair next to the window which served as a ladder. She climbed up first, peered into the nest, and then it was my turn. Sure enough, there were two blue speckled sparrow eggs. "Wow! So small."

Back on the couch we passed the glass back and forth for an eternity of lazy minutes. I explained to her the importance of her never touching the eggs. "When you touch the eggs Da, it's like trying to interfere with the normal process of things." My cautions were all gibberish to her and she dismissed me with a playful squirm. I powered up the laptop and began selecting tunes to compliment the moment. I settled on Cocteau Twins, Blue Bell Knoll. As *Carolyn's Fingers* filled the room with her ethereal gloom, Lyda turned and greeted me with her most beautiful scowl. "What this bullshit, huh? What language she sing? *Tzzz*. Why you not play some real music?"

She stood and abruptly turned her attention back to folding clothes while I dissolved into a reverie, contemplating the sting of her constant and static disdain. In the moment, nothing could have been more perfect. Her proverbial *Tzzz* leaving me chocking on my own self-inflicted misery. I loved my misery with her. I'd long ago given myself over to her emotional vacancy and verbal lashings as a sort of purging for my own lack of emotional potential. I'd died years ago, and since had become reliant on her hate to remind me I was still alive. I'd become her inert and unlovable plaything. Her stigmata martyr.

I reached for the bag and selected another rock. A gentle but deliberate knock sounded at the door. Having received no texts and anticipating no visitors, my heart collapsed. Before I could speak to remind Da of our chaos, she unlatched the dead bolt and opened the door.

Chapter Fifteen

Phnom Penh
April - May 2015

A man who I had never seen before stepped cautiously into the room with a sick cartoonish smile spread wide over his thin whiskered face. Dressed in jeans, black shit-kickers and a black leather jacket entirely out of season, he bore an uncanny resemblance to a young Stephen Baldwin, the actor; could have passed for his twin. I stood. "Can I help you?"

He turned, shut the door quietly and faced me for a silent and uncomfortable moment, smiling at me like an old friend. I could see Lyda in the bedroom. She had the chair pulled up to the window and was checking on the eggs again. She had no angle on our new visitor. "Can I help you?" I repeated. The man just stood there creepy and smiling. An adrenaline rush swam over my face. "Listen, I don't know who you are and I-"

"-But I think I know who you are." The guy answered slowly, choosing delicate words with a saccharine kindness, as if suddenly figuring out the answer to a riddle. "You must be Aaron. Am I right?"

"I am. And who the hell are you? I've never met you or seen you before and you're standing in my house uninvited. So, I'm going to ask you to please leave."

He held out his hands in a motion for me to calm down. "Now, now. No need to worry. This will only take a few minutes. I have a situation I think you can help me with." He began crossing the room, circling around the coffee table. "Why don't we just take a seat and talk for a few minutes?"

I moved with him in a slow, cautious dance, keeping the coffee table between us. "I'm not sitting or talking with anyone I don't know. And again, you're uninvited. So, unless you tell me your name-"

"Fair enough." He sighed. "My name is Danny." He introduced himself without extending his hand. "I'm known around town as Double D. Got that nickname because I like to play blackjack. And when I play cards, I like to double down. It adds an element of tension to the game, don't you think?"

Lyda came oblivious through the room carrying an armload of clothes to the machine. Passing us, she tossed a silent glance at Danny and continued onto the balcony. Danny watched her move through the room. "Hey, I know you!" He then turned his smiling attention back to me, pointing to Da with his thumb like a hitch hiker trying to flag a ride. "I know her." He assured me. It was the worst thing he could have said. The fact that he'd been with her sent my already scrambling brain into a whir and churn of protective and jealous rage.

He took a slow seat on the couch and scanned the room. "Nice little place you got here."

"What do you want, Danny?" I asked, still standing.

"What I want is for this here visit to go smoothly. What I want is for you to sit down." He patted the space next to him. "C'mon Aaron, have a seat. This should only take a minute." It was then I noticed the ring he wore on his right hand, middle finger. It was a silver band, with a single cone-shaped spike protruding out about a quarter inch.

I took a seat on the far end of the couch. "That's right." He assured. "Just relax." He spoke to me like I was a child. "Now. To get right to the point, I'm here to discuss some business with you. And I'm here on behalf of an associate of mine. You know Gabby, don't you?"

284

"Cut the bullshit, Danny. You know I know Gabby. And you obviously know that he and I are in the process of trying to sort out a business deal. So why don't you let us resolve the issue and get the fuck out of my house."

He took my reply in perfect stride. "Well, I appreciate your forthright answer, Aaron. And now that we have that cleared, if you don't mind, I'm going to call him on the phone right now. He's very close by. In fact, he's waiting down on the street just in front of your place. And as I understand things, he's been wanting to meet with you. He'll be happy to know you're here and wanting to resolve the dilemma."

Danny punched Gabby on speed dial, signaled him with a single ring, then hung up. He then turned his attention back to me and tried filling the tension with small talk while we waited for Gabby to arrive. "So, how long have you and your girl been here? What's her name again? Linda? Lina? I can't seem to remember..." As if on cue, Da walked back through the room on her way to the bedroom. "Excuse me Miss. What's your name again?" She passed him silently without a glance. The mental screws he was turning were excruciating. Intimidating. Wearing me down completely on a shattered Sunday morning.

An eternal minute later, without a knock, without a word, Gabby entered the room. He appeared as usual wearing jeans, red sport shirt and his proverbial scowl with brow furrowed low over his dark eyes stabbing me from across the room. Like Danny, he turned and closed the door behind him without a sound. Danny and I stood in unison. Gabby moved slow through the room around one side of the coffee table. Danny moved around the other; the two of them closing in on me like buzzards circling down on their prey. Backed into the corner, my last thought was to raise and wrap my arms around my head.

Lyda's screaming voice. "No... no... stop... now!" I focused in. Saw the vague shape of her slender and gorgeous legs in a flurry of dance. I was on the floor. Staring strangely at the place where the drainpipe from the kitchen sink connected into the wall. I felt her thin arms pulling me to my feet. Instantaneously I was transported across the room. When I woke to full consciousness I was standing at the door. Gabby on my left. Danny on my right. Both with their arms laced under my shoulders, holding me upright like brothers in arms.

"Easy there... easy..." It was Danny's voice soothing me. "I must say Aaron, you took that really well. Steady there. You okay?"

"Okay." I mumbled. Da stood stoic directly in front of me swabbing my face with a bloody towel. My scalp and face felt sticky and wet. I reached up and ran my fingers through my hair. Everything sticky and warm. "I'm bleeding."

"You'll be okay." Danny assured. "Your girl is taking good care of you... whatever her name is."

I focused in on Da and her thin fingers working on me like a disenchanted nurse. Danny, serving as a crutch, walked me to the couch. "Ok, now that the hard part's over why don't we all take a seat and figure some things out." Danny continued with his pseudo mafioso persona while Da left us to mop up my blood off the floor. Gabby sat pouting in his continued silence. "Okay Aaron, here's where we're at. Gabby has told me everything from start to finish. And you owe him some cash."

"And you're here to try and collect?"

"See there, I knew you were bit above the average guy. That's exactly right. We're here to collect."

"Well that's typical." I slurred. "You come into my home on a Sunday with guns blazing, knock me around and then sit me down to take my cash and all on the testimony of a one-sided story? You and your visit stinks of bullshit, don't you think?"

Danny raised his eyebrows. "Do you have a side to the story?"

"Fuckin-A right I have a side to the story." I shot back. "And I've told Gabby my side of the story a million times. And it's obvious that in telling you his side, he neglected to tell you mine."

Danny glanced at Gabby and Gabby looked away. He then reclined, crossed his arms over his chest. "Well now, go ahead Aaron. I'm listening. Tell me your side."

"What's the use?" I moved to the kitchen to exchange my bloodied towel for a new rag. "You come in here, fuck me up and then ask my side of the story?"

"No, no. You have a point here. Perhaps I should have..."

Seated back on the couch I spent the next few minutes recounting verbatim the deal gone bad with Hout. I detailed my role as middleman, emphasizing Gabby's error of irresponsibly placing his product into Hout's hands ripe for the taking.

Danny sat nodding his head. "I must say, that's pretty much the same story that Gabby shared. Thank you for your honesty, Aaron."

"So, if Gabby fucked up by laying the entire stash out on the floor—an amateurish move at best—then why am I being held accountable?"

"Because like you said, Aaron, you were the middleman on this one. And you must take a share of the responsibility." Danny answered.

"A share? How much, exactly?"

"Well, that's exactly what we're here to discuss. How much compensation do you think is fair? The sale was for five grand. And after talking it over with you both, I think that half of that would be an adequate compensation."

"Minus the ass kicking I just received? Exactly how much does a pound of flesh go for these days?"

The whole gig was a farce. Nothing more than a shakedown that Gabby obviously didn't have the balls or the spine to negotiate himself. He sat there silent, cowardly, wringing his hands like a pathetic drug fiend hiding behind his hired thug, hoping for the payout.

Without missing a beat, Danny answered, "Well, I see you have a nice bike parked out in front. That could be worth what, say... a grand?"

"I'm not giving you my AX-1." I answered flatly.

"Well, you're going to give us *something*. Otherwise, we're going to have to repeat these visits in the very near future. And believe me, I'd rather spend my Sunday's doing a hundred other things rather than making house calls." It was a threat. Clean and clear.

My only thought at that point was to get them out of the house. To secure myself and Da away from Danny's constant stares. The entire time he'd been there, Danny's sick and roving eyes had focused as much on me as on Da. "I don't have any cash here. I never keep money in the house."

"Where do you keep it?"

"In the fucking bank, Danny. Where do you think?" Before he could answer, I offered, "I have exactly one thousand in my account. Nothing more, nothing less. I can give you that, but anything beyond that will have to be discussed further. Call it a good faith payment." My offer was exactly what the two miserable junkie thugs had come for.

The three of us stood in unison. "Give me a minute. I want to get cleaned up." Gabby and Danny stood by the door while I disappeared into the bedroom.

Da sat small and cross-legged on the bed. "You need me help you?"

I dismissed her with a nod and slipped into the bathroom. Splashing water over my face and scalp, residual trails of blood stained the porcelain. Danny's spike ring had left minor cuts across my forehead, and a deep hole in the second joint of my middle finger on my right hand. Curiously, the injury wasn't bleeding. Tendons and muscles had been torn apart and left creeping out of the hole like strands of spaghetti. Da appeared at the door and stared at me. "You stay here, Da. I have to go with these guys to the bank."

"How much you need to pay?" She asked with a sweet innocence.

"A thousand."

"No!" She whispered. "I come. When we get to the bank you tell them you owe me three hundred. That way you only pay them seven." Da thinking on her feet. I brushed her cheek with a kiss and seconds later, the four of us filed out the door.

The ATM was a few blocks away. On the street, we walked in pairs; Da and Gabby ahead of Danny and me by a few paces. After a silent block, Danny turned and began spilling out a colorful monologue as if filling the Sunday afternoon with a breath of fresh air. "You know, Aaron. This whole predicament reminds me of a funny situation that happened many years ago. I was young. Freshly arrived in The Penh, I quickly joined up in business with a guy, a Frenchman he was, who decided to take me under his wing. He was my first contact into the business and set me up on my first job running a few kilos in from S. America. We started out very well, and built up a good rapport throughout the first few months, but after that, things started-"

"-Listen Danny. I couldn't care less about your history. And I don't give a fuck about listening to your pseudo-Mafioso vignettes where you try and share your stories in a lame attempt to teach me some abstract lesson. If you guys had any balls, you'd go directly after the guy who ripped you off. Why haven't you and Gabby gone directly after Hout, huh? I know the answer to that one. You guys fear him because he's Khmer. You come after me for the compensation because I'm much easier to deal with. Gabby's nothing more than a slimy opportunist who doesn't have the spine to solve his own problems. And you're nothing more than his hanger-on hired thug. I'll give you a payment today because, as you've pointed out, I *was* the middleman in this deal, and my integrity tells me that I should bear a bit of the debt. But beyond this, I'm not beholden to you or Gabby for any future payouts. So spare me from all your Don Corleone moral teaching crap. The only lesson I've learned through meeting you today— you're both nothing but cowards. So, if it's all the same to you, I prefer to walk in silence."

The four of us approached the ATM. With perfect timing, Da stepped into her role. "You pay me now? Huh? I wait one week and you not pay me!"

Regarding her as an annoying and insignificant interference, I asked, "How much?"

"You owe me one week! Three hundred!"

With a tired glance at Danny and Gabby I entered the ATM. Minutes later I emerged with the cash. After pealing off three hundred to Da, she parted in a huff, hailed a moto and sped off in the opposite direction of the house. I turned to Danny and Gabby. Gabby stood aside with hands in pockets, shifty, staring absently into the passing traffic. Not even enough balls to accept his own payment. I counted seven bills into Danny's hands. "There you go. That's all I got. Seven hundred. A good faith payment that Gabby will finally leave me alone. It's more than I feel obligated to give. Don't come to my place anymore."

Danny accepted the payment without a word, turned silently towards Gabby. The two of them walked off slow into the direction of GSM.

Walking up to the house, my heart melted to see Da waiting patiently on the street sucking contently like a small child on an ice cream cone. "You Okay?" She asked. I took her by the hand and entered the salon. The two daughters greeted us with suspicious eyes. Being a Sunday, it was rare to see them in the business space. No customers; but they appeared to be working, tidying up the place. They spoke to Da in quick Khmer. Da gave a curt answer to their inquiries, then led me up the stairs and back into the flat.

"The house owners, they ask why those men come. They heard the noise. They want to know why you bring trouble to the house."

With no mental space to process the situation with the house owners, I dismissed it outright. I collapsed onto the couch while Da prepared an icepack in the kitchen. She joined me seconds later, placing the pack on my head. I showed her my finger. She went into the bathroom and returned with a small bottle of

Hydrogen Peroxide, cleaned the wound, then wrapped it in gauze. With all the doctoring over, she handed me two-hundred fifty of the three I'd handed her at the ATM. Her keeping fifty was her unspoken commission for thinking on her feet. Over the next few hours we burned through a solid half G, enjoying what was left of the day. Curiously, Da voiced no inquiry regarding Danny and Gabby's visit, or the extortion. She accepted it as just another commonplace and terrible incident in our lives.

Danny and Gabby's unexpected theft had trickled me down to nothing. All the cash from the Nigerian score now gone. I still had about nine G's stashed away. And the AX-1 was still parked in front of the house. Aside from that, I was back to zero. It wasn't cash I so much worried about. It was the fact that I had no current supplier to pull from. All ties broken with Master Hout, with the Nigerians, and now certainly with Gabby. Product was everything. Money came from product. In a week, Da and I would suck down the remaining rocks, and then we'd truly be in serious trouble.

Later that evening Da asked me to take her out for *tok-a-loc*; a Khmer sweet drink concocted from blended fruits, condensed milk, an egg, all chilled with crushed ice. Her favorite stall was just around the corner from Mighty's place near the central market. Taking seats at our usual table on the street, I ordered a small plate of fried dumplings with a side of sweet n' sour for us to share. Minutes into our midnight snack, a terrible clash of metal grinding metal came from the street. We looked over and saw headlights of a stopped car illuminating a twisted moto with a small man lying next to it on the pavement. Within seconds, a small crowd of on-lookers assembled around the wreck. Da quickly stood and sprinted the ten yards over to the carnage. I could see her in the headlights, acting as security, arguing fiercely with the crowd, occasionally pushing them away. I thought to go and help her but there was no need. She had it all under control. Her sentry duty lasted until a tuk-tuk rolled up about ten minutes later and agreed to take the injured man to a nearby clinic. She helped load the wounded guy and his damaged moto into the carriage, then returned to the table. She took down the last of her shake and stared at me.

"What was that all about?"

"Man was hurt."

"I know that, Da. Why did you go over there?"

"If I not go then all people steal the man's money and take his moto." She stood with a sigh, tucked her shirt into her jeans, then cast a brief and exhausted glance up and into the starless Cambodian sky. "Okay. Now you take me to GSM. I want to drink a beer." In that moment, I loved her more than ever.

Da and I wandered into the crowd, took a table on the vast patio outside the Swiss Bar and ordered beers. The scene was typical for a Sunday evening, with the ever-present ex-pat drunks getting rowdy with the working girls. I sat watching Da as she wearily watched the scene. I was enamored. She had been amazing today. Carrying herself tall and stoic under Danny's lustful stares. Poised amidst the violence in the house. Calculating under pressure of the extortion. Gentle in her doctoring of my wounds. Thoughtful and protective of her injured compatriot who'd gotten slammed in the street. And now, sitting silent sipping a beer while staring reflective over the hideous neighborhood of GSM; the hotbed of The Penh's flesh trade. The neighborhood she'd relied on for so many years of selling herself to survive. But not now. Now, she was sitting with me, separate and away from the horror. Albeit, it was a thin line, but for the moment, she sat safe, nonetheless.

"You Okay, Da?"

"Yeah, I Okay."

"You need anything?"

"No, I not need." Da took a sip of her beer, then leaned across the table. "Aaron," she asked in a whisper, "Why that man look hard at you?"

"Who, Da?"

She tilted her head to her right, then rolled her eyes to the left. After a pause, I moved my eyes towards the direction of her agitation. Seated three feet away at the next table, Sand sat smiling at me. Close enough to reach out and lightly graze Lyda's hair. Close enough to insert an accurate bullet into my head. No way out.

"Da." I whispered. "You go now. Meet me at the house in thirty minutes." The words had scarcely left my tongue when she stood without question and disappeared into the crowd.

Deciding to meet the dilemma head on, I turned to face Sand and greeted him with a handshake. "May I join you?"

"Please do." He slid the empty chair aside and invited my presence. Tilting his beret, he narrowed me with an expressionless face. "I've been trying to track you down for a few days now, Aaron. I saw you here the other day with your friend, but you ran. Why did you run from me?"

I ignored his question. "Your name is Sand, yes?" He gave a subtle nod. "Well Sand, I think the better question is why are you tracking me?"

"Business." He answered, flatly. "I wish to speak business with you."

"So, speak." Heart thumping, mouth dry, I did my best to maintain composure.

"May I buy you a drink?" He asked. He ordered two Cokes. "Firstly, I know everything that happened between you and Stan."

"I doubt you know *everything*," I challenged.

"I know enough. I've taken the time to gather the whole story. I've spoken with many people involved. You may be pleased to know Stan is no longer in Cambodia." My ears pricked up. "He's been relocated to Singapore. Still working for the organization, but in somewhat of a lesser and remote position." He paused for my reaction. When I gave none, he continued. "I neither approve or condemn what you did. It's not my place. But I can say this. I understand *why* you did what you did. It all comes down to what we must do."

I took this as his silent endorsement. I couldn't believe what I was hearing. The enormous weight of paranoia I'd been carrying over the past couple months was evaporating off my shoulders. I countered the sudden rush of adrenaline by maintaining my best poker face. "So, where does that leave us?"

"I want you to work for me." He answered flatly.

"Sorry Sand. I appreciate your offer. Sincerely. But after all that's happened, I promised myself I will never work for the organization again. Thanks, but the answer's no."

He returned this with a slight smile and pierced me from across the table. "There is no organization, Aaron. Just me. I work independently. You can look at this as a sort of joint business venture between just you and me. I'm what you'd call a *start-up*. And I need a man like you who has experience, has a local clientele already established, and who knows the business."

"You want me to run locally for you?"

"Yes, for starters. And as far as international runs are concerned, I'm putting a job together in Taiwan that will happen sometime in the next few months."

After warming up to his details, I finally asked, "What's your price on a G?"

"What were you paying to Stan?" He answered.

"Too much."

"Well, I have a reliable local supplier, and strong buying power. How does $33 per unit sound?"

I'd been paying Stan much higher than that, and then had moved on to Gabby paying $43. Since first throwing myself into the game two years ago, Sand's price was by far the lowest I had ever been offered—one step away from the rock bottom wholesale rate. I'd finally made my way up the ladder only one rung away from the main source. "Good price. But with a price like that, I naturally doubt the product."

Sand coyly removed a sac from his pocket and slid it under the table. "Try it out for yourself. If you don't like it, then we simply walk away. No cost for this, by the way. A gift on the house." After exchanging phone numbers, Sand and I shook hands and parted ways.

Keying into the flat, my mind was racing. All in a matter of minutes, I'd been exonerated wholly and completely from all things associated with the Nigerians and had gained a line on a new supplier and potential employer. Sliding the deadbolt, I called Da. She answered with the sound of buzzers and whistles chiming in the background. She was at the fish game. "Da, I need you at the house. Come now." She showed up a half hour later and went immediately to check on her sparrow eggs. I could hear her in the adjoining room, oohing and aahing over the eggs soon to hatch like an expectant, jubilant mother.

I weighed the pouch Sand had passed me. It came in just slightly over three grams! A fine and admirable gesture. As I crushed the smallest of Sand's rocks and began preparing the glass, I called to her. "Da, come here! I want you to try this out and let me know what you think."

Da took a deep inhale and passed the pipe. I did the same. The rush was immediate. I looked over at Da for her approval. "Yeah, it's good. Where you get?" Without waiting for my answer, she took another hit, and then another. Before long we were both humming around the flat in full speed with the clock nearing 3:00 AM, busying ourselves intently on everything and nothing in particular.

I sent Sand a text just as the sun started bleeding its way through the blinds. `<Would like to meet to discuss things further.>`

He replied immediately. `<How about this morning at 9:00? I am always available for you.>` And just like that, I was back in the game.

Sand was already seated when I arrived. I eased slowly into the booth. "Are you Okay, Aaron?"

"Ah, good enough. I have a hernia, Sand. It appeared a couple months ago, and it seems to be getting bigger. Just a bit uncomfortable, you know?" Truth was that in the past weeks the hernia had increased from the size of a golf ball to the size of an apple, and the bulging deformity had forced me to forgo wearing a belt, putting a noticeable handicap on my movements.

Sand offered a nod of concern. "You must get that checked out. A hernia does not get better with time, only worse."

I dismissed his caution, thanked him for the gesture and complimented him on the product. "I'd like twenty more." We arranged to do the drop later that afternoon in front of the Lucky Burger on Monivong.

"This is a good location for me." He explained. "The street is busy with many side streets leading from it. Here's how it will work. Our drops will always be done in the same manner. If the drop is scheduled for let's say, 4:00 pm, then you will show up at a few minutes to four. You will park your moto in an inconspicuous place and wait for my arrival. I will show up on time, *always*. I will roll by slow. When you see me, you will pull out and follow me down the first side street I turn. I will slow to a stop. You will come up beside me and we'll do the exchange with no discussion whatsoever. Every exchange should only last a couple seconds. We'll then part ways, you in one direction and me in the other. Don't worry about the weight. My weights are *always* accurate, and the potency is *always* clean." I liked Sand from the very beginning. He was a world away from Stan's entitlement and loquacious arrogance. Sand's words were *always* brief. *Always* true.

The drop went exactly as Sand instructed. I rode immediately over to Mighty's and threw the bag on the scale. It weighed slightly *over*. And the kick was enough for Mighty to snap up half of it on the spot. "This is really good shit. You think this'll be regular?"

"Yep. Just met up with the guy last night and we did our first drop today. He says he'll be as consistent as my orders. Looks like we're off to a good start."

I returned to the flat but Da wasn't there. I made my way over to GSM and found her loitering at the fish game just down from The Walkabout. A dangerous place for her and a tense predicament for me. She'd long since blown through the fifty she'd skimmed off Danny and Gabby's extortion and asked me for a ten.

I handed it to her and watched her blow through it in a matter of minutes. She then asked me for ten more. It was a never-ending dynamic. Her asking for money to gamble away. And if I didn't pay it out, she and I both knew that she could and would walk the twenty yards down the street to The Walkabout and start soliciting for a John. It was as simple and as excruciating as that. I needed to get her out of the neighborhood. "C'mon, Da. Let's walk down to Swiss Bar. I'll buy you some crab legs." I reached for her hand and she pulled away. "Wait! Five more. I play another five and then I go." Twenty-five bucks gone all inside of ten minutes.

Setting Lyda up with a drink at the Swiss bar, I walked over to the crab legs stall and placed the order. With Da's addiction in full swing, I didn't even trust her enough to send her there carrying any cash herself. I brought the order back to her and she started in. Out of nowhere, Srey Leakh, a working girl regular, appeared and sat dawn. "Trouble at Peter and Lin's." She whispered. "Big trouble. Many police there!" Immediately, I paid the bill while Da wrapped her snack to go. We then followed Srey Leakh through the traffic on 51 down to the corner of 174.

The three of us peered around the corner. My heart sank. Halfway down the block a cluster of cop cars were parked directly in front of Peter and Lin's building, blocking all traffic on the street. Lyda started walking toward the melee and I pulled her back. If surveillance of the place had triggered the raid, then Lyda and I would surely have been noticed coming and going from Peter's building. After monitoring the commotion for half an hour, Peter and Lin eventually emerged from the building in cuffs and were placed into separate police cars. Parting ways with Srey Leakh, Lyda and I returned to the flat. After sucking down the last of her crab legs, she reached for the glass and asked for a rock. I selected some shavings off the bottom of the bag. "Is that all?" She pouted, lighting the flame to the bowl. We were both nearing three days without sleep.

"C'mon Da. Time to sleep."

Peter and Lin's arrest came with little surprise. The flow of drug traffic they maintained coming and going all hours was off the charts; far thicker than anything I would have ever dared. The following day, both the *Khmer440* and *Cambodiaexpatsonline* reported the arrest.

The anti-narcotics task force cracked down on the dealing and usage of illegal narcotic drugs at house number 57-59 E1, Village 5, Street 174, Sangkat Psar Thmey 3, Duan Penh District, Phnom Penh and arrested 3 people. 01. Name: Sim Lin, Nationality: Cambodian, D.O.B: born 1984, Profession: waiter (ringleader) 02. Name: GOLD PETER RICHARD, Nationality: British, passport number: 707479947 D.O.B: 1947 Profession: Businessman (facilitator) 03. Name: Lee Sovanna, Nationality: Cambodian D.O.B 1988, profession: Waiter (SLir) and confiscated the following evidence 1. Methamphetamine class narcotics (ICE) 2 packets that equal 4.69 grams 2. Marijuana 18.44grams, scales for weighing drugs, 2 passports, 5 bank passbooks, and a quantity of paraphernalia for taking drugs.

At 17:25 on the same day the (police) forces joined together to search another rented room at House Number 91, Street 110, Sangkat Wat Phnom, Duan Penh District, Phnom Penh and arrested one suspect called Iem Seng, Cambodian, born 1975, unemployed (drug caretaker) and confiscated Methamphetamine class narcotics (ICE) 2 packets with a weight of 2.57grams, 1 telephone, 1 motorbike, and a quantity of drug taking paraphernalia.

Peter and Lin were truly fucked. I could see by the report that at the very least they were staring wide-eyed down the barrel of a five-year sentence. I felt sorry for them, sincerely. It had been a rough month. Danny and Gabby's assault and theft; and now Peter and Lin's arrest. It was a blow, truly, but I quickly brushed it off. As long as I had Lyda and access to rocks, life was bearable. Sand's daily drops at the Lucky Burger were proving both convenient and profitable.

One evening in the flat, Da and I were going about our usual. We'd been up for a few days and I could see the fringes around her beginning to darken. The hole in my knuckle had grown over and the finger had healed itself into a discomforting trigger finger.

Da's phone rang. She withdrew it from her purse. Checking the number, she went into the bedroom and closed the door. A minute later she emerged carrying her curling iron and make-up kit and started to doll up. I stared at her incredulously. "What are you doing?"

"I go out." She answered.

"What do you mean *you go out*? It's after twelve on a Monday night and you haven't slept in two days." She answered by plugging in her iron and lining up her essentials: Blush, lipstick, various tubes and compacts and her small packet of fake eye lashes that I hated. After a minute of watching her putting the glitz on, I repeated myself. "Da, what the fuck are you doing?"

"My friend called. I go meet him."

"Meet who?"

"My friend. He live in Sihanoukville. Now he come Phnom Penh. He want to see me."

Reaching over, I unplugged her curling iron and began replacing her trinkets back into her purse. "Da, are you insane? You're not going anywhere. You think I give you this place to live and give you food and ice and take care of you so I can sit here and watch you make yourself up to go meet another man? Are you out of your mind?"

She took in this reality check without expression. After reaching for the pipe and taking another inhale, she stood, entered the bedroom door and slammed it shut. I reached for her phone that she'd left on the table, scrolled down to her received calls and copied the number. Minutes later she emerged from the bedroom fully dressed and stood by the door with her purse slung over her shoulder. "You let me out."

I stood and began pacing the room. "Da, you need to understand something. I *provide* for you. I *give* you everything you need..." It was a speech that I'd given a thousand times before. And listening to the words spilling out once again, I suddenly felt devoured by an overwhelming fatigue.

The expression on her face mirrored my exhaustion. Her lovely, curled hair shadowed her face, her eyes circled black and clouded over in a severe nimbus hue. Without warning, she slammed her purse down hard on the floor and whirled on me, unleashing full fury. "You think I happy here? You think I not have to *work?*" She was screaming now, her shrill stabs bouncing off the walls and through the open windows into the silent neighborhood. "You not fuck since they come and beat you! And they beat you like a little baby!" She crossed the room to the very corner I had stood in where Gabby and Danny had launched their assault. She then threw herself into a hurtful pantomime, playing the role of me getting pummeled. Bringing her award-winning performance to a finish, she picked up her purse and whirled on me once again. "You think I want a man who not fight back, huh?" Her stiff fingers stabbed me repeatedly in the chest, her hateful and unforgiving eyes blazing, melting me to puddles. Inside of thirty seconds, she had emasculated me in every way. I collapsed onto the couch, covered my face and began sobbing.

She offered a few steps and stood over me with all the compassion of an elegant egret, wings extended, gazing down on the final movements of a shimmering minnow.

In complete and pathetic surrender, I spoke in a fit of uncontrollable dyspnea, "Da, it's so hard to be with you. I love you. *Sincerely* love you. And I want to give you everything you want, but sometimes I can't. And I try to keep you here with me but I..."

I felt the weight of her small body next to mine. Her voice, impossibly sympathetic. "This life not good life for us. Sometimes I feel like I die here. Like you die here. This not a good life, Aaron. I have to go and find my own life. Sometimes I think I need to just go away and find myself. Some days I think I go far away from you, far away from everything, and maybe I go far away into the provinces where no one knows me. And maybe there, I find my life without you. Without Phnom Penh. Without everything. *Just me.*"

Her perfect poetry filled my head with a tender overflow; all my frustration and anger suddenly subsiding into the curl of an unexpected eddy, sucking us both into a short lull from our usual fury of frantic activity.

Wiping my eyes, I could focus on nothing but the clear view of Da stripped naked laying on some sodden mattress in some filthy three-dollar room, her slender fingers gripping the corners of sheets while some gigantic slob got the best of his menial offer of a twenty-dollar bill in exchange for an hour of her tired body. Articulating my gutter fears as best I could, I felt her arms suddenly cradle around my head. "I never know where we stand, Lyda," I sobbed. "I never know where you go… what you do. I never know if what we do is ever *real* for you."

After minutes of combing her fingers through my hair, she shattered the silence with a whisper. "It's always real with you." She stood and walked to the door. "Please you let me out."

I stood, unlocked the door and together we walked the narrow stairs and down through the dark salon to the front door. Before opening it, I tried to throw in one last threat with the hope that she'd stay. "Da, if I open this door and you leave, then I never want you to come back. You understand?" Turning the lock, she slipped into the street. I watched her walk the full length of the block in the direction of GSM, then turn the corner, never once looking back.

Da's desertion was the worst thing that could happen; leaving me to face the impossibility of my being alone. The concept of *alone* was so horrifying that I'd trained myself to dismiss the mere notion of it. I loathed mine and Da's destructive dynamics and the certain slow death it promised. The constant misery and torment of living with a working girl, our addictions, our day-to-day cycle of poverty; the entire maggot infested cornucopia was better than being alone. For nearly two years Lyda had been my lover, my hater, my partner in crime and addiction, the locus of my obsessive focus and my convenient source of distraction. I hated the reality we were slowly killing each other, leading each other to an early grave. I hated her for leaving even more and yet, I understood it with perfect clarity. Da wanted what all working girls want—what everyone wants: A life without *fear*. Walking out the door, Lyda displayed her willingness to pursue her life without me. Hers was a towering display of strength I knew I lacked, and it left me wandering mute through silent rooms contemplating the hollow and haunting absence of literally, *everything*.

I trudged the stairs, past the glaring eyes of my landlord and the two sisters dressed in their nighties and gathered on the darkened landing. As I passed, they mumbled something definitive in Khmer, eyeing me with disdain. Back in the flat, I reached for the glass and then replaced it onto the table. Wandering into the bedroom, I shut off my phone, turned out the light and lay in the darkness.

I woke hours later to the sounds of birds—not the usual chirping of the sparrows—but of a new sound of babies screeching for food. I pulled the chair up to the window and peered into the nest. Two new-born chicks peered up at me with their mouths wide open. Da had waited three weeks for the chicks to hatch. And now she was gone. The sorrow of this was incredibly dense and spurred me to the bathroom where I spent the first minutes of the day retching into reality. Wiping my face and sitting naked on the toilet, I examined my hernia. It was growing and becoming more painful by the day. I then examined my trigger finger, trying to extend it, only to have it snap back into its grotesque, abnormal angle. I was looking at two impending surgeries. With Da now gone, my only focus was to distance myself as far from reality as possible.

A soft knock on the door. Scrambling into clothes, I walked fast to the door hoping to gather Da back into my arms. Instead, the landlord and his entire family stood expressionless. The father handed me a piece of paper, awarding me my fourth eviction in the past fourteen months. The eldest daughter translated the sentence. "Our family want you not stay here no more. Please you and girlfriend leave." I stared directly through the paper, past the scribbled words, beyond the moment, surpassing the reality. The family stared at me with sheer contempt. When I gave no reply, the daughter applied the screws. "You go one week. You understand?"

This tenancy had lasted three months. I closed the door softly making the good family disappear. Tossing the eviction onto the table I thought, *an ironic shame that Da isn't here to receive it with me.* I did everything I could to push her from my mind. I spent the second night of her absence purging the place of any and all reminders. I gathered all her clothes and personals, bagged them up and tossed them into the back of the closet. I scoured the entire place thoroughly; gathered her hair from the shower drain and washed the sheets and pillowcases to rid the bed of her scent. Her absence spurned me to spend as little time at the flat as possible.

GSM was my natural draw. After meeting Sand for my daily pick up, I'd moto over to the mall, spend a few hours dishing hoons and quarters, and then around 1:00, I'd select one of the working girls and bring her back to the flat for company. I loved the girls; I liked the idea of getting them off the street if even only for a night. I enjoyed cooking hot meals for them, offering hot showers, a place to wash their clothes. I loved getting high with them and listening to music. I loved them as they lay naked on the bed; loved giving them massages and listening to their memories of their family and friends back in Kampong Cham; stories about their mothers and sisters and their children they no longer saw. That entire week Da was gone I must have entertained half dozen girls. Their company had *nothing* to do with sex. My hernia had increased to the size of a shot-put bulging from my groin. I was self-conscious about the abnormality and always kept my pants on. Their presence had *everything* to do with the fact that without their laughter, their simple movements and their companionship I would have gone mad contemplating Da's excruciating absence.

Alone again, I spent the days posting all my belongings onto the local buy and sell sites and making appointments with potential buyers. Lyda now gone, I wanted *everything* gone. I wanted to sell off all the remaining furniture and anything else I was carrying that was impeding on my hell-bent path to final destruction. By the end of the first week in May I'd liquidated nearly everything. And with no focus or energy to line up a new place to relocate, I was looking at moving back into the Lucky 2, paying a weekly room rent, embracing with wide arms a season of transient uncertainty.

My highest achievement of that week was meeting with Gloria at Clinic *Sokhapheap Thmey*. Stretched out on the gurney, Gloria rolled down my pants and rolled her eyes. "This needs immediate attention, Aaron. *Surgery like now*. Can't wait any longer. Your intestines are protruding through the fatty tissue."

"I can live with the pain, Gloria. What's the worse-case scenario?"

"Have you been experiencing nausea? Vomiting? A burning sensation around the area?"

"All of the above."

"Incarceration. Which means that within a month you'll more than likely experience a bowel obstruction. And if you can't shit, then you die. So, assuming you're not ready to die, let's get your surgery scheduled."

I lay mute on the gurney staring at the ceiling.

"I'll call my colleague over at *Visol Sok* Hospital. He'll do the surgery. I've known him for years. You'll be in good hands. The surgery will be inpatient and take about an hour. Post-op recovery will last four to six days."

"And the cost?"

"Assuming no complications, you're looking at somewhere between six and eight hundred."

Gloria left the room while I pulled my pants back on. She returned with a few pamphlets on hernia surgery and all the pre-op instructions I would need to follow. She'd taken a moment to specifically highlight one of the bullet points:

Eat normally on the night before surgery but take no alcohol after 8PM and nothing to eat or drink after 12 midnight except prescription medications.

"See that?" She asked through a biting and wry expression. Without waiting for my answer, she concluded, "That includes *non-prescription* drugs as well. When I took your vitals today your bp was off the charts. Might want to think about laying off the drugs, Aaron. Your current lifestyle will only result in three things: Prison. Death. Rehab. And I strongly suggest you opt for the latter." She turned and left the room. Given the circumstances, I contemplated death. Death by hernia? There were certainly worse ways to go.

My final night in the flat, I sat alone on the floor next to a candle burning through a new pick up I'd received from Sand. The minty inhale coated my mouth with the familiar tingle of slug-tongue and the rush scrambled my brain into a thick and appropriate quagmire. The place was empty, the rooms cavernous, with everything I owned shoved into my backpack, and some random kitchen items packed into two boxes. My phone rang. Number unrecognizable. "Hello?" Da's small voice leaked into my ear like burning acid. She said something about her clothes... something about wanting ice. She said she was standing on the street.

I held the door for her. Locking us in, I took my place on the floor next to the candle and loaded another glass. She stood still for a minute, then began wandering the empty rooms, absorbing the deadness of the place. "Where my things?"

I pointed to the closet. She opened the door, pulled the trash bag out and began rummaging through it. She then took a seat next to me and waited for me to pass the pipe. In an hour we plowed through an entire half G. Knowing she had no answers, I voiced no questions. We smoked in a pure and apathetic silence. With the glass cashed, I laid down flat on the hard floor.

She reached over and poked me playfully in the ribs. "Why you not speak me?" Her voice was calm. Sincere.

I bit my tongue against all sarcasm. *How was your time with your friend in Sihanoukville? Did you both enjoy a fun week? Did he pay you well? Did it feel good? Did you ever once think of me?* "Do you remember the eggs in the nest, Da? Did you forget? The eggs hatched, Da. The babies came a week ago, the day that you left. The babies are in the nest now. Go see." I whispered.

She disappeared into the bedroom. I heard her pull the chair to the window. "Ohhh, they so small. So beautiful. Come see, Aaron. Come look with me."

I wanted to share the moment with her, but something about it felt too painful. Staring at the ceiling, I silently declined her offer.

I loathed the sun's first threats; those silent moments when the first pink hues began thundering through the blinds with all the gentle sincerity of another day; crawling over my skin like an impending execution. I loved the feeling of my naked back on the floor. I sensed Da within reach and took comfort in not reaching for her. We'd passed the entire night not speaking but a hundred words; our mouths full of nothing to say.

I did one last lap through the house making sure it was thoroughly vacated. Da waited at the door. Hoping to avoid the walk of shame, I wanted to slip out before the family woke so we wouldn't have to endure their glares. Shouldering my pack and carrying the boxes, I motioned for Lyda to lead the way. She started out the door, then suddenly dropped her clothes bag to the floor. She walked quickly back into the bedroom, pulled up the chair to the window and withdrew the bird nest from the jamb. She then placed the nest holding the two baby sparrows inside her purse, picked up her clothes bag and made her exit. Leaving the key at one of the workstations in the salon, Da and I stepped out into the street.

We passed the awkward moment on the sidewalk. There was nothing more I wanted than for her to come with me. I stood silent waiting for her to speak. "So, where you go?" She finally asked.

"Not sure. Probably over to see Mighty. Maybe leave my things at his house while I look for a new place to live." It was a lie, but one my integrity was forcing me to tell. Aside from the ice, Lyda had become my second addiction, and having attained a week's worth of sobriety, I was determined to stay clean of her. Another part of me also wanted to give her what she had asked for. Over the past year I'd given her my every possible effort, provided her with food, fed her unlimited addictions and provided her a place to live. I'd handed her my heart to annihilate, and recently had come to understand that these things were not her necessities, but merely her conveniences. What Da ultimately desired was her freedom. Her freedom to come and go as she pleased. Her freedom to work, fuck, fail, survive and wither away on her own terms. Freedom to move about without any restraint, unbeholden to anything or anyone. She craved to embrace her own world with her own attempts. Her own downfalls. She hoped for her own chance to circulate through her own orchestrations, despite any potential truths to be realized, with all consequences left to the wind. The ability to live, lie, steal and love on her own conditions. All reasonable terms. And because I loved her, I agreed to let her go.

She was waiting for me to ask where she was heading. I remained silent. After a minute, she flashed sad eyes. "Okay. I go now." She took a few paces and then turned. "Aaron, maybe you can help me a little bit?"

"What do you need, Da?"

"Maybe you give me a little money to get a room?" In one motion I hailed a tuk-tuk and together we loaded our belongings and went rattling down the street.

I checked her into one of the cheap $6 rooms near GSM. I paid her room for the week. I followed her into the cubicle where she dropped her clothes bag onto the floor, closed the curtain and placed her purse gently on the nightstand. She withdrew the nest and laid her babies onto the center of the bed. Together, we sat staring at the two fledglings. They stared back with their small beady eyes, screeching through wide open beaks, demanding food.

"What do they eat, Da?"

"I go now. Buy rice." She returned minutes later with a small bag of rice and began pulverizing it into meal. Dipping her finger into the paste, she took turns feeding each bird until they appeared satiated. I stood, kissed her head, and moved to the door. She gave no notice to my leaving.

I returned to the flat to retrieve the AX-1. Balancing the boxes on the gas tank, I made my way slowly over to the Lucky 2 and checked into room 206. I knew the neighborhood well, and it was centrally located to both my pick-up point with Sand and to most of my regular customers. After situating and hurling through a hoon, I called Sand for my daily re-up. His return text came as a surprise, variating our normal routine that I'd come to enjoy. `<I want to meet you for lunch. Business to discuss.>`

Sand I had fallen into a comfortable and convenient rhythm; one that ensured both our mutual anonymity, and along with it, our mutual profits. For the first time in a year, I was making a comfortable living with daily pick-ups from Sand and drop-offs to Mighty for a gain of about a hundred dollars per day. Minus my forty dollar a day habit, I was still clearing enough to keep the rent paid and bread on my lonely table.

Sand and I showed up at the same time at an Asian fast-food joint near City Mall and took seats in a booth near the buffet table. Neither of us were keen on food. I ordered a Coke while he settled on green tea. Over the past weeks, we'd done about twenty drops together, each one like clockwork. Sand *always* on time. "I appreciate you meeting on such short notice. I know you are busy, as am I." I thanked him for his professionalism and told him how happy I was to be working with him. I admired his decorum. His etiquette and standards far surpassed anything that Stan had ever displayed. After small talk he leaned across the table and asked in a hushed voice. "Are you up for some real work, Aaron? The job in Taiwan is ready. It's a turn-around trip. Three days, and two nights."

"You know my history and my experiences with Stan when he used to send me abroad. We got a good thing going here. I don't want a bad experience to complicate what we have now."

Sand sighed. "I understand your apprehensions. And they are well founded. But believe me, I would never do anything to put you in jeopardy like Stan used to do. I think you can already see that I do not work like him."

"Yeah, but given my experiences, I simply won't agree to go unless certain things are in place."

Sand held out his hands as if presenting me the world. "Tell me what you require."

"Well first off I need a flight itinerary that includes a return flight. No *open-ended* return date like Stan used to arrange. I need tickets in hand, to and from."

"Done. What else?"

"$50 per diem, per day. All hotels booked and pre-paid for."

"Done."

Sand nodded patiently and thoughtfully while I outlined all the details and trimmings of the trip. And systematically, he checked all the boxes. "When will I be going?" I finally asked.

"That all depends on your hernia. I noticed you're still limping. Still in a bit of pain? I don't want you flying until that medical situation is cleared up. I need you in perfect condition."

"Surgery is scheduled a week from now, next Wednesday on the 27th."

"And how long will the recovery time be?"

"Doctor says I'll be up and running within a week or ten days after the operation."

"Very well." Sand nodded. "Then we'll be looking for you to fly sometime in mid-June." So far, he'd proven true to his word and precise in his deliveries and I had no reason to second guess his scheme. Before paying the bill, he slid me my order of twenty G's under the table.

Walking through the lobby of the Lucky 2, the boy at the desk stopped me, greeting me with his subversive grin that all young Khmer boys wear so well. "Today you move rooms." He instructed.

"Why?" I asked.

"Today you move rooms." He repeated, stretching his stupid grin to infinite proportions; a typical Khmer situation I had no patience to negotiate. After living in The Kingdom for eight years and having not mastered the language, I'd learned long ago that it was far easier to agree with an uncertain situation rather than proffer an argument. "You move please—room 408. You move now please." It only took minutes to pack and load everything onto the lift and settle into the new room. The cubicle on the fourth floor was a mirror image of my room on the second; the only variant being a new and elevated window perspective that afforded a more expansive view of the neighborhood.

The mid-day Orussey Market area was in full bustle, streets clogged with tuk-tuks parked and awaiting fares, food vendors filling the air with smoke from burnt chicken and beef skewers, and all forms of desperate survival evident in a proverbial ant farm urban scurry. Scanning the neighborhood layout, I was drawn to a curious sight. Directly across the street was an unremarkable two-story building. Grey and dingy, the building fell into perfect sync with all the other buildings on the block. But what caught my eye was the dilapidated structure perched on the third floor.

It was a one-story traditional Khmer wooden house. Nothing more than a shack, really, situated atop the two-story modern cement structure in the center of Phnom Penh. Amidst the surrounding urban sprawl and nearby towering skyscrapers, the tiny house was entirely out of place. The inverse would be like walking down a deserted beach and suddenly running into a small industrial complex. It was a curious sight. An object of intrigue. A somewhat cute and charming architectural anomaly built snug and hidden in the middle of the concrete jungle. I took a quick photo and enlarged it onto the laptop screen. The magnified photo

310

showed a small *For Rent* sign displayed on the door. Typical Khmer advertising. Whoever the idiot landlord was who'd hung the ad had failed to understand that the sign—*the entire house*—was invisible from the street. I copied down and called the number. A man answered. After thirty seconds of complete English/Khmer communication failure I hung up and made my way over to GSM to find a translator.

Rolling onto 51, sunset collapsed over the neighborhood, dousing the street into its familiar ambiance of enticing pleasures and promising hedonism. Small clusters of early working girls were assembling outside the bars in all their gorgeous splendor; the tables filling up with the regular and eager ex-pats ordering their first beers of the night, preparing for yet another evening of drunken and soulless pursuits.

Rounding the corner near Pontoon Bar, I collided with Kanya; a little waif of a girl who I'd partied with on numerous occasions. Dressed in dirty ripped jeans and a near threadbare AC/DC T-shirt, she came storming out of one of the fish game arcades with a dark scowl on her face. She threw into a short rant about losing her last five bucks. I explained what I needed, told her she'd be compensated for her time and followed her back to her one room hovel in ice alley.

She keyed the deadbolt. I followed her into the room. The sights and scents of her poverty smacked me full in the face. Her husband was sprawled out snoring on the bed in his underwear; Her infant son crawling around unsupervised on the floor. Dishes piled high in the sink. Roaches scurrying. Toilet filled with pungent piss. Kanya took up her baby, moved to prepare a bottle while I sat on the floor and loaded a hoon into the water pipe. Kanya passed me the baby and a bottle. I cradled the infant in my arms and fed her while her mother sucked down the rock. After the feeding, I handed back the child. Kanya placed the babe into a rudimentary crib then called the number to my future landlord and arranged the meet.

The next morning my phone rang. Kanya's cheery voice announced, "I'm here." I ran down to the lobby and brought her up to the room. After burning a quick hoon, I opened the blinds and pointed out the small wooden house across the street.

"The house owner will meet us at 9:00." Over the next half hour Kanya and I raced non-stop through another quarter G while waiting for the landlord.

Kanya and I approached a grey Mercedes SUV parked on the street directly in front of the building. A middle-aged man dressed in immaculate white pants and a red polo shirt stepped from the car and extended his hand. On three of his fingers, he wore gaudy gold rings; more wealth on one hand than Kanya would see in her lifetime. Kanya translated and introduced me. "Aaron, this is Mr. Hua, the house owner."

The three of us walked up the external staircase that ascended along the side of the house like a sort of fire escape. Coming to the entrance, Mr. Hua fumbled with an enormous ring of keys and unlocked the door.

Stepping into the front room of the small wooden house, we were immediately assaulted with the pungent odor of shit. Mr. Hua quickly unlatched the shutters and threw them open. The sudden sunlight sent a legion of roaches scattering and shed light onto the endless clusters of rodent poop littering the floor.

A short hall ran the length of the house from front to back, connecting a small common area, a small bedroom, a kitchen and a bathroom. Along with the piles of rodent shit, the tiled floor throughout was discolored with a thick layer of dirt. The kitchen counter was black with grime. And the bathroom was entirely spun over with an eerie dream of cobwebs. Mr. Hua spoke rapidly. Kanya translated. "This is the first time the house has been opened in six months. Mr. Hua apologizes for the filth and the condition. He has many other properties around the city that he would like to show you. Very nice properties... much nicer than this one."

"This house is great! I'll take it." To both Mr. Hua's and Kanya's dismay, I asked to sign the lease immediately. Locking up the place, the three of us adjourned to a small coffee house down the street and sorted out the paperwork. I handed Mr. Hua the security deposit and the first month's rent and by the end of the afternoon, I'd checked out of the Lucy 2 and into my new, little wooden Khmer house.

Chapter Sixteen

Phnom Penh, Taiwan
June - August 2015

I loved the new place. Its filth. Ugliness. The real selling point was its anonymity and the way the house couldn't be seen from the street. I imagined the look on Lyda's face when I would finally give her the tour through each room and the way she'd scowl and call me stupid for renting such a crap hole. I loved the idea of finally disappearing into the invisibility of everything and securing my own extinction.

After picking up my daily drop from Sand I headed to the hardware down the street. Armed with a gallon of bleach, liquids, powders, sprays, scrubbies, towels, rags, and a face mask I returned to the new house and set to work. With plenty of ice and nothing on the schedule I launched into a twenty-four-hour non-stop cleaning marathon. Once the place was scoured, I took inventory of the physical needs of the sad house. The plastered walls were an eyesore and needed a complete caulk, sanding and paint job. The tiled floors were discolored in a greenish-yellow grime. The kitchen and bathroom needed a complete plumbing overhaul and new pipes. The lighting was sparse, dark and dingy and I mapped out a plan to rewire the electricity to illuminate each of the rooms. As I took a complete inventory, I made a list of tools, supplies and intentions. Number one on the list was to keep my new location hidden from Lyda for as long as I could. She had largely been the reason for my last few evictions. I loved my new little Khmer hideaway and was determined not to lose it on account of her psychotic shenanigans.

Taking a break from the cleaning, I saddled up the AX-1 and went over to her guesthouse to check on her. She opened the door half dressed. The room was dark, illuminated by the glow of her afternoon soap opera. Empty Styrofoam carry-out containers littered the nightstand. She crawled back into the sheets and began flicking through channels. I sat on the bed next to her. "You Okay, Da?"

"Yeah, I fine. Where you stay now?"

"At a guesthouse, near Orussey."

After an awkward silence, she rolled over and slid the drawer of the nightstand open. Her two little sparrows fluttered out onto the bed. "You see? Now they start to fly a bit."

"Wow Da, that's great! You're taking good care of them. What do you feed them?"

"Rice. Sometimes chicken."

The tiny birds hopped and fluttered around on the bed, testing their wings. Lyda picked each of them up easily, toyed with them, then placed them into my hands. "This one very loud. He screams all night. But this one more shy. He sleep a lot." Sitting there in the ambient glow of the TV, I was entranced at Da's gentle observations, her attention to detail, her sincere focus on something other than herself. I watched her play with her babies, enamored at the way she picked them up and held them closely to her eyes.

"Have you given them names?" I asked.

She placed her birds back in the drawer and closed them away. She then let out a deep sigh and answered with her lovely scorn, "Aaron, why you talk like that? Birds not people. They not have names. They free." Enduring another awkward silence, she rolled from the sheets and sat up. "Okay. You go now. I want to sleep. I so tired." I leaned over and kissed her on her head, then opened the door. As I was closing her away, her small voice leaked through the dark. "You come see me again tomorrow?"

On the way back to the house I stopped again at the hardware and loaded up on tools for the renovations. A hundred feet of 18 AWG gauge electrical wire, an electric sander, a hand-held mini circular saw, five tubes of caulk and a stack of sandpaper. A call came in from Mighty. "Where you at?"

"A hardware near Orussey. Just moved into my new place. Want to swing by?"

By the time I checked out of the hardware and returned to the house, Mighty was waiting for me on the street. I keyed in and gave him the quick tour. "Well, it's certainly a complete and utter shithole. Lots of room for improvement."

"Exactly." I answered. "That's why I took it. I need a project, you know? Something productive and positive I can devote my time and attention to."

Mighty took a seat on the floor and began preparing a glass. "Where's Da?"

"Not here." I answered. "That's the point, Bro. That girl... you know I love her more than I love myself. But she's the reason for my last countless evictions! I've come to the understanding that I simply can't stay with her anymore. I mean, I'll still see her. But it's got to be on my own terms, not hers. I certainly can't live with her; you know what I mean? She's proven time and time again to be my death knell. And she's probably better off without me anyway. You know it. I know it. Everyone around town knows it." Mighty nodded patiently as I reasoned through my endless mazes of hollow logic. My words were simply words. No conviction. Nothing more than a hollow pep talk convincing myself of the impossible.

"Word that." He mumbled, handing me the pipe. "I'm glad to finally hear you say it." After sharing a hoon, he purchased five G's and was on his way. Returning attention to the house, I spent the nocturn hours smoking incessantly, taking measurements, mapping out the vision of my new home.

At exactly 9:13 the next morning the hazardous hints of the last seventy-two hours of sleep deprivation and consistent sucking on the glass started appearing. Quick and sudden movements out of the corners of my eyes, peculiar echoes whispering through eardrums and random mental flights of grandiosity were cluing me in that it was time for a break. Riding through the residual rush hour morning traffic, I pulled up in front of Lyda's guesthouse and parked in my usual spot. The familiar street kids swarmed me, asking for the usual payout to look after my bike. Shelling out handfuls of Riel, I walked to the nearest vendor and bought two large orders of *bai sach chrouk*. Entering the lobby, I gave my usual nod to the boy behind the desk and ascended the stairs to Da's door.

Her room was in complete disarray and held the sweet scent of decay—the *aloneness* she had demanded. I walked to the window, opened it but kept the blinds drawn. Lyda rolled over with a groan. I sat on the bed and shook her lightly. "Wake up pretty girl." I whispered. "I brought you breakfast."

Waiting for her reaction, I pulled open the drawer to the nightstand to release the birds. Like small pieces of chalk, they lay dead in their nest. I closed the drawer gently, laid down next to her, placed my palm on the curve of her hip and crawled into sleep. A couple hours later I felt her stirring and opened my eyes. Her face was just inches from mine, her doe eyes staring at me. "They die, Aaron. First the quiet one, the one that sleep a lot. Then an hour later, the loud one."

I kissed her forehead and pulled her tight. She eventually pulled free and sat slumped over her breakfast. We ate in silence.

When her food was gone, she asked for smoke. "Go shower Da. I'll pack a glass and we can smoke when you're ready to go."

"Where we go?"

I knew of a Buddhist shrine built next to the Mekong down off Sisowath Quay. Each day, hundreds of monks, lay people and tourists made pilgrimage to the shrine to purchase caged sparrows. Once purchased, the birds were then released. The Khmer custom was known as *Fang Sheng*. According to tradition, it stood as an act of compassion and was believed to increase karmic merit and cleanse one's sins.

Lyda and I sat next to the river and watched the crowds milling about. When she was ready, she withdrew the dead birds from her pocket which she'd wrapped neatly and carefully into a napkin. She handed them to me. I walked alone down to the river's edge. The swift current carried the white napkin a short stone's throw before swallowing the dead babies away.

Re-joining Lyda, I lit a cigarette. She sat silent, staring at the water.

"Da, I need you to do something for me." When she gave no reply, I continued. "You know I've been sick for a while with this hernia. I'm going to the hospital tomorrow. The doctor told me I must stay there maybe four or five days. I want you to come with me to the hospital tomorrow and stay with me after my operation."

"I not do that," she snapped. With a huff she added, "You think I your mother?"

"They're going to cut me open, Da. I need someone there to help me through the days after my operation. It'll be hard for me if I'm there alone. I'll pay for you to stay with me in my hospital room. You don't have to pay for your room at the guesthouse."

"So why you ask me, huh? Why you not call one of your other girls to take care you?"

"Because I don't have any other girls. I want you to be there. Just a few days. That's all."

After a moment of thought she answered, "Okay. Maybe I be there, maybe I not." It was more than I'd anticipated.

Lyda's sparrows. So much potential. It's almost that she'd actually conceived them herself. She had desired them. Discovered them in their gestation. She had missed their birth, but had returned to adopt them just a week after they'd hatched and begun to breathe. Together we had listened to their first cries, and for the next countless weeks she had carried them around the city from guesthouse to guesthouse in her purse; nurturing, loving, hoping for the best. All her rare glimpses into joy resulting in nothing but two tender deaths.

Dropping Lyda back at her room I returned to the house, plugged in the electric sander and began the lengthy task of sanding the grime off the floor and smoking myself into a frenzy. Following Gloria's instructions, I set the pipe down at exactly 11:30, powered down the sander and ordered a large pizza with extra cheese and shrooms. It was my best effort at physically and mentally preparing for my surgery scheduled for 9:00 the following morning.

On zero sleep and riding full agitation withdrawal I presented myself at *Visal Sok* Hospital at 8:00. After checking in and signing various forms, I agreed to pay an extra two hundred to have provisions brought in for Lyda. Two young orderlies then ushered me into my private room. The room was spartan, save for the bed shoved snug in the corner, a medical station on wheels complete with an IV drip and monitors, and a small wooden desk shoved into the corner. The smiling staff rolled in a second bed and a nightstand for Da. Left alone to endure both wall-crawling anxiety and dry-mouth withdrawal, with one eye on the clock I waited for her arrival.

At quarter to nine a flurry of activity entered the room. Intelligent looking hospital staff dressed in white carrying clipboards, followed by orderlies pushing a gurney. After introducing himself, the young handsome Doctor pointed to his colleague. "This is Doctor Heng, the anesthesiologist. So, if you are ready, we'll begin prepping you for the procedure." Both the doctors were half my age. Reeling with reluctance and eyeing the door for Lyda, I tried to stall for time.

As if on cue, she appeared like an angel and walked into the room. The doctors turned their attention on Da and exchanged a flurry of dialogue in Khmer. I sat up to hug her as Dr. Heng slid the needle into my arm. "Hi Da. Look! They brought you a bed!"

She bent over me, dousing me with a rare and gorgeous smile. "When you wake up, I be here waiting." Counting backwards from ten, her small face evaporated pleasantly into a haze of stars. It was everything I imagined death to be. Beloved death. Lyda's face disintegrating into a zillion velvet explosions. I lifted my arms to hold her, but they wouldn't move. I think I laughed, and then everything dissolved beautiful into lovely and silent black.

The first moments of waking were like trying to swim up through a pit of quicksand, arms and legs weighted down with sludge. Shadows shifting on the undersides of my eye lids. Sounds echoing and fading like wind blowing through dense skeleton trees. Tongue slurring words. My mind folding over and over into itself, trying to escape out of a peculiar and somewhat frightening nitrous and ketamine buzz. Dipping in and out of consciousness, I eventually found myself laying still, eyes focused on the rectangle ceiling tiles. I counted them up to ten, then rolled my head to the left. I focused in on Da sitting next to the bed. I watched her for a silent minute playing some game on my iPad.

"Ohhh, you wake now? Mmmm, you sleep long time! Your body hurt?"

"Yeah, I think so. I can't really move. I feel numb."

She left the room and returned minutes later with an orderly trailing behind her. After sucking on some ice chips, I listened to the staffer recite all the precautions of the post-op care to Da, who in turn translated as best she could. An hour or so later a man from the financial department came in and presented me with the bill. It was just as Gloria had estimated; an even $800. I reached for my backpack and fished out Turgenev's *Sketches from a Hunter's Album* where I'd hidden eight one-hundred dollar bills between the pages. The money was gone. I looked over at Da who sat gaming away on the iPad, scowling with concentration.

"Da?"

"Hmmm?" She answered sweetly.

"Where's the money?"

"I take the money to Naga. I tried to win. Money all gone." Suppressing the urge to vomit, I dismissed the man from the financial department. Asked him to come back later. I wanted to kill her, but with an eight-inch scar swollen and bulging with stitches, there was little I could do from the gurney. "How could you do that, Da? That was all the money I had to pay for the operation!" She answered this by completely ignoring me, her little thumbs hammering away at the game. To her, it was always a game, every situation a win or lose; and she did everything to win, every time, leaving any and all random casualties strewn beaten and bloodied behind her.

When I was finally discharged, I returned alone to my wooden house and posted the AX-1 for sale online. AX-1's were in high demand among the ex-pat biker community. A Japanese import and long out of production, there weren't many of them in the country. Responses from interested buyers came flooding in immediately and it only took a matter of hours to sell it off. Returning to the hospital, I settled the bill, retrieved my passport, then returned home to continue with house repairs.

By the end of June, I'd made a full recovery from the surgery and had caulked and sanded all the walls in the place. I'd also brightened the rooms with a full electrical overhaul, complete with soft indirect lighting. Regular daily pick-ups from Sand continued and I'd nearly recovered the eight hundred that Da had scammed from me while under the knife. I missed her something terrible, or rather, missed something about her. What exactly, I couldn't quite put my finger on. I certainly did not miss all her stunts, or her pejorative comments, her callous thievery, or the constant and pure mental torture that came from living with a woman of her profession. Perhaps it was her rare moments of sweetness that I caught here and there, or the brief glimpses of sadness that I'd observe leaking from the corners of her eyes when she'd suddenly let out a deep sigh in the silent nightfall hours. Living with her proved constant torment. But living without her was at times, equally relentless. I did everything I could to push her from my mind. My concentration and efforts reconstructing the house helped considerably. But there were many waking nightmare stretches when memories and images of Da ushered me slow but sure back into mental landslides of near madness. Imagining the worst—her living on the street, hungry, strung out, images of her sadly entertaining other men, living in her dark reality—I'd suddenly leave the house in the middle of the night to cruise through GSM.

I knew her usual haunts. I found her at 4:00 am one morning shooting pool at The Walkabout. The bar was near empty. I slipped into a seat in a dark corner and watched her and her John play pool—some scraggly looking American hillbilly dressed in cut-off jean shorts, a Hawaiian flowered shirt and sporting a mullet. They were both drinking beer. After each of her shots, the John would point out what she did wrong, offering drunken drawl advice about what she could have done right. He'd then take his shot, and if the ball sank, he'd circle the table giving himself a round of applause as Lyda appeased him with fake smiles. She was playing quite well, and the game eventually came down to the 8 ball. When she sunk it, the guy came around the table to rack the next game, pausing to grab her firmly on the ass.

I shot from my seat and came into view. "Hi Da."

Her response was one of both shock and relief. "How you?"

"Fine. Let's go. *Now*. I want to show you my new house." She tabled her cue and followed me to the street. Her date came after us, waving his pool cue in the air. I whirled on him and told him to go to Hell.

After weeks of sobriety from Lyda, I'd relapsed, giving myself what would prove to be a slow, full and near lethal injection.

Given all that had happened, Lyda ingratiated herself slow and subtle back into the swing of things with all the coy and cunning of a rabid panther. Like a panther, she wore no clothes, emerging fresh and glistening each morning from her shower, preparing and spoon feeding me deliciously naked meals, lounging for hours in bed, sharing the glass and silently moving from room to room with thin trails of smoke steaming from the corners of her lips in the form of evaporated words and noxious smiles. It wasn't until two weeks had passed when she began speaking again, frowning again, in fits of hysteria that left me once again pinned to the floor in my very best crucifix pose, demanding nails.

And indeed, the nails came, as if fired from the barrel of a nail gun. They came in the form of late night phone calls which she'd take in the next room; and after hushed negotiations lasting mere seconds, she'd leave the house sometimes for hours, sometimes for entire days. Then my phone would ring, and I'd answer to her small voice telling me she needed a meal, a shower, a place to sleep. And I always took her in, each time opening the door wider to my misery. She'd return, looking haggard, but wearing a new dress that I'd never seen, or with a new pair of shiny earrings dangling from her small lobes.

A most welcomed reprieve to the lethargic and debaucherous monotony came one night when I rolled up to retrieve my nightly pick up from Sand.

"Tomorrow, can you meet?" He asked.

"Sure. When and where?"

I arrived at the Russian Market KFC at 10:30 sharp. Sand was in line waiting to order. I slipped into the line next to his and waited my turn. Together we convened in a booth and began laying plans.

"How do you feel? Are you ready?" I loved the way he entered conversations. No preludes or small chat. Straight for the gut.

"Physically? One hundred percent. Fully recovered from the surgery. Mentally? Completely shredded. Problems with my girl, as always. She'll be the death of me, Sand."

He shook his head. "Are you fit to travel?"

"Absolutely. Is the Taiwan gig ready?"

"Whenever you are. Perhaps some time out of town will help clear your mind."

Absolutely goddamned right. Eight months had passed since my last trip to Saigon, and almost a year since my last mule run to

Brazil. My existence in The Penh had become an endless treadmill of Lyda-fueled bullshit, wandering the never-ending labyrinth of dead-end disappointments and utter misery. I'd been drowning in a self-imposed quagmire for months; an endless arctic season, waiting for the sunrise that never came.

While Sand illustrated all the details of my next escape, I nodded blindly like a thoroughbred chomping at the bit. Over the next few days, the job slowly crystalized via email.

I rode over to Mighty's, dropped off enough product to tide him over for a few days, then spent the rest of the early evening doing small drops around town. At quarter-to-nine I padlocked the house and took a moto taxi over to the Lucky Burger on Monivong. At a few minutes past nine an old beat-up Honda Civic slowed to a stop. Sand gave me a nod through the passenger window. Climbing into the back the car rolled into traffic. I was introduced to the elderly looking man driving the car. "Aaron, this is Papa George." The man shot me a quick glance in the rear-view. With a weathered black face crowned with a nap of grey hair and wearing a permanent frown, he reminded me of Fred Sanford. Sand handed me a small black and yellow backpack over the seat. "Put all of your clothes and personal items in here. This is your luggage. Do not check this when you go to ticketing. Just tell the agent that you have no bags to check. You'll carry this directly onto the plane. Everything you need is in there. This is the backpack you will give to your contact once you arrive in Taipei." The empty backpack was heavy. I estimated its weight at around three and a half to four kilos. I filled the pack with my outfits for three days.

"Who packed this?" I asked.

"Papa George did. He is the best packer I've ever seen." Papa George gave a silent nod.

"Guaranteed?" I asked.

"One hundred percent," Papa George affirmed.

The ride to the hotel, largely silent. After twenty minutes we rolled up to one of the small and unassuming guesthouses that surrounded Phnom Penh's International Airport. Tucked down a dark side street, the hotel had been perfectly chosen for its anonymity. Sand handed me an envelope. "Your tickets, and your per diem. $150 for three days. Your room here is already settled. Your two nights in Taiwan are also paid for. You leave tomorrow morning. Do stay in tonight. Get a good sleep. In the morning go directly to the airport. Please send me a text tomorrow when you are boarding the plane. And then another text letting me know you arrived. Do you have any last questions?"

I settled into the room just after ten and immediately set to loading the glass. I'd been awake for two days and figured another night wouldn't matter. I'd be able to sleep on the plane. I hadn't brought any product to travel with, just enough to get me through the night and onto the flight. At that point, I was feeling my body demanding and teetering somewhere between death and sobriety. I was looking forward to a relaxed night of solitude. A bit of room service. Perfect anonymity away from the daily treadmill grind. I relished the fact that no one knew where I was. Not even God. I loved the idea of dissolving. Extinction.

My flight routed through Hong Kong with a slight delay. I managed to float through fragments of surface sleep, but depressing thoughts of Lyda and menacing images of Gabby kept tormenting. The sun was setting in splendid color when the plane made its final descent into Taiwan's Kaohsiung International Airport. With my pack slung loose over my shoulder, I approached Customs and Immigration in perfect form: Sleep depraved, hung over, suicidal, robotic, strung out and completely distracted from the task at hand. A perfect cocktail resulting in pure apathy. I presented myself, laid the pack onto the conveyer, proceeded through the metal detector and emerged on the other end to greet the young TSA official. She was a cutie. Thin as a toothpick. Her starched uniform tailored to make her appear boyish. Handing me my pack, she placed her small hands in supplication. And in her perfect Asian/American accent and sweetest smile she offered her frail bow. "Welcome to Taiwan."

Settling into the FX Hotel I ordered an enormous spread of seafood hot pot, oyster vermicelli noodles with a side of sticky rice, dumplings and wontons. The following morning, I woke refreshed and had a taxi deliver me to Kaohsiung's central train station. Settling into my seat, I immediately passed out. The next thing I knew I was being roused by one of the train orderlies. "Sir, please gather your things. Welcome to Taipei." Reaching speeds of 300 kph, I'd crossed the entire three hundred fifty kilometer coastal length of the beautiful island, past Sun Moon Lake, through scenic towns, majestic mountains, waving rice fields, and hadn't seen a thing.

I staggered from the station, hailed a cab and reached the Imperial Hotel in a matter of minutes. Walking into the lobby I immediately saw I was way out of my league. Enormous windows bathed the expansive reception area with natural sun. Skylights. Marble floors. A circular staircase. Banquet rooms. Multiple restaurants and bars. Every inch of wall space covered tastefully in Asian murals. Everything opulent and luxurious. Five star all the way. Presenting my reservation at the front desk, the young man clicked away at the keyboard, then finally shifted gears. Eyeing me up and down, he chimed in his best polite condescension. "I'm sorry, Mr. Reed. But it appears you are not in the system. Would you like to book a room now? We have a few economy rooms left for the day." Working this long with the unpredictable cartels, it was a presentation I knew too well.

"How much?"

"The economy rooms left are currently priced at 2,970 TWD. That converts to $96 U.S. dollars."

"Thanks for the info. I'll let you know in a few minutes." I shouldered my pack and sent Sand a text from the street. <Bro, I just tried checking in at the Imperial. They say there is no room reserved in my name. Am I missing something here? Please advise.>

Sand's reply came before I could finish my cigarette. <Very strange. I reserved the room in your name. No

worries. Just pay cash for a room and I will reimburse you.>

I crushed my smoke and lit another. <Negative. The room is $96. I only have a hundred left. I am not willing to put myself in the position of being in a foreign country with only $4 in my pocket. Sand, I do not need to stay at such an expensive hotel. I will scout the neighborhood and find a less expensive place. Understand? Please advise.>

He responded. <Brother I am sorry I have put you in this position. I don't know why your reservation is not in the system. Pay for a room with your cash at the Imperial Hotel. You must TRUST ME! Get a room there and then call the number I gave you. The man will come and then you will have all the money! I repeat... Trust me!>

After roaming the neighborhood for nearly an hour I made the decision. It wasn't fear, but rather, acute lethargy that moved me to accept and follow Sand's directives. Anything could go wrong, and in my experience, probably would. An unforeseen delay—the buyer never shows—buyer shows up with counterfeit cash and deal goes south and a hundred other possible scenarios of fuckery. I reasoned there were worse places than Taiwan to finally discover my impending homelessness. Back at the front desk, I approached the familiar clerk and checked in.

The room was over the top quaint and decked out in all forms of candy-apple blossoms and excessive fluffiness. Everything tucked and detailed to perfection. An enormous flat screen hung opposite the bed, assaulting all awareness. Freshly cut flowers clogged my nose with pungent pink aroma. An array of tourist pamphlets littered the desk offering everything from massages to a church mass, to a para-sailing adventure. Everything anyone could ever want crammed into a cell-like arena, clean, polished and starched to immaculate perfection. Tossing my pack on the bed, I collapsed next to it and felt like I was drowning. Profound exhaustion. Nausea flowed through body and brain like liquid lead. A tidal flow of venom ran sudden and swift through

327

all senses and all I could think of was being back among the dead in The Penh crawling through the dark alleys and howling and weeping sincerely among the needles and straws and dead eyes contemplating mere survival. A brief flash of Gabby's terrible face increased my hate. A flash of Lyda standing small on the street. I sat up, reached for the phone and dialed the number to my contact. A soft but serious voice answered. "Hello?"

"I'm here. Imperial Hotel. Room 808."

"Room 808?"

"Yep."

"I will come now."

I ducked into the enormous bathroom for a quick splash. The room phone rang as I was drying off. "Hello?"

"Good afternoon, Mr. Reed. This is reception calling. Are you expecting a guest?"

"Thanks, send him up."

I'd barely gotten my pants on when the knock came. I opened the door to a young Taiwanese kid standing in the hall. He walked in, shut the door softly behind him and latched the dead-bolt. We shook hands without exchanging names. I measured him in his late teens, twenty at best. Young enough to be my son. Dressed casual but business style in Khaki's, dress shoes, a long-sleeve Oxford and a smart summer jacket, I noticed curiously that the backpack slung over his shoulder was identical to mine. Same brand, same color. A perfect replica. I pointed to my backpack on the bed. "It's all there."

The youngster smiled and asked permission to sit. I joined him on the bed. Reaching into his backpack, he took out a bundle of cash. With effeminate hands he slowly and carefully counted out the hundreds into five stacks. He looked for my approval. "OK. Now you count, please."

Reaching into each stack, I randomly withdrew two bills and held them up to the lamp to authenticate the security strips. "Looks good." I stood. The boy smiled. Shook my hand again, then shouldered *my* backpack and made his silent exit. The transaction had taken less than four minutes.

The entire gig, from my last night in The Penh with Lyda until now had all passed in whirlwind and flash. I could barely recall walking through security upon arrival back at Kaohsiung International. My night at the FX hotel, the train ride, nothing but one big blur. I sat on the bed and recounted the cash. The easiest three grand I ever made in my life.

Securing the cash in the safe, I slipped a hundo into my pocket and sent Sand a text. <Done deal. All is well. Depart tomorrow morning. Will call you when I land.> Without waiting for his reply, I left the phone in the room and went for a walk to clear my head. Emerging from the hotel, the balmy evening swallowed me whole with temperature at a near perfect 80 F. A bit sticky, but the slight wind felt cool against my skin. Broken clouds collided beautifully with the descending dusk. A five-minute stroll landed me at *Shuangcheng St.* Night Market: a hundred booths and carts offering the very best of Taiwanese street food. A burst of colors and odors churned from a flurry of bustle and noisy activity; the endless vendors offered up fresh fruits, steaming veggies, soup concoctions in exotic blends of oyster or squid rice noodles and raw meats waiting to be skewered. Ordering enough food for three people, I took a seat on the street and slowly stuffed myself. After eating, I ambled around the neighborhood for a half hour, enamored at the hushed and still Taiwanese ambiance. Boredom and exhaustion quickly took hold. Retracing steps back to the Imperial, I marveled at the city's peculiar silence. For being such a grand metropolis, Taipei held an intimacy that I'd never before encountered in all my global wanderings. Perhaps it wasn't so much silence, but a peculiar peace.

I angled down a dark, deserted side street and paused outside a window slightly ajar. Through the slats of an opened wooden shutter, I caught sight of a family huddled in a cubicle around a small, candle lit wooden table taking supper. A balding man sat slumped in a black suit with his yellow tie loosened, close to his spouse dressed in a loosely fitted night gown. The stout woman slowly stirred and then blew breath on hot soup before spooning it into her infants pursed lips. The baby smiled and clapped her hands. I stood paralyzed on the street, staring into a perfect and balanced aquarium, utterly transfixed. Wanting to die. The purity of it all hammered my skull. The man looked up and caught sight of my invasion, stood quick and slowly closed the blind.

Rounding the corner to the hotel, a weathered and ageless monk sat tending a small shrine of candles. I handed her coins in exchange for three sticks of incense. Lighting the sticks into swirling aromatic smoke, I placed them appropriately and departed with her blessing. Back in the room I fell heavy into bed, hoping to merge quickly with any and all coveted spirits of the dead.

On the last morning of July, I woke in the luxury of the Imperial Hotel thoroughly revived and hustled into a taxi to make my flight out of *Taoyaun*. My connection through Kuala Lumpur was smooth without delay and I touched down in Phnom Penh late afternoon. I'd made the physical landing, but exiting the airport and walking back into the familiar streets, I felt thoroughly fragmented, like I'd left my soul back in Taipei, and my mind evaporating over the ocean, perhaps in the stratosphere or somewhere in between. A tuk-tuk delivered me to the house. I unlocked the door and went directly to the hidey-hole, withdrew the stash and sat on the floor with the glass. Those first hits after a few days hiatus were always the sweetest.

I shot off a text to Sand affirming my arrival, requesting an immediate meet both to pay him off and re-up with a 20 G order. An hour later he rolled past the Lucky Burger and I followed him around the corner. Handed him an envelope. "There's two thousand for you, minus a hundred for my room at the Imperial. It was a very good trip. Aside from the hotel reservation mix-up, everything went well. Thanks, Sand. It was a pleasure to work for you. Sincerely."

Pocketing the envelope, Sand handed me my order with a smile. "Don't settle in too much. I've got another job for you."

"Yeah? When?"

"Two weeks. I will call you in the next two days and we will meet." Before I could ask details, he sped off down the dark street.

The following days were productive, trying once and for all to get my act together. After meeting with Mr. Hua and settling two months' rent, I returned to the house and spent the late morning scouring the local buy/sell web pages for used furniture. With the house renovations nearly completed, it was time to start detailing the space.

I loved my new place, and spent the entire evening streaming tunes, strolling through the rooms, smoking myself silly, pleased with the renovations, admiring the new furniture additions, forcing thoughts of Lyda far and away, sincerely happy in my self-inflicted solitude. For the first time in a year, things were looking quite good, especially with Sand's promise of another gig. When I finally met up with him to discuss particulars, I wasn't pleased with the details. "Colombia. It's a long trip, but I assure you, you won't be there more than ten days."

The KFC was empty, save for a few young teenage lovers giggly kissing and feeding chicken tenders into each other's delicate mouths. I sat frowning over my mashed potatoes. "Sand, I've been to S. America twice already. It's a difficult run... very far. There's gotta' be another local gig here in Asia. Why not another run to Taiwan?"

"I can send you to Taiwan again, but not until much later. Perhaps near Christmas if you want to wait that long. The trip to Colombia is nearly ready. Just a few last details to sort out."

"My daughter's turning six next month." I confided. "I haven't seen her for a long time. I miss her terribly. I'm seriously thinking of flying back Stateside to be with her on her birthday."

"It's a very good idea. If you agree to go to Colombia, you'll come back with a bit of cash. Just think of how you could spoil her. You could take her to Disneyland!"

Colombia. South America, again. Nothing but a nightmare. But the idea of getting in another trip so quickly certainly held its appeal. Sand and I departed on no certain terms. I told him I'd think about it. Sand's idea of my daughter and me at Disneyland seemed like an unattainable fairy tale, but the image was enough to motivate me to roll over to my favorite travel agent on street 19. A half hour and $900 later I walked out with tickets back to the States. I sent short emails to my parents and to my now ex-wife in California letting everyone know I was coming. My mom's and Li's reply was surprisingly positive.

Riding back to the house I felt rock solid with how I'd spent my Taiwan payment: Rent paid, new furniture, and now tickets to return Stateside to reconnect with my family and celebrate my daughter's birthday. It was a trip that I would never take.

The last sound sleep I'd gotten was back at the Imperial Hotel in Taipei City. Two… three days ago? The clock read 4:07 AM. I reclined naked on the couch with Asian porn streaming on the laptop and reeling from meth overdose. The first notes of Sonic Youth's *Bad Moon Rising* came burning into my ears, ushering me into the first glimpses of minor auditory and peripheral figments of trickery. Muscles had long surrendered to involuntary tics and spasms. In that isolated and peculiar slice of night, when the first notes of birds chime and the dawn begins devouring the silent noir, all nightmares begin dissolving into fragmented vignettes of hallucinogenic and careless hilarity. Staring blank and wide-eyed at the ceiling like an idiot grinning, I heard a noise—a foreign *clang* that seemed to come from the direction of the balcony running the side length of the house. The sound of a woman's exhale quickly followed. Unmistakable. My feet hit the floor. I tip-toed across the room and put my ear to the wall. Stepping cautiously, I moved slow onto the balcony, muscles taut, eyes wild and alert, prepared to confront some crazy Khmer junkie thief. I approached the ledge and looked down to see Lyda's wide-eyed elfin face staring up at me.

The staircase ascended three stories from the street—fire escape fashion—along the side of the house and up to my place. Lyda had made the death-defying acrobatic leap from the second-story staircase up to grip the rail of my third story balcony, her tiny hands gripping the railing. She hung dangling from the rail, arms extended, her orange purse draped over her shoulder with nothing under her but fifty feet of air separating her feet from the cement below. She smiled. "Hi."

"What are you doing, Da?"

"I come to see you."

"Why are you hanging off the balcony? Why didn't you come and knock on the door like a normal person?"

"Because I think you have a girl here. I want to see."

"There's no girl here, Da. Just you." I reached down clasping her forearms, pulled her up and over the rail and she followed me into the house.

I could clearly see she was as shredded as I was. She took her clothes off and headed straight for the shower, emerging minutes later glistening and wrapped in a towel. After blowing through a hoon and the necessary small talk, we collapsed into sweet unconsciousness.

After hours of dead sleep, I woke to pee. Da was breathing steadily, deep and away. I opened her purse and fished out her phone. I went into her inbox to check where she'd been and what she'd been up to since I'd last seen her.

0965239547: <Lovely Lyda, can you come now? I stay at the usual hotel, room 303. Please say yes.>
0964093160: <All night I want to talk with a beautiful woman and sweet person. Please call me.>
0964093160: <Why don't you call now, honey? I miss you.>
0177039711: <Lyda meet me now I want to fuck!>

Those were the first messages, followed by an infinite list of more. Slipping the phone back into her purse, I rolled onto the mattress sinking slow into a deeper level of madness. She stirred and gave half effort to push me away, then eventually succumbed to my frantic sorrow as I wrapped my legs and arms around her like a straight-jacket.

Dawn brought me curling into the arch of her back. A beautiful time of day devoured by a treacherous condition. Funny how Da's unexpected arrivals always served to blur and obliterate my optimism. Even funnier how I always invited her back in. Her presence in the day's fragile hours triggered my automatic reaction of disdain. I hated the day. I hated the songs of the birds and the memories of Lyda's dead sparrows. I hated the impending motions of the day. The very thought of making tea—filling the small pot with water and heating it to boil left me exhausted. I hated the idea of waking and showering and meeting Sand and Mighty and shelling out hoons to the girls at GSM. The thought of standing with them in dark alleys, waiting and watching them count out their small, crumpled Riel notes for their fix… too much to take. The imaginary sound of a woman's high heels clacking hard on imaginary pavement, the imaginary notes of my daughter's lost laughter, and the thousand other unreal fantasies my infected mind reluctantly entertained made me want to sleep for a thousand years. I hated imagining the countless subtle mental and facial nuances required to get me through the day, and in a fit of pure refusal, I burrowed further into the warmth of Lyda's back. She recoiled with a delicate sigh, leaving me to absorb it all, alone.

I woke, late afternoon. Lyda was gone and my pockets were emptied once again. After sucking through a quarter gram, I took inventory of the house and saw that in addition to rifling my pockets, she'd made off with my laptop, my second power sander and my glue gun. After blazing through the GSM fish games and coming up bare, I sped over to Naga and began combing the casino. It didn't take long to spot her perched on a stool with one hand pulling at the quarter slots and the other clutching a handful of cash. I crept up behind her and grabbed the money out of her hand. She turned, startled. Seconds later, two monstrous security guards approached. Turning to them I pointed at Da. "*Jao*! My girlfriend is a *jao*!" Biting her lip, she turned to the security thugs and dismissed them with a few sentences of Khmer. I took the stool next to her. "I'm so tired of it all, Da. Every time I let you back in you take my money and steal my shit." She sat small, taking my redundant scolding like a pouty schoolgirl. "Give me the pawn tickets." She pulled the tickets from her tight jeans and handed them over. "Sick of it, Da. So fucking tired."

Hard as nails, that girl. I continued to love her out of pity. I loved her with genuine concern. I loved the fact that she'd come to possess me like a pinned butterfly, reducing me to nothing but her plaything on some lonely and random Wednesday afternoon. I loved the idea that perhaps, because of my Christ-like persistence and personifications, she'd one day suddenly begin to love me back. I especially fell in love with her inability to love, knowing this would never happen. My sins had rendered me born again, yet unlovable, curled beneath Lyda's winter branches, content in a pathetic mortuary stasis. I applauded it all with a raucous standing ovation.

She followed me out of the casino and into the market. The street was underway in full mid-day swing. Vendors selling racks of meat and pigs' heads swarming with flies, hawkers offering fruit, fried crickets and tarantulas, beggars lifting bowls, saffron-robbed monks from the Wat seeking alms, uniformed school kids skipping home for lunch. These were Da's streets. She'd worked them since her early teens; followed by her crazy pathetic spineless drug-dealing *barang* boyfriend. Everyone knew who we were; they'd all witnessed our violent public displays of affection.

Nearing the center of the bustling market, with my arm extended, I stabbed her with a pointed finger and announced to everyone, "*Jao*! Look at the *Jao* I have for a girlfriend!" As the words left my mouth, all activity froze on the street. Every eye fell on me and Da. I circled her, forcing her to slow her pace. "*Jao*!" I continued, "Lyda, my *Jao* girlfriend!" Jao is the Khmer word for thief. In Cambodian culture, to publicly condemn someone as a thief is the most scathing thing imaginable—the worst experience a Khmer can endure. With the single word, I had entirely shifted our power struggle, instantly gaining the upper hand.

Victorious, I turned and began walking back to the moto. She turned with me and kept pace a half-step behind. Out of my peripheral, I saw her stoop over and pick something up from the ground. Turning just in time, I caught the blur of her arm as she smashed me full force in the face with a brick.

The back of my head smashed against a wall; knees turned to jelly. Blurry moments later, I woke dazed on the ground. Da sat cross-legged in the alcove of a back-alley shop cradling my head in her arms. I focused in on her, my head nuzzled against her breast like an infant gazing up at its nursing mother. "You fucked up, Aaron. You so stupid to call me like that!" She scolded in a soft, exhausted voice. "Why you call me like dat, huh? All the people looking, why you call me like dat?"

I don't recall at all the ride back to the house where Lyda and I shut off our phones and spent the rest of the afternoon silently passing the glass and listening to a streaming mix of Madonna, Gustavo Santaolalla and White Stripes. At that point in the game, I had endured so much abuse that a brick in the face was nothing more than a tickle under my chin.

My love for Lyda had become certain death. We'd died long ago and had since become nothing more than fossilized relics. Dead sparrows floating down a muddy river. In those last days, I kept a running log of her activities:

Last $50 taken from my pocket while I lay sleeping
Phone stolen
Heat gun stolen
Keys stolen
Clubbed in the face with a wooden plank
Large rock thrown at me injuring my arm
Watched her ride off with another man to a guesthouse where

she went in and stayed the night and all the following day

I wrote the log as a sort of obituary; a loving release to all we had hoped for and all we had failed to achieve.

I met with Sand many times, and many times rejected the Colombian gig, until finally—enticed by the idea of my early grave—I agreed.

Death saturated my final days and nights in The Penh, spent alone in the little wooden house streaming Asian porn with my fingers soaked in KY jelly; my last remaining efforts for pleasure and my final attempts at finding God. I'd warmed to the idea of death, licking it off my fingers, tasting the shit. Boarding the plane en route to Bogotá, I walked stiff as a corpse, carrying a pure and enthusiastic misery, quite aware of the fact I had little left to live for.

Chapter Seventeen

La Modelo Prison, Bogotá
25 August 2015 - February 2016

I'd be lying to say there wasn't an intrigue. Finally walking into the big house held a certain fascination; one I'd pondered over the past years; one I'd fantasized about, even role-played on certain occasions. Chained hand and foot, I shuffled out the front door of the Bogotá airport jail with my head held high. I wasn't pride, but determination. Willing to collide and integrate with any and all.

After spending two days in a small police station cell, I was led through the front door of La Modelo just after 9:00 in the morning and ushered into a large 20x30 foot holding cell. Windowless, the only light bled down from a skylight carved into the ceiling. Looking up through the dirty glass I could see the silhouette of a guard standing on the roof balancing a machine gun on his hip. The room held around sixty faces that all turned to evaluate my entry. Fat faces bulged from ripped and grubby T-shirts. Thin and emaciated faces of the homeless were content to be there, looking for nothing more than three hot's and a cot. Young teen-aged eyes stared wide and painted in fear, homicidal lust and all expressions in between. Dead eyes, evasive eyes, scurrying eyes regarded me with absent porcupine stares. Eyes eaten out and left vacant and hollow by life's sad and endless film reels.

I entered the dungeon. Returning the weighted stares, I walked unhurried to an empty corner of the cell, preparing myself for the assault. The shakedown came in the form of two men.

Once I'd settled myself on the cement floor, they quickly approached. One was abnormally huge; well over six feet. It wasn't his size that alarmed me, but rather his face. His enormous head set square on broad shoulders. Fat cheeks pushed in on a button nose and pouty lips, and his eyes were grotesquely small, as if someone had placed a chubby baby's face onto the body of a giant. When I stood to face him, he loomed over me and spoke in short syllabic grunts. I shook my head. "I don't speak Spanish." I answered. "*Yo no hablo español.*"

The 220 pound half-witted toddler glanced over at his sidekick. His partner: a young and crazed-looking gangster type broke into a wide smile. His four front teeth were missing. "*Ahh, tu Americana? Tu Gringo?*"

"*No hablo español.*"

My English seemed to excite them and they backed me tighter into the corner. "*Parce, ¿Tienes algo de lucas para nosotros?*" I scrunched up my nose and shook my head. "*Moonnee, Gringo. Give me moonnee!*"

My *no comprende* pantomime ended there. I knew what they were after, and they knew that I knew. I fished out my last 20,000 Peso note from my shoe and handed it over. From that moment, I found myself among friends.

Using my small bag of clothes for a pillow, I curled into a ball on the concrete floor, closed my eyes and began breathing.

Around noon I startled awake to the clang of the cell gate opening. Guards dressed in blue and black camo with army boots on their feet lumbered in carrying milk crates. Styrofoam boxes were distributed. I flipped the lid to a cold chicken leg buried in a cup of white rice, two boiled baby potatoes and a small heap of lettuce with a single slice of beet. No salt, no seasoning, incredibly bland but not bad. Not bad at all. After the lunches were devoured, the ambiance in the cell returned to its tense and static hum.

Just past 2:00 the door crashed open to another flurry of activity when the cell was suddenly filled with a rush of guards all carrying guns. A surreal procession of beautiful young women dressed in white scrubs paraded into the cell. With the guard's fingers on their triggers, the girls set up makeshift interview stations and all prisoners were instructed to form lines. The women were from the prison hospital, here to create the new prisoner's intake biographies. Name. DOB. Ethnicity. Allergies. Blood type. Family medical history. Etc. With my limited Spanish I fumbled through the interview—not able to understand or lend appropriate answers to the questions.

Just as the sun began dousing the cell into a bleak gray, a guard appeared at the gate and began barking names from a clipboard. A small line of prisoners began to form. The announced roster created a thick and immediate tension throughout the cell. After five minutes the guard stumbled through his pronunciation. "*Aron... Michel... Red!*" I shuffled into the queue. Asking those around me if anyone spoke English, I was greeted with blank stares, shakes of the head and masochistic grins. Having been clunked into the system for the past three days, I'd come somewhat resigned to the abrupt churns of the cogs and the terrible whine of the machine. But still, my inability to communicate and understand what was happening on a minute-to-minute basis was crippling. The constant unknown, unnerving.

I was filtered into a group of nine other guys. In the middle of the line, I shuffled into a long, dimly lit cement corridor that seemed to stretch forever. With backs against the wall, a parade of ten guards stood facing us and began screaming instructions in Spanish. The men around me quickly began disrobing down to the skin. I followed suit. After a quick and thorough body search, I pulled on my clothes. I was fingerprinted, filtered through an electric body scanner, and handed a small scrap of red paper with a six-digit number printed on it.

From there, and under the constant screamed instructions from the guards, I followed the guy in front of me down the harrowing corridor like cattle herded down the chute in a light jog towards the slaughter and came to another gate leading to intersecting hallways. Here I was issued a plastic bowl and spoon, and a *kit* containing a toothbrush, toothpaste, a bar of soap, a sachet of deodorant and a roll of toilet paper. I was then paraded in front of a video camera where I was prompted to stare into the lens and read my number aloud. Assuming my best posture, I recited my number in English. The guard slammed his truncheon against the wall, barking at me like a crazed dog. In my best *Español*, I stammered, 3.7.1.7.9.6.

With a sick and wicked grin, the guard pointed his stick to his right. "*Patio Tres!*" I followed the direction of his baton into the hall extending left and eventually came to another guard standing sentry at a large gate. Regarding me with a bored glace he opened the gate allowing me to pass, then locked it behind me.

Alone in a spacious, dark patio and craving a cigarette, I found myself standing in front of a peeling statue of Mother Mary. A young black man in civilian clothes materialized out of nowhere. "I'm Angel. Welcome to Patio Three." He whispered his words in a thick Caribbean accent.

Shrugging off the surrealism, I offered my hand. "I'm Aaron. Is this where I'm going to stay?"

"Yep. For the moment. Things can change pretty quick around here."

Standing there with Angel, I was suddenly overcome with a surge of fear. I'd finally made it to the end of the road. No more slipping over borders, narrow aversions or back-alley escapes. I knew that within minutes I'd finally be led into the lion's den. Fears of media-fed rectal prison initiations flooded my brain. "Angel, just one thing. I'm not a troublemaker. Not interested in violence."

He gave a weak sigh. "You're in a good place. This is Patio Three. A lot of foreigners here."

I followed Angel about ten yards to another gate. He unlocked it and I entered the hall. He then locked the gate behind me and spoke through the iron mesh. "You're in hallway three. Find a guy named Ali. He's the *monitor del pasillo.*"

"He's the what?"

"The guy in charge of the hall. He'll get you settled and help you get whatever you need. See you tomorrow morning." And with that, my Angel was gone. I turned, started down the hall and began walking. Passing the cells, I could see in periphery guys standing in their rooms. Some guys were pacing the hall. A group of five were camped out in front of an ancient television watching some show in Spanish. I approached them. "Hello. Any you guys speak English? I'm looking for Ali."

One guy shrugged, then screamed over his shoulder. "Maaaaax!"

A young guy with a kind face appeared from a cell and approached me. "Hey, I'm Max. You just got in?"

"Yeah, I'm Aaron." We shook hands. "I'm supposed to find Ali." Max led me to a room halfway down the hall where Ali welcomed us both into his cell and offered us seats on his cot.

Ali was black, tall, handsome and spoke broken English with a thick French accent. Max was from Guatemala. Both narco-traffickers. From their passable English they re-affirmed what I'd already put together. I was in La Modelo, Patio Three, Hall Three. I listened closely as they outlined my orientation.

La Modelo. The 'model' prison. One of the largest prisons in the country. Built to house 2,900, it was bursting at the seams with a population of 8,000, obscenely overpopulated at 37%. Fucked up. Gangs. Murder. People die. *Keep your head down and your mouth shut.*

Patio Tres. One of eight patios. Patios 1A and 1B were filled with all the rapists and pedos. 2A and 2B made up the 'infermos,' all the guys with physical handicaps, the criminally insane and the guys with HIV. Patios 4 and 5 were crammed packed with the worst of the worst; repeat offenders, the poor with no resources left to rot in terrible conditions.

"What do you mean by terrible?" I asked.

Max and Ali exchanged glances. Max explained. "It's like this... Where you are now—patio three—we got about three hundred guys living here. Patio four is the same size as patio three, but over there, there's over twelve hundred guys. Here we got two or three guys sharing a room. Over there in patio four, they fit five or six or even seven into the cells. There's no room over there. Guys sleep in the hallways on the floor no bed no blankets no nothing they find any place they can and try and survive. No electricity. No toilets. Rats. People die over there every day."

Ali took over Max's monologue. "Here, patio three, relaxed. Chill. Lots of foreigners here. Guys from Spain, France, England, from all over Europe. Everyone from another country, but also a lot of rich Colombiano's who pay the bribe to be moved here. Here is safe, not much violence. Patio three, the best patio in the country."

"That's what Angel told me." I offered. "The guy who met me at the gate."

Pasillo Tres. Ali continued. "There are sixteen halls in this patio. Each hall has twelve cells. This is hall three. There's currently twenty-eight guys in the hall. Tomorrow morning I'll show you around and introduce you to Brazil. He's the *Pluma*."

"The Pluma?"

"The feather! The man in charge. He runs the patio. He'll tell me which room to put you in."

"And for now?" I asked. "Where am I supposed to sleep? And where can I get a mattress, a blanket and pillow? The air in here is cold!"

Ali asked Max if he had an extra mattress. Max went off and returned minutes later carrying a thin mattress rolled up under his arm. "For now, just put your mattress down anywhere in the hallway."

"And you can use my bathroom until you get your room assigned." Max offered.

I set up camp at the far end of the windowless hall, away from the foot traffic and the headache from the blaring Spanish television. A few guys introduced themselves while pacing past my camp, but no one was really interested in my arrival. I liked it that way. Laying on my mattress, I enjoyed my anonymity. As the night wore on, the hall traffic died down with most of the men disappearing one by one into their cells. At 9:00 the TV volume was turned low. By eleven, the last of the viewers turned off the set, found his room and closed his door. The hall was empty and miraculously quiet. Wearing my ever-present apathetic grin, I settled into my first night in prison.

Dead night, I woke to severe abdominal cramps. Clutching my stomach, I walked quick to Max's room. A snoring roar came from behind the locked door. I paced back to my camp, located my food bowl, pulled down my pants, squatted against the wall and filled the large tupperware with my chicken leg, rice and potato lunch in explosive diarrhea. I dumped it all into the trash bin at the end of the hall and curled back fetal position, shivering into my jacket.

The sound of broom bristles scraping cement lulled me awake. I opened my eyes and saw the blurry figure of Max looming over me. He was sweeping and mopping the hallway. "Wake up." He whispered. "Everyone has to be out in the courtyard by 6:30."

"What time is it now?"

"Six."

"What about all my stuff? I just leave everything here in the hall?"

"Yeah. I'll make sure no one fucks with it."

Those first few mornings in the yard when I walked out to assemble with the general population for breakfast were difficult. I knew no one and stayed within sight of Max like a wide-eyed puppy. The ebb and flow of the patio seemed to hold a sort of orderly semblance, but with an ever-present current of potential explosive turmoil simmering under the façade. Brazil, the *Pluma*, was the orchestrator of the gloss that kept the patio intact.

After waiting in line to receive my bread roll, an orange, and a slice of mystery meat, I wrapped the food into a piece of paper to save for later and set out to find Ali. I spent the morning pestering him to help me settle in. Enduring all my frantic questions, Ali possessed the classic *je ne sais quoi*, proving himself a complete gentleman.

He led me up to the second floor of the patio, to *Pasillo* 8. There was a sentry stationed at the entry to the hall and Ali asked permission for us to pass. The sentry then walked to the far end of the hall to a table where a group of men were seated. Returning a minute later, he said Brazil would see us. It was like trying to get an appointment with the Wizard of Oz. Walking down the hall, I immediately saw it was a world away from my hallway downstairs. *Pasillo* 8 was Oz! In contrast to the windowless dungeon of *Pasillo* 3, the entire hall and each cell I passed was well lit and painted in crisp white. Each room was immaculately clean, as opposed to the rooms downstairs that resembled overcrowded crack dens. *Pasillo* 8 was outfitted with multiple cooking stations where men dressed in designer clothes stood smiling and frying late breakfasts of sausages, bacon, hash browns and eggs.

Ali and I approached a small group of well-groomed and dressed men seated at a table, laughing heartily over their tamales, omelettes and bacon—food brought in from the street not available to the common population. A chubby faced-bald man was at the center of it all—holding court among his inner-circle. Ali gave him a subtle wave and he acknowledged our presence with an annoyed nod. After waiting ten minutes, the breakfast broke up, each man shaking hands and going his separate way. The man named Brazil then turned his attention on us and held out his hands for us to sit.

Brazil accepted my hand into his warm, soft palm and offered me a weak smile. He appeared like a cross-breed between a pig and a pit-bull. Bald as a cue-ball, he wore his shiny scalp like a hardhat crowning his pudgy face. He never made appropriate eye contact. His beady eyes were in constant motion. Flickering. Cunning. Alert. After talking with Ali and me for a few seconds, he dismissed me with a clap on the shoulder, then disappeared into his cell and shut the door.

Back down in my hall, Ali helped me move into my new room. There were two concrete bunk beds crammed into the cell. I climbed up into one of the top bunks and began journaling.

24-26 August '15

Finally found the dead end. Transferred to La Modelo, Bogotá. Sick and miserable with diarrhea, cramps and vomiting. Given essential toiletries. Spent three hours in the prison Sanidad waiting with a hundred other prisoners to see the doctor who spoke no English. After receiving two hydration packets returned to the patio and Ali showed me into my new room, cell #4. Felt better by evening. Given blanket and bedsheet. My two roommates speak no English. No communication. I know nothing about them and they inquire nothing of me. Three men living incommunicado through constant tense and uncomfortable silence in a 13x17 ft cell. Luis showed up and I was led out of the patio into a small dark and dingy quarter where prisoners yell through bullet-proof glass at their lawyers. I signed him on as my legal rep. Luis called mom and dad and told them what has happened. He said they were sad but took the news well. I'm dreading speaking with them.

27 August '15

Woke and rushed out to a light morning rain— nearly a mist—veiling my face and arms. The men standing around me didn't hear my soft laugh. The drizzle felt beautiful and washed away my worry. Men stand in the yard in small clusters and nudge each other as I pass. Everyone knows I'm new because I have no shoelaces. Everyone knows I'm a gringo. There's a group of guys in the hall who all live together in the same room just a few cells down from mine. Tito is from Guadalajara and Fernando from Nogales. Jordy and Maelo are Colombiano. All young kids in their twenties, all narco-traffickers. Drug fiends like myself. Kind guys who've taken me under their wing. They invited me in to share some lines. Stayed up all night playing Monopoly.

Forking over $200 for B&O Railroad, Fernando handed me the deed, delicately balancing a fat line of coke. After snorting the blast, I asked, "So who's this Brazil guy anyway?"

The moment I voiced the question, the light and frivol atmosphere in the room turned dark. Fernando answered simply, "He the man."

Cutting more lines out onto the tray, Tito added, "He's in charge. Nothing happens unless he says it happens. Brazil controls everything."

Slightly confused I stated, "But he's just another prisoner, like the rest of us."

"Yeah," Jordi corrected, "but connected. Very powerful. He works with the guards to keep the patio safe. In the other patios… people die. Violence every day. Brazil's like the God Father, our Don Corleone. He keeps everything safe and smooth."

Maelo chimed in, summing it all up. "Brazil runs this patio. He pays the guards to leave us alone. Big money every month. *Milliones*! The guards don't control things here. It's all mafia! Brazil holds all the power."

I kept silent through those first days. Absorbing everything. Trying to get my bearings. Giving best effort to assimilate to my new life in lock-up. I often sat alone, distanced and reluctant to integrate, always keeping a keen eye on Brazil.

Cute like a pig, Brazil was always foraging around, digging into anything and everything. Brazil and his small inner circle of six or eight henchmen were referred to as "The House," and ruled the patio with an iron fist. Brazil laughed a lot—a high, tittering laugh—always at the expense of others. And whenever the

Header: Aaron Reed

occasion presented, he'd simply give the order to his lackeys to exert his undisputed power through violence, often assaulting the impoverished and most desperate of inmates if they didn't meet his insatiable, financial demands. This often resulted in the poorest of inmates sexually whoring themselves in order to make their monthly rent payments. Brazil proved to be one of the most vile people I had ever met, demanding my ultimate respect.

Most governing entities in Colombia run under a system of covert corruption. In 2018, the U.S. News and World Report ranked Colombia as the second most corrupt country in the world, behind Nigeria. Among the endless civic, political and governmental organizations, one needs to look no further than Colombia's prison system as a microcosmic example of the abject corruption that runs pervasive and reckless throughout the entire country, defining the country's disgraced global identity.

Throughout my entire stay at La Modelo, the daily functions of the prison were implemented and enforced by two governing bodies. The National Penitentiary and Prison Institute (INPEC), a branch of The Ministry of Justice and Law, shared a collusive balance of power with the Mafia. Each month, Brazil extorted as much money as he possibly could from the prisoners. Fake raffles were often held where prisoners were obligated to buy tickets to win prizes that simply didn't exist. Each prisoner was required to pay "rent" by the 5th of every month. If a prisoner refused or couldn't pay for any reason, they were terrorized and on occasion, beaten by Brazil's gang of thugs and threatened to be expelled from the safety of the patio. A large slice of this income went to pay the prison guards. In exchange for this payment, the guards were expected to do the mafia's bidding. As long as the cash was paid, the guards left well enough alone. But if the payments were delayed or withheld, then the guards ran ape-shit on the prisoners. The electricity and water were turned off and the guards came into the patio like gangbusters, tossing cells, stealing anything of value. After making the monthly payment to the guards, Brazil and his small circle of minions then pocketed the rest.

348

Within a month I was able to define both sides of the argument. Nothing more than a career criminal, Brazil was a ruthless and tyrannical dictator, but also an established mafioso with far reaching social and political connections. Indeed, he kept a benevolent order in the patio that thrived on the absence of physical violence (aside from the violence that Brazil himself exerted,) and this was appreciated by the masses. He was also a skilled parasite that sustained his existence and derived millions by sucking off the meager assets of the poor. The order he ensured came at the price of the terrified commoners he lorded over. His power was immense. And he certainly held the credentials to govern like he did. For obvious security reasons and motivated by self-preservation, "Brazil" kept a strong and secure hold on his real name. Throughout my time in the jail, I tried to pick up bits and pieces along the way, but not until my final months in lock-up was I able to discover that Brazil was actually Eduardo Alberto Villareal Rivera, charged with multiple accounts of conspiracy, terrorism, narco-trafficking, arms dealing, and trafficking substances to produce narcotics. He'd been arrested in mid-May 2014 in a syndicate involving fourteen other people. A real piece of work.

28 August '15

Maelo took pity on me and hired me to wash his laundry in exchange for a pack of smokes. I also agreed to sell my hammer and sickle T-shirt that I bought in Laos to some Russian guy for another pack of smokes. Everything here is cash, cash, cash!!! My biggest challenge for the moment is staying in cigarettes. $2.00 a pack and I have no money. On serious daily cigarette ration! I need to place that dreaded phone call to my family soon and ask them for support. There's a little library here in the patio that holds about 1,500 books. The English section has about 200 titles. I checked out *A Bend in the River*, by Naipaul and *McCarthy's Bar* by

Pete McCarthy—a slice of humor to keep a grin on my face. Another Russian named Roland gave me some shoelaces. Wrote a six-page letter to Curtis, a letter to Lin and one to my parents letting them know I'm okay. Also met with a pastor.

I was drawn to Don Carlos from the very first day. Standing over six feet and despite his frail age, I was attracted by the way he strolled slow through the patio, giving his time and personal attention to anyone who sought it. His eyes were kind, and his charisma loomed large. I immediately saw there was something different about him. A glow. An aura perhaps? Five days after entering La Modelo, I approached and introduced myself.

He invited me to sit with him at a table in the yard. After pleasantries, Don Carlos explained, "There's a little church here that meets every morning. I'd like you to come. The services are in Spanish, but I think you would enjoy meeting the men. It's a simple service—about a half hour long. We sing a few songs, and then a word is given. It would be a good place for you to meet good people."

"Church? Here in the patio? Can I see it?"

He led me to one of three small classrooms situated directly across from the library. The room held about thirty chairs. We took seats, taking a moment to absorb that universal silent and mystic ambiance that all houses of worship hold. The walls were adorned with large oil canvases depicting tragic religious scenes. The paintings were rudimentary, amateur at best, reminding me of the paint-by-numbers kits that I'd occupied myself with as a child. Saint Peter standing amongst the flames of Hell chopping Satan's head off with a large, disproportionate sword. A primitive effort of the trinity, illustrating the Holy Spirit as a furious wind, Christ shown as a dove, and God portrayed as a bearded old grandpa. Another painting showed Christ staring down at the viewer with large glass-like tears streaming from his eyes. "Prisoners painted these."

"I can see that." I answered. Don Carlos asked me what had brought me to the prison. I gave him an abbreviated version and then returned the question. With a twinkle in his eye he answered, "Well, I may have forgotten to pay my taxes."

A tax evader and a narco-traficante sitting in a small prison church. It was a surreal moment. "What does this church mean to you?" I asked. "And why do you want me to come?"

Without pause he answered, "This is a place where men come to heal. And I want you to come because I'm the pastor."

"Pastor Carlos, I appreciate your invitation, but let me be honest. I was raised in the church by my parents since birth. I was trained through Catechism. I know the Bible well and can recite scripture, but over the past years, I've come comfortable with the fact that my relationship with God has come to a standstill. And the last thing I need right now is a *Jesus loves me* lesson. After everything that's happened, I'm not sure I believe in God anymore."

Don Carlos smiled tenderly and nodded, "Well, I'm sure he still believes in you."

Looking over Don Carlos' shoulder, I caught sight of Fernando standing just outside the door. He made eye contact, tapped the side of his nose, then walked off quick into the direction of the hall. "Pastor Carlos, I just remembered, I have to meet with some of the guys in my pasillo." The pastor stood to full height and gave me an unexpected hug—a sincere hug that melted away my callous frost. "It's very good to meet you, Aaron. Think about coming to church. I think it will be good for you." The tenderness in his voice cracked my spine and left a lump in my throat.

Back in the hallway, I came to Fernando's closed door with Jimi Hendrix blasting behind it. I slapped my palm hard against the iron and the music immediately silenced. "*¿Quién es?*"

"It's Aaron."

The door opened, and I was immediately enveloped in a dense cloud of sweet marijuana smoke. As soon as I'd secured the door behind me, Jimi's *Machine Gun* was cranked back to full volume. The room was in complete chaos. Jordi, dressed in jeans and dark sunglasses was dancing with himself in the bathroom, attempting to shave his adolescent whiskers without a mirror. Fernando sat on his bunk next to a small mountain of coke, cutting multiple fatty lines onto a small broken mirror he'd taken from Jordi. Perched next to Fernando, Tito, shirtless, looked up at me with thin face and glassy eyes and a mile wide grin. He screamed over the music, *"¡Bienvenido a nuestra fiesta del viernes por la tarde!"*

It was a Friday, just past 10:00 AM, and indeed the party was fully underway. I took a seat on Jordi's bunk and spent the late morning mediating a random and passionate debate. Led Zeppelin, Pink Floyd, Jimi? Who was the best rock n' roll band in the world? At one point Fernando asked why I had been meeting with Pastor Carlos in the church. After giving sound bites of the discussion I'd shared with the pastor, Tito stood up in the center of the cell, lit a fat joint, spread his arms wide and proclaimed, *"¡Esta es mi iglesia, y la marihuana es mi Dios! ¡Amor, alegría, paz entre todos los hermanos! ¡Amén!"*

I looked to Fernando for the translation. "This room is our church… marijuana is our God… and we wish love, joy and peace for all our brothers."

Throughout the day, Tito and Fernando blessed me with gifts. Equal to sharing their kind company, they each took inventory of their wardrobes and selected clothes items from their stacked milk crates that they thought I could use: A couple T-shirts, a pair of over-sized house pants, a pair of socks, and a sweater. They assembled a care package consisting of items they'd collected from the prison store: foot powder, a few slices from a vanilla cake, a huge pack of saltine crackers and a few sachets of deodorant. Fresh into the jail, they knew I had nothing. I could tell by the way they were living that they had little more than I did, and yet, they gave to me for no apparent reason other than to accelerate their own joy by giving out of their poverty.

The party lasted all day and into the night; The five of us destroying our septums with multiple blasts of the harshest coke I'd ever snorted. The high was intense, but the product had been stomped on by secondary ingredients that left my eyes watering and nose on fire. In-between blasts I asked, "So how do you guys get your coke and dope into the prison?" Tito, Fernando and Jordi each took turns educating me on the dynamics of La Modelo.

Drugs were everywhere. Majestic mountains of coke and endless acres of weed. Under the blind eye of César Augusto Ceballos, the prison Director, the guards smuggled in and delivered kilos of pot and cocaine to the drug kingpins who employed poor prisoners to peddle the mess around to the general population. Acid tabs and other designer drugs like ecstasy and 2C-B were also widely available. All contraband was attainable including weapons, store bought liquor, cell phones, *even people*, but always at a price. Everything was purchased through Brazil. On Sundays, prostitutes were admitted into the prison and pimped out to anyone who had the cash to pay. César Augusto Ceballos and his administration turned a blind (albeit exacting) eye on the endless dynamic. Throughout my entire time at the prison, Director Ceballos ran the jail like a mammoth cannibal dynamo, skillfully directing endless avenues of extortion and negotiating human rights violations through which he profited immensely.

Jose L. Rey, a rep from the U.S. Embassy's *American Citizen's Services* division referred to La Modelo as "The most negligent, most dysfunctional and corrupt prison in the entire country."

Director Cesar Augusto Ceballos was arrested in January of 2019 on charges of illicit enrichment and conspiracy to commit a crime; charging inmates millions to smuggle alcohol, drugs and women into the prison.

At the end of the day when the last lines had been snorted and the last joint crushed, I thanked all the guys with a sincere hug and staggered down the empty hall back to my room. Three hours 'til wake-up. Giving best effort not to disturb my snoring roommates, I slithered into my bunk and entered the familiar and excruciating hour of the come down. It was time to sleep but I couldn't. The last six lines of coke I'd blazed continued broiling my brain and surging through my veins like a vast and white-capped reckless river shattering all dams I attempted to construct. Time to empty my head from all the experiences of the day but the funny and endless film excerpts and nightmare experiences plagued my brain with the vengeful and static hum of a zillion swarming bees. I tossed, turned, wrestled the sheets, reached for a tissue and spent the next seventy-four minutes sneezing out chunks of my bloody mind. Shoving wads of toilet paper up my nostrils, I gave lame attempt to clog the deluge and silence the memories of the night. The million half-welcomed experiences of the evening continued to creep and devour my brain like fire ants. A sick and utterly depressing place to end the day. And yet, the fangs of addiction punctured my thin skin demanding my full and committed participation. I'd always regarded coke as a miserable drug. In a room full of cokehead's, no one laughs. Everything elevates to a level of fake intensity, leaving you feeling mentally annihilated and physically destroyed.

After years of loathing and avoiding the church, I'd attended two churches in one day, and found myself spiraling into dualistic vacuums. My primitive lust kept me awake, replaying all the pomp and hilarity of Tito's church. I found it interesting that in his drug induced frenzy he'd demonstrated the first three Fruits of the Spirit. With his thin arms held high over his head, he'd announced *love, joy, peace,* and was living them in his fullest.

Pastor Carlos' church had silently whispered into my ears… something about surrender, about grace; foreign concepts I understood in the abstract but currently had no capacity to grasp.

1 September '15

A woman showed up from the American Embassy's Citizen's Services to check on me today. When I entered the small room I was shocked to my core and taken completely off guard. She was gorgeous… Asian… her long black hair cascading over her forehead, hiding her eyes as if she was Lyda. She introduced herself as Cassandra Payton and offered her hand. INPEC guards stood by with their fingers on their triggers. The first words out of her mouth: "There's nothing we can do for you other than make sure you are being treated humanely."

"Where do you set the bar to measure humane treatment? Basic human rights are not recognized in here."

After a stutter, she replied, "I guess we're to make sure that you're being treated with the same treatment as the other Colombian prisoners."

"With abuse? Constant extortion? Neglect? With no adequate medical services? Well, then I guess you can say I'm being treated fairly well!"

Cassandra demurred, scribbled a short notation in her log and then handed me a garbage bag filled with random mini bars of soaps and shampoos that had been taken from hotel rooms, and a pair of socks. "I know it's not much, but it's all we have to offer."

My second care package in as many days. I couldn't help but compare the contents to what my friends from Guadalajara had offered. Tito and Fernando had shared their time, acceptance, their friendship and their resolutions at being human. They'd displayed—like the woman illustrated in the scriptures—love out of their poverty. My countries' Embassy—the richest and most powerful country on the planet—had provided me with a six-minute meeting, leaving me with a handful of free hotel toiletries. I accepted the package with a weak smile and a thankful nod to the United States of America. Making my exit I turned and asked, "Can you please send a note to my family letting them know that you saw me and that I'm Okay?" Cassandra made another scribble in her log and wished me well.

It took me nine days after orientation to find my spine and finally call my parents. The phone card Pastor Carlos gifted me allowed me five minutes. Dad answered. "Hi Dad. How's mom?" His voice was tender. Patient. Weak. The thousand tongues of apologies swarming through my head couldn't be translated into English. I wept, hushed and exposed through awkward stretches of dead air while my father listened and loved me, forgiving me throughout our remaining minute of terrible silence.

Our call the following day involved more practical discussion. I needed cash to survive. Explaining the dynamics of prison life and all the Mafia involvement it entailed, my father exclaimed, "But that's extortion!"

"Exactly, Dad. It's the way things work here, and I need to survive!" After a lengthy debate, he agreed to send $150 to my prison store account every quarter. A hundred and fifty bucks every ninety days translated into surviving on a dollar and sixty cents per day. His financial pledge was a pittance, but after all the pain and frustration I'd inflicted on the family over the many years, I knew it was more than I deserved.

The days leading up to September 13th—my daughter's 6th birthday—were excruciating. I'd bought my ticket to return to celebrate with her when I had returned from Taiwan. I'd promised her a happy reunion. I'd promised her a birthday party with all the frills. I'd promised her Disneyland! She had been anticipating my arrival. I had no choice but to call her and tell her I wasn't going to make it. Hearing her burst into sobs and then reassuring her with lies that I would see her soon was my own indescribable punishment—far worse than being locked up in the jail. Speaking with her locked me into a reality that I couldn't alter, knowing that in her confusion, she was suffering far more than I was for the sins I'd committed.

I decided my daughter was too young to be given the truth of my circumstances. I constructed a story of half-truths to shield her from the raw reality that her father was soon to be a convicted felon and now serving time in a foreign prison. *Papa is now living in S. America studying Spanish, and for now it's very difficult for him to come to visit.* My parents and ex-wife agreed to support the ruse.

28 September '15
Quiet morning in Patio Tres. Multiple stabbings in Patio 1-A. 12 injured and one dead. Entire prison under lockdown. Cops everywhere. Sequestered in the hall and not allowed to go out to the patio for breakfast.

October defined a torturous dimension of the prison experience. *Separation.* Prison isn't so much about being locked in, but more about being *locked out and away* from the experiences of loved ones. The few times I was able to speak with my daughter on the phone, she squealed with excitement and anticipation for Halloween. She went trick-or-treating dressed up as a pink crayon. Her innocence, and my inability to participate left me melted in a myriad of feelings I had neither the will nor the capacity to process. November. Alone in my cell, chewing on beef gristle and cold rice, I shut out images of family and friends gathered and seated around warm Thanksgiving dinner and conversation, of which I had neither. And then Christmas. The season of gifts. My parents sent me an additional hundred dollars to my prison store account. In return, I had nothing to offer but the continued pain that I'd given them for the past three years of my reckless existence. And to my daughter, I gave yet another year of an empty chair at the table along with a head space to try and figure out why Papa wasn't around.

Throughout those first months of incarceration, Luis visited frequently. About twice a month the prison crier would call my name and I would rush out to the visiting area—a dark hall lined with six separate cubicles. Luis was always waiting with a smile, and I would spend a few happy minutes yelling my sincere thanks through the streaked and smudged bullet-proof glass. He advised me to make a plea-deal which he would present to the prosecutor.

"If I do that—admit my guilt—how much time am I looking at?"

"If the prosecutor agrees and we submit the plea to the judge, then the judge will decide between the minimum and maximum punishment." Luis began scribbling on a piece of paper and then handed me a diagram through the window slot. "The maximum the judge can give for your offense is ten years and six months." As I was falling off the stool, Luis quickly rescued me. "The minimum is five years and four months. We will of course, argue for the minimum."

"And what are the chances for the minimum, Luis?"

"Everything is up to the judge. We just need to trust in God."

"Do you believe in God, Luis?" I asked with sincere curiosity.

"Of course." He answered. "I am *Cristiano.*"

After a moment of indecision, I asked, "Will you pray for me?"

My unquenchable thirst for escape continued. Escape from both the prison and escape from myself. Whenever Tito and Fernando invited, I leapt at the chance of blowing through endless lines of coke and blowing my mind apart in a futile effort of escape and finding none. The physical walls around me were three stories high, guarded by INPEC commandos toting machine guns and pacing along turrets coiled with razor wire. Far worse were the impossible mental impasses constantly reducing my mind into dungeons of solitary and mental stalemate. Suicide, enticing. Lights out, Baby. Agnosia. Hallucinogenic nihilism. Raw telepathic desire transmitting to nowhere. Psych block freeze and cerebral stalemate leaving me coiled through endless nights reclined on my side dipping fingers into my bowl of cold soup and licking them to the bone.

Each morning, walking into the yard, I gave conscious effort to avoid Pastor Carlos, passing the small church, ignoring its existence. Miserable and fighting my hangover, I loathed the gnawing option of church, crawling back to the God who for so many years I'd held accountable for my misery. My God, forever tormenting me with His relentless forgiveness and torturous and indiscriminate love.

The day after Christmas a team of women dressed in white smocks came into the patio to take the vitals of the prisoners. After waiting in line for two hours I stepped onto the scale. I'd lost twenty pounds in four months. Sitting in the yard, I stared up at the slices of clouds moving through the razor wire and tried to imagine the animal images that my daughter might have seen. I couldn't see anything resembling reality. Just concrete walls and dead ends. In a moment of epiphany, I settled on the fact that there was no going over, under or around the walls. No more opportunities to evade circumstances. These were walls that I had no other option but to work my way *through*.

Friday, January 1st.

Due to the holiday and the scarcity of guards (no doubt sleeping off hangovers,) the prison was in lockdown. Morning spent locked into the Pasillo with a breakfast of a bread roll and an orange distributed through the bars. Happy New Year! Finally let out around noon to wander the patio, I was passing by the library when Don Carlos' voice called my name. I looked up. A book came fluttering down from his second-floor hall and I caught it with both hands. A Bible.

The following day Pastor Carlos asked me to his room. He paid to live alone, and his room was painted white and thoroughly spotless. He'd paid to have cupboards built onto his walls. His concrete floor was covered in a large shag carpet. He even had his own coffee maker. He took a seat on his neatly made bed and I sat on the other which he'd fashioned into a couch. "Have you had a chance to read?"

I shook my head. "No, Pastor Carlos. The last time I seriously studied scripture was back when I was living in Half Moon Bay. That's in California. I was in a small men's Bible study group. Nine years ago." He handed me a small chapbook: *You'll Get Through This*, by Max Lucado. I glanced over the preface then read aloud.

> *You'll get through this.*
> *It won't be painless.*
> *It won't be quick.*
> *But God will use this mess for good.*
> *Don't be foolish or naïve.*
> *But don't despair either.*
> *With God's help, you'll get through this.*

Staring at the word *through,* my eyes began to tear up. I kept my head down hiding my face.

"Would you like to read more?" He invited. I didn't want to read more. The only thing I wanted to do was find Fernando and Tito and spend the rest of the retched day and my miserable eternity snorting drugs and melting my face off my head watching my mind spiral and pool down into the drain.

The Pastor's voice was impossibly kind. Fighting all impulse to ditch and run, I spent the next half hour reading and discussing the story of Joseph being thrown into the pit, and how God used his bleak circumstances to save a nation. I clearly understood the story analogous to my circumstances. After stammering through the scriptures, I stood to make my anxious exit. Pastor Carlos melted me with his soft voice and kind eyes. "May I pray for you?"

My first six months at La Modelo were spent living in a sphere of pure culture shock. Not having the language, everything around me was in a constant swirl of confusion. I held no understanding of Latin or Colombian culture and had no desire to learn. I took a peculiar comfort in *not* being able to communicate, and often used my ignorance as an inroad to solitude. Surrounded every waking moment on all sides with excessive noise, grown men bellowing, shouting and posturing like apes in a concrete jungle and I had no desire to participate. I spent time absorbing only necessary information and focused on my survival.

One random morning Luis showed up toting a collection of letters and photos my family had sent. He'd taken the time and expense to print them out. I took them into my hands like treasured pearls. Images of my daughter visiting with my parents seated and smiling around a Christmas feast. Pictures of my parent's recent trip to Yellowstone. A photo of a birthday card my daughter had drawn for me—offering a pile of cinnamon rolls and an overflowing fruit salad. I spent a half day searching around the patio halls trying to locate a roll of tape. As I was arranging the photos onto my concrete walls, Fernando wandered in and told me to take them down.

"Why?" I asked, incredulous.

I listened intently to Fernando's lesson on *Essential Prison Behavior, 101*. "You have no family here." He instructed. "You don't talk about your family. You don't tell anyone about your family. If someone asks you about your family, you say they are dead. If people know you have *gringo* family, then they think you are rich. They try and locate your family. And if they find where your family live then they say they fuck your family up unless you pay them money. Big money! No pictures. Take them down. Keep them under your bed. You have no family here. Only in your mind." Fernando's instructions were completely bizarre, but as I processed it, it all made sense. He shook his head like a learned professor and outlined my orientation with subtle pearls of wisdom. I could clearly see this wasn't his first rodeo. A wake-up call of sorts that I was no longer in Kansas anymore. "Be smart!" He added. "Don't make friends here. Everyone here is a fucking snake!" Under his tutelage I quickly discerned that my best existence was *non-existence*, and from then on, gave every effort to ease invisible through each day, silent, un-noticed and under the radar.

Friday morning, 12 February, I dressed in my best clothes to endure a 6:00 AM thorough strip search. I boarded a prison bus, cuffed into a line of thirteen other prisoners. Rolling through Bogotá morning traffic, I stared out the window into the other cars, studying the expressions on the faces of commuters heading to work, mothers scolding children.

Arriving at the *Paloquemao* courthouse, the commandos stopped traffic, and under the guidance of their guns I shuffled into the basement of the building. Sequestered into a 30 x 30 foot cage with sixty-eight other prisoners, the tension was enormous. Failed men crammed into life threatening situations, pacing and frantically waiting for their sentences to be read.

My name was called. I was ushered up an institutional stairway, down a long hall and into a formal courtroom. Luis was waiting and greeted me with a hug. The judge entered and began reading my case in Spanish. I sat mute, comprehending nothing, everything lost in translation. After a half hour of listening to the gibberish, Luis finally leaned over and whispered, "The judge accepted our plea. You are sentenced to 64 months."

The tension in the room evaporated. The audience ended. The prosecutor shot me a weak smile and began filing her papers into her briefcase. The judge focused his eyes hard on me and leveled me with a statement. Luis translated. "The judge says… if you wish to say anything to the court, please say it now."

I stood and leaned into the microphone. "I would like to thank you, Your Honor, for your time and attention to my case. I know that the country of Colombia has its problems and issues with drugs and narco-trafficking. I would like to offer the prosecutor and the country of Colombia an apology for adding to this problem. Please accept my apology."

Two weeks after my sentencing I woke to the clang of the first guard unlocking the Pasillo. I dressed silent and carried my journal into the yard. Staring east, I examined the growling sun crawl over the sharp edges of the Eastern Cordillera range of the Andes, painting the high concrete walls of my prison in a strange orange glow. Alone in the yard, I absorbed the large and empty space. I walked over to the trash bins and fished out the largest cigarette butts, sat on the concrete bench and smoked. Looking up and pondering the morning clouds, my eyes froze on a black kitten dangling by its small furry arms, crucified and dead on the coiled razor wire.

Saturday 27 February '16
I *feel* myself slowly coming to terms with facts and events. I was sentenced on the 12th: 64 months. I'm fine. Even thankful to some extent, knowing the alternative to being here would most certainly have been my death. Divine intervention? Perhaps. All my life my family has observed that I make my decisions based too much on my feelings and not enough on pragmatic logic. Over the years I've come to own this fault. Events in Cambodia led me to a place of no feeling at all, pure apathy. Apathy being the most dangerous and corrosive place of all. I'm beginning to feel the peculiar sensation of feeling again. I'm *feeling* several things—some good and some not so good. The prison itself is a real crap hole. Everything here broken, bound together with wire and duct tape. Electricity flickers from dim 40-watt bulbs hanging by live and exposed wires casting everything in a putrid yellow. The walls are crumbling. A few days ago, TIME magazine reported that at least a hundred butchered bodies had been discovered in the sewers that run under the prison. Violence and killings seem to be a weekly if not daily occurrence. The rooms are infested with roaches and microscopic bed bugs. Rats run freely in the yard. Broken bodies everywhere. Young fathers

limp together in mourning counter-clockwise around the yard trying their best to turn back time. Grandfathers holding faded books weep openly in the library. Young scarred, tattooed boys sit in the yard smoking dope and carve toy guns out of scavenged wood with their shanks. Believers pause on their way to chapel and bow to the four-foot statue of the deteriorating Virgin. This place is full of broken bodies. I'm here in this place with them. I am them. My body equally broken; another fallen piece from a chaotic mosaic laying scattered on the concrete prison floor.

After breakfast I wandered to the library and spent the morning browsing the English titles. The selections were mostly dime novels—trashy potboiler crap. Shelved between pulpy mysteries and ancient romances, I managed to discover some gems. That evening, while thumbing the pages of Theroux's *Dark Star Safari*, I underlined *"Ruins especially lend themselves to invention; because they are incomplete, we finish them in our imagination."*

On the last day of the month, the prison crier called my name and I ran anxiously to meet Luis in the dark visitor's hall. He was there waiting with his ever-present smile and armed with a de-brief of the sentencing. "So, where do we go from here?" I asked.

"There are many things we will do. First, we will file an appeal and try and get your sentence reduced. Second, because this is your first offense and you have no criminal record, we will file for *la detenzione domiciliare.*"

"Luis, English please."

He smiled. "Home detention. I have talked it over with my mom. We can give the court our address so that you can come and serve your sentence in our house."

I stared at him through the dirty glass, mute and bewildered. He had known me for only seven months, and to him, I was nothing more than a criminal that had fallen into his legal lap. From our very first introduction, he'd blessed me with pro-bono representation, and now he was inviting me to come and live in his house? "Why, Luis? Why are you blessing me like this?"

"It's what we do." He answered simply. Before I could discuss further, he glanced at his watch and announced his quick departure. "Aaron, I have another appointment. Before I go, I have a note from your daughter. She sent it last month." He gathered the letter from his briefcase and slid it through the slot. I hid the letter into my pocket. Luis asked if he could pray for me. Joining our palms against the thick partition, he prayed blessings over my safety and God's guidance over my legal process. I, in turn mumbled thanks for his involvement in my case and a blessing over his mother—the first sincere prayer I had uttered in six years.

Carrying the letter in my pocket, I danced through the day. Wandering through the halls of eternal concrete, I laughed in the face of the dead-ends. I collided and gushed *into* everyone around me with an extraordinary detachment and a hilarious peace, focused entirely on my evening's moments of rare solitude when I'd finally pull the curtain to my bunk and be alone with my daughter. My Ex had taken the time to transcribe my six-year-old daughter's diction into a stream of stunning prose.

Jan 31, 2016
Dear Papa,

I love you. I miss you so much. I want to climb into this paper and jump out to see you. I hope to see you soon. When I see you, I will give you a really big hug. I got a new bicycle for Christmas from Aunty Ali, Bubba, Liam and Avery. I have two wiggle teeth on the bottom and in the front. I can run faster now that I am 6 years old. At Christmas I went to Arizona to visit Ahmu and Peepaw, Aunty Heather, Uncle David, Erin, Alex, Evie, Uncle John and Aunt Ronnee. Me and mom drove to Arizona and back. It was a long drive but I safely made it. I am learning how to play piano at home when mom and Aunty Nan teach me. I hope to start learning the guitar too. I also started a gymnastics class this month and continue to take art. In kindergarten I am learning addition and subtraction, sight words, high frequency words in reading, PE, outdoor education, science, music and drama. I got all my spell-a-thon words correct and raised $600 for my school. Here are the words I can spell: horse, mouse, noodle, tiger, the, to, can, is, a, go, me, my, octopus. I want to talk with you very soon.

Love, Mei.

Chapter Eighteen

La Modelo Prison, Bogotá
March 2016 - June 2017

March 2016

Hi Aaron, just want to let you know that Mei received the drawing you sent and it encouraged her a lot. I'm not sure you want to continue "Spanish classes" as the reason for your absence. She will still feel abandoned in thinking you chose to take classes instead of being with her. For now I have respected your decision not to tell her anything else but as time goes on she may come to other conclusions. She also can't fully grieve the loss of your absence during this time frame as she doesn't know what is going on. I very much want you both to have the father daughter relationship that you both need. I hope that after your release you will be able to take more of a part in her life. We pray for you nightly. For your health and safety. I pray that your bond remains strong and that you both are secure in the love that you have for each other.

-Li

My ex-wife's words were simple, but the concepts were nearly impossible to fathom. I'd desecrated our marriage vows through unfaithful deceit. Lashed her with my tongue. Abused her with lies and ultimately abandoned our marriage in my insatiable pursuits of drugs and selfish abandon. And she was offering herself as a continued bridge of support and love between me and my estranged daughter? Praying for me? Li's pearls of grace felt like burning coals falling onto my head, singeing my hair; the power of forgiveness burrowing into my mind leaving me inert, cleansed and contemplating renewal.

One early April morning, 2016, after another all-night binge with Tito and Fernando, I stumbled out of my cell with the intention of capturing the first glows of the empty day, alone. I hated coke and the miserable after-effects were nearly impossible to bear. The comedown felt like death. But the cheap buzz and party time with other guys served as a desirable alternative to spending nights alone in my cell. Stumbling into the open concrete yard, my anticipations for a single solitary moment were razed by a large man pacing furious laps. A new inmate, or one I'd never noticed? Rounding the yard corner, he spotted me, paused, then began walking towards me. His face was disfigured. One eye missing, folded over by a haunting skin graft. Nose canked askew. His one functional eye floated, giving the impression of a 15th century Quasimodo, resurrected.

I side-stepped his advance. He swayed, keeping himself positioned in my path. I angled again, and he again turned with me. As the distance between us lessened with each step, I readied myself for the impending assault. The terrible dance brought us face to face. Staring into his one eye, I threw out my hands. "¿Qué pasa?"

In a quick and fluid motion, the stranger wrapped his huge arms around me, holding me tight. He whispered into my ear in his broken English, "Dios love you." After returning the polite hug I relaxed my arms to break the embrace, but the man continued to hold me repeating over and over, "Dios love you… He love you so much… so much Jesus love you… Dios love you…" His words washed over me like waves; howled in a most violently tender tidal flood and every muscle in my body and all defenses in my mind instantly dissolved into sinuous surrender.

With a sudden crash, I felt the levee inside me break. The man held me for a minute as I wept uncontrollably like a small child against his chest. I'd later learn that the stranger, Omar Gómez, was in for multiple murder counts. He'd been a member of Colombia's right-wing *paramilitary* and his mishandling of a grenade had blown off half his face.

Each morning a group of about twenty men gathered in the little church. I enjoyed the ambiance, but my attendance was sporadic. Everything was in Spanish and I understood little. What I did absorb with a pure intensity was the universal language of the *Holy*.

The three Abrahamic religions agree upon the concept of the Holy Spirit. The Hindu trinity translates the Holy Spirit into the name, *Shiva*. Buddhists also absorb the idea, beautifully stressing the Spirit into everyday life application. Raised in the church, my childhood and early adulthood resulted in an injured distrust for religious division and pluralistic thinking. My recent antics and experiences in Cambodia had motivated me to declare a deliberate and clean severance from any relationship with God; waging an all-out unholy war against anything *Holy*. Entering the little church each morning, the *Holy* safety that permeated the room was a direct relief to the constant impending doom that, throughout each minute of every day, threatened to crush me from all sides. For thirty minutes each morning I knew a sanctified area was available for me to enter, where the daily screams, proverbial miseries and constant threats of violence and doom were suspended into a very real sensation of pure peace.

Lingering one morning after service, I spotted a CD labeled *Musica Cristiana*. I popped it into the DVD player and spent the following hour hypnotized through live performances by Christine D'Clario, Jesus Adrian Romero, Marcela Gándara, and Ricardo and Eva Luna Montaner. My discovery of the music became my primary motivation for attending the morning services. I would sit, waiting patiently for the service to end. The men would file out and back to their rooms to ready themselves for the day. Left alone in the little church, I'd steal some coveted alone time listening to the gorgeous and transformative notes before the room was overcome with the academic classes scheduled for the day. Alone with the music, these precious moments became my daily baptism.

Throughout the first year in *La Modelo*, I learned how to endure the constant brutality of the INPEC guards along with the relentless weight of Brazil's Mafia. The crushing reality became my treadmill normalcy. One day and for no apparent reason, Brazil showed up in my cell and announced that I was moving rooms. I relocated up to the fourth floor, Pasillo 15. For two months I enjoyed a good cell with Brian, another narco-mule from Jersey, before I was abruptly uprooted again and tossed back down into Pasillo 3 and made to live for a month with Hector, a Colombiano and Victor, a guy from Mexico City who both held a certain disdain for foreigners. After a few tense weeks, they together concocted and presented an elaborate story to Brazil that I was a "…filthy Gringo who never bathed and never washed his clothes." After a public and humiliating expulsion from the pasillo I was moved again up to hall seven and into a cell with the most flamboyant queen in the Patio.

The only thing Pacha loved more than himself was his gay identity. Every thought floated from his mind, each syllable that dripped from his carefully painted lips, and every gesture was saturated in his flaming *gayness*. I sincerely admired his passion and found myself fully intrigued and entertained by his melodramatic *everything*. His entire circle was made up of all the coke-head queens who paraded to and from our cell all hours of the day in a constant fashion show whir, displaying their recent acquisitions of feminine apparel: thongs, compacts, panties, dresses, perfumes, bras and anything else they were able to smuggle into the prison. I enjoyed the colorful array of characters, their frequent gushing emotional displays, and especially their cheap coke which they shared freely. I only stayed with Pacha a week, my time with him cut short by two defining circumstances.

Saturday night. The last of his girlfriends had left the room. Pacha was climbing the walls and out of his mind zooming on a three-day X/coke binge. The last thing I'd seen before going to sleep were his zany and lustful eyes flickering around the room looking for something to do. Mystical valleys and moors later, I awoke to a blurry fairy-tail landscape of Pacha licking my ear. Shaking sleep, I sat up quick and grabbed him by his shoulders. Holding him at arms-length, I stared hard into his delicate eyes, making it perfectly clear I held no interest. I threw him gently back onto his bed and flicked the light. He sat small, his face beet red staring at the floor, crushed at my rejection. I wasn't offended in the least by his advances. On the contrary, I was a bit flattered. I liked the guy and wanted to maintain a stable roommate situation, as opposed to being moved to a new room again. Absorbing his embarrassment, I took a seat next to him and offered him a cigarette. We smoked silent through the delicate tension.

The next morning was Sunday—female visit day—the most sacred day of the week where multiple rules were set in stone to ensure the safety and enjoyment of all the wives, mothers, grandmothers and daughters who came to see their loved ones. The rules were militant, enforced by *The House* with a zero-tolerance policy. 1. All men with no visitors must stay in the patio from 8:00 until 3:00. Once all visitors have left, men can return to their rooms. 2. No selling or doing drugs of any kind. 3. Smoking cigarettes only allowed at the far end of the Patio near the trash cans. 4. No use of televisions or radios. 5. Do not look at or speak to female visitors unless they are your family.

I woke to the sounds of Pacha singing in the shower. Moments later he emerged and dressed while dancing around the room. When I finally opened my eyes, he was sitting on his bunk filling in his eyebrows. I could see he still hadn't slept, riding into day number four on his drug-fueled rollercoaster. He was wide-eyed and manic, multi-tasking around the room in a half dozen useless activities. After breakfast, we both gathered our belongings for the day and left the room by the time the first women visitors arrived.

Every Sunday visit day, the little church was converted into a small movie house where all guys who didn't have visitors congregated to watch DVDs. I spent the entire day in the little church, counting the hours until 3:00 when I'd be permitted back up to my cell.

3:00 and all the visitors had gone. Dinner was served and by 4:00, all prisoners were locked back into their *pasillos*. Everything was routine in the hall. Guys were sleeping, strolling the hall, visiting room to room. TV's blaring at full volume. A normal Sunday evening. Around 6:00 the gate at the end of the hall clanged open and Brazil appeared flanked by all his thugs. They paraded down the hall in their typical menacing stomp and came to a halt just outside my room. Both Pacha and I sat up in our bunks. Brazil began firing questions at Pacha. Apparently, while I'd spent the entire day in the church watching movies, Pacha had chosen to pass his day by violating every rule on the Sunday Rule list. Multiple complaints had been levied against him by many other prisoners. Under the supervision and blessing of the guards, *The House* proceeded to beat Pacha senseless, dragging him moaning half dead down the hall and out of the patio, never to be seen again.

The following day, in an effort to empty the cell for *Colombiano* inmates willing to pay the big cash, Brazil moved me into a cell further down the hall. The cell was a dump, darkly painted with a leaky toilet and infested with chinches. My new cellmate proved to be the perfect nightmare.

Omar was Colombian and spoke no English. I knew from the first moment meeting him that the situation wouldn't last long. He was the spooky type, with no interest in cohabitating or communicating with anyone. A complete loner. Omar had been rounded up and charged with multiple murder counts as one of Pablo Escobar's assassins. Having been in the system for over fifteen years, he'd become entirely institutionalized and was looking forward to his impending release.

Enduring the first night's awkward silence, I learned that Omar insisted sleeping with the light on. Burrowing under the blanket, I eventually drifted off only to wake hours later in the dead of night suffocating in thick smoke. I sat up and focused in on Omar crouched over a small bonfire blazing in the center of the tiny cell. He was staring into the fire, tossing scraps of newspaper and fanning the flames. "¿Qué carajo?" I asked. This translated loosely into "What the fuck are you doing?"

Omar glared furious and made hand motions to silence me, then leapt onto his bed and began examining the walls of the cell. Processing this as complete insanity, I jumped from my bed and lugged my mattress into the hall where I set up camp.

The next day, I confronted Omar through Cheeky Charlie; a bilingual British drug mule who lived down the hall. Charlie explained through a smug grin, "He says the room is infested with *chinches*... He says the smoke makes them less active. He thinks that building a fire every night and smoking them out is the only way to deal with the situation."

"It's completely insane, Charlie! How am I supposed to live like this? My roommate sleeping with the light on, building a bonfire in the room every night? Tell him it's unacceptable. Completely fucking insane!"

Charlie translated. Omar shook his head and left the conversation. Charlie clapped me on the shoulder and invited me to his room where he explained, "Nothing you can do, Aaron. Omar's crazy. He's due to get released soon. Probably in the next few days. Just tough it out. Sorry for laughing, dude. But Omar's a fucked-up guy. Been in jail for a long time. He'll be gone soon and then you'll have the room to yourself."

Much to my relief, Omar was indeed released a week later, but counter to Charlie's prediction I was not awarded the room to myself. I was again evicted by Brazil and moved over to Pasillo 12 so the room could be sold to an inmate willing to pay for his own space. Throughout my first eighteen months I lived in twelve different cells with seventeen different roommates, until I was finally moved back down to the dungeon, Pasillo three where I'd first started. Tito moved out of the patio of his own volition because he hated Brazil and didn't want to continue paying Brazil's extortion demands. So, Fernando and I moved in together, and for the first time I was able to enjoy the stability of a good room with a cellie who I sincerely liked.

Fernando was from Nogales; a scrappy and depressed border town just three hours south from my parent's home in Phoenix. I'd made many trips down to Nogales for the cheap thrill of the wild Mexican fiesta. I knew where Fernando came from. If Nogales offered anything to its quarter of a million poverty-stricken residents, it was a glimpse through the border wall into the illusions of the Land of Plenty. La Modelo was Fernando's second rodeo. Back when he was eighteen, he'd been popped crossing into Arizona carrying 220 kilos of Mexicali brick weed. After being detained State-side for a month, the authorities had deported him back over the border.

Fernando was kind, though a bit reckless. He had a short fuse and a lethal temper, willing to throw punches with anyone who looked at him cross-eyed. He also had a raging coke addiction, which I quickly learned to live with and completely ignore. By that time, I'd successfully kicked all addictions save for my half-pack-a-day habit. Cold turkey. It was easier than I thought it would be. In fact, committing to the decision proved more difficult than the actual kick.

Weaning off the drugs was a pleasantly painless process. Pragmatically, it was an easy decision. The drugs in the jail were terribly dirty, cut with junk. Plaster scraped from the walls. And the high always resulted in a haunting morning hangover with my heart completely annihilated and my nose and mouth filled with blood. On top of that, I simply didn't have the financial resources to continue supporting the destructive routine. And after years of abuse, to finally release the habit revealed as a blessing, and not the curse I had always feared.

In the confines of our cell, Fernando and I agreed to leave each other well enough alone, with an invisible line of tolerance dissecting the room. While he did his blow, I spent my hours lying in bed reading or listening to my music. Our laid-back personalities and mutual respect created an excellent and functional ambiance, allowing us to cohabitate perfectly.

A year in La Modelo and I was fully ingratiated into prison life. Living in lock-up was all about *survival.* Mental survival. Physical survival. Spiritual survival. Financial survival. The pressure to constantly hand over money and bribes to *The House* was enormous and relentless—a prison within a prison. Everything was centered around cash, or in my case, the lack of. Wealthy inmates worried for nothing, sleeping in, and lounging in their single cells all day while making payments to The House to be left unmolested. Intent on maintaining their lavish lifestyles, they also made payments to the guards for luxuries and benefits to be smuggled in. Anything could be bought and delivered for a price. Expensive groceries purchased from the outside, hotplates for cooking, coffee makers and cookware, shag rugs, expensive cologne, smartphones, prostitutes. The possibilities were as endless as the cycle of bribery and extortion.

After receiving payment, the guards then smuggled in the goods. A week or so later the same guards would show up and confiscate the items they had just delivered and then re-sell the items back to the inmates for a price. Inmates with little resources lived with the eternal fear of being thrown out of sheltered *Patio Tres* into the jaws of the common prison population, and so spent every minute of every waking day hustling around for any job that might pay some cash. Under Brazil's relentless threats, the poorest of the poor resulted to whoring themselves for cash in order to make their monthly "rent." Through my connections, I found myself both lucky and blessed.

Pastor Carolos and his rich friends up in *Pasillo* 8 hired me on as their personal dishwasher. Each day the pastor cooked lunch and dinner for himself and his three millionaire cronies. Salmon steaks, filet mignon, *spaghetti frutti di mare*. After their feast, I attend to their dishes, scouring a half hour after lunch and a half hour after dinner for their paltry pay that rounded out to about .28 per day. My most lucrative position came when I became the *Pasillo's Limpiador*, responsible for keeping the hall clean. This involved mopping the hallway morning and afternoon. My duties were performed in exchange for my monthly rent. The relief of not having to fret about where my rent was coming from was an enormous relief and allowed me to exist without worrying about Brazil and his merciless regime. For everyone (except for the rich,) paying the monthly rent was an excruciating process, but there was always the invisible incentive of staying safe *and alive* that made the exercise bearable.

On June 14th, 2016 multiple stabbings occurred in Patio 4. I walked up to Pasillo 15 which afforded me a glimpse at the carnage. All prisoners had been beaten back and locked into their halls. A few hundred guards milled about in full riot gear armed with batons, machine guns and tear gas launchers. Multiple and random pools of blood scattered over the concrete. Four makeshift triage tents had been constructed to tape up the wounded. Guys waiting in line gripping their wounds, blood flowing freely through their fingers.

An hour later, *Mario Grande* hit in our patio. Everyone herded into the yard and forced to sit on the ground while the *Dragoneantes* conducted a systematic strip search of all prisoners. During the three-hour shakedown, the Commando's tossed our cells. When Fernando and I returned to our room, we saw the cell had been trashed like never before. Our mattresses had been ripped open, along with our pillows. Everything once standing upright was toppled. The bathroom was smeared with shampoo and toothpaste. Every item in the cell had been left strewn around the room as if scattered in the wake of a cyclone. While tossing the room, the guards had helped themselves to refreshments. The sodas and the snacks I'd purchased from the prison store had been devoured; empty bottles and cellophane snack wrappers left scattered over the floor.

Second only to the constant requirement to survive financially came the effort to simply live. The prison clinic consisted of a pathetic handful of ill-trained staff responsible for taking care of a population of eight-thousand criminals. The medical facilities were abysmal and underfunded in a filthy environment that bred contamination and illness. Cold and flu symptoms were constant and widespread throughout the jail. Food poisoning cases were a daily—no, hourly occurrence. On the multiple occasions when I contacted food poisoning there was nothing to do but hunker down in my bunk for two or three days and sweat it out.

Five months after walking into the jail, the eagle-eye vision I'd enjoyed all my life suddenly began to decline. When I put in a request for a vision exam and glasses, the clinic staff simply shrugged. My vision continued to deteriorate to the point of having to hold the printed page at full arms-length in order to simply read. By the end of September, a rash began appearing on my fingers and hands. Multiple trips to the prison clinic awarded me a couple tubes of low-grade topical creams which did nothing to alleviate the infection. Entering the holiday season, the rash had advanced into deep slits weeping blood and blisters oozing pus. The clinic had no Band-aids. The lack of bandages resulted in my stealing rolls of masking tape out of the library and fashioning my own bandages with tape and toilet paper. Washing and doctoring my hands for a half hour became my morning routine; a ritual that I would perform for the duration of my sentence.

Along with the first strings of Christmas lights, an ominous pall swallowed the prison whole. The holiday season threw everyone into a state of crushing and unbearable depression. Makeshift decorations and ornaments were put up around the prison, casting everything in an eerie glow of sadness. The more people tried to brighten up the place, the darker everything became.

Early December, the patio crier summoned everyone to the Patio to enjoy a Christmas coral concert given by the Ladies Guild of the *Ministerio Carcelario Biblico Bautista*: The Prison Ministry of the local Baptist Church. It was a grand assembly, with *todo mundo en el patio* required to participate. Under the watchful eye of the guards, all three hundred prisoners gathered together in best behavior for the festivities. The elderly choir of six silver-haired ladies opened their mouths and began singing "The Carol of the Bells." A fellow prisoner who I knew distantly as Camillo suddenly took the opportunity to scale the fence and spider-web his way along to his delusional freedom. In the broad glow of daylight, Camillo's attempted escape scattered the entire patio into holy chaos. A squad of Commandos assembled pointing their rifles at Camillo while another squad surrounded the old women. The ladies at once lifted their arms and began howling prayers and speaking in tongues as they were sequestered into a corner of the patio for protection. Ignoring the multiple warning from the guards, Camillo was shot down off the fence in a hailstorm of rubber bullets. The concert ended just seconds after it had begun with all prisoners violently herded and locked back into their halls to contemplate the horrors of being separated from their loved ones and the impossible implications of the impending holiday season.

With intense feelings of separation, regrets, frustrations and gloom, general violence in the prison escalated dramatically. The days following Camillo's valiant attempt, two other prisoners gave it a go, only to be thwarted, beaten and buried deeper into the system with six additional years added to their sentences.

Children all over the world, including my own daughter, had begun the magical countdown for the arrival of Christmas day. In prison, everyone was counting down the days for it all to be over, and for the New Year to begin. On the evening of New Year's Eve while smoking in the hall I caught sight of Brazil and his minions assisting the guards smuggling in 20 black plastic bags of booze for the New Year's festivities. The wealthy inmates would welcome in the New Year with celebration and oblivion while the rest of us would pass the hour alone in our cells calculating time.

Throughout that first year, Luis visited regularly and fought tooth and nail for my release. His bimonthly visits filled me with hope and sustained my endurance, but his every effort was blocked by the courts. Ten months after my arrest, in June of '16, Luis filed for my *domiciliario*, house arrest, on the grounds of my clean history, good behavior and my chronic illnesses which the prison refused (or had no resources) to treat. Shortly after the petition was filed, Sofia Del Pilar Barrera Mora, the judge handling my case sent two social workers to interview me. The court sent for my medical records from the prison clinic. It took an entire year for the court to review my application, and in June of '17 I received the rejection. I took the news surprisingly well, and asked to give a word in the church, using my rejection for home jail as an example for others not to give up hope when we don't get what we want; to trust God and "...lean not on our own understanding."

The Colombian legal system presented itself as a sadistic rollercoaster. Every few months an announcement was given, or info circulated from Colombia's mainstream media regarding benefits being given to prisoners. At one point I was called out to meet for a second time with social workers sent from the court informing me that I was eligible to receive a 50% reduction off my sentence. No reduction was ever given.

The following month a notice was posted on the prison kiosk signed and dated by The Ministry of Justice. Everyone gathered around to read the notice and threw into a frenzy about the impending reduction of sentences for foreign prisoners that the Colombian Congress would soon vote for. The notice created a huge buzz throughout the patio. The vote took place, and in the end, all benefits were rejected.

In my fifteenth month of lock-up, I received a positive letter from the court informing me that I would soon receive a 72-hour freedom pass. The letter described in detail that because of my excellent behavior and time served, how I'd be released once every three months for a period of 72 hours, after which I'd return to the jail and continue my sentence. A week after receiving the notice, another letter arrived informing me that because I was charged as a narco-traficante, I was not eligible for the benefit. *You won the lottery!* No, you haven't. The constant promise of freedom, countered by the constant rejection leveled out to a proverbial flatline of counting creeping months, the slow days, empty hours, ticking minutes and all the countless seconds that filled the large calendar hanging on my concrete wall.

The daily prison gossip concerning impending and possible benefits, combined with the constant and conflicting information delivered from the courts was an absolute mind-fuck that I eventually learned to ignore. Luis informed me that I'd be eligible for my conditional release in April, 2018. Those were the hard numbers; the ones I began counting by.

January 2017. Brazil and his henchmen ushered in the New Year by intensifying their constant and unrelenting fear campaign. A string of meetings ensued where it was announced that certain prisoners had been writing letters to the prison Director complaining of the constant extortion. The House responded by making examples out of seven suspected prisoners and kicked them out of the patio. They also announced that they were increasing the monthly rent payments from 20,000 Pesos to 50,000 per month—a 150% increase. Three months later, all the American prisoners (there were six of us at that time) in the Patio were assembled and were made to sign a letter Brazil had authored stating that our experiences in the Patio were perfectly normal and we remained *unmolested.* "This letter will be sent to certain Colombian politicians and Senior INPEC Agency Officials and to the Ministry of Justice," Brazil Announced. "You must sign the letter! If you are interviewed, say nothing about having to pay your monthly rent. Rent does not exist here! There are no drugs here! No extortion! You are happy! You have no grievances! This is the best patio in the country, and you are lucky to be serving your time here. If you don't sign the letter, I'll find space for you over in Patio 4!"

Prison was a cesspit plagued with roaring whirlpools that tried to suck you to the very bottom of the deep river every minute of every day. By the end of my first year, I'd learned the ropes, assimilating both physically and mentally into the prison culture. I'd learned when to lock eyes and when to speak up; when to shut up and when to look away. The perpetual and violent threats of extortion snapped my resolve. Awareness of the lack of medical services initiated a daily lifestyle of caution and hypersensitivity to impending illness and possibly injury. I learned to ignore the constant din of deafening television volume, cut to commercial, back to the never-ending reality show of guys fighting over whose turn it is to clean the toilet; grown men threatening to kill each other's mothers over endless and trivial disputes. The dysfunctional legal system offered nothing but exasperation and disappointment. I learned to walk the tightrope of maintaining hope and expecting nothing. It was a nightmarish conundrum. Excruciating isolation. Depressing separation. Endless pragmatic frustration. Fear.

Despite all the darkness, there were moments of reprieve and encouragement. One Sunday, Luis's mom showed up. Alba Liz, a woman who I knew only by name came on a Sunday to spend the entire day with me. When she arrived, I took her arm and walked ten feet tall, glowing through the patio. She arrived carrying an enormous lunch that Luis had prepared in his kitchen—Mexican fajitas, with all the trimmings. I invited my friends Bob and Chinche to share the wealth. After lunch, Alba Liz and I attended church and then spent the afternoon chatting with the help of Bob's rudimentary Spanish translations. When it was time for the visitors to leave, I escorted her to the gate and embraced her in tears. It was my first visit after being locked up for two years. Alba

Liz returned the next month toting salmon steaks, frijoles con carne, tortillas, buttered potatoes, and more of her selfless care and love.

My communication and healing with my family continued. Saturday was the highlight of my week. I rented an hour on a smuggled cell phone and enjoyed video conferences with my parents and my daughter. After giving me her update on her week in school, Mei and I began writing together, collaboratively inventing characters and applying curious plots and hilarious conflicts into funny short stories. Our joyous and torturous face time always ended the same. "Papa, when will you come? Why can't I come see you? When will I see you again?" Back in my cell, I'd lie in my bunk recalling her every word, phrase and nuance until the burning tears came.

I always had an excuse or a deflection ready. After a year and a half incarcerated, I called, and Li answered. "Aaron, she's figured it out. She put it all together on her own. She knows you're in jail." Before I could catch my breath, she handed the phone to my daughter.

"Hi Papa, are you Okay?"

"I'm *very* good, baby girl. How are you?"

"I'm sad, Papa."

"Mei, I know you know where I am. And I want you to know that I am very safe and nothing bad is going to happen to me. I will be out soon, and as soon as I'm out I will come straight to see you and hold you in my arms and smother you with pug kisses!"

"Oh Papa, please come. I miss you soooo much!"

"I will baby. But for now, I'm sure you have some questions for me. And I want you to know that you can ask me any questions you have, and I'll answer them."

Following a long pause her small voice asked, "Papa?"

"Yes?"

"Did you steal something?"

"No baby, I didn't steal anything."

After another long pause, she continued. "Did you hurt someone?"

"No Baby. Papa would never hurt anyone."

"I don't want to know what you did, Papa. I just want you to know that I love you and I want you to come home. Please come home soon because I don't want to grow up. I want to keep small so when we see each other again I'll be the same size as when you last saw me." I covered the receiver so she couldn't hear my crying.

Absorbing my family's forgiveness was difficult. Mei's innocent and pure forgiveness was even more painful. Her forgiveness demanded that I first roam again through the many rooms of my past to discover my ability to work through the process of forgiving myself: a *growth demand* that involved a long and painful stare into the mirror. Stepping cautiously through the front door of the hideous funhouse, I saw my skeleton bent over my crying wife, weeping over our broken marriage vows. Ascending the stairs, I came to the room littered with drug paraphernalia: pipes, glass and endless mountains of meth and an infinite calendar marking my years of poor and cowardly choices. Walking up to the third floor, the mental browse continued with a horrific tour through the long halls. Rooms trashed and left bloody as a result from my tumultuous life with Lyda. Empty rooms littered with receipts of my financial ruin. Rooms left in sadness and confusion in the wake of all the lies I'd used to alienate family and friends. My most horrific escapades leaping out around every turn; all dark corridors filled with frightening spirits and painful memories.

Everything had finally come to an end. A life changing end. I knew with perfect clarity that landing in La Modelo was the best thing that could have ever happened. Without my detour into prison, I most certainly would have died before my forty-sixth birthday.

Throughout my prison experience, my daughter flooded me with notes, photos and texts, anxious to offer me her unconditional everything. My Saturday hours with her on the video calls were the very best moments. My weekly connections with Mei and my family, along with my devoted study of the scriptures and filling my head with the sounds of *Hillsong* all intertwined into a rock-solid foundation on which to stand. Confronting my physical healing, I continued to maintain my sobriety.

The process of separating myself from drugs involved an automatic re-evaluation of friends and acquaintances. Environmental control was the key. I placed myself in the center of a new social circle that simply didn't accept drug use. After my cold turkey success, I was able to whittle down my social interactions to a tight circle of three intimate friends.

Bob was a burly farm boy and long-haul trucker from the N. Eastern plains of Colorado. Erik was a science teacher from San Jose. Bob and Erik were both small load narco-traficantes doing small time who'd gotten pinched for one reason or another. And Edgar, the only Colombian in our group, was a chemistry teacher who'd been charged with having an "inappropriate encounter" with one of his students. The underaged girl had come on to him after class in the chem lab. Edgar and the girl had made out for a few minutes before the girl returned home and began chatting the news of her tryst on the phone to her girlfriends. Her parents overheard the conversation and alerted the police. Edgar had been found guilty, and the Colombian judicial system had issued him a ten-year sentence for *making out with a minor.*

Bob, Erik and Edgar were good men with sharp minds whom I enjoyed passing all my time with. I was most fond of Edgar, just a young nerdy kid in his mid-twenties who only in the last few years had devoted himself to an authentic spiritual quest, developing a whip-crack knack for memorizing and interpreting scripture. This commonality solidified our bond and in short time Edgar and I became inseparable. We both loved music, and spent hours listening to the music DVDs in the church, discussing lyrics, analyzing scriptures, searching for meaning and life applications.

The prison church for me became a safe house—a sanctuary away from all the noisy bullshit and annoying daily riff-raff. I understood little of what was being said but found myself immersed in the Spirit I felt there. The church service itself was boring and methodical, and eventually my attendance tapered off. My church became the yard where Edgar and I would spend hours together. My church became my cell where I'd sequester away pouring through the Bible Don Carlos had given me. For the first time in my life, I wasn't just reading scripture. I was analyzing it, dissecting it. And with Edgar's prayer partnership, I began exerting conscious efforts to center myself and apply my life efforts to its much-needed repair.

Along with Don Carlos' Bible, two other books fell into my hands that smacked me upside the head. I discovered a tiny and antiquated paperback in the library titled *God Calling*, written by "Two Listeners." It was a mind-blowing daily devotional. Each morning I'd read the dated passage and focus my mind and moral compass before stepping into the chaos. Jen Hatmaker's *Interrupted: When Jesus Wrecks Your Comfortable Christianity* challenged me to redefine my spiritual identity and shift my perspectives away from the treadmill activities of the boring church and into *active* community service. One morning, Pastor Carlos approached me and asked if I would consider leading the Saturday morning services. When Edgar offered to be my translator, I readily agreed.

The prison experience tends to reduce one's focus to viewing everything through two lenses: Self-preservation and achieving freedom. Everything else becomes peripheral. Hatmaker helped me shift the focus and attenuate my efforts to other guys around me in the jail rather than obsessing about myself and my own legal process. This involved taking the baby steps of emptying myself, inviting God to work through me, replacing my wants and desires and concentrating on encouraging those around me rather than focusing on myself—an impossible platform to achieve in jail (and in life for that matter,) but a daily goal to focus on, nonetheless.

Aaron Reed

I eventually came to define the prison experience as 10% physical and 90% mental. Every day presenting itself as a game. On one side of the board, my deteriorating body leaned forward, constantly studying my options with blurred lucidity and failed vision. On the other side, I gave best effort to remain poised and focused into repairing myself spiritually, strategizing through the muck. Negotiating myself through the experience, the turning point arrived when I stopped trying. It was all about *surrender*. And as I gradually and painfully learned to dissolve myself closer to nothingness, another Spirit revealed and eventually took control.

I recall the moment it happened with perfect clarity. A typical morning in June, I woke in my dark cell listening to the nocturne noises of the waking jail. Distant echoes of clanking chains and locks and slamming gates and inaudible conversation—the night shift exchanging with the morning guards. The swish swish of someone sweeping the hall. A distant jumble of morning Spanish talk show radio. Fernando snoring softly. I showered and dressed in the dark, then slipped from the room and into the deserted patio. I was the first one out. Sitting on a concrete bench I lit a cigarette and watched the sun creep slow over the high and distant *Cerros Orientales*, the Eastern Hills, bleeding its warmth into the shy, low clouds. After enjoying a few moments of perfect solitude, other guys began appearing, straggling into the day. Within the half hour the patio was filled with a few hundred prisoners milling about waiting for breakfast.

7:00, I took my usual seat in the small church and greeted the other men. Familiar faces I'd grown to know. Aside from my friendship with Pastor Carlos, my relationships with the other twenty or so men were superficial. Everyone was Colombian, and aside from our shared language of worship and prayer, we held nothing in common. The service began with a song by Jesús Adrián Romero and Marcela Gandara playing on a DVD: *Dame Tus Ojos*—Give Me Your Eyes—a simple song with gorgeous harmonies. I did my best to mouth the Spanish and was doing well until the middle of the song when my knees gave out and I

386

collapsed into my chair. Tears were streaming down my eyes. I leaned forward, hiding my face in my hands. The song ended. The men sat. Alvaro, some guy I didn't know, took the podium and began delivering the message while I continued to muffle the sounds of my weeping.

The more I tried to stop, the more reckless the tears flowed. I tried to stifle my sobs and they only became louder. This went on for several minutes to the point of my becoming a distraction to the service. Sobbing uncontrollably. The sense of immense loss, regret, defeat, sadness was overwhelming. Five minutes into his sermon, Alvaro stopped speaking and spoke my name. I tried to pull it together, my face smeared with tears and snot, and looked at him. "What are you feeling at this moment?" He asked.

In my fit of dyspnea, I managed to mumble a single word. "Broken."

Alvaro quit his sermon and instructed everyone in Spanish. The church surrounded me in hugs and prayer.

The world of addiction has produced a myth that misguided professionals have termed "rock bottom." This term leans on the premise that addicts cannot begin to find their recovery and healing until they've found themselves financially destitute, emotionally decimated, abandoned by all friends and family, laying alone in some alleyway drooling saliva from their mouth with a dirty syringe dangling from their arm. In my experience, "rock bottom" was not the point of finally reaching physical annihilation, emotional hopelessness, or even spiritual collapse. When I found myself sobbing in the church that day, I was clean for the first time in five years. Rock bottom for me, is an ironical phrase that describes the moment when I realized that the success of my habilitation and finding my life again wasn't born by my hitting face first in the dirt or smashing my teeth out on the curb, but rather, waking calm one morning, processing the epiphany that I no longer needed to try and control things.

Surrender. If there exists such a thing as a rock bottom moment, this was mine.

Chapter Nineteen

La Modelo Prison, Bogotá
2018

The pragmatic and emotional rollercoaster of April came to a full stop when Luis showed up on the last Friday of the month carrying a letter from my honorable judge, Sofia Del Pilar Barrera Mora. The letter denied all my requests for *domiciliario,* home jail. The letter denied all my requests for a 72-hour leave, along with receiving any and all benefits I had accrued from my good behavior. The letter was a total slam to all expectations. A complete and utter mind scramble. All hope disintegrated on a single printed page.

After reading the letter, I simply recited a quote from Joel Houston, the lyricist of Hillsong. *"I feel we're at our best when we're broken because that's the moment where God gets to be made evident. He gives us an opportunity to love and to trust and to operate from his strength, not our own."*

I then thought of Christine Caine's illustration of *endurance.* Greeting Luis with an enormous smile, I asked if he'd pray with me. With my footsteps planted firm on Psalm 40, instead of processing the letter as a dead-end, I invited the opportunity to wait patiently, exerting best effort to laugh in the face of the judge's relentless scorn.

"So now we will file directly for your conditional release. Your parole." Luis affirmed. "You have served enough time. I will file the petition this week." After praying with Luis, I returned to my cell unfazed, defiant and ready to continue forward with emotional and spiritual precision.

I knew I was to be freed soon. I'd fulfilled the three-fifths of my sentence necessary for my paroled release. My behavior in the jail was flawless. The new Turkish narcos from down the hall somehow got word of my impending release and one evening called me into their cell for a meet. It turned out to be a recruiting conference. Apparently, they still had packages waiting outside and wanted to hire me to mule their loads back to Turkey. The plan was detailed, thorough, complete with contact numbers on both ends. They promised guaranteed security, and the payday was huge. Their proposal took me completely off guard. But I couldn't help thinking: *If your security is guaranteed, then what are you guys doing sitting in here with me?* It was strange to even imagine being back in that world again. I politely declined their offer.

Wrapping up the meeting, a text arrived for me on the Turk's phone. A message from Mighty.

`<Hey sorry to be the bearer of bad news. Lyda got busted selling dimes for the Nigerians. She's locked-up down in Sihanoukville. Sentenced to four years. Thought you'd want to know.>`

I walked back down my long hall; sidestepped the guys laughing around the television. Footsteps on concrete to my dark windowless cell. Doused the light. Collapsed onto my thin mattress. The thought of Da locked up in a Cambodian jail brought the tears streaming. Throughout the ecstatically treacherous years I'd known Lyda; enduring her, loving her, loathing her, weeping for her, experiencing cellar addiction with her, interchangeably fucking and fighting her, trying to teach and disciple her, defending her, living and dying with her, I often tried to imagine how it was all going to end. I always imagined it would be her death, my death, or one or both of our arrests that would once and for all dissolve the sandcastle I had tried so hard to build over and over for the both of us. I thought of our little wooden house. The last place we'd lived together. The endless script of lies.

Our slow and excruciating deaths. Our days spent drowning together in addiction, one failing to rescue the other due to our impotence to rescue ourselves.

On the eve of my departure to Bogotá, she'd stolen my passport and had held it for ransom, demanding I pay her a hundred dollars. She arranged to meet me outside one of the fish game arcades. She appeared walking up the filthy street strung out, dressed in dirty jeans and a T-shirt. After taking the cash she sheepishly returned the document. I watched her ride away poised perfectly on the back of a moto driven by some scummy Khmer dope-head whose face I never saw. As they approached the corner about ten yards away from where I stood and made the turn, she looked back at me, waved small, then disappeared. I remember her face in that moment, scorched like a photograph into my memory; the image of a small delicate schoolgirl with drooping eyes and crinkled nose looking confused like not knowing the answers to the questions. That was the last time I ever saw her.

Sitting up from my bed and trying to find composure was like extracting teeth out of the tender gums of infected memory. Prying myself away from the reality of total loss, I stood, flicked on the light. Bracing myself against the wall, I steadied myself against the images of Lyda squatting in some dark and forgotten Cambodian dungeon. Strangely, there was a vague comfort that came with the image. The fact that she was locked up erased the torment of imagining her being led sad and silent into random rooms around the city by men she didn't know. And I held no doubt as to her safety in the jail. She was savvy in any situation. Street smart and cunning. A melancholic smile spread across my face. I knew that within a month she'd be running the place.

Death is often a requirement in order to behold the fields of renewal. In mine and Lyda's case, we both went kicking and screaming. My process proved excruciating; the pain swirling around my neck and nearly drowning me. Standing there, in the silence of my dingy cell, I prayed her experience to be less painful, leading her to stand stoic, only knee deep (or perhaps waist-deep) in her tears. No wonder our story ended with both of us in lock-up. A blessing, really; a painful, albeit necessary alternative to death. I committed to pray for her daily—for her strength, resiliency and focus.

Two months after Luis filed for my parole, I called him to check on the status. I could tell something was wrong the minute he answered the phone. "I will come to the jail to see you tomorrow."

"Luis, just tell me what's going on."

"...I just have to check some things on the computer regarding the petition. I will be there tomorrow afternoon."

He showed up at 3:00 the following day. After our usual small talk, he delivered the news with a sigh. "The petition for your release that I filed at the end of April has been lost."

"Um... what do you mean... lost?" His words simply didn't compute.

"I filed the motion, but when I check your file in the computer, there is no record of the filing. The file has somehow been lost in the system."

I stared at him, mute. I couldn't find words. After a long silence, I stammered, "That was two months ago, Luis! For two months I've been sitting in here with no movement on my case?"

He absorbed my frustration nervously. "I am filing a *tutela* tomorrow-"

"A tutela?"

"An emergency petition. The courts must acknowledge that they received it within three days. We will receive the judge's answer at the end of July. I am confident you'll be released."

As always, we ended the meeting in prayer. But there was no meaning in my words. Just mumbled recitations uttered from my dead heart. I staggered back to my room, cut the light and collapsed into bed. At this point, my incarceration was no longer a result of my crime, but rather, a by-product of a corrupt and inept judicial system that couldn't even process their paperwork.

The answer to Luis' tutela arrived at the end of July. The Patio Crier called my name and handed me the letter. I immediately sought out Edgar to translate. We sat alone in the yard and I listened intently as he read. My dis-honorable judge, Coño Sofia Del Pilar Barrera Mora, expressed herself with a curt and personal subjectivity and unprofessional bias. *"Aaron Michael Reed... you have fulfilled three-fifths of your sentence... your prison record is perfect... you are eligible for your conditional release... I deny your conditional release... you are guilty of a terrible crime... you are a terrible person and I expect you to serve your entire sentence in the prison..."*

Another crowbar bludgeoning my senses, leaving my mind squirming. Despite fulfilling my legal requirements, I continued to squat, discarded, paralyzed. In the developed world, a legal process like this would have been sliced off at the tongue. I was far from the States. I'd landed in backwater Colombia where the judicial process was improvised at best. Colombian jurisprudence constantly violates its own Constitution, playing it by ear as it bumbles along with missing pages of testimony littering the floor, inconsistencies commonplace, resembling little more than a kangaroo court in Banana Republic where no one really cares one way or the other.

Despite all of my spiritual focus and *ommmm* attempts, a peculiar and terrifying feeling began festering over my skin which I colloquially defined as my *Colombian Cancer*. I finally and clearly understood the phrase that I'd heard others recite so many times before. *Buried in the system.*

Luis arrived the next day to help me process the information. "Your judge 14 has a very bad reputation," He explained. "She has a reputation as one of the meanest judges in the system. I did not want to tell you this before because I did not want you to lose hope. Now we will file another appeal, and your case will be transferred to a new judge. This is good news. We are now finished with Judge 14. Your new judge is number 47. He has a good reputation. He is fair. Just another month or so and we'll get you out of here."

Reciting another string of vacant prayers, I left Luis. Back in my cell I fell into bed and dispersed myself into the darkness. My body tumbling inert near dead swallowed by the relentless currents. My mind and flesh cut to shreds along the sharpest coral prongs jutting from the darkest bottom of a forgotten sea. I curled like a baby into my radio. Hillsong. *Another in the Fire.* The only remedy I knew to reach for.

Insult to injury came at the end of August in the form of Bob's release. He came grinning into the yard and showed me his papers announcing his conditional freedom. Enduring the sensation of my disintegrating heart, I embraced him with strong arms. I was happy for him but could only process his release as another impossible mental blow. Bob arrived at the prison two months *after* me. He had received the same sentence as I did. He was now being released while I was ordered to continue my incarceration. The Colombian judicial system is not based on justice. The concept of due process is nothing but a struggling abstract. The functions of the courts are little more than random and arbitrary proceedings; attorneys rambling Jabberwocky with the hope of gaining the nod of the corrupt and grinning judge hoping for the payout.

August 30th was a Thursday. Bob walked out of La Modelo while I remained crushed and chewed up in Colombia's dysfunctional gears and rusted cogs. In response, I entered an *active* season of fasting based on Isaiah 58, praying constantly for freedom from the oppression, praying to become more aware of the needs of those around me, praying for continued spiritual illumination, and to obtain a response to these prayers.

My new judge's office acknowledged receiving Luis' petition for my conditional release in the second week of September— nearly five weeks after it was filed. The following day the Embassy showed up for their quarterly visit. I sold my Centrum vitamins for 50,000 Pesos, about $16. Immediately after pocketing the cash, the Patio Crier call my name. I reported to the gate.

Another visit to the clinic for reasons I couldn't understand. Making my way through the *prisión central*, INPEC Inspector Fredy Briceno appeared out of nowhere, threw me up spread eagle against the wall and began patting me down. His fingers reached into my pocket and pulled out my cash. Chalking it up as a total loss, I gave a wave and continued toward the clinic. Briceno grabbed the neck of my shirt, pulled me into the central office, handcuffed me to a chair and began the interrogation. Seconds later, Inspector's Juan Marin and Mario Morales joined in the circle.

Inspector Briceno barked at me. *"No puedes llevar dinero en la prisión. Esto es una falta grave."*

"Lo siento, pero no entiendo español." I tried playing the *I don't speak Spanish* card, but I knew exactly what they were saying. Carrying money in the prison was forbidden, and they were trying to bust me for carrying cash. Inspector Marin took a moment to scribble out an official form and then slid it across the table along with a pen. An *Informe*—an official prison report documenting a prisoner's infraction to the rules. Once signed, it became a permanent stain on a prisoner's record. The infraction was then sent to the judge's office, automatically disqualifying the prisoner from any benefits, parole, or any other release programs. Signing an *Informe* was signing one's own death certificate.

The entire situation was nothing but a pathetic farce. Inspector's Fredy Briceno, Juan Marin and Mario Morales were the same guards who were paid on the black market to receive Western Union money transfers and then smuggle thousands into the prison each week and distribute the fistfuls of dollars to anyone willing to pay for the clandestine service. My shakedown was nothing but a *let's fuck with the gringo* effort; a perfect example of the random corruption that permeated the system.

I spent the entire day cuffed to the chair, pleading my case. Having missed both lunch and dinner, and worn down by their bull-headed badgering, I finally signed the paper. Returning to the patio in a total mental breakdown, I called Luis and told him what happened. "I had to sign it." I explained between sobs. "I had no choice. And now my request for parole will be denied!"

"Not necessarily." He assured. "Our petition has already reached the judge's office. It's already under review. The *informe* will probably take a week or more to reach the judge's office. Maybe the judge will grant your freedom before he sees the prison report."

Necessarily… probably… maybe… Empty words I'd heard countless times before. I collapsed into bed mentally drained from the day, with Luis' suppositions swirling through my head like an eternal toilet flushing shit. Out in the hall I could hear a party starting. Eduardo had produced a batch of freshly brewed Chi-Cha. Fernando came storming into the room along with two other guys. After rolling fatty joints and blazing down, they left the room clouded in a dense swirl of thick and pungent smoke. An hour later, Alex threw some porn flick into the DVD player. I returned to my cell, hunkered down. Plugged into Hillsong to drown out all the sounds. I could think of nothing more depressing than guys locked up in prison swaggering up and down the hall high and drunk listening to the moans of cheap Euro-porn blasting from speakers.

On the morning of the 12th I was summoned to the gate. For the millionth time I trudged down the endless hall into the dark recess of the meeting room. On any given day, the room was swarming with activity; inmates pushing and shoving their way to the gated windows to discuss their cases with their lawyers. On this day, the room was deserted, except for the presence of a single inmate stooped silently, half asleep on a stool. His dirty jeans were held in place by a piece of twine tied around his waist. His shirt was torn at the sleeves. Blurry prison tats ran the length of his arms and up both sides of his neck. Definitely from Patio 4. I offered a nod as I passed. He returned my greeting with a grunt.

The woman at the window was sharply dressed, obviously from the court. She greeted me with a pleasant smile. Asked me my name. She then slid a few papers through the slot while speaking in rapid Spanish.

"*Lo siento, señorita,*" I answered. "*Pero no hablo español.*"

She slid a pen through the slot and motioned for me to sign the docs.

Again, I hesitated, and tried to explain that I didn't understand what I was signing.

Casting her stare over my shoulder, she addressed the young thug seated behind me, asking him if he spoke English.

He lifted his head. His voice was little more than a raspy growl. "*Buena Gringo. Buena...*" Through his two-word translation, I knew that my conditional freedom had finally been granted.

The 13th of October was a Saturday. I sat with Edgar and Erik on the afternoon of my one thousandth, one hundred and forty seventh day of incarceration. The guards had just completed the four o'clock count. All inmates were milling about doing their thing. Young kids shooting hoops. Stoners buying, rolling and passing joints. Guys strolling their endless counter-clockwise circles around the yard. Everyone waiting to be let back into their halls. Over the patio din I heard my name called and walked to the gate.

Hormiga, one of Brazil's minions in charge of my hallway walked up and handed me a small red card. The word LIBERTAD was printed in caps; the card stamped 13/10/18 and signed with an illegible signature. I stared blank at Hormiga. "Freedom?" I asked.

"*Si.*" He answered.

"When?" I stammered. "*Cuando?*"

"*¡Hoy! Alrededor de las 6:00. Prepararse.*"

I returned to Edgar and Erik and showed them my card just as the guards opened the gate and everyone began filing back to their rooms to prepare for dinner. After quick good-byes, I made my way through the crowd over to the dope corner and hugged Fernando.

He greeted me with his ever-present kind and glassy eyes. "Congratulations, bro! Call me when you want to come see me in Nogales!"

I then ran over to the pay phone and called Luis. "Bro, I just got the notice. I'm going out!"

"Wow, that was fast! When?"

Grinning through the irony I answered, "Today. They say around six o'clock! In an hour and a half or so. Can you come get me?"

"Yes, I will be there!"

Rushing into my cell, I set a bucket of water to boil for my last shower. Cleansed, I dressed in my best clothes and began rifling through my belongings, creating two piles on my bunk. My books, journals, letters, photos and a few clothes items created the *take* pile. Everything else fell into the *leave* heap. I left my beloved radio and data card to Erik, and a few of my books for Edgar. As I was busy throwing my life's essentials into a trash bag, the best moments of my prison experience began flashing like cinematic snapshots through my memory.

My entry into the prison had come through the passage of complete chaos, failure and suicidal rage. Per God's usual modus operandi—using the best of the worst of us—I'd been handed my reminder of His unfailing love by Omar, a one-eyed freak and convicted murderer. Once I had gained my orientation, I was brought back into the church and His family by Pastor Carlos, a wealthy merchant and convicted tax evader. And finally, I'd been given a new family in the form of other narco-traficantes to surround me with the love and acceptance and encouragement to enable me to find myself again.

A few minutes after six the guard unlocked the gate. *"Aron Michael Red!"* With my life in a trash bag slung over my shoulder I exited the patio and was ushered into a small holding cell. I waited for a half hour with three other guys for my paperwork to process. After a final finger printing, I followed the guard to the front door.

The street running the length of the front of the prison was empty. Three merchants were still open, their small stores illuminated by single light bulbs hanging from wires. I set my bag down on the concrete outside the nearest shop and sat on an empty milk crate. I stared at the pebbles around my feet. Stared up at the starless sky, imagining the thunderous explosion, the acrid scent and celebratory image of fireworks. The street was dark. Deserted. Silent. Beautiful.

The headlight of Luis's motorcycle rounded the corner. He coasted to a stop in front of the shop. Balancing myself on the back, I held my arms out like wings, warm wind on my face, soaring through the night streets of this random South American city.

©Leslie McCoy/Mac Photography

Made in United States
North Haven, CT
08 October 2021

10225052R00223